READING INDIA NOW

Ulka Anjaria

READING INDIA NOW

Contemporary Formations in Literature and Popular Culture

TEMPLE UNIVERSITY PRESS
Philadelphia • *Rome* • *Tokyo*

TEMPLE UNIVERSITY PRESS
Philadelphia, Pennsylvania 19122
tupress.temple.edu

Paperback edition published 2024
Cloth edition published 2019

Library of Congress Cataloging-in-Publication Data

Names: Anjaria, Ulka, 1979– author.
Title: Reading India now : contemporary formations in literature and popular culture /
   Ulka Anjaria.
Description: Philadelphia : Temple University Press, 2019. | Includes bibliographical
   references and index. |
Identifiers: LCCN 2018030500 (print) | LCCN 2018052302 (ebook) | ISBN 9781439916650
   (E-Book) | ISBN 9781439916636 (cloth : alk. paper)
Subjects: LCSH: Indic literature—21st century—History and criticism. | Popular culture—
   India—History—21st century.
Classification: LCC PK5405 (ebook) | LCC PK5405 .A55 2019 (print) |
   DDC 891.4/007—dc23
LC record available at https://lccn.loc.gov/2018030500

ISBN 9781439916643 (paperback : alk. paper)

021524P

For Rehaan, Naseem, and Jonathan

Contents

Preface

The majority of this book was drafted in 2015–2016, during a yearlong research leave spent in Mumbai. As the year progressed, the place where I was writing grew to shape the project. I spent the days mostly at our rented apartment, in front of my computer, following a schedule typical of my life at home in Cambridge. At first, that seemed silly; living in Mumbai should have inspired me to do lots of new, different things. But this similarity, in fact, gave me the conceptual questions around which this book began to coalesce.

The time in Mumbai was a time of routine: waking up, making breakfast, taking my kids to school, going to the gym, shopping for food, and then writing for several hours. Sometimes the landlord stopped by to collect the rent or discuss repairs, and other times I went back to school for a teacher's conference or performance. The parents' WhatsApp group for my kids' class provided me a running commentary on school-related anxieties as well as practical advice on how to do class projects and where to buy supplies. Traffic-light vendors, bookstores, and social media kept me updated on new releases in fiction and other genres. Some days I crisscrossed the city in taxis and trains. Other times I waited in interminable lines at the bank or to pay my electricity bill. At night, after the kids were asleep, I watched videos, both news and entertainment, on the Internet, along with films and comedy shows. None of this was exceptional or extraordinary. But it was, for the most part, the time in which my writing took place.

That year was also marked by a number of important national-level events, some of them disturbing and violent: for instance, the assassination

of Kannada writer M. M. Kalburgi in August and the Award Wapsi movement that followed, where dozens of writers protested the government's
increasing indifference to mob violence by returning their national literary
awards. A beef ban was instituted in Maharashtra, resulting in instances of
violence against individuals suspected of carrying beef. There was a racially
motivated attack on a Tanzanian student in Bangalore, the suicide of a Dalit
student in Hyderabad, and a toxic fire in a garbage dump in eastern Mumbai
that produced a cloud of smoke and haze that engulfed our neighborhood
for days. These were some of the things that made headlines, reminded us
that history was still very much alive in India, and troubled all those who
worried about the future.

But in between these events, everyday life seemed to go on, not just for
me but for many people. I read a lot about these events as they were unfolding, and then reading about them also became part of my routine. This led
me to think more about the relationship between the two. Do the routines of
a place simply constitute the backdrop against which important historical
events play out, or might they also be important on their own terms? Why is
the unspectacular, everyday present so often overlooked as a significant
realm of experience for the study of India? Is this an issue particular to
places like India, where the big problems seem too pressing for the everyday
to matter?

As I returned to the texts I was writing about for this book, it struck me
that many writers and cultural practitioners were in fact trying to carve out
a space for the representation of the present, with its unspectacular aspirations and its at times banal desires. What I had been reading as the dissolution of postcolonial form now became clearer to me as a collective engagement with reimagining how literature and cultural production could be
something altogether different from what it has long been, specifically by
being open to the present in a cultural sphere in which the present is so undervalued. These texts were writing spaces of freedom, love, and small-time
aspiration into a context more concerned with what Arundhati Roy famously called "Big Things" (1997, 165). Sometimes they touched on political
topics, but when they did, they presented new forms of politics that were
folded into the routines of everyday life rather than being radical or revolutionary. The problem was not with the texts out there, I realized, but with the
lens I was bringing to them, which was always seeking out themes of historical import, global significance, or a deeper meaning rather than letting
the everyday speak, as it were, for itself. That is how I was trained; that is how
I was used to convincing my students and colleagues in neighboring fields
that literature matters. I began to consider how much of my previous work
on Indian literature—and so much work on India in general—overlooks the

unexceptional state of the present. When it is considered, it is often done so solely as a way of lamenting how bad things have gotten. This might well be the result of the disproportionate influence of diasporic scholars (which I am a part of as well) on the field of postcolonial literary studies, whose relationship to India is marked by periodic visits to see family and friends, attend conferences, and do research rather than by participation in the routines of everyday life. In these visits, the past often becomes the primary lens onto the present. But it goes deeper than that: for most scholars the mundane present is also seen to have no inherent politics; it often does not bear the weight of history and does not offer transformative visions of the future, and thus, for those who see ourselves as politically inclined and our work as potentially consciousness raising, it seems irrelevant on its own, without the explanatory shadow of history. Moreover, as the Indian present becomes more imbricated in consumer economies, studying it might seem a distraction from, or even an impediment to, the real work of progressive, critical scholarship.

This book, then, is an effort to outline what literary criticism might look like when it becomes attuned to the everyday lives that people live in India outside the shadow of history. This endeavor has taken me beyond the novel, which is where I began, to multiple genres and media, crossing the divide between "high" and "low" fiction and between languages. My intention is not to supplant the study of transformative events in India, which remains needed and important. I intend, rather, to supplement it, by illuminating, by bringing to the foreground, a time that is everywhere but virtually invisible—a time that I am calling the Indian contemporary.

Acknowledgments

The year I wrote the majority of this book was supported by an American Council of Learned Societies (ACLS)/Charles A. Ryskamp Fellowship, without which timely completion of this project would have been much more difficult. Research, writing, and publication were also supported by the Theodore and Jane Norman Fund for Faculty Research at Brandeis University, a subvention grant from the Dean's Office at Brandeis University, and a visiting fellowship at Delhi University.

I thank the Brandeis English Department, the Dean's Office at Brandeis, and Lisa Pannella for their constant support of me and my work. My three research assistants, Courtney Pina Miller, Gina Pugliese, and Daniella Gati, were immensely helpful in this project's early stages.

Portions of this book have been presented at conferences and talks in Champaign-Urbana, Illinois; Dhaka, Bangladesh; Durham, North Carolina; Evanston, Illinois; Ithaca, New York; Lahore, Pakistan; London; Leuven, Belgium; Mauritius; Mumbai; New Delhi; New York City; Paris; Philadelphia; Tokyo; and Utrecht, Netherlands, as well as in various contexts at Brandeis University. I thank all the interlocutors in those domains who contributed to making the work better.

Parts of this book have been published in different forms as Ulka Anjaria, "Notes on the Indian Contemporary," *South Asian Review* 38, no. 3 (2017): 57–61; Ulka Anjaria, "Realist Hieroglyphics: Aravind Adiga and the New Social Novel," *Modern Fiction Studies* 61, no. 1 (2015): 114–137; Ulka Anjaria, "Chetan Bhagat and the New Provincialism," *American Book Review,*

September–October 2015, pp. 6–22; and Ulka Anjaria, "Amitav Ghosh and Aravind Adiga: Two Ways to Write English in India," *Scroll*, August 9, 2015, available at https://scroll.in/article/747269/amitav-ghosh-and-aravind-adiga-two-ways-to-write-english-in-india. Portions were also published as parts of Ulka Anjaria, "The Realist Impulse and the Future of Postcoloniality," *Novel: A Forum on Fiction* 49, no. 2 (2016): 278–294, and are republished here by permission of the copyright holder and the present publisher.

I thank all the friends and colleagues with whom I have discussed my ideas and shared work and who have supported me at different stages of this project, especially Aliyyah Abdur-Rahman, Susan Andrade, Jerónimo Arellano, Amita Baviskar, Laura Brueck, Mrinalini Chakravorty, Zahid Chaudhary, Lindsey Collen, Kavita Daiya, Emma Dawson Varughese, Jennifer Derr, Shani Ellis, Jed Esty, Ajay Gehlawat, Lauren Goodlad, Sangita Gopal, Michaela Henry, Margaret Higonnet, Priya Joshi, Sudhir Mahadevan, Saikat Majumdar, Anita Mannur, Julie Minich, Satya Mohanty, Lucinda Ramberg, Raka Ray, Sangeeta Ray, Geoffrey Sanborn, Sambudha Sen, Naghmeh Sohrabi, Eli Park Sorensen, Harish Trivedi, and Alex Woloch. In my department I thank Caren Irr, John Plotz, Dawn Skorczewski, David Sherman, and Ramie Targoff, with a special thanks to Paul Morrison and Faith Smith, who have been true allies.

Additional special thanks go to Shilpa Phadke for her hospitality in Mumbai, to Naresh Fernandes and Arunava Sinha at *Scroll*, and to Paromita Vohra for her generosity with her work. Paromita also gave me permission to reprint the kiss map from Agents of Ishq; R. Raj Rao kindly gave me permission to cite his poem; and Atul Dodiya generously allowed me to use his stunning image as my cover. I also thank Marinanicole Dohrman Miller, Rebecca Logan, and everyone at Temple University Press and Newgen for all the effort they put into this book. Special thanks go to Sara Jo Cohen for her faith in this book from the beginning, her thoughtful editorial eye, and her guidance through the different stages of its publication.

The biggest thanks go to my family. I am grateful to my parents, Nishigandha and Shailendra, and my sister, Keya, whose support is always unwavering. Jonathan, my partner, has supported me as a colleague and as a friend. Together we spent many evenings in many parts of the world dissecting the ideas that are now part of this book. I cannot imagine having done this without him. My sons, Naseem and Rehaan, have been such good spirits throughout this whole writing process, offering words of support when I needed them and reminding me, at other times, that there is more to life than work. Their complete and unhesitating embrace of the Indian contemporary during our yearlong stay in Mumbai is part of what inspires this project.

READING INDIA NOW

Introduction

In Search of an Indian Contemporary

n June 2015, acclaimed Indian novelist Amitav Ghosh toured various cities to promote the third novel of his Ibis trilogy, *Flood of Fire*. In Mumbai, at the event I attended, he spoke in the auditorium of the National Gallery of Modern Art (NGMA). The auditorium was quickly filled to capacity, and closed-circuit cameras broadcast the event to the upstairs gallery and even to the porch outside, swamped with premonsoon humidity. Ghosh was in his usual fine form. He spoke to the event's host, Shobhaa Dé, about the extensive research he did for the three books, the hospitality he received during his travels in China, the Indian Ocean's cosmopolitan past, and the relations between India and China in the nineteenth century. He spoke of the centrality of the opium trade to building the fortunes of the world's wealthiest families. He spoke of the hours he spent poring over old documents in libraries and his interest in paleography, the science of deciphering handwriting on manuscripts. In answer to a question about why the trilogy is named after the ship the *Ibis*, he underlined the way communities are born on the ship itself, in the multiple crossings it makes over the course of the three novels. These answers met with enthusiastic response. Outside, the monsoon rains were about to begin. The air was heavy with impending turmoil. The traffic circle was full of cars, scooters, pedestrians, hawkers, and revelers, and Mumbai's incessant honking was in the air. The city was moving at its usual frenetic pace. Inside, the air was conditioned, calmer, and more refined.

Then, breaking the spell, one audience member asked Ghosh what he thinks can be done to improve current India-China relations following the historic visit of Xi Jinping to India the year before. Ghosh hesitated a bit, then said that very little can be done because both countries are thinking only about wealth. With this dismissal, the conversation mostly got back on track. But the unanswered question hung in the room, a flash of the contemporary in an atmosphere otherwise oriented toward the past.

Against Ghosh's fascinating account of historical interconnections, the audience member's question animated an alternative space, asking not a question that Ghosh could not answer but rather one that he would prefer not to, a question where the known space of postcolonial writing meets the more unsure time of the contemporary. For Ghosh, the past is a series of stories that can be woven together by the strength of an evocative metaphor: the shadow lines, the sea of poppies, the river of smoke. This past and the transactions of imperialism, the role of translation and transit in forging community, cultural hybridity, the modern art museum, and even the Colaba neighborhood of Mumbai in which the NGMA is located occupy a demarcated space of postcolonial legibility in which Ghosh perfectly fits, in part because he helped create it. But the unfinished questions of economic policy, territorial squabbles, and competing growth rates signify less literary concerns. More fitting for newspaper editorials or policy debates, these remain outside the purview of the litterateur.

What would happen to our understanding of today's Indian literature if the doors to the NGMA were figuratively opened and the sea air, and the smells of the city outside, were allowed to pour in? If the hawkers selling pirated pulp novels, the snatch of a film song, the hum of millions of satellite dishes, the twenty-four-hour newscast, Twitter, and the smell of rupees exchanging hands—if those were allowed to enter and disrupt the quiet spaces sanctified by literature and cosmopolitan history? What kinds of texts would be discussed, and what kinds of questions would have to be answered? How would that compel us to think differently about literature's relationship to the world outside? How would that compel us to think differently about literature more generally?

This book argues that over the last several decades, we have seen a gradual diminishing of the distance between the world and the text. On the one hand, this is a global phenomenon (Brouillette 2017, 281), brought on by the rise of social media, book releases, literary festivals, and other venues in which authors and practitioners are called on to engage with a range of issues of contemporary relevance more frequently than ever before. Moreover, the expansion of reality television, the Internet, blogs, and other user interfaces has increased a culture of participation in what we read and consume. But in India this shift is even more profound. The growth of the Indian publishing industry and of the reading middle class over the last two decades means that there is an ever greater demand for accessible books, especially those that tell new, relevant stories (Mallya 2016).[1] The recent popularity of homegrown pulp fiction from romance to mystery to fantasy fiction,[2] as well as the phenomenon of commercial authors who publish one or even two novels a year,[3] means that the temporal gap between stories and their reception is diminishing. Even Hindi cinema, known for its escapist plots, is telling more contemporary stories. The past seems less and less relevant to contemporary cultural production.[4] The literature of authors like Amitav Ghosh, which deliberately resides in a space apart from the present, is increasingly the exception rather than the rule.

Some critics have lamented this change as the loss of India's "modernist counterculture" (Mishra 2014) resulting from its turn toward capitalism and neoliberalism,[5] which have commodified art and literature and shorn them of their critical edge. No longer skeptical of these changes, critics say, new literatures and cultural productions are entirely products of the new India and thus cannot reflect critically on them. Today, writes Pankaj Mishra, "neo-liberalism creates its own human subjectivity. So everyone—whether writers, cotton farmers or mere tweeters—is supposed to turn into an entrepreneur" (Mishra and Sethi 2015).[6] To these commentators, the fact that popular authors aggressively market their works and write novels using Bollywood formulas has left little space for fostering art as political dissent. Literature is all about money now, they argue, rather than great ideas or great books. Moreover, this new obsession with the present has made us myopic. By ignoring the past, we are doomed to repeat it, as evident in the resurgence of Hindutva politics and the increasing encroachment of religion on private life.[7]

While recognizing the importance of these critiques, this book offers an alternative view: Although contemporary literature and popular culture in India might seem complacent, artless, and entirely the product of capitalism, their openness to the world outside allows them to offer significant insight into the experiences and sensibilities of contemporary India. But to receive this insight, we need to shift our understanding of what we mean by literature and what we imagine it to do. To understand today's literature as a product of and reflection on the present, we need new tools, moving away from a valorization of counterculture and looking instead at the myriad microcultures that, while not always fully oppositional, nevertheless reflect boldly on the various questions of our time. Insofar as critics are accustomed to looking to literature and art as a bulwark against myopism, provincialism, and the market, we end up missing all the complex ways in which writers engage with the present and, often, imagine alternatives to it. Authors in India today write from within a capitalist system, much as their counterparts do in the rest of the world.[8] But that does not mean their works are simply a by-product of capitalism. Rather, these authors remain *ambivalent* with regard to the changes India has undergone in the last twenty-five years; they find some of them limiting and some of them enabling. They do not necessarily valorize the past as a refuge from the present but find faults and benefits in both. Their politics is eclectic because they are open to the contested landscapes of the present and the possibility that something new and not entirely known lies just around the bend. This openness allows them to reflect on crucial contemporary questions in a way that the earlier Indian English novel, with its inbuilt mistrust of the present, was never able to.

Thus, even without the liberalism, secularism, and cosmopolitanism that have characterized modern Indian writing (Sunder Rajan 2011, 204), recent texts across a range of media are innovatively considering a number of questions that concern India's present: What is India's future on a world stage? What is the fate of the poor in India's big cities? What is the continuing role of caste and religion in public life? What does it mean to be a feminist? Where is there space for everyday life and for love and desire? What is the nature of freedom? These pressing, *contemporary* questions sometimes extend to offer political critique and at other times do not, remaining open and unanswered. From the perspective of literary criticism, today's texts often seem unfinished or apolitical. But rather than lament this as the end of literature, we might see how these new texts compel us to rethink our conventional readerly paradigms. Rather than look for a coherent politics, we might read them as extending the space between the tentative expressions of aspiration and desire and the confidence of political certainty or ideology.

I use the term "the contemporary" to name both the time of the present and this new optic that recognizes and reads literature as of and for the world rather than as inhabiting a space apart from it. Insofar as the contemporary is merely another word for the present—or more specifically, "a condition in which the moment of cultural production and reception are identical" (Carroll 2015, 19)—there have been many contemporaries (T. Smith 2006, 696), in India and elsewhere, and many contemporary literatures. These include the fiction of the late nationalist period (1920–1940), the topic of my first book, which anticipated an independence that was not yet realized (U. Anjaria 2012). They include the *sathottari* poetry of 1960s Bombay, which "was trying to capture the fast-moving present of the lived experience by [offering] . . . an assault on literary, textual, and printing conventions all at once in the hopes of getting through to some other, inexpressible side of things" (Nerlekar 2016, 56). They include the "angry young man" films of the

1970s, which registered the profound uncertainty and disillusionment brought on by the declaration of the Emergency in 1975, as well as Dalit literature of the late twentieth century, "with [its] emphasis on the documentation of the violence, oppression, and structural inequality engendered by casteism" (Gajarawala 2013, 1–2). However, insofar as the contemporary is an optic, a mode of reading, a dissolution of literature's distance from the everyday, and partially a product of a newly instituted market economy, I use the term specifically to refer to *this* moment, in the early 2000s, a moment that, in India, we might otherwise call post-postcolonial.[9]

In this sense, the contemporary exists in contrast to the postcolonial, which, particularly in Anglophone theory, has been the dominant optic in the study of Indian literature and culture for the last several decades and, as we saw with Ghosh, a dominant attitude that approaches the present with skepticism.[10] Postcolonial theory was field changing within literary criticism for drawing attention to power and to the role of language in consolidating epistemes, for shifting focus from nations to borders, and for modeling an account of literary history that was cosmopolitan, democratic, and secular.[11] However, these very qualities make postcolonial criticism largely unable to account for the literature and cultural production in India today, with its setting in the present and its indifference toward the past, its representation of aspiration and desire, its pragmatic rather than idealist politics, its interest in the banal and the everyday, its investment in new political subjects beyond those based in caste and religion, its refusal of metaphor and allegory, its new demands on how we read, and its new conception of the role of the critic. From the postcolonial perspective, these traits most often appear as capitulations to capitalism or a decline of progressive thought rather than as literary, cultural, or epistemological positions in their own right.

This book argues that reading for the contemporary begins by recognizing the political and cultural contradictions of contemporary India, which is witnessing a right-wing resurgence and increasing communalization, wealth inequality, and consumerism but also housing new alternative cultures, queer spaces, publishing venues, readerships, and future imaginaries. We need to see these contradictions, even if we dislike them, as *productive* of the present. Reading for the contemporary means not coming to texts with an idealist sense of what would make the best society but attempting to understand the contradictory reality that actually constitutes society. It requires not reading with skepticism, working to expose the exclusions and silences of texts, but reading inductively to see how texts construct new imaginaries. In all these ways, and because it goes against the grain of dominant political and theoretical trends, I argue that *the contemporary in India is counterintuitive* and thus cannot merely be stated but must be actively

asserted. The contemporary offers us new and at times problematic formations; it is where the high and low meet, where conventional generic and
formal categories break down, and where the sanctified literary dissolves. In
this sense, the contemporary is necessarily impure—even, as Nietzsche
called it, "untimely" (quoted in Erber 2013, 39)[12]—exceeding the conventional classifications of literary criticism to register "the existence of mutually contradictory worlds" (C. Holmes 2013, 149).

The book's subtitle, *Formations of the Contemporary*, encourages us to
read the contemporary as heterogeneously constituted across the hundreds of
new texts that have appeared in India in the last two decades in a variety of
genres and media. The contemporary is not one thing but appears in multiple
forms. What unites these texts is that they respond to, cathect, reflect, question, criticize, and assess the present to offer new accounts of it, along with
new imaginations of the future. These works are not closed, "never . . . in the
past tense" (R. Williams 2009, 129), but always potentially open, in process.
As Rachel Carroll writes, the contemporary's "richness resides in its status as
crucible of the near but as yet unfixed future; in its analysis we can see the
forces at work in the making of possible future histories, including forces
implicated in inequalities of power" (2015, 19–20). Thus, we are called on not
to lament the glimpse or the formation as a degraded consequence of capitalism or a digital age but to recognize it as a product of thinking across previously distinct lines of inquiry. Thus, we can see how recent Indian literature,
films, nonfiction, and other cultural products imagine new geographies outside the first world–third world and urban-provincial binaries, new publics
built on political alliances outside the traditional subaltern-elite dichotomy,
new forms of representation, and new relationships between writers and critics. Neither progressive nor right wing, neither elite nor subaltern, these texts
offer insight into the myriad open-ended questions that make up India's present and, in doing so, generate tentative insights into new possible futures.

The following discussion highlights the major obstacles to a full account of
the Indian contemporary. These include postcoloniality's emphasis on the
past and its concomitant skepticism of the postliberalization present, which
have resulted in a lack of serious engagement with the literary and cultural
products that are circulating in India today. The anticontemporary thrust of
postcolonial theory is only strengthened by the implicit limitation, in global
literary theory's Western centrism more generally, on who gets to be contemporary and who and what count as the legitimate subjects of non-Western
writing. Having framed the theoretical landscape in this way, the book then
proceeds to reading for the contemporary in a range of new literatures and
cultural products published since 2000.

The book's three parts explore different characteristics of the Indian contemporary: the locations it imagines, the publics it engenders, and the forms of representation it makes possible. Reading for the contemporary requires grouping texts as generic, formal, and thematic constellations that frame new questions rather than along the older lines of language, medium, or genre. Thus, each part includes texts across these various categories. Part I, for instance, shows how recent commercial novels and nonfiction books offer a rethinking of place in India today, when villages and small towns are associated with India's backwardness, and the cities with India's emergence and futurity. The two chapters consider how these assumptions are reconfigured in recent writings, engendering a new geography of the Indian present. While postcolonial chronotopes have included borderlands, ocean crossings, and diasporas, contemporary fiction by authors such as Chetan Bhagat and Anuja Chauhan has shifted focus to India's Tier-II cities and less fashionable regions, resulting in what I call, in Chapter 1, a "new provincialism" that reimagines the future as one in which young people realize their aspirations in India rather than only abroad. Chapter 2 examines what forms best represent the sprawling Indian megalopolis, often considered either entirely transformed by capitalism or as a dystopic example of urban decay. Because the very structure of narrative brings with it its own temporality, city writings make various attempts to reconfigure narrative itself to queer or otherwise call into question these simplistic narratives of India's emergence and decline.

Part II identifies new, experimental political formations in the popular Hindi visual media. While these media are often criticized for their star culture, their epical and melodramatic stories, and their over-the-top sentimentality, recent texts use these modes of affective engagement to imagine new publics in a political context in which the old categories of religion, class, and caste might be ceding to new demographics whose characteristics are as yet unknown. Moreover, in the context of a middle class that is historically apathetic, these texts envision a new civil society enriched by libidinal attachments. While Chapter 3 shows how recent popular Hindi films pursue the elusive but imaginatively rich category of the "common man," Chapter 4 shows how Aamir Khan's new television talk show *Satyamev Jayate* mobilizes the charisma of the Bollywood superstar to construct new affective publics around issues of contemporary importance.

If Part II gestures toward the creation of new publics across class alliances, Part III approaches the contemporary from an epistemological angle and asks: What alternatives do we have to the postcolonial view of representation as an act of power and of reading as a means of exposing silences and exclusions? What is the role of the critic in the Indian contemporary? What would it mean to read alongside, rather than only against, the grain of texts—even to read with "a loving eye" ("March on Women" 2016)? Chapter 5 focuses on a set of recent novels that transcend the themes and tropes of classical postcolonial fiction to ask what lies on the other side, so to speak, or beyond the pale of Indian English fiction as it has been globally received and celebrated. Chapter 6 offers a reading of the multimedia work of documentary filmmaker Paromita Vohra, whose insistent experimentation with form and genre allows her to ask new questions about feminism and everyday love and desire outside received categories such as "feminist" or "political." Vohra's critical writings advance a new model of reading born of intimacy rather than distance, which pushes us to consider how the contemporary is not only a literary project but also a critical one.

The book is not a comprehensive study of all contemporary literature and cultural production and certainly does not cover the range of languages in which people write and create in India today. But it does cross a number of genres and media in Hindi and English, ranging from "high" to "low" cultural forms and extending across fiction and nonfiction, film and television, documentary and melodrama, literature and journalism. All these texts offer formations of the contemporary in India through formal, generic, and epistemological innovations that might not be recognizable using the old critical lenses. Thus, the book is meant to be an outline, an incitement to further study, rather than a full assessment of the Indian contemporary. It tries to model what a renewed literary criticism might look like in a context in which representation is understood as experimental and receptive to the world around it, even at the cost of critics' long-held beliefs regarding what counts as literary and what it means to be political. Thus, in each chapter I read for the fullest potential of the text rather than for its limitations. While my account does not intend to be naïvely celebratory of the present, it does dispute the dominant sense among many scholars that the literary and cultural sphere in India today is in grave crisis. Without underplaying the serious problems India continues to face, the book argues that the solution to these problems might not necessitate a complete dismissal of the literature and cultural products of the present. Rather, these new formations may also contain tools for alternative futures, not despite but precisely because of their imbrication in a new commodity culture—potentially offering new representational possibilities from within its midst.

Postcolonial Time and the Problem of the Present

"I had been mysteriously handcuffed to history, my destinies indissolubly chained to those of my country." So wrote Salman Rushdie in 1981, in the voice of Saleem Sinai, and in doing so inaugurated a new consciousness in the Indian novel in English. This sentiment and the novel that introduced it have shaped literature and literary criticism since 1981. Through this formulation, Rushdie registers the tie of both Saleem and the novel to history. From that point forward, the Indian novel's primary role seemed to be to illuminate the myriad ways in which the past continues to shape the realities of the present (U. Anjaria 2015, 22).

Midnight's Children marks the birth of what I call "postcolonial time."[13] Following its success, many of the Indian English novels that have elicited international fame have similarly described the overwhelming influence of history on the present: for example, Anita Desai's Clear Light of Day (1980); Amitav Ghosh's The Shadow Lines (1988), In an Antique Land (1992), and The Glass Palace (2000); Rohinton Mistry's Such a Long Journey (1991) and A Fine Balance (1995); Vikram Seth's A Suitable Boy (1993); Arundhati Roy's The God of Small Things (1997); Kiran Desai's The Inheritance of Loss (2006); and Jhumpa Lahiri's The Lowland (2013). Whether it is capital-H History and the Love Laws (Roy), historical events such as the Partition (Ghosh, Seth) and the Emergency (Mistry, Rushdie), or other forms of state violence (Desai, Lahiri), these works collectively suggest that engagement with history is the primary role of the Indian novel (Tickell 2015; Sunder Rajan 2011, 203–204).

For many writers and critics, accounts of the past serve as an important corrective to the confident temporality of an emergent India (Kaur and Hansen 2016, 266). As Jyotsna Kapur writes, "We are told that India has no use for history because it is in the midst of reinventing itself as a global economic power" (2013, 3). The rhetoric of "emerging India" espoused by the state—especially the current Bharatiya Janata Party (BJP) government—the corporate media, and some economists (Bardhan 2013, 2), grew out of the liberalization of the Indian economy in the 1990s, which gave rise to new social dynamics premised on consumerism and aspiration rather than the older Nehruvian ideals of restraint and deferral of desire. This rhetoric sees India's high economic growth, buoyed by foreign investment, relaxed import restrictions, and an expanded consumer economy, as promising a new role for India on the world stage. It is supplemented by the increasing influence of a militaristic Hindu nationalism, which has consequences in a range of domains, from the ongoing occupation of Kashmir and parts of the northeast, to the threats to religious minorities and the increasing suppression of free speech. In such a context, calling attention to history—whether it is to cataclysmic events such as the Partition (Zamindar 2017) or to the philosophies of secularism and socialism that formed the Indian polity—seems an important rejoinder to a myopic presentism.

But turning away from the present for fear of implicitly condoning its violence has the consequence of overlooking the vast diversity of cultural production that has emerged in the last two decades, including films, television, graphic novels, chick lit, fantasy fiction, romance novels, and mysteries, in English and in the bhashas (Shobita Dhar 2014), in addition to myriad new translations from the bhashas to English ("Major Focus" 2018) and new forms and themes in literary fiction. This proliferation of new texts, spurred by the growth of international publishing houses in India and the increasing number of small presses (Mallya 2016), has changed the face of Indian literature. For instance, there are entire series of popular fiction, such as Penguin India's Metro Reads, targeted to the commuting reader and priced around one hundred rupees (Pal 2012; Suman Gupta 2012, 52), as well as new serial novels in a landscape earlier occupied only by imported series from the United States and the United Kingdom. There are new kinds of films enabled by the growth of Indian multiplexes, which no longer need to rely solely on high-revenue blockbusters. These new forms live side by side with the new cultural productions that flood the Internet every day: interactive media, music, podcasts, webzines, stand-up comedy, spoken word, satire, journalism, blogs, web series, spoofs, remakes, and countless others. While these works are "a mixed bag" in terms of quality and approach (Suman Gupta 2012, 52), they nevertheless mark a flourishing of cultural production outside the erstwhile elite centers of artistic and literary value.

Yet critics' alarmist sense that Indian counterculture is in decline often impedes their ability to read and understand these new forms as anything except expressions of that decline. The view, as Pankaj Mishra (2017b) wrote on the seventieth anniversary of India's independence, that "India . . . seems to have missed its appointment with history" pervades the progressive public sphere, as well as academic writing. In an earlier article following Narendra Modi's electoral victory in 2014, Mishra (2014) explicitly linked the current literary landscape to Modi's "new India," contrasting Vikram Seth's 1993 novel *A Suitable Boy*, which for him marked the more innocent and optimistic side of Indian democracy, with today's cultural production, characterized by a vacuous press, "a spate of corporate-sponsored literary festivals," a "degenerated" popular cinema, and the demise of what used to be a rich "modernist counterculture." In this view, contemporary literature is read only as proof of how bad things have become.

Many other critics share this sense. Recent cultural production is constantly criticized in reviews and scholarly accounts for being saturated with market values and for reflecting capitalist sensibilities such as ambition, pragmatism, and self-help. New phenomena such as literary festivals, the so-called Bollywoodization of the novel (Gopal 2015, 360), market-driven publishing, and shallow, antiliterary prose are taken as further examples of this decline.[14] As art historian Geeta Kapur writes, art today no longer has its "agonistic function" and is nothing more than the "reified . . . exchange of spectacular, consumer-driven signs" (2008, 32). Novelist and critic Anjum Hasan (2014) laments that the "potential diversity" of new Indian literature "has been straitjacketed by the idea of 'genre.' Genres are being created in assembly-line fashion, and are received as such by readers."[15] For novelist and critic Amit Chaudhuri (2006), "[today's] Indian writing in English reflects [India's growing prestige] and imperialist ambition. I would be happy with a writing that is more ambiguous about its own position and wish it would be less triumphant." In another interview, Chaudhuri (2016) criticizes literary festivals as places where "there is celebration but you do not really find the literary." His criticism hinges on a distinction between literariness and the market that has become an essential component to this new anticontemporary ethos. In a recent roundtable in the web-based *Public Books*, Anjum Hasan wrote:

> The murmur of the market . . . has amplified in this time as the big publishing corporations have set up house [in India], and as the English-speaking middle class, increasingly cut off from the languages of their parents and the kinds of progressive literature that generation might have read, acquaints itself with a younger, often more functional, definitely less discomfiting writing in which they might recognize themselves. The market has certainly created one model of literary relevance, a model new to this country, and yet one we've embraced as ineluctable. (Quoted in S. Majumdar 2016)

In another piece, Hasan (2014) similarly avers, "Alongside the growing writerly concern about the market taking over is the rise of the writer as entrepreneur, for whom marketing and writing are not discrete activities at all, and the book more an isolated, potentially profit-making product rather than something belonging to a complex network of associations called literature." This view is stated even more strongly by another critic:

> If writing literature is an act of social responsibility, the new-breed writers display total disregard towards readers' finer sensibilities. . . . These books are mindless narratives—like a TV serial, is the opinion of many who have grown reading "real" literature. . . . When books do not challenge, disturb and agitate the mind, when they stop questioning the reality, the norms, when they do not reflect social and personal conflicts, they sound the death-knell for the age of reason.

At best they offer entertainment, at worst, they promote escapism. (V. Shukla 2016)

And for novelist Aatish Taseer, the commercialization of literature is a reflection of Indian backwardness; when asked about the phenomenal success of best-selling novelist Chetan Bhagat, he responded, "He might just be a symptom of the fact that in English, India is basically a semi-literate country and Chetan Bhagat is the best it can do" (Tiwari 2015).[16]

This sense that today's literature and cultural production mark a diminishment of an earlier literary sensibility because of the influence of the market is widespread and pervades literary criticism, commentaries, and book reviews. It is true that some commercial writers talk at length about marketing and publicity and move directly from authoring books to starting publishing houses, such as best-selling romance novelist Ravinder Singh's Black Ink (S. Chakraborty 2015). Sometimes, as Chetan Bhagat is, they are proud that their works do not qualify as art ("I'm Battling" 2016).[17] But when scholars criticize such practices, they implicitly valorize literature's "independence from the mechanisms of cultural commodification" (D'Arcy and Nilges 2016, 4) and idealize, in the tradition of Western modernism and India's own history of progressive writing, "the true artist [who] was noncommercial, struggling on the fringes of human existence, with neither society nor companions (and hardly any publishers), alone with his indomitable self" (Braudy 1999, 615).[18] This nostalgic image of the writer uncorrupted by the market fails to acknowledge that artistic cultures change over time. Indeed, criticisms of contemporary writing and cultural production, although well-intentioned, are often advanced with such insistence that they start to resemble the "left melancholy" Wendy Brown describes among progressives worldwide as "not only a refusal to come to terms with the particular character of the present . . . [but also] a certain narcissism with regard to one's past political attachments and identity" (1999, 20).

Moreover, when scholars read new texts, they do so through the old lenses. For instance, in a recent book in which two chapters were specifically devoted to contemporary postcolonial fiction, both presented historical analysis as the means to understand their contemporary texts, suggesting that the project of writing the contemporary in the postcolony is an impossible one because it comes up against "colonial residues" that it cannot wish away (Luckhurst and Marks 1999, 8).[19] Alternatively, scholars focus on the exclusions and the "narrative marginalization" (Guttman 2017, 270) enacted by new texts rather than on what they do or the new worlds they imagine. Conferences, workshops, and journal special issues continue to ask the same questions, even when addressing new literatures. Across postcolonial literary study, especially in the Indian context, critics concur that exhaustively studied and documented themes such as the nation and its fragments, exile, melancholy, memory, violence, and trauma are the best and most politically astute optics for reading and interpreting Indian literature. The result is an overall uniformity of scholarship on Indian literature even in the face of a massive diversity of political, formal, and epistemological viewpoints.[20]

What is left out or dismissed in these approaches are the various new themes broached by contemporary texts, themes such as aspiration, everyday life, sexuality and desire, dreams for better selves, dreams for a better India, provincialism, and new futures. While some of these bear the imprint of capitalism or Hindu nationalism, none is entirely the product of these. In fact, many writers and cultural producers use these themes to assess and criticize current conditions, not out of an ascetic or progressive imaginary that remains distantly critical of the present they describe but *through* their intimate coexistence with that present.

Refusing to acknowledge the importance of aspiration in contemporary India—which affects, for instance, everything from the books people read to the leaders they vote for—might have significant costs for progressive criticism. By dismissing aspiration as one of the biopolitical techniques of self-making demanded by a neoliberal regime, critics simplify the nature of desire and find inexplicable the language in which many Indians imagine their lives and futures. Historian and cultural critic Vijay Prashad (2014) suggests that the inability of left-wing parties to understand aspiration left them largely unequipped to contest the right-wing BJP, perhaps contributing to the latter's historic win in 2014:

> Why were the Communists not able to capitalise on their critique of neoliberalism? Neoliberal policy not only drives inequality, it also produces aspirations. Malls, filled with shining new commodities, have been built in the large cities and small towns. Television shows and films have produced a culture of goods—fancy houses, jobs that pour money into their employees' banks, which hand out credit cards to buy anything in the malls. These neoliberal desires have over the course of the past 20 years had a marked impact on the Indian imagination. It is no longer a society formed on the values of the anti-colonial movement or of the Nehruvian period of national development. The core values of the present are personal consumption and career advancement. . . . The left struggles to find a way to both critique the inequality of neoliberalism and to appeal to the public for an alternative future. This is the conundrum of the left around

the world. The red flag has come to represent protest against the present. It does not yet indicate the pathway to the future.

Prashad's diagnosis of the failure of the left to understand and channel people's desires for better lives is applicable in literary criticism as well, where many recent writings and cultural forms are dismissed because they do not subscribe to a preexisting idea of what constitutes progressive politics. This is all the more important in the case of art, which, as Prashad has written elsewhere, "must be free to engage with contradictory consciousness without a predetermined end. . . . If a political line drives the process of elaboration, then we would know the answer to our question before we began our studies" (quoted in Nowak 2016). Taking contemporary writing seriously on its own terms, even when it seems apolitical or populist, is not a concession to the current right-wing shift but potentially its antidote.

Admittedly, focusing on literature and cultural production that centers on everyday life and aspiration will not in and of itself solve the major political crises of the twenty-first century. Likewise, it is not my aim to deny that there are many who contribute to Indian literature and cultural production from outside the world of consumerist aspirations—enriching the public sphere with the perspectives of the poor, the marginalized, and the subaltern. But dismissing texts from the outset because they might show us aspects of society that we would prefer not to acknowledge can be considered another form of elitism. Rather than seek out a literature or a subaltern voice uncorrupted by the market, we might read the impure contemporary to see what new possibilities it offers us. It might not resemble the literature we are used to; it might even mean, as Anjum Hasan (2016) writes, "a rejection of literature." But if that is not a problem for so many readers, why does it continue to be one for us?

Whose Contemporary?

One of the biggest challenges to representing the Indian contemporary is that the contemporary is implicitly seen as a time inhabited by the West.[21] This is evident in the term's common usage without geographical specification (as in "the contemporary" or "contemporary literature") when it is referring to Western texts and with a qualification (as in "contemporary Nigerian literature") when it is used for non-Western contexts.[22] Moreover, it is considered legitimate for books and articles to have titles such as "XXX in the Contemporary Novel" even when they include only Western texts. Even uses of the contemporary in fields such as art history end up conflating the Western experience of the present with a universal one. Thus, the term's associations with postmodernism are emphasized, and the contemporary becomes another word for the artistic avant-garde (Ivanova 2009, 35). A text is contemporary if it is radically formally inventive or iconoclastic; rather than "explanatory totality," this version of the contemporary offers us "proliferating differences" (T. Smith 2006, 704), and rather than "'strong' affective scenarios" in forms such as the painting or the novel, we have "less robust assemblages of life, affect, and form in their wake" (Vermeulen 2015, 3). As Peter Osborne writes, contemporaneity is "a coming together not simply 'in' time, but *of* times" (2013, 17). Language such as this reflects a very particular understanding of the contemporary, as a highly networked, late-capitalist, postindustrial time that is not experienced globally and indeed in probably very few economically and culturally advantaged pockets in the West. It privileges the contemporary as an aesthetic or philosophical concept rather than a time founded in the experience of everyday life. This very specific usage is belied by the term's universalizing gesture.

Even when progressives critical of Western solipsism attempt to talk about the present in spaces outside the West, they often do so in terms that further displace these spaces' contemporaneity. This was epitomized in the hashtag #firstworldproblems that trended on social media around 2011 and has become a common phrase since then. The hashtag, defined on *Urban Dictionary* as "problems from living in a wealthy, industrialized nation that third worlders would probably roll their eyes at," was initiated to poke fun at privileged Westerners' myopic complaints about their lives on social media, with the suggestion that they should put their problems in perspective. To make the point, "first world problems" were opposed to so-called real problems, such as, in a Louis C. K. skit, "where your life is *amazing*, so you just make shit up to be upset about. People in other countries have *real* problems. Like—'Oh, shit. They're cutting off all our heads, today!' Things like that." A Tumblr post similarly defined first world problems as "had to park far from door," "too much goat cheese in salad," and "your show isn't in HD," in contrast to "real problems": "hunger," "cholera," "rape" ("First World Problems" 2011). The intention of the meme is to compel those in the West to realize how good they have it, but it does so at the cost of a complex sense of what life is actually like in the rest of the world. The repetition of this meme thus effaces the existence of the middle classes of the so-called third world, those who might also have "first world problems" but cannot be included in the category of first world. As it does poor people who live in the West, this construction leaves that group doubly overlooked: they are neither the first worlders with illegitimate problems nor the third worlders with real ones.

These examples suggest that even in an age when knowledge travels more than before, there are still some parts of the world whose narratives get defined by others and whose claim to contemporaneity must always contend with the power of those definitions. Even though people know in theory that there exists a range of socioeconomic classes in every country, images of the non-West remain largely static and one-dimensional. Thus, someone who wants to represent the contemporary from these locations always has to explain herself. A recent article on African architectural innovations had to apologize at the outset for talking about architecture "when so much development still needs to happen on the continent" (Chutel 2017). Nicole Amarteifio (2014), whose YouTube-based television series *An African City* focuses on five women who navigate friendship and romance in contemporary Accra, has to constantly defend her show against the claim that it is not "African 'enough'" because its protagonists are middle class (Karimi 2016).[23] Kenyan author Binyavanga Wainaina (2011) is even more blunt, defending his choice to leave politics largely out of his memoir, *One Day I Will Write about This Place*, by cutting through liberal platitudes: "I was just trying to have sex in South Africa at eighteen . . . as was everyone who was eighteen in South Africa. They were not sitting down beating their chests about the fall of apartheid" ("Guardian Books" 2011). In these examples, authors have to legitimate their claim for everyday life in Africa in a context in which there seems to be simply no room for other representations aside from abjection or political assertion.

So how do writers, artists, and cultural producers reclaim a contemporary that is continually denied to them? It involves regaining control of their own representations, which in turn requires refusing the dominant idea of what is significant and important and what counts as a legitimate position for non-Western literature to take. It means embracing contradiction and at times refusing to choose what aspect of life—the personal or the political—is most important. As Toral Gajarawala writes of contemporary Dalit writer Ajay Navaria, "Beyond the question of the landlord and the peasant, upper-caste atrocity and village exodus, in Navaria's writings, there is the office space, the birthday party, urban anomie and existential reverie" (2015, 374). This juxtaposition of seemingly incongruous realities asserts a range of experiences, some abject and some merely banal, as an antidote to the pervasive idea of lower-caste life completely overrun by violence. It not only rejects global assumptions of what life in India is like but also refuses to be simplistically narrated or understood; it claims to be *all those things at once* and does not ask for permission to move between them. It portrays life as diverse and irreducible—the opposite of #firstworldproblems. And it is that restlessness around fixed definitions that becomes the marker of the contemporary.

In Gajarawala's seemingly simple description of Navaria's writings lies a radically different form of representation from what has come to be expected in Indian writing and cultural production. It is born in daily life, it is not always spectacular (although sometimes it is), it is often banal, it is at times affected by history and at other times free of it, it is partially complicit with capitalism, it is contradictory and heterogeneous—it is, in a way, just like contemporaneity everywhere. But like the African cases described previously, the Indian contemporary always has to prove itself and render itself legitimate; it is inflected by its own inevitable difference even while what it asserts is unspectacular similarity. Thus, the Indian contemporary is never self-evident but must be actively claimed, in writing, in cultural production, even in literary theory, against sedimented forms of thought that continually deny its existence. In the process of these assertions, we see the birth of new forms, new political sensibilities, and new relationships between text and world. This is evident across media and genre: attempts to represent the Indian contemporary even while knowing that it cannot be accommodated without some form of epistemic battle. "It takes imagination and courage to picture what would happen to the West . . . if its temporal fortress were suddenly invaded by the Time of its Other" wrote anthropologist Johannes Fabian (1983, 35), and indeed, representing the contemporary requires both. This is in part the reason that contemporary texts are so formally innovative, finding inspiration from unlikely genres such as self-help books and journalism; are generically transgressive; and are incessantly questioning what it means to read and understand literature at all. This restlessness around preexisting categories and writerly sensibilities, this seeming need to represent *something else* entirely, is the consequence of a contemporary that is experienced and understood in practice even while it is incessantly denied in theory.

The ability to clear some space for everyday life, momentarily free of the past or of a predetermined idea of what counts as political, is one of the characteristics of a theory of the contemporary that is truly global rather than a purely theoretical idea of the contemporary as "a kind of incessant incipience, of the kind theorized by Jacques Derrida as *à venir*—perpetual advent" (T. Smith 2008, 9). This is true not only for India and Africa but also for those within the first world whose narratives continue to be partially controlled by others. For instance, in recent African American popular culture we see a similar desire to represent a middle-class life that is not always handcuffed to history alongside the continuing effort to recognize and memorialize black history and culture. This is evident in the recent proliferation of television shows featuring African American characters in which political issues sometimes surface and sometimes do not, much as in Navaria's writings. While these shows can be criticized for not being political enough or for not taking race and the legacies of racism seriously enough, these are reductive critiques that overlook the contemporaneity of these shows as precisely their intervention.

For instance, in the successful television series *Black-ish* (Barris 2014) and *Insecure* (Rae 2016), we see across the episodes a productive oscillation between regular life and political critique. Issa Rae, the creator of HBO's *Insecure*, is quoted as saying that "in spite of her personal allegiances—[she] had no desire to make an overtly political show. She never wanted Insecure to be, as she says with a generous eye-roll, a story about 'the struggle' or 'the dramatic burdens of being black'" (Mulkerrins 2017). Of course race surfaces at times, but at other times the show is about other things: romance, sex, friendship, work (Wanzo 2016, 50–51). ABC's *Black-ish* similarly demonstrates how middle-class African Americans must constantly negotiate between the unspectacular routines of everyday life and the historical significance of being black in America (Moore 2014). Rather than choose one or the other, the show foregrounds the process of living with both: of trying to go on with everyday life in the context of increasing racial strife in the nation at large. The show reflects the contradictory desires elicited by culture and community, on the one hand, and the routines of an unmarked middle-class life, which are now available to the Johnson family, on the other. Both *Black-ish* and *Insecure* alternate between representing political issues and just depicting people living their lives, and it is that alternation that is so freeing, offering an alternative to our current "moment [in which] the relation between the aesthetic and the political can often feel restrictive and claustrophobic" (Lee 2017, 263). These shows neither assert race as a consistent defiance of white American norms nor conform to a melting-pot multiculturalism. Or, we might say, they subvert dominant norms precisely because they represent the contemporary, showing black life as it is lived rather than as it is imagined from the outside, as either abject or explicitly and always political.[24]

We see an even more extended presentation of contemporaneity in Chimamanda Ngozi Adichie's novel *Americanah* (2013).[25] *Americanah* marks a contrast to the more classically postcolonial aesthetics of Adichie's earlier novel, *Half of a Yellow Sun* (2006), which is set in the past and unfolds under the shadow of history, in a nation-state still haunted by the specters of colonialism. *Americanah* is set in the present and is largely lacking the spectacular instances of poverty and violence that have come to define Nigeria in the global novel. The novel centers on Ifemelu, a young woman who moves to the United States from Nigeria and writes a blog on her experiences with race there. At the end of the novel she returns to Lagos to reunite with her lover and to continue her writing. There are two aspects of the novel in particular that register its contemporaneity as a break from preformed assumptions about what constitutes African literature: first, Ifemelu's blog on race in the United States and, second, her return to Lagos at the end. The blog, which appears in snippets throughout the text, puts pressure on the literary aesthetics of the global novel, particularly, as we saw in regard to Ghosh, its tendency to reside at a distance from the vagaries of daily life. The blog is a casual, colloquial, open form, which even while discussing historical issues such as race, has an unfinished aspect to it that is perennially subject to revision and modification, in the form of editing, follow-up posts, reposts, and readers' comments. The blog's contemporaneity is emphasized because what it describes is the unresolved question of the meaning of race in the United States today, along with the vexed relationship between African American and African perspectives on race. The difficulty of finding the language to represent this contemporary landscape is legible in the blog's self-consciously bulky title: "Raceteenth or Various Observations about American Blacks (Those Formerly Known as Negroes) by a Non-American Black," which is in marked contrast to the pithy summative metaphor that has long defined the postcolonial novel. This purposeful resistance to ideological or sociological analysis contrasts dramatically with the pathos-infused writing of *Half of a Yellow Sun*.

Likewise, Ifemelu's move back to Lagos at the end of the novel offers a new mapping of migratory geographies from those usually on offer in the postcolonial novel. Such a move requires the representation of Lagos as a *livable* space in the present rather than the dystopic site it is usually considered. In this way, Ifemelu's return makes Lagos into a site of futurity rather than only an exit point for emigration—the site of the resolution of the romantic plot and the restoration of her mental health. The inscription of "Afropolitan" spaces (Y. Goyal 2014, xv)—Ifemelu's heritage house in Ikoyi; the office of the women's magazine where she works; and Jazzhole, Lagos's top café bookstore—contests the representation of Lagos in global crisis literature such as Mike Davis's *Planet of Slums*: "Tragically," Davis writes, by 2020, West Africa "probably will . . . be the biggest single footprint of urban poverty on earth" (2006, 6). The representation of everyday spaces, unmarked by abjection—the "non-Afro-pessimist representation . . . of Africa" (Y. Goyal 2014, xiv)—might thus be redescribed as an epistemologically "revolutionary" act (Mohutsiwa 2016).[26]

Americanah's contemporaneity is born of these disruptive qualities that operate at the level of both style and plot. Its refusal of the acceptable aesthetics of the global novel is evinced in Janet Maslin's *New York Times* review in 2013, which contrasts its "less authoritative" register with the "gravitas" of *Half of a Yellow Sun*. Maslin ends the generally critical review by noting that "the plot ultimately feels like an excuse for the venting of opinions—and the opinions carry far more conviction than the storytelling does." Another reviewer similarly commented that Adichie's "blog posts . . . have a deliberately preachy flavour, more parable than anecdote"; and later, "The story often feels like a vehicle for the discussion" (Lowdon 2013). In expressing their discomfort around the lack of formal cohesiveness in the novel and the casual venting of the blog posts, these reviewers reveal unstated expectations of what postcolonial literature should look like—the very expectations that Adichie is trying to refute. *Half of a Yellow Sun* is more accessible to a Western reader precisely because its time is not contemporary. Failed states, sexual violence, war, and disillusionment keep Nigeria safely in another time. *Americanah*, in contrast, erupts into its readers' world: through the blog, through its commentary on U.S. race relations, and by mapping Lagos through bookstores and offices rather than slums and refugee camps.

What unites this range of texts is their representation of characters doing everyday things and living unspectacular lives in contexts where readers have come to expect images of abjection or political revolt. All these texts refuse to conform to a preexisting idea of what it means to write political literature or to have a progressive politics, which often means representing the postcolonial (or African American) present as always and continually under the shadow of a violent and traumatic past. But this idea is increasingly being questioned. As popular Indian author Chetan Bhagat (2014a) writes:

> My simple stories are set in contemporary India and reflect society as it is today. And that may be one reason why the West is not so interested in me. I write the actual reality of India, versus the exotic India Westerners would rather read about. My characters are looking for jobs while falling in love. They are career-oriented, ambitious and have modern values. Who wants to read about such Indians—those who work in multinational banks and shop in malls?
>
> The India that has sold abroad is typically India with lotus ponds and simple villagers. Those who ride elephants and climb up coconut trees and that is all they want to do in life. You won't find them in my books. If there is a villager in my book, chances are he will be visiting a cyber café, checking his phone or trying to get ahead in life. Don't know if the West is ready for or interested in that India.

In refusing a static image of what constitutes the legitimate subject of the global novel, many contemporary authors create new epistemic and political possibilities. By reading the texts for these new possibilities rather than for what they do not represent or leave out, we can begin to see the outlines of a truly global contemporary.

Reading India Now

This book deploys a reading methodology that highlights experiments and unfinished aims rather than criticizes texts for what they exclude or for their lack of fully developed ideologies. I aim to read alongside texts rather than against their grain. This is in part an attempt to establish a new relationship between text and critic founded, as Chapter 6 discusses, in intimacy rather than distance, as an alternative to the somewhat repetitive nature of postcolonial literary criticism as it has been practiced over the past two decades, which subjects every new text to a similar, prefabricated critique and assumes that reading is a self-evident practice rather than one generated at least in part from the text itself. It is important to remember that when Gayatri Chakravorty Spivak published her groundbreaking reading of *Jane Eyre* in 1985 and Edward Said his reading of *Mansfield Park* in 1993, they took the academic world by storm because they offered a new way to read older and oft-read texts. Three decades later, the reading practice they advocated—exposing the silences of seemingly apolitical texts to reveal the violence of imperialism underlying them—has ended up generating readings that ironically lack any critical edge. As Rita Felski argues of ideological critique more generally, what used to be radical, against-the-grain readings have become ubiquitous and commonplace: "The danger that shadows suspicious interpretation . . . is less its murderous brutality than its potential banality. For several decades it has served as a default option in literary studies. Its gestures of demystification and exposure are no longer oppositional but obligatory. . . . It singularly fails to surprise" (2015, 115–116). Mitchum Huehls similarly writes that "the left's capacity for political and social critique has run out of steam. Those argumentative descriptions of the world that aim to defamiliarize, disillusion, and debunk our commonly held beliefs, values, and norms, exposing their ideological or discursive construction, their aporias and contradictions, their constitutive blind-spots, their racism or economic self-interest—those representational acts are not as effective as they used to be" (2016, 13–14). Yet despite its exhaustion, ideological critique is "entrenched as a professional protocol and a disciplinary norm in its own right" (Felski 2015, 119), relegating other modes of reading to the domain of the apolitical or conservative.

What can critics do besides ideological critique, as an alternative to reading literature as either complicit with or resistant to power? Or, to put it in Felski's terms, "If one is no longer 'digging down' to expose hidden meanings invisible to all others, if one is no longer 'standing back' by de-naturalizing things that everyone else is held to take for granted" (2015, 386), then what options are left? In a recent book on nationalist literature from the 1930s, Snehal Shingavi (2013) argues that the assumption that nationalism is an inherently violent discourse obscures how Indian novelists of the 1930s used the concept of the nation to envision new, radically democratic formations, even if, in the end, those visions were never realized. Anand Pandian (2015) has written what he calls an "anthropology of creation," looking at how Tamil filmmakers use cinema to imagine new worlds. These two alternatives suggest that part of what is lost in the overdetermined political reading of literature is an emphasis on representation as a *creative* and *imaginative* practice rather than as one that merely subscribes to, rejects, or subverts preexisting power relations. But to grasp this creative process, we need different models of reading from those conventionally practiced in postcolonial studies. Rather than see language as the site of the consolidation of discourse, we might consider it as a terrain of striving, of working out political positions. Likewise, rather than read texts as reflections or subversions of hegemonic norms or unequal social relations, we might read them as tentative considerations of alternative futures.

Thus, this book reads inductively, advancing a theoretical paradigm generated in the texts themselves rather than from the perspective of a distant and suspicious critic. This allows us to see not only what texts exclude but the places where they try and fail. As Christopher Holmes writes in a discussion of Zadie Smith, "The architecture of literature is not constructed merely to house ideas, but as well to give rise to thinking, to give birth to future ideas as of yet unimaginable, and to create what Virginia Woolf admonished were 'the new forms for our new sensations'" (2013, 141). From this perspective, fictional texts might also be read as works of literary criticism, and literary criticism might be understood as an act of representation, but not one with a higher value than the texts it describes.

While not all literature published since 2000 could be called contemporary by the definition laid out here, I suggest that reading for the contemporary offers new perspectives on seemingly self-evident texts. Several recent novels retain a postcolonial sensibility: for example, Jhumpa Lahiri's *The Lowland* (2013), Amit Chaudhuri's *Odysseus Abroad* (2014), Sarnath Banerjee's graphic novel *All Quiet in Vikaspuri* (2015), Mirza Waheed's *The Book of Gold Leaves* (2014), and of course Ghosh's own Ibis trilogy. But other recent texts try to bridge the contemporary with the postcolonial in innovative ways. For instance, Hansda Sowvendra Shekhar's *The Adivasi Will Not Dance* (2015) merges political resistance with the everyday through its representation of contemporary Adivasi life (de Souza 2015). While the title story documents the exploitation of Adivasi performers, others, such as "They Eat Meat!," "Blue Baby," and "Eating with the Enemy," are written from the perspective of middle-class Santhals. The inclusion of both marginalized and middle-class characters demonstrates Shekhar's interest in representing Adivasis not only as political victims or subaltern voices but also as regular, flawed people, with domestic squabbles and at times petty complaints, including the classically bourgeois complaint of bothersome servants. In fact, in "Eating with the Enemy," it might be said that the story chooses an Adivasi perspective over a subaltern class perspective, as the maid Salochana is presented as resolutely silly and the narrator's aunt has nothing but contempt for her. Here, Adivasi life is not only abject, although at times it is plagued by discrimination and violence. Likewise, Lavanya Sankaran's novel *The Hope Factory* (2013b) alternates between the stories of Anand, an entrepreneur eager to expand his automobile parts business to foreign contracts, and of Kamala, who works in Anand's house as a maid. In an interview at the end of one edition of the book, Sankaran says that of the two characters, "Kamala came easily to me; her story and her struggles seemed to flow from the pen. . . . [However,] getting to the truth of [Anand's] character was much more difficult for me" (2013a, 355). This is striking given that Sankaran was an investment banker before launching her career as a writer and would thus seem to have more in common with Anand than with Kamala. But her difficulty in representing Anand suggests that it is paradoxically easier for middle-class writers to represent subaltern characters than characters closer to their own class. Kamala is a type that has been oft written about: the noble, hardworking servant who, despite her poverty, has dreams of her own. But Anand, who aspires to navigate India's new capitalist economy, lies largely outside the Indian English novelistic imaginary. Sankaran finds Kamala easier to write because Kamala has become domesticated by the Indian novel in English, whose particular politico-aesthetic vision is exactly suited to representing her. By contrast, Sankaran's inclusion of Anand reflects her attempt to supplement that vision with something new.

Reading for the contemporary means reading for such contradictions, even when they remain unresolved in the work. Sankaran's uncanny discomfort with Anand's similarity to her suggests that surprises might be found closer to home. As journalist Aman Sethi writes, there is a tendency among progressives to look for alternatives to our world somewhere out there, "among remote, marginalised communities who have somehow developed anti-bodies [to neoliberalism] in the form of . . . an 'older ethos of restraint and limitation.' . . . In this narrative, knowledge and power always lies outside and elsewhere. . . . Everyone else has been enfeebled or co-opted" (Mishra and Sethi 2015). This fantasy of a pure, uncorrupted political resistance precludes attention to the varied ways in which people mount micro-resistances from within their "co-opted" lives. The shifting and unstable narratives produced in this process envision better futures but eschew the language of revolution. Thus, they easily fall below the progressive radar. Attending to these narratives suggests that the present is not so bleak as it might seem. There are new political imaginaries everywhere, but we have to know how to read for them.

PART I

Locations

1

The New Provincialism

N ear the end of *Half Girlfriend*, the 2014 novel by best-selling Indian writer Chetan Bhagat, the protagonist Madhav travels to New York to take up an internship with the Bill Gates Foundation. There, he gets introduced to life in the United States and reunites with his lost love, Riya. After the internship is over, Madhav's friends encourage him to stay in the United States and "make a new life" for himself there (Bhagat 2014b, 228). However, Madhav refuses and returns home to Bihar instead, using a foundation grant to upgrade a school his mother has been running in his natal village, Dumraon. As the novel ends, there is no regret or sense that Madhav has missed something by returning home. In fact, it is just the opposite; he has perennially felt like an outsider in both the United States and Delhi, where he went to college and held his first job. "*You belong to Dumraon in Bihar,*" he keeps telling himself. "*That is who you are, Madhav Jha . . . and that is all you will ever be and need to be*" (94; emphasis in original). Despite opportunities elsewhere, Madhav eventually realizes that the best opportunity is waiting for him right at home. Fittingly, then, the novel's epilogue shows Madhav three years later, running a fully equipped school in Dumraon, with Riya and their son by his side. This fruitful coincidence of enterprise, romance, and return becomes one of the hallmarks of the English-language commercial novel in the first two decades of the twenty-first century.

It seems like a simple gesture, coming home to find one's future in India, but it flies in the face of literary paradigms born in the postcolonial novel's love of cosmopolitanism, border crossing, and exile. How does this inversion of standard postcolonial geographies reflect contemporary discussions around aspiration, futurity, and youth in India? How does it reimagine the popular novel to accommodate this new sense of possibility?

As the Introduction to this book illustrates, coming home goes against the grain of the cosmopolitanism that has been dominant in the Indian English novel since the 1980s, which emphasized travel, transit, and routes over roots.[1] Salman Rushdie's *The Satanic Verses* (1988) begins jubilantly in the liminal space over the Atlantic Ocean; and when characters do return home, as Rahel does at the end of Arundhati Roy's *The God of Small Things* (1997), it is often presented as dystopic. Indian English writers themselves were, in the 1980s and 1990s, also transnational, as captured in the excitement with which the *New Yorker* described the photograph of eleven Indian English novelists featured in its special fiction issue in June 1997: "The photograph . . . was taken in London on the morning of May 30th. Two weeks earlier, the plan had been to have it taken in New York. In truth, the photograph could have been taken just about anywhere . . . anywhere, that is, except India" (Buford 1997, 8).[2] That issue of the *New Yorker* was published in the year Arundhati Roy stormed the global literary scene with *The God of Small Things* and four years after Rushdie's *Midnight's Children* won the Booker of Bookers. This marked a high point for the Indian novel in English. Not only did English make the Indian experience globally accessible, but for many writers, English was the perfect language in which to express frustration with the failures of the nation-state. As Rajeev Patke writes, "English is an antidote to provincialism and narrow-mindedness; it is the language of translation and access to the world's literary cultures" (2016, 296). In the 1980s and 1990s, "exile," "diaspora," and "cosmopolitanism" were the privileged terms of the Indian English imagination (Lau and Dwivedi 2014, 7).

From this perspective, Madhav's return to India might be seen as a reverse trend: an instantiation of patriotic nationalism, a refusal of exile, a turning inward. But seeing it only as a reactionary gesture overlooks the contemporaneity of this return—specifically, how coming home offers a new imaginary of India as a livable place rather than one to be abandoned for better prospects elsewhere. This reimagination requires the help of a number of emergent discourses: the potential of India's youth, new opportunities for the middle class, self-help, and enterprise, which in turn require new literary forms different from those of the classic postcolonial novel. We can see these new forms in a range of commercial fiction by authors such as Bhagat, Amish Tripathi, Durjoy Datta, Ravinder Singh, and Anuja Chauhan. Unlike the group pictured in the *New Yorker*, all of these newer authors live in India and write in English, primarily for Indian audiences. Their works are translated into Indian languages but few European ones, and they will likely never win any international prizes. While these new commercial fictions are often criticized as evidence of a decline in both political engagement and literary quality since the 1990s, we can alternatively see them as part of a new imaginary that is actively redefining what India means for Indians today and what new literary forms might represent it. Thus, against the association of English with exile, today, "as English percolates to a more general level of writerly usage, it makes itself more at home in India" (Sunder Rajan 2011, 218).

This chapter argues that the new English-language commercial fictions reorient postcolonial geographies that valorized exile over nationalism to offer a new representation of India for their Indian readership.[3] They do this in part by locating livable futures not only in India's megalopolises that more easily exemplify capitalist aspiration but also in India's less fashionable regions and provincial towns, such as the Bihar to which Madhav returns. These works resignify those spaces from sites conventionally associated with decay and backwardness to ones of contemporaneity and even hope. While much of the criticism of economic liberalization in India focuses on the closing down of futures—cosmopolitanism narrowing to nationalism, idealism narrowing to pragmatism—these texts offer the ability to see the future of India anew. They seek alternatives both to the secular cosmopolitanism of the Rushdie generation of Indian writers in English and to a statist nationalism built on nepotism, tradition, and the status quo, one that is suspicious of youth and change altogether. In this way, these fictions mobilize the impulse evident in earlier experiments with provincialism, such as those of Indian novelists R. K. Narayan (Hasan 2015b, 6; Amitava Kumar 2012, 66–67) and Phanishwarnath Renu (K. Hansen 1981, 282), both of whom used the idea of the local to write new futures for India in the early postcolonial decades. Even the early twentieth-century concept of *swadeshi* (one's own country) might be seen as a form of provincialism that offered an alternative to nineteenth-century modernity. However, in mobilizing current discourses around the potentiality of India's youth, self-help, and enterprise, and in writing specifically against the cosmopolitanism of the postcolonial novel, today's texts present a *new* provincialism fitting for a new India.[4]

In this way, and like the various other instances of contemporaneity discussed in this book, the new provincialism is epistemically significant, a reconceiving of Indian English writing as not intrinsically tied to exile and loss, as it was in the 1980s and 1990s, but as potentially imbricated with new forms of aspiration—entrepreneurialism, social mobility, financial independence, individual success—that had little place in earlier Indian fiction. The new commercial fiction could be said to work as what Zadie Smith calls "antiliterature," a body of work that "evacuates ideas from the novel and engages in a dynamic process of building, razing and rebuilding structures for thinking" (C. Holmes 2013, 151). Although seemingly simplistic in terms of plot, characters, and style, the new commercial fiction entails a rethinking of what literature is, the role of its readers, and its relationship to the world it describes. Far from being a mere expression of market forces, it serves as a means of assessing how new conditions might generate new limitations and new possibilities. Attending to these texts as imaginative and creative reveals the epistemic significance of the new provincialism, against critics' alarmist sense that it marks the definitive end of progressive secular culture or "great literature" in India.

This chapter focuses primarily on controversial Indian novelist Chetan Bhagat, a former investment banker whose six novels have won him millions of readers, especially among middle- and lower-middle-class Indian youth (M. Jain 2014). While Bhagat is not by any means the first pulp writer in India (Khair 2008; Mongia 2015; Kaur 2012), his immense success and his appeal to a wide range of readers across the country have made him somewhat of a phenomenon in the last decade. While selling hundreds of thousands of copies of his first book, *Five Point Someone* (2004), "in a market where you don't need to reach even the 10,000-mark to qualify as a bestseller" (Singh 2009, 27), Bhagat's success has transformed Indian publishing and English-language reading countrywide.[5] Yet his outspoken and often reactionary comments on contemporary political and social issues in interviews and on social media have made him unpopular among progressives and more-educated readers.[6] He has criticized taxes and agricultural subsidies and has enthusiastically championed a culture of enterprise, as demonstrated in his nonfiction books *What Young India Wants* (2012) and *Making India Awesome* (2015). He endorsed the right-wing political party BJP and its prime ministerial candidate Narendra Modi in the run-up to the 2014 national election (T. Joseph 2014). He is also criticized for his occasionally sexist comments,[7] as well as for seeming at times to fan the flames of communal discord (Bhagat 2013; Akbar 2013; F. Ahmed 2011; D. Goswami 2017). Because of this public persona, very few critics have engaged with his novels themselves either to interrogate their appeal or to treat them as literary and aesthetic experiments with representing the contemporary in India.

I argue, however, that Bhagat's works are so crucial to understand precisely because of their rejection of cosmopolitanism and postcolonial literary aesthetics and the wide, populist appeal of their English. His version of the new provincialism involves stories such as Madhav's return to Bihar, contemporary settings such as call centers and malls, and young people trying to make their way in a landscape at times hostile to youth. These make "the characters that populate Mr Bhagat's novels, the preoccupations they have, the ambitions they nurse and the obstacles they encounter . . . all endearingly those of today's real-life India" (Balakrishnan 2013). But his project extends even deeper into rethinking the novel itself as a contemporary form, one open to the present rather than erudite and distant. Thus, we see throughout his works a series of formal and aesthetic experiments that have been largely absent in the Indian English novel before his, such as formulaic characterization, an aesthetics of self-help, an interpellative form that stages a dialogue with his readers, and the vernacularization of English, bringing it closer to the polyglossic speech of young urban India. Moreover, Bhagat's works are avowedly "antiliterary" (P. Joshi 2015, 312); he famously said that he sees his strongest competition not in other books but in "apps like Candy Crush or WhatsApp" (Kapoor 2014a). These aspects of Bhagat's works combine with his contemporary stories and settings to offer something new to Indian readers and, indeed, to the Indian novel in English more broadly. Rather than use an elite form remaining at a distance from its reception and from the vagaries of the contemporary world, Bhagat reinvents the novel by turning the present into an aesthetic possibility.[8]

At the same time, Bhagat's continuing investment in a wounded masculinity and his undertheorized female characters, who rarely engage in the same extended struggle as his male protagonists, also mark a limit in his oeuvre. Although he is read by young women as much as men, and looks less like a "lad lit" writer than some of his best-selling counterparts,[9] his novels consistently present a world in which men are aggrieved protagonists and women are merely the aloof objects of their advances. There is little room in Bhagat for female sexuality; what we have instead are cold, unwilling partners of awkward but well-meaning, sexually frustrated males. Thus, his success in writing the struggles of young men seems to be predicated on the effacement of their female counterparts.

It is in this context that I read the female-centered popular fiction of Anuja Chauhan as a rejoinder to Bhagat's limitations. Chauhan's hugely popular "chick lit" novels,[10] in which her young characters navigate the vicissitudes of the new India, also advance a new provincialism; but while Chauhan similarly revalues India as a place of futurity rather than backwardness, she does so through the figure of the woman who can have it all—professional success and romance—thus writing female desire as central to a successful life and a happy ending. As in Bhagat, in Chauhan a return home marks a break from the valorization of exile seen in the earlier generation of Indian English fiction. But by criticizing the way female desire is often seen as distracting from professional success and by writing a protagonist who manages to reconcile the two, Chauhan imagines a contemporary that is not merely a space of earnest masculinity but also one of fun and female desire.

The Challenge of the Commercial

As noted earlier, the recent widespread popularity of English-language commercial fiction in India, when discussed at all, has been used by critics and commentators as evidence of the decline of literature, a takeover of the market, and the end of a culture of political dissent in the public sphere. These novels' focus on middle-class characters is seen to reflect an increasing indifference to India's poor and disenfranchised in the new India (Philips 2015, 108). Phenomena such as new author Savi Sharma selling one hundred thousand copies of her book *Everyone Has a Story* (2015) in one hundred days (K. Gupta 2017) and romance writer Ravinder Singh claiming that he had not read much at all before becoming a multiple best-selling writer (Hasan 2016)[11] support the idea of the new fiction being entirely market rather than quality driven: "Rather than successfully selling branded shoes, cosmetics, clothes etc., the trained marketing executives are writing and selling books" (V. Shukla 2016). Vandana Shukla continues:

> Serious writers would sometimes take a decade to write a classic; revising, editing, rewriting umpteen times, [whereas] these bestsellers are produced dot on a fixed deadline. And they are written with total disregard for grammar, syntax and spellings. The writers know the pulse of the texting, whatsApping generation. . . . In one of the sessions at the Jaipur Literature Festival-2015, packed with cheering young fans—mostly in school uniform—[Chetan] Bhagat declared writing like Shakespeare or Salman Rushdie is easier because ". . . these guys sit with dictionaries and use the most difficult word where a simple word would do to earn literary respectability. I write from the heart!" If our books write our cultural history, these books are creating disturbing trends.

In contrast to these views, I argue that the phenomenon of Indian commercial fiction in English offers a new perspective on some of the long-standing concerns of Indian literature and postcolonial criticism. While in the twentieth century pulp fiction was much more developed in the bhashas than in English (Khair 2008), the new commercial fiction represents a shift whereby, for the first time, the most successful English books in India have very little, if any, market outside India.[12] In addition, these titles reach a much larger number of Indian readers than Indian English or bhasha fiction has, including those outside the metropolitan cities and first-generation English readers, meaning people raised in the bhashas, who are "English/ Hindi bilinguals . . . and yet they are uncertain of how well their English meets external, global standards" (quoted in Suman Gupta 2012, 52). As

Bhagat has confirmed, "[English] is not my first language, and for my readers it's not their first language. These people are constables, drivers, the class of people you would never associate with reading an English book. The guy who frisks me at the airport, he tells me: 'I'm trying to read your book. It's taken me a month'" (quoted in Dhaliwal 2014). The books' low pricing also ensures that they reach readers from a range of socioeconomic backgrounds (Viswamohan 2013, 20–21; Kapoor 2014a). As Rashmi Sadana confirms, "Bhagat's novels are not only sold to people who already read English novels, but to thousands upon thousands who might never have read one before. . . . The fact that his novels are not literary means most critics dismiss them, but what cannot be dismissed is that his novels represent a new readership whose relationship to English and to their own class identities is markedly different from before" (2012, 176).

In this way, today's commercial fiction picks up on an alternative tradition in Indian English writing, exemplified, for instance, by the romance novelist Shobhaa Dé, who wrote novels throughout the 1990s and 2000s but never gained (or sought) an international audience and was never included among the list of writers who brought Indian literature to the world. As Padmini Mongia writes, the exclusion of a writer like Dé from the category of Indian Writing in English (IWE) says a lot about the prejudice of the field toward "literary rather than popular concerns. . . . Dé's popular fictions are written for consumption by local readerships in India. They belong neither to the postcolonial category nor to vernacular ones. . . . Her oeuvre thus complicates our understanding of the implied tension between vernacular worlds and cosmopolitan imaginaries" (2015, 105).

While commercial fiction is deemed "inferior" for its nonliterary qualities the world over (Harzewski 2006, 36),[13] Deborah Philips writes that "the [new commercial] novels are not without their contradictions" (2015, 109). Reflecting the professional and romantic struggles that constitute life in contemporary India, these fictions capture the popular imagination on a scale unthinkable for literary fiction. Commercial fiction thus poses a challenge for critics. Seemingly market driven and antiliterary, commercial fiction nevertheless reflects large-scale changes in Indian society, including a rethinking of the assumption that English-language publishing is always oriented westward.

"Over and Over Again"

One of the features most often criticized in Bhagat's novels—and indeed, in commercial fiction more generally—is their formulaic plotlines, which, in Bhagat's case, inspire comparisons to Bollywood films rather than literature.

As Fredric Jameson writes, "Where the modernist novel sought to flee repetition, or at least to translate it into something more lofty and aesthetically worthy, mass culture thrives on what used to be called the *formulaic*: you want to see over and over again the same situations, the same plots, the same kinds of characters" (2010, 366). Very much embracing this sameness, Bhagat's novels present social and political problems through recognizable characters and tropes: for example, a male protagonist (with the exception of Bhagat's most recent novel, which features a female protagonist [U. Anjaria 2017a])—often a loser or misfit—who has professional aspirations; faces intergenerational conflict; seeks out friendship and romance, which is not always requited; and faces ethical and moral challenges. The books follow this protagonist through the various hurdles of professional and romantic life and adulthood in what is supposed to be a new India but in which some of the qualities of the old remain. Their struggles thus have mixed results; even as the formulaic structures often mean a happy ending, there is equally an investment in questioning what it means to be "happy" in the first place.

Bhagat's use of these formulas has led some scholars to classify his works as "lad lit," a global genre characterized by "masculine insecurities, competition at college or the work place, sexual fantasies, drug addiction, relationships, heartbreaks, family issues and obsession with sports" (Viswamohan 2013, 19) or as "inspi-lit," because they "narrate stories about 'triumph[s] over personal trauma'" (Subir Dhar 2013, 161). But fitting Bhagat into such categories ignores how his use of formulas serves his interest in the Indian contemporary. Indeed, by creating a *type* out of otherwise unremarkable young men, Bhagat imagines a new demographic comprising young, aspirational men with common experiences across geographic, class, or other divides. *Five Point Someone*, his first book, describes the intense pressures of student life for India's aspiring engineers at the Indian Institute of Technology (IIT), India's most prestigious engineering college. *One Night @ the Call Center* (2005) is set in a business process outsourcing (BPO) office that offers the promise of financial success for young urban Indians but for which they pay a price in terms of their self-respect and dignity. *The 3 Mistakes of My Life* (2008) features three friends in Gujarat who start a sporting goods store but get caught up in the anti-Muslim riots of 2002. In *2 States* (2009) a Punjabi man and Tamil woman face challenges as they try to convince their families that they should get married. *Revolution 2020* (2011) is a look at the business of Indian education through the eyes of a protagonist who cannot pass the competitive engineering exams and ends up starting his own coaching center. And *Half Girlfriend* (2014) is about a student on a sports scholarship who comes from Bihar to Delhi and faces limitations because of his strongly accented English.

While the settings and stories of these books vary, they share features that allow Bhagat to underline commonalities between different parts of India and different class positions. Many scenes across the novels are set in new consumerist spaces such as call centers, multinational banks, shopping malls, coffee shops, and lounge bars, which represent to critics the shiny new manifestations of an exclusionary capitalism. But far from celebrating these spaces, the novels show their protagonists struggling to navigate them, realizing that although the spaces promise new futures, they continue to hold out new and older obstacles. These spaces are not presented as self-evident but as aspirational and problematic. The characters are rarely at ease in them but attempt to reconcile their own versions of themselves—flawed, insecure—with the dominant discourse of a new and shining India. Across these works, the spaces of the new India are presented as sites where the conflict between promise and reality play out.

These unspectacular stories of everyday Indian lives refrain from asking big questions about the relationship of the individual to history, as did so much Indian English fiction of the earlier generation; instead, they present repeated formulas with small variations to write the insecurities of middle-class life into the space of the novel. In presenting stories that actively refuse the universal significance characteristic of "good" literature, the novels are not expressions of a predetermined ideological position. They let everyday lives speak for themselves and, in doing so, open up the novel to a larger range of experiences. Their contemporaneity thus lies partly in their use of formulas.

Character Types

Along with formulaic plots, Bhagat experiments with character types to criticize certain aspects of the new India. Some scholars see these as stereotypes; for instance, in *One Night @ the Call Center*, Aysha Viswamohan argues, Bhagat gives us

> Shyam, the "loser" hero on the verge of losing his job as well as the woman he loves . . . ; Priyanka, the self-righteous and upright girl; Esha, the aspiring model; Radhika, the sari-clad housewife who knits during office hours while her sales manager husband cheats on her; Vroom, the "misfit" who loves living on the edge . . . ; Military Uncle, a retired army man, abandoned by his son and daughter-in-law; Bakshi, the unscrupulous and lecherous boss. (2013, 24)

The characters Viswamohan describes are certainly recognizable, which is Bhagat's hallmark. But a closer look at *One Night* shows that even while

Bhagat employs character types, his novels also play with the idea of type-casting and stereotyping. The nickname "Vroom," for instance, derives from his obsession with cars. "Military Uncle" is the designation the young people give their older, strict colleague at the call center because he used to be in the army. In fact, all of the characters, because they work in a call center, have real names as well as American names they have to adopt so that their callers can pronounce them. So Shyam becomes Sam, Priyanka becomes Pearl, Esha becomes Elizabeth, and so on. In this way, Bhagat uses character types to call attention to the lived experience of being typecast.

We see this attention to the dangers of labeling people in Bhagat's other novels as well. For instance, in *2 States*, Krish's and Ananya's families—Punjabi and Tamil, respectively—harbor negative stereotypes of each other's cultures, especially the Punjabis, who cannot stop themselves from calling Ananya's family "Madrasis." Even after they have accepted the interethnic marriage, they continue to utilize this language, leading Krish to lament: "National anthem, national currency, national teams—still, we won't marry our children outside our state. How can this intolerance be good for our country?" (Bhagat 2009, 102). In *Revolution 2020*, Gopal suffers from being typecast as a "loser" because of his low rank on the engineering exams. This label haunts him: "We are losers. We don't get things easily. Marks, ranks, girls—nothing is easy for us" (Bhagat 2011, 79), making him jump at the opportunity to succeed, even when it involves acting immorally. In both these novels, typecasting is not just bad writing; it is a cultural problem that India needs to overcome.

But it is in *One Night @ the Call Center* that the consideration of types is most complex. The angst that this novel's characters face working in a call center is precisely that they have been typecast, relegated to a role that has been determined for them in advance. This leads to a feeling of stagnation in their lives that counteracts the discourses of the call center and of economic liberalization more broadly, discourses that ostensibly celebrate innovation and movement. Even beyond the individual racism they face from their American clients, *One Night*'s characters are boxed into the particular role reserved for Indian labor under global capitalism. Despite striving to embrace the sense of futurity that working in a call center promises, the novel's young characters quickly discover that they are in fact bodies invented to fill a need in a "global" capitalism that is actually driven by the West; they are the faceless labor force who will make American multinational companies more profitable. Conforming to this type has hollowed out their own individuality, leaving them unsure of who they really are. As Vroom observes, "'I like jeans, mobiles and pizzas. I earn, I eat, I buy shit and I die. That is all the fuck there is to Vroom. It is all bullshit man'" (Bhagat 2005, 214). Globalization fails to deliver on its promise to the young Indians it seduces:

> We don't have jobs that make us work to our potential. . . . There is so much to do. We should be building roads, power plants, airports, phone networks and metro trains in every city like madness. And if the government moves its rear-end and does that, the young people in this country will find jobs there. Hell, I would work days and nights for that—as long as I know that what I am doing is helping build something for my country, for its future. But the government doesn't believe in doing any real work, so they allow these BPOs to be opened and think they have taken care of the youth. (209)

Here we can see how flat characterization is a thematic as well as formal choice, representing a world in which some types of individuals are valued more than others. This is not a wholesale critique of capitalism, as it imagines a world in which capitalism *will* live up to its promise. However, it is not an unnuanced celebration of capitalism either. Through its formal play on character—choosing who gets to be an individual and who remains a type— the novel registers the various obstacles to *inhabiting* capitalism from the frustrated perspective of those whose lives it promises to transform.

The ideal of individual character also suffers, Bhagat's novels suggest, in a cultural context in which the intrinsic wisdom of the elderly is valued more than the drive of the youth. This is a theme that appears in all of Bhagat's novels and in his nonfiction work, *What Young India Wants*, as well (C. Jeffrey 2013). Many of Bhagat's protagonists are fatherless or, as in *2 States*, have an estranged father, indicating a dearth of role models from the older generation. Instead, various representatives of the older generation step in to play the role of father—such as Om's Hindu nationalist uncle in *3 Mistakes* (Avinash Kumar 2013) and the corrupt Member of the Legislative Assembly (MLA) Shuklaji in *Revolution 2020*—but significantly, they end up leading their "sons" off course. There are also misguided plans by India's elders to advance the country, but at the expense of youth rather than in collaboration with them. In *One Night*, the call center represents a misguided form of inclusion into the global capitalist system; rather than tap young India's potential, it yokes India's youth to a system geared entirely for the benefit of others: "Our government doesn't realize this, but Americans are using us. We are sacrificing an entire generation to service their call centers" (207–208). In *3 Mistakes*, Hindu chauvinism is portrayed as exerting a negative force on India's youth, as an ideology that traps young people into bearing the historic grudges of Partition and Hindu-Muslim violence—grudges that threaten to distract them from their own futures: "I checked myself from dreaming again. India is not a place for dreams" (115). In *2 States*, the older generation takes two forms: professors who want to turn all innovative ideas into solvable equations, and parents who are more interested in marrying off their children than in making them happy. "They are all frustrated," Krish tells Ananya regarding their professors. "We are half their age but will earn twice as them [*sic*] in two years. Wouldn't you hate an eleven-year-old if he earned double?" (12).

Bhagat, then, presents character not as a given but as something that young people must actively claim for themselves to forge their own futures. Bhagat novelizes the question of India's "progress" into the struggle between society and the young person whom it disempowers—not only politically but also psychologically. Often, his protagonist does not have access to the best education and cultural capital and thus is multiply disempowered. Reading Bhagat reanimates the connection between literary character and social mobility, a connection often forgotten in the literary novel, in which characters have the privilege of being rounded from the outset.

Self-Help Fictions

How does a Bhagat character go from being disempowered to feeling a sense of agency over his or her own life? And how must the novel form bend to accommodate such a transition, when enacted within the restricted parameters of formula fiction? For Bhagat, who has little interest in philosophical or aesthetic concerns, these questions have a simple, pragmatic response: self-help, a utilitarian, antiliterary genre of writing that offers individuals stuck in their circumstances a set of steps to move forward. Self-help writing has risen in popularity in India since economic liberalization, and indeed, one of the criticisms that Bhagat's novels most often receive is that he uses a "typical self-help guide style" (Viswamohan 2013, 24) that simplifies the process of empowerment to one that can be completed in a series of steps. Self-transformation is one of the repeated formulas of his fiction: In *One Night* Shyam realizes he cannot work for a call center any longer but must take the plunge and start his own business; in *2 States* Krish acknowledges that he has to forgive his father; in *Revolution 2020* Gopal realizes he must apologize to his former best friend, and so on. But far from the "unapologetic, self-confident, brash" sensibility that Purnima Mankekar identifies in aspirational youth cultures in contemporary India (2013, 28), these protagonists are wracked with self-doubt, and it takes a significant amount of struggle for them to motivate themselves out of it.

The rise of self-help cultures globally is generally associated with a neo-liberal regime in which care of the self becomes the new expression of biopolitical discipline. As David Harvey writes, "Neoliberalism is in the first instance a theory of political economic practices that proposes that human well-being can best be advanced by liberating individual entrepreneurial freedoms and skills"; thus, the "'conduct of individuals themselves'" is tied to overall economic development (quoted in Gooptu 2013, 7). Self-help is generally seen as representing an abdication of the duties of the state, so the language of universal rights is replaced by the language of strategic maneuvering and profit: "self-help teaches . . . marketing strategies to use on ourselves" (Simonds 1996, 25). Self-help guides, ever popular under this new regime, present "an ideal self . . . [who] will internalize and biographize her social circumstances, and perceive discontentment, ranging from mild unhappiness to considerable psychological distress, as a temporary setback to be turned into useful fuel for ongoing work towards future successes" (Brouillette 2014, 44).

From this perspective it is easy to find neoliberal resonances in Bhagat's novels of enterprising youth struggling to define their identities and professional futures against the various challenges of family and society. Given Bhagat's own advocacy for individual empowerment as a means for India to progress (as in his nonfiction book *Making India Awesome*), such interpretations are understandable. But to read the novels as straightforward expressions of neoliberalism overlooks the particular obstacles against which Bhagat's protagonists struggle, as well as the function of self-help in the novel form more broadly. Unlike the protagonists of the male-centered romance novels of Durjoy Datta, for instance, who change very little from beginning to end, all of Bhagat's characters need to undergo some transformation for their stories to be resolved. In some cases, characters need to transform themselves to get the girl. For instance, in *One Night*, only when Shyam speaks up to his incompetent boss, quits the call center, and decides to start his own company can he win Priyanka back (272). "No one wants to date a loser" is the message of *Half Girlfriend* as well, and only when Madhav becomes proud of his Bihari identity can he reunite with Riya. In *Revolution 2020* we have a slightly different version: Gopal gets Aarti, the romantic partner he has long desired, but realizes that he won her from Raghav, his former friend, through deceit and an immature desire for revenge, and thus he ends up concocting a plot to get Aarti and Raghav back together, while he ends up alone. In this outlier, self-transformation is not a means to romance; rather, romance is sacrificed to self-transformation (Anjaria and Anjaria 2013a, 202).

To say that these novels work to discipline their readers into a certain sense of self that benefits an aggressive, market-oriented nationalism misses the complexity of these representations. It also reads the texts narrowly as power-laden discourses rather than as more open terrains of conflicting viewpoints. As Rita Felski argues, while language can in many cases "be used to police, control, or exclude," that does not mean that it always or necessarily does so:

> After all, people seek to articulate and understand themselves in different milieus and to very diverse ends. . . . Some of these speech acts, no doubt, are inspired by self-delusion or misperception; others may bully, browbeat, or exclude. Yet they can also forge new attachments and solidarities, renounce or reaffirm past histories, offer fresh angles of vision or reaffirm crucial but long-forgotten insights. They serve differing needs and have countless uses. (2015, 79)

Felski urges attention to speech acts in "specific cases" (2015, 79)—and indeed, the use of self-help in Bhagat calls for such a sensitivity to context rather than designates his works as neoliberal from the outset. We might read his self-help formula in relation to the question of character discussed previously, in which self-transformation becomes a contemporary version of what Lauren Goodlad calls, in the context of Victorian fiction, building character. For Goodlad, nineteenth-century novels operated on "a prescriptive notion of character in which every human being was, in theory, endowed with the potential to develop the most ennobling governing qualities" (2004, 134–135). In its twenty-first-century incarnation, self-help might be seen as a democratic discourse that, by helping build character, allows those on the margins of the middle class to imagine their way into a world to which they would otherwise be denied access.[14]

Discourses of empowerment, despite their neoliberal resonances, have been central to a range of writings by and for marginalized groups. Feminist tracts such as Gloria Steinem's *Feminine Mystique* and bell hooks's *Sisters of the Yam*, for instance, argue "that self-esteem is the necessary foundation for social action" and that "we cannot fully create effective movements for social change if individuals struggling for that change are not also self-actualized or working toward that end" (Simonds 1996, 24). Paul Gilroy, a deep critic of neoliberalism, nevertheless admits that the long history of antiblack racism "seems . . . to have inclined people towards the solutions proffered by neoliberal styles of thought. . . . In other words, the history of being denied recognition as an individual has actually enhanced the appeal of particular varieties of extreme individualism" (2013, 35). The importance of self-transformation as a prerequisite for political transformation is evident in the differences between white American chick lit and what Lisa Guerrero calls African American "sistah lit" featuring middle-class black protagonists. As Guerrero writes, sistah lit's protagonists' "struggles are marked by much more than just *how* to get a man in order to fit into socially constructed ideas of womanhood; because of their race, they are first forced to forge their own sense of womanhood" (2006, 93; emphasis in original). Whereas a mainstream chick lit novel like *Bridget Jones's Diary* ends with Bridget finding happiness in the perfect man, Terry McMillan's *Waiting to Exhale* "ends with each woman finding a place to begin to stake her claim to self and happiness. . . . Unlike Fielding, whose final portrait of Bridget's becoming coupled with Mark Darcy marks a triumphant *end*, McMillan shows her four heroines' ultimate relationships to men . . . as *beginnings*" (100; emphasis in original).

Bhagat's novels, too, end in beginnings, emphasizing self-transformation as a prerequisite for a successful life. *One Night* ends with Shyam and Vroom starting their own company; *3 Mistakes*, with Ali's recovery and the beginning of a cricket career; *2 States*, with Krish and Ananya's marriage; and *Revolution 2020*, with Gopal's new life apart from Aarti. Just as sistah lit characters "realize that their responses to men, romance, and relationships have led them, in part, to their current lives, and that galvanizes their desire to change themselves" (Guerrero 2006, 95), Bhagat's characters find that they too are partially responsible for their failures in the professional and romantic domains. Whereas in the African American women's case, this is in part because of "society's ideals of beauty" (95) and the historic devaluation of black women, in Bhagat it has to do with a range of factors that Bhagat diagnoses as the ills of contemporary India: social hierarchies and favoritism, the devaluation of youth, middle-class conservatism, a cutthroat educational system, government corruption, and so on. Bhagat's protagonists must transcend these limitations to imagine a successful life; and at times, like their sistah lit counterparts, they even have to give up the possibility of a romantic resolution for this empowerment to take place.

Despite what seem like formulaic romantic plots in Bhagat's novels, therefore, the resolution of the romance plays a more marginal role than in other current romance novels such as those of Durjoy Datta and Anuja Chauhan. Any reader of Bhagat will notice that the love story often gets resolved impossibly quickly at the end. The reason is that the romantic problem, the problem of how to get the girl, is in Bhagat recast as part of a larger problem of low self-esteem and a depleted sense of agency. In *One Night*, Shyam loses Priyanka not because he is not a good boyfriend but because of her mother's view—shared by Priyanka as well—that "her daughter was stuck with a loser" (141). The moment Shyam stops being "a mousepad" that "people are rolling over . . . everyday" (151), Priyanka takes him back. Thus, at the end Shyam can say, "As for me as a person, I still feel the same for the most part. However, there is a difference. I used to feel I was a good-for-nothing non-achiever. But that is not true. After all, I helped save lots of jobs at a call center, taught my boss a lesson, started my own company, was chosen over a big-catch NRI groom by a wonderful girl and now I even finished a whole book. This means that i) I can do whatever I really want ii) God is always with me and iii) there is no such thing as a loser after all" (284).

The only one of Bhagat's novels that is primarily a love story is *2 States*, but it too links love with an empowered self. The novel begins with Krish visiting a psychiatrist for depression; he has reached this low point after he and Ananya broke up as a result of the lack of understanding among their parents, and it is fixed only by Krish's estranged father taking the uncharacteristic action of interceding on his son's behalf. This, in turn, could happen only when Krish forgives his father for his earlier mistakes. Romantic love here is once again seen as the outcome of self-empowerment, suggesting that it is not until one can see one's own life clearly that romance will fall into place.

In *3 Mistakes*, self-transformation is represented by sports, which runs against cultural norms that value security and financial success over health, the body, and entrepreneurialism. In the novel, the three protagonists open a sporting goods store in defiance of the more traditional professional aspirations their parents have for them. They constantly face difficulties because sports is considered frivolous and risky: "Middle-class parents . . . [are] so scared of losing money, they want their kids to serve others all their lives to get a safe salary" (111). When the young men visit a municipal school to sell sports equipment, they are told it is not a priority for the school since so many of the kids are poor and need material advancement rather than sports. When the protagonists visit Australia, however, they learn that the government offers scholarships for talented youth of all income ranges to attend sports camps. The novel has characters repeatedly lament India's abysmal sports record as a product of the older generation's conservatism: "Sports is the wrong choice in our country" (124); "What an idiot I am? Why couldn't I open a sweet shop instead? Indians would always eat sweets. Why sports? Why cricket?" (125). In the face of these prejudices, their commitment to the sports shop is represented as an act of personal resilience that will potentially lead to a more balanced set of priorities for India's future.

In *Revolution 2020*, the meaning of empowerment is more complex. Gopal is so obsessed with overcoming his "loser" characterization that he partners with a corrupt MLA to build a coaching center. When Raghav, his journalist friend, exposes the corruption, Gopal looks the other way when Raghav's office is ransacked in retaliation. His flaw is not his enterprising spirit but that he stumbled on the wrong model of what success is. Only when he realizes that he has acted badly can his story resolve itself. *Revolution* is particularly interesting because it has a second protagonist, Raghav, who despite his excellent placement in an engineering college decides to become a journalist and work on behalf of the country instead. At first Gopal derides Raghav's decision but gradually realizes that the latter's moral choice is better than his own immoral ones, even if the markers of success it brings are less visible. *Revolution* is unique because the protagonist does not get the girl, but Raghav does—a character whose perspective we never see and who undergoes no self-transformation. In this novel, the romance plot is separated from the self-help plot altogether.

In all these books, self-help is generative of new selves rather than a reflection of a preexisting national discourse. To be more precise: it *is* nationalist, but for the country that could be rather than the country that is. This is a patriotism that has as its prerequisite a certain self-transformation or self-betterment. The "loser" protagonist becomes a representation of the "loser" India, which, with a change in mentality and a simple will to succeed rather than a contentment with failure, can occupy its rightful place as a "winner" once again. But as Gopal's case shows, winning does not just mean reaping the fruits of a successful life but acting with morality even when it means having nothing to show for it.

This view can be criticized for what seems like a simplistic diagnosis of a host of social ills and a reduction of social action to a set of self-help mantras. Indeed, in some of these novels, the actions the protagonists undertake at the end to gain control of their lives—the false terrorist threat spread over phone lines to help boost the call center's call volume in *One Night*, the murder of a gang of Hindu nationalist thugs in *3 Mistakes*, and Gopal's staged encounter with two call girls in *Revolution 2020*—are fantastic if not outright absurd. But the reader is asked to overlook these lapses in the novels' otherwise realistic quality because they allow for the moral universe to right itself. These endings read as narrative bulges in what are otherwise economized and sleek texts; they contain an excess of absurdity that cannot be resolved into the otherwise squeaky-clean self-help manual. In this sense, they distinguish the novel from a straightforward how-to guide and leave open a set of questions about the pragmatic difficulties involved in actually making a better world that in his nonfictional writings Bhagat can easily ignore.

"My Readers, You That Is"

Bhagat's interest in self-transformation allows him to transcend the generic boundary between the novel and the self-help manual. His novels are not only stories of self-empowerment but are themselves empowering stories. Besides their insistent narrativization of self-transformation, Bhagat's novels attempt to involve the reader in the story in ways that break down the conventional distance between the novel and the world. Viswamohan sees

Bhagat's writing as "'how to' reading" (2013, 24), and indeed, his works elicit much more participation in and affective commitment to the text than does a conventional novel, specifically in the sense that the text provides lessons that are meant to inform a reader's own life. A self-help book or manual, characterized by a "standard expository formula . . . in which an 'expert' specifically describes a problem or set of problems and then sets out a program for resolution" (Simonds 1996, 16), is a particular kind of text that operates, unlike a traditional novel, with language as performative rather than descriptive, inciting in readers a desire to act on their own lives in textually prescribed ways. While novels can incite action, they require interpretation to link a character's story with the reader's life, and different readers are likely to have different relationships to them. Self-help, in contrast, does not require this level of interpretation; it is often written in the second person, addressed to a particular kind of reader with a particular kind of problem, and offers an easy takeaway, perhaps in the form of a quiz or checklist of suggested actions.

Seen in this way, Bhagat's novels can be read as actively interpellating their readers into their worlds in ways uncharacteristic of most literary fiction. Before the start of *One Night*, Bhagat offers an untitled author's note: "Before you begin this book, I have a small request. Right here, note down three things. Write down something that i) you fear, ii) makes you angry and iii) you don't like about yourself. Be honest, and write something that is meaningful to you. . . . Okay, now forget about this exercise and enjoy the story" (ix). The activity serves as a generic pronouncement that adjusts the reader's expectations, "an implicit contract that prescribes a particular kind of emotive engagement" (Lauren Berlant, quoted in Vermeulen 2015, 7). It suggests that unlike other novels, this story should not be read from a distance but connected directly to the reader's own life—that the characters' fears and insecurities might be directly tied to the reader's own. Thus, when God asks Shyam to consider "what you really want and what you need to change in your life to get it" (228), the reader is primed to ask those questions of her life as well. The distance between a novelistic world and that of its reader is here bridged to create a new community forged across the diegetic divide. The reader is asked to self-reflect just as Shyam is; the reader is compelled to act on her desires just as Shyam does; the reader's success is tied to Shyam's. As the storyteller tells Bhagat in *One Night*'s epilogue: "It is one of those rare stories that is fun but can help you as well" (285).[15]

The prologues and epilogues that have become characteristic of Bhagat's fictions are by far the most significant manifestation of this generic transgression (P. Joshi 2015, 315). Although *Five Point Someone* has an authorial prologue in which the author, sitting with the protagonist Alok in an ambulance, reflects, "If Alok makes it through this, I will write a book about our crazy days, I really will," it is really with his second book, *One Night @ the Call Center*, that the prologue/epilogue format takes hold. *One Night*'s prologue begins with Chetan Bhagat on a train, heading to an invited talk, when he meets a woman who recognizes his name and then proceeds to criticize his earlier novel. She claims she has a better story for him, but she will tell him only if he promises to make it the basis for his next book. The formula of getting the idea for a novel from a fan or reader of one of his books is repeated in his future works. In *3 Mistakes*'s prologue, Bhagat, at his home in Singapore, receives an e-mail from a fan on the brink of suicide: "I'm an ordinary boy in Ahmedabad who read your books. And somehow I felt I could write to you after that. . . . Sorry to bother you with this. But I felt like I had to tell someone. You have ways to improve as an author but you do write decent books" (xii). Bhagat feels compelled to fly to Ahmedabad to hear the young man's story, which becomes the basis for the novel. In *Revolution 2020*, Bhagat meets Gopal during a motivational speech he is giving in Varanasi and goes out for a drink with him, only to be drawn into the story that becomes the novel's plot. And in *Half Girlfriend*, the prologue describes Bhagat being hounded by Madhav in the former's hotel room in Patna, asking him to read the journals of his "half-girlfriend." At first, Bhagat throws the papers out, but ultimately he cannot help himself: "The journals bothered me. Sure, they lay in the dustbin. However, something about those torn pages, the dead person and her half-boyfriend, or whoever he was, intrigued me. *Don't go there*, I thought, but my mind screamed down its own suggestion: *Read just one page*" (4). From there, Bhagat is hooked, and the novel follows.

In all these cases, Bhagat presents himself as a character of sorts in his novels, writing the purported discovery of each story as part of the story itself. Repeated in most of his works, it is another formula, something that has become a part of his distinctive style. Some critics have read this as a self-aggrandizing gesture, by which Bhagat "strategically position[s] [himself] as a counsellor figure . . . a prophet of sorts" (Subir Dhar 2013, 167). But I read these prologues as a marker of the works' contemporaneity, as they situate the creative act in a place of dialogue and interface between readers and the author. This reflects a very different representation of the act of writing from what we saw in regard to Ghosh or what we see in conventional *Künstlerromane*. In Bhagat, the artist does not find his inspiration in a space apart from the everyday, as in James Joyce's *Portrait of the Artist as a Young Man*, for instance, but in the contemporary moment, in the very world of his readers, in the everyday spaces of the home, the train, the hospital room. This banalization of the act of creation is central to Bhagat's rendering of the contemporary. The implied connection between author and reader potentially democratizes the space of literary writing and strives to rewrite the novel as an everyday domain in which reading and writing exist together.

First-person reflections on the writing process also offer an alternative account of the source of writerly creativity. The only Bhagat novel presented as a fictionalized autobiography is *2 States*, where Krish, working for Citibank, tells people that eventually he wants to make enough money to quit banking and devote full time to writing—a path that, as readers will know, Bhagat himself ended up following. But *2 States* ends when Krish and Ananya get married and therefore refuses the closure of the *Künstlerroman*; we see a portrait of the artist as a young man but not the birth of the art itself. Thus, we have a paradoxical structure across Bhagat's fiction: the novel that is most explicitly a *Künstlerroman* fails to represent the birth of the work, and the more clearly fictional texts are the ones that render visible the act of creation. The role of the artist is not fixed, despite the novels' formulaic structures, but constantly reassessed.

This writerly contemporaneity is also evident in Bhagat's acknowledgments sections, which occupy a unique place for a novel: at the beginning, before the prologue, rather than at the end of the book. This happens first in *3 Mistakes*; Bhagat thanks "my readers, you that is, to whom I owe all my success and motivation" (ix). In *2 States*, he extends the thanks further: "My readers, you that is, have made me what I am. Last time I mentioned that I wanted to be India's most loved writer—and you gave me that. Thank you. Please continue with your support, and if possible, give me a tiny but permanent place in your heart" (vii). Similar statements of thanks begin *Revolution 2020* and *Half Girlfriend*. The language of these acknowledgments resembles self-help language—"success and motivation"; "you have made me what I am"—and is somewhat overwrought as well. But by moving the acknowledgments section to the front and by hailing the readers in this direct address, Bhagat furthers the sense of the readers' participation in his text and of the novel as a generative space of social formation rather than something distant and aesthetically sanctified.

Provincializing English

Smells of mustard, curry leaves and onions reached us. If this was one of those prize-winning Indian novels, I'd spend two pages on how wonderful those smells were. However, the only reaction I had was a coughing fit and teary eyes.
—Chetan Bhagat, *2 States*

In the Introduction, I argue that contemporaneity in the novel is a specific rejoinder to the politics and aesthetics of postcolonial writing as it had been advanced by the internationally celebrated Indian novels of the 1980s and

1990s (Lau and Dwivedi 2014). This is nowhere more clear than in the works of Chetan Bhagat, for both their antiliterary populism and his pointed refusal, as a public figure, of liberal politics. I argue that Bhagat's fictions expose a certain impasse in progressive writing in India, which is its marked inability to merge social and political critique with an attractive vision for the future. As simplistic as Bhagat's novels may seem, with their inspirational takeaways, their flat characters, and their formulaic structures, their tremendous popularity indicates they need to be read as a significant intervention in a fraught public debate around the future of India.

Thus, I propose that we read the passage quoted from *2 States* in this section's epigraph not only as an underhanded dig against "prize-winning Indian novels" or as a management of Bhagat's embarrassment around his own lack of literary prizes but as a legitimate critique of postcolonial aesthetics that is widely shared by contemporary Indian readers and writers, if as yet undertheorized. The smell of spices is the kind of evocative, exoticized image that has been a central feature of the Indian novel in English. Even when not specifically spices, as in Chitra Divakaruni's *The Mistress of Spices* (1997), images of home cooking abound from Anita Desai to Jhumpa Lahiri to Amit Chaudhuri, along with the various extended pickling images and metaphors in *Midnight's Children* and *The God of Small Things*. In contrast, Krish's coughs at the smell of cooking turn those images of exoticism and difference into something banal and even unpleasant, from the perspective of someone who encounters them daily. The quotation suggests that in the smoke-filled kitchen, where cooking is pragmatic rather than metaphorical or nostalgic, the images of difference that have sustained Indian writing in English are reliant on the suppression of their contemporary reality, especially for those who live in India itself.

We see this interest in the local throughout Bhagat's writings. In the prologues discussed previously, for instance, we see an intense specificity of place: the layout of the long-distance train berths, the new Ramada Hotel in Varanasi, the malls of Gurgaon, the streets of Mylapore. These spaces are never explained for a foreign reader but assumed for local ones. This has the effect of undermining the supposed universality of the novel, the genre's ability to appeal across time and space. Bhagat refuses such wide reach; for him, universality itself is the function of an elite literary sensibility with little purchase on regular Indian readers of the twenty-first century.[16]

Bhagat thus represents the contemporary as potentially untranslatable, at least in the way translation is commonly celebrated, which is the ability for a text to be understood by readers in the West. Bhagat has few readers outside India; his novels have been translated into a handful of European languages, but they are far more widely read in other South Asian languages such as Hindi, Tamil, and Sinhala (Griffin 2009). But interestingly, in most of these cases, the translators seem to have retained the novels' English titles, merely transcribing them into the second language; for instance, *One Night @ the Call Center* in Hindi is called वन नाइट @ द् कॉल सेंटर; and *Revolution 2020* in Gujarati is રેવોલ્યુશન ૨૦૨૦. The simplicity and straightforward descriptiveness of the titles seem to preclude translation, while highlighting the multilingual nature of Bhagat's enterprise—the fact that code-switching irreducibly constitutes the world of his characters and readers. In contrast, Amitav Ghosh's Hindi versions use translations of his poetic titles, so *Sea of Poppies* is *Afeem Sagar* and *The Glass Palace* is *Sheesh Mahal*.[17] Even though translation is a key trope of cultural connection across linguistic difference in Ghosh's novels, in their translations, language is still presented, at least in the title, as a transparent container of meaning. Bhagat's original texts, however, are peppered with Hindi and other bhasha words that suggest that translation is not a transformation of one text into another but itself part of the daily life of the Indian contemporary (Orsini 2015). By transcribing rather than translating his titles, retaining the English phrases in the bhasha novels, Bhagat refuses "to be explanatory and demonstrative in the way that literary fiction, with a potentially international readership, feels it should be" (Suman Gupta 2012, 50). Moreover, he reorients conventional notions of translatability from their associations with cosmopolitanism and universalism, offering the provincial as a capacious category for linguistic mixing. (A similar move would not make much sense for a French translation, for instance—and indeed, *The 3 Mistakes of My Life* is translated into French as *Les trois erreurs de ma vie*.) This reimagining of the richness of intra-India linguistic exchange becomes another marker of the new provincialism.

This local sensibility offers a new geography of the Indian provinces. If Rushdiean cosmopolitanism was a modernist celebration of exile and a critique of the nation, the new provincialism is based in India, specifically in its smaller towns rather than its global cities. Bhagat recasts these spaces from places of "decay and degradation" (Amitava Kumar 2012, 60)—as were Ayemenem in *The God of Small Things*, rural Bihar in Aravind Adiga's *The White Tiger*, and Shillong in Anjum Hasan's *Neti, Neti, Not This, Not This*— to places of growth, both economic and personal.[18] In *3 Mistakes*, for instance, the protagonist builds his enterprising dream in Ahmedabad. One critic writes that Ahmedabad is "quite incidental" to the narrative; "it could be any other city in India and the tale of grief and pain and suffering would replicate itself exactly in the same manner" (Suparna Chakravarty 2013, 99). But I think that is understating Bhagat's investment in literary provincialism. Or rather, Ahmedabad's genericity *is* its significance; Ahmedabad is an Indian anytown in the way Mumbai is not, and it is this sense of replaceability that drives Bhagat's fiction. Likewise, in *Revolution 2020*, Gopal fulfills his professional dream in Varanasi. In *Half Girlfriend*, in which the theme of provinciality is most explicit, Madhav leaves a lucrative job with a multinational bank in Delhi to run a rural school in Bihar. Here, Bhagat is clear about his intentions, dedicating the book in the following way: "For my mother/For rural India/For the non-English types."

In these plots, entrepreneurial achievement requires not migration to global or national centers but a change of perspective that sees the provincial peripheries as offering their own possible futures. In Delhi Madhav felt socially inferior because of his Bhojpuri-accented English; back in Bihar he stops judging himself by elitist, Delhi standards. Once he stops worshipping Delhi and loving where he came from, he is able to mature as a young man and prosper at the same time. Bhagat's works thus imagine India—all of India—as a place of possibility, and for a nation where the English-language novel has been tied up with a sense of loss and disappointment, this is no small feat. The contemporary requires *living in* and *contributing to* India itself, which does not mean telling Indian stories with universal appeal but forging a livable existence in regional centers. It requires not idealistic commitment to the idea of India—which many earlier authors had, even as they resided abroad—but a more pragmatic combination of criticism, aspiration, and commitment that would allow a young person to construct a life for herself in India. This explains Bhagat's interest in individual empowerment and entrepreneurialism, his critique of the bureaucratic state, and his proposal to teach simple English to all Indians, which he believes opens up avenues of social mobility: these are utilitarian rather than ideological solutions to the nation's problems. Provincialism thus becomes a pragmatic means of envisioning India's future.

Bhagat's use of English also reflects this new, pragmatic provincialist imaginary. Ahmedabad, Chennai, Varanasi, and Patna are more conventionally associated with their respective bhashas (Gujarati, Tamil, Hindi, and Bhojpuri) than with English; but by telling their stories in English, Bhagat writes these towns into a story of Indian futurity. His is not, of course, the literary English of Ghosh or Rushdie but a stripped-down English that reaches a wide, nonfluent audience. From a sign of globality and cosmopolitanism, then, Bhagat transforms English into a practical vehicle for self-transformation. In *What Young India Wants*, Bhagat summarizes this perspective: "English helps me face an interview, read the best academic books available and access the world offered by the Internet. Without English, progress for a middle-class youth is heavily stunted" (2012, 114–115). This is not a love for the literary beauty of English—for what it represents—but rather language as a means to an end.

Bhagat's use of simple English is often an object of scorn for critics because his style is often clunky, economized, and standardized; this is an English shorn of Rushdiean excesses, as in this passage from *Half Girlfriend*:

> "Why not?" I said, reaching for a chocolate myself.
> "Because Riya's dead."
> My hand froze in mid-air. You cannot pick up a chocolate when someone has just mentioned a death. (2)

There is little artistry in this prose; it relies on cliché ("in mid-air"), banal theatricality (a hand freezing in mid-air), and a self-evident morality that has a faint trace of irony ("you cannot pick up a chocolate when . . ."). But this is part of Bhagat's intervention; while Rushdie's style, inspired by modernism and the rambling idioms of premodern Indian writing, was a response to what was considered the staid, political realism of Indian English writing in the 1930s, Bhagat's, in turn, is an innovation on Rushdie. As Shyam announces in *One Night*, "My English is not that great. . . . So, if you are looking for something posh and highbrow, then I'd suggest you read another book which has some big many-syllable words" (14–15). While Bhagat's might be bad writing, it is bad writing with a purpose: by taking English away from the elitist sphere of art and into the populist domain of economics and self-help, Bhagat produces a popular, indigenized English that is not only a counterpart to Rushdie's esoteric "chutnification" but language that reflects how many Indians actually speak.[19]

In this way, the new provincialism regionalizes Indian English. The decades after independence saw the flourishing of *anchalik sahitya* (regional literature) that was rooted in Indian villages and counteracted the modernizing impulses of nationalism through an appreciation of the provincial and the folk. Anchalik writers embraced linguistic difference by making use of regional languages and, as Toral Gajarawala writes, by being "veritably untranslatable, moving from dialect to dialect, making careful note of vagaries in caste/class-bound speech, invested in the cadences as well as the politics of orality" (2013, 99). While it might seem that Bhagat, with his generic English, is entirely opposite to this impulse, we can also see how at times, his new provincialism looks similar to the anchalik, for instance, in *Half Girlfriend*:

> "Would you like to order anything?" I said.
> The three girls froze and then began to laugh. It dawned on me that they were laughing at me. My English had sounded like this: "Vood you laik to aarder anything?" I didn't know this was such a cardinal sin. (27)

Indian accents are largely absent from Indian English prose; here, Madhav's tonality comes to the surface in a rare act of phonetic transcription. This is a moment of shame for Madhav, experienced because one kind of Indian English is valorized over all others. Shame here is presented not, as it was in Rushdie's *Shame* (1983), as a form of provincialism but dramatically the opposite: as a by-product of cosmopolitanism, as suffered by those excluded from it. By representing Madhav's Bihari accent, Bhagat calls attention to the implicit normative English assumed in Indian English narrative more generally: from Delhi, not Bihar. When we read "Would you like to order anything?," his readers from elite institutions might think it sounds one way, and his bhasha readers, another. This is simultaneously a critique of elitism and a revaluation of this denigrated speech. Like the anchalik Hindi writer Phanishwarnath Renu (1921–1977), who also included "misspellings" of Hindi words in his writings, here too Bhagat "is playing with the reader's perceptions of language, pointing a finger at the gap between what the ear hears and the eye sees. . . . Spelling according to sound forces the reader to mouth the words . . . [thus] mak[ing] the reader leave the security of the printed page and enter an oral universe" (K. Hansen 1981, 277–278). By forcing us to *hear* Madhav's accent, the text gives space for a range of languages and tones. In this passage, therefore, Bhagat both exposes the complicity of Indian English fiction with the marginalization of provincial India and offers a rejoinder to it (Dhaliwal 2014).

This new kind of vernacularization, this bridge between English and the bhashas at the lower end of the literature/popular culture continuum, sheds new light on some of the old debates central to postcolonial literary criticism in the 1980s and 1990s, which pitted IWE and its global audience against bhasha writers and their local ones (M. Mukherjee 1993; V. Chandra 2000). Here, this contradiction is collapsed, as English no longer represents solely a foreign perspective with roots elsewhere, and the vernacular is no longer the only idiom in which to express an authentic Indian voice. In this way, the new provincialism is not a move backward to another, more traditional time but a disruption of some of the epistemological premises of the Indian English novel. In its seeming distance from conventional literary aesthetics, it imagines a new kind of future in which the traditional hierarchies between center and peripheries begin to break down. It valorizes an idea of home, not in a romantic or sentimental way but pragmatically, attempting to replace the perennial image of India as a dysfunctional place one leaves with a new image of an India where it is possible to make one's future. The melancholic critique of nationalism that marked the postcolonial Indian novel has thus morphed into a pragmatic critique of the inefficient state—pragmatic because rather than wishing for an India that never was, it lays out the policies and attitudes that need to change for India to become better. Indian English is central to this critique, but in its most pared-down, deaestheticized form. Idealism has been replaced with utilitarianism, and consequently—ironically—Indian English is now a platform of possibility rather than only of loss.

"Bloody Haarmoans": Desire and the New Provincialism

The fact that most of Bhagat's novels are love stories and meld professional success with romantic resolution suggests that the contemporary has a psychosexual dimension as well. However, in Bhagat's works, this is cast as a crisis specifically of masculinity. Across his novels, the female characters generally resemble one another in their frigidity and distance: *One Night*'s Priyanka is superficial and needs to be impressed before she can return to Shyam, Aarti flirts with Gopal but keeps giving him the cold shoulder in *Revolution 2020*, and Riya cannot seem to decide whether she is interested in Madhav in *Half Girlfriend*. The overall sense across these novels is that women are confusing or hard to read, that they are one of the hieroglyphic components of the new landscape—willing to engage in flirtation, perhaps, but ultimately unreadable, much like an engineering exam, inherited religious discord, or other aspects of social and cultural life that young aspirational men must navigate without completely understanding. Such a view not only foregrounds a male perspective and reads women as passive rather than potential movers and entrepreneurs in their own right, but it also offers a vision for Indian futurity in which sexuality and desire remain a male prerogative.

How might approaching aspiration and desire from a female perspective enrich the new provincialism? I now focus on another popular writer of commercial fiction, Anuja Chauhan, whose five novels—*The Zoya Factor* (2008), *Battle for Bittora* (2010), *Those Pricey Thakur Girls* (2013), *The House That BJ Built* (2015), and *Baaz* (2017)—offer a rejoinder to Bhagat, even as they are part of the same contemporary phenomenon. Chauhan's novels are often considered chick lit: they feature strong female protagonists who navigate sex and romance, pressure from their families, professional ambitions, and their own character flaws. Like chick lit around the world, they reflect a context in which "the roles of sex, love, marriage, domesticity, motherhood, and success ha[ve] been radically transformed" (Guerrero 2006, 90).

However, calling Chauhan's novels chick lit and thus linking them to a global genre, while interesting, has the potential to overlook the similarities between Chauhan and authors such as Bhagat, especially in light of the new provincialism. For instance, Chauhan, despite writing seemingly universal stories of the Bridget Jones variety, also makes little attempt to market her

novels abroad. Even more than Bhagat, she uses a mixed Hindi-English vocabulary that is less interested in translating itself for an international readership that knows little about India than in making visible the richness and
nuance of Indian English itself as a variably accented language, using forms
of linguistic humor that, for the most part, only Indian readers will understand. Like Bhagat's, Chauhan's English is relatively simple, and the stories
operate largely as formulaic melodramas. Chauhan also actively cultivates
this antiliterary quality; as one interviewer writes, "Chauhan has no qualms
in admitting that Salman Rushdie is too hard to understand, except his children's books" ("Anuja Chauhan" 2015). This deliberate rejection of erudition
affects the orientation of her literature and her literary career; she seems to
have little interest in winning international prizes or asking universal questions in her writing but celebrates the value of local settings, themes, and
audiences. Fittingly, then, all her texts are set in India, where her modern
female characters find professional as well as romantic success.

Chauhan's second novel, *Battle for Bittora*, is particularly useful for illuminating what the new provincialism might look like from a gendered perspective. Jinni Pande is a young graphic designer in Mumbai, in charge of
creating the animated germs that appear in toilet bowl cleaner, antimalaria,
and other television advertisements. Hailing from a political family, her
grandparents were both involved in the Pragati Party (a thinly disguised Congress Party), and Jinni was schooled in Delhi, after which she went to Toronto
for her graduate degree and then returned to work in Mumbai. Already, this
offers a different imagination of exile and return than what we see in the Indian English fiction of the 1980s and 1990s, where professional success is
generally found abroad. Jinni's mother, in fact, still lives in Toronto because
of her disillusionment with life in India, specifically the corrupt political system in which her parents were involved: "Amma and [my grandmother] just
didn't see eye-to-eye on the whole lying-about-your-age and pretending-you-
had-been-to-prison and accepting-expensive-presents-from-shady-
industrialists thing" (18). Her mother's lack of interest in moving back to
India contrasts with Jinni's desire to build her life there, marking a significant
generational gap that underlies the new provincialism.

Jinni's politically connected family has roots in the "dusty badlands" (9)
of the fictional state of Pavit Pradesh, in the constituency of Bittora. When
her grandmother, longtime political representative of Bittora, gets sick, she
convinces Jinni to run for the position in her stead. At first Jinni is hesitant
but decides to do it, with fond memories of election time from her youth (24).
But in one of the first evenings of the campaign, she runs into her childhood
crush, also from Bittora, Zain Altaf Khan, who—coincidentally—is running
for the same seat from the opposing party (the IJP, a thinly disguised BJP).

Jinni immerses herself in the political contest but is nevertheless torn because of her attraction to Zain, rekindled after almost a decade apart. As the election nears and it is clear that it will be a close race, the personal attacks between the two parties increase, as well as paid incentives to step down and other illegal machinations. Although Jinni and Zain clearly have chemistry between them—they can barely keep their hands off each other whenever they meet—Jinni is constantly unsure whether her feelings for Zain are distracting her from the election and, conversely, whether Zain is trying to gain advantage in the election by seducing her. They have a few passionate encounters, but she forces herself to keep her emotional distance from him. She maintains this distance until she wins the election by a mere six hundred votes, at which point, in the final chapter of the novel, she goes to meet him and they reconcile. The novel's epilogue narrates Jinni's swearing-in ceremony and her commitment to her new role, with Zain by her side, cheering her on.

Jinni's transition from urban, career-minded young woman to dynastic rural politician seems counterintuitive—and indeed it is that sense of surprise that motivates Chauhan's narrative. As a graphic designer living on her own in Mumbai, Jinni is thoroughly a product of the new India. She is embarrassed by her old-fashioned name—Sarojini, after Sarojini Naidu, a significant nationalist poet—and prefers to go by the more trendy "Jinni." She works late and orders pizza in the office with Rumi, her best friend and colleague, who is gay and with whom she discusses everything, including sex. On the very first page, for instance, they casually debate whether "every superhero is a homosexual struggling to break free from the shackles of society." From the perspective of this urban world, the kind of politics represented by her family is outdated, bloated, and corrupt; thus, she hides her family dynasty from her friends, worried that "they'll instantly start making snide *your-nani's-security-costs-the-state-exchequer-three-crores-a-year . . . cracks*" (9). Indeed, the world of rural Pavit Pradesh seems far from the slick world of Mumbai; at one point, a Mumbai journalist asks her, "Don't you find all this a bit disorienting? Bittora, Pavit Pradesh? Bittora means Heap Big Pile of Cowdung, by the way, did you know?" (13). When Rumi comes to visit Bittora, he is constantly "moaning on and on about the *smells* and the *mosquitos* and the *heat*, like some city-bred diva. He complained that the AC hissed hot gas and the shower had no pressure"; Jinni too has to make some adjustments, although her outlook is less "pampered" than her friend's (274). There are several comedic scenes, for instance, when she tries to digest the greasy coffee served with fresh unpasteurized buffalo milk in the village—which she dubs "Bhainscafé" (127), a play on Nescafé using the Hindi word *bhains*, meaning "buffalo." The representation of Pavit-accented English is also comedic—"our" written as "aawar";

hormones as "haarmoans," naïve as "nave"—even as it quite lovingly represents the heterogeneity and richness of the various dialects of Indian English. And indeed, the comedy is not meant to mock; rather, the novel advances a new image of futurity that suggests that a more globalized lifestyle in Mumbai ironically turns the aspiration of the middle-class protagonist toward India itself rather than, as one might expect, toward the West. It is precisely Jinni's confidence as a young successful woman comfortable in her own skin and largely free to live as she likes—rather than, as the earlier Indian novel in English might have had it, a woman craving freedom—that makes her interested in reclaiming her family's political heritage and giving back to the country. Although it may not seem modern—a move backward or toward less freedom—Chauhan counterintuitively presents the village as a further development of Jinni's identity rather than a place where she might lose it.

Thus, importantly, Jinni does not have to become someone else in rural India—demure and conservative, for instance—but rural India is where her true self, including her true sexual self, can flourish. This includes her ultimate union with Zain but, more important, the journey she has to take to get there. Indeed, the primary conflict in many of Chauhan's novels is between a strong young woman's pride and sense of her own value, on the one hand, and her feelings of desire and sexual agency, on the other. How much of ourselves, Chauhan's female protagonists ask, do we have to give up to fall in love? The protagonists of the various novels mistrust the desire they feel because they value themselves as smart and independent women, and their romantic emotions cannot at first be contained within that self-perception. *Those Pricey Thakur Girls'* Debjani is perhaps the most extreme example; because of her professional ambitions, she thinks that love is not for her, even after she meets and is attracted to Dylan. Debjani's niece, Bonu, protagonist of *The House That BJ Built*, feels the same way. Jinni's continual paranoia about Zain's intentions is similar; she is attracted to him but mistrusts her feelings, worried that they will distract her from winning the election.

While some critics claim that works such as Chauhan's represent the conflict between "tradition" and "modernity," or "generational clashes between the protagonists and their elders" (Turner 2012), especially in the arena of gender roles, such a reading misses the point of her works. Tradition—in the form of a patriarchal family or limits on sexual freedom, for instance—does not really feature in these novels; it is not the case that these women "selecting their own partners is disruptive of the traditional social order" (Turner 2012). The conflict Chauhan's protagonists face is not the pull of tradition on otherwise modern women but a contradiction embedded in modernity itself: how to reconcile one's professional ambitions and individuality with sexual desire and feelings of love? In *Battle for Bittora* Jinni is plagued by this question, as her interactions with Zain are dominated by desire. When she first sees him again, after nine years, she is immediately drawn to his "lean but muscular forearms . . . sinewy wrist . . . [and] seriously sexy mouth" (42). Every time she meets him, she cannot help noticing his physical attractiveness, "making [her] heart pump like that of an aging Praggu cabinet minister in desperate need of bypass surgery" (47). But all these moments cause her self-doubt. She is not afraid of her own desire but constantly worries that it is leading her down a self-defeating path. After they kiss that first evening, Jinni questions herself: "What was *wrong* with me? . . . Here I was, behaving like some feisty, get-on-the-carousel-boys chick and unbuttoning achkans like I did it every day of my life. . . . [I] sipped my drink and then sniffed the glass suspiciously. Had they laced the sherbat with some kind of aphrodisiac?" (57). The reference to the aphrodisiac, although funny, also underlines Jinni's feeling of giving in to impulses she wishes she could control. This feeling persists throughout her interactions with Zain, especially as the campaigns heat up: "What kind of loser are you, anyway," she reprimands herself, "mooning over a guy when there's a whole parliamentary constituency to be won?" (106). She tries to focus on the election even though her mind "kept looping back to all the non-intellectual elements of our conversation—like how he'd said *Don't go* with that glowing look in his eyes and how sinewy his forearms had looked below his rolled-up sleeves" (170). She is increasingly paranoid that their physical chemistry is actually a manipulation on his part: "Obviously, my so-called childhood friend had struck like a snake last night, while I'd been hugging my pillow, dreaming about his stormy eyes. More fool I" (178). And when a manager of Zain's campaign offers her money to withdraw from the election after a passionate encounter, she doubts herself once more: "They had lured me in here, bathed me, fed and fêted me, rendered me incoherent with lust, and now they were closing in for the kill" (235). These anxieties culminate at her grandmother's funeral, when, feeling lonely and vulnerable, she rushes up to hug Zain, who has come to pay his condolences. The reaction is so strongly negative from her constituents that it threatens to cost Jinni the election. As she worries, the election "had been within arm's reach till I screwed it all up with my stupidity. Bloody haarmoans, I thought bitterly, they'd led me up shit creek good and proper" (354).

Jinni's fear of giving in to her romantic desire marks a seeming incommensurability between female empowerment and female sexuality, especially for someone waging a political battle. Campaigning for Jinni means traveling around to the different districts of Bittora and meeting her constituents, many of whom are poor and marginalized. But even then, Zain proves a constant distraction:

I really didn't know what was happening to me. At one level, I was
campaigning . . . , promising water, jobs and healthcare to the common man. At another, I was in a permanent state of hyper-awareness,
constantly hoping to hear the *khatakhatakhata* of the blades of Zain's
low-flying chopper. . . . No way could I deny that I was a hopeless,
seething mass of frenemy alerts and pheromones. Which was not
only loser-like but also supremely shallow. Seriously, what kind of a
sicko was I, wandering through the homes of malnourished and suffering people in a state of continuous, feverish lust? (195)

Here, Jinni's desire appears to her self-critical eye as hypocrisy. Her fixation
on Zain in the midst of the campaign could be criticized as reflecting the
indifference to the plight of most Indians characteristic of the out-of-touch,
urban middle class. But the novel's interest in Jinni's desire suggests that we
not read this as hypocrisy but as the bifurcated reality of being a young
woman with political ideals. The ascetic figure of Gandhi dominates the image of the Indian politician, and what Jinni fears is that because she is not
morally upright or a saintly figure—because she is not *pure*—she cannot
contribute to the nation. In fact, as we learn, her "haarmoans" do not detract
from her political commitments; they make those commitments more
human.

For what Jinni seeks, increasingly, is not only to win the election but
actually to participate in the political process of India's provinces. Her
grandfather had been a freedom fighter, but after his death her grandmother,
who took over his constituency, joined a party system whose morality was
dubious at best. Pushpa Pande thus became associated with the bloated, corrupt Pragati Party, which won elections through complex vote-counting
strategies, semilegal negotiations, and occasionally bribes. This is the world
Jinni's mother wanted to escape by moving to Canada. But whereas her
mother had left, Jinni proposes an alternative. For instance, she notices that
most politicians in India are very old:

It's sick how old some of these pollies are. Guys in their *fifties* are still
in the Youth Pragati. Guys in their sixties are referred to as Young
Turks. And every time there's a party meeting at the Akbar Road
office, the driveway gets jammed because there are so many wheel-
chairs toiling up the hill. Some of them are so decrepit that you're
scared they may actually *die* on you while you're talking to them at a
function. You'd be sparkling and going all *so-how-are-you-uncle* at
them and suddenly you'd realize the uncleji's so quiet because he's
popped it. (37)

In such a context, in which capital-P Politics is seen as the prerogative of the elderly and the youth are not invited to participate but are actively mistrusted, Jinni's political career has an element of idealism to it—not because she has put aside her complex personality, which includes moments of irrational desire and lust, but because she has embraced it. After the debacle at her grandmother's funeral, a television talk show hosts a debate

> about whether the influx of so many young people was destroying Indian politics. [The debate] featured half a dozen geriatric MPs, all agreeing with each other, saying the same thing again and again. Would you want a young, inexperienced doctor to operate on you? No! Would you want a young, inexperienced lawyer to fight your case? No! So why would you want a young, inexperienced MP, whose hormones were totally out of control, to represent you? . . . Take it from us, they declared, all these young people, who think erection is more important than election, are going to rip apart the moral fabric of the country! (338–339)

Jinni disrupts the world of party politics precisely because she brings her personality and youth, including her hormones, to a domain traditionally reserved for elderly men who don the mantle of sainthood. In a twist on the traditional chick lit romance, the protagonist's hormones here become the site of a new political imaginary born in the new provincialism *and* the centrality of female desire.

Indeed, for Jinni and Zain to end up together, she must relocate to Bittora permanently, bringing together the political and romantic plots. This move from the city to the provincial town, this coming home, replicates what we saw in *Half Girlfriend*. When Jinni begins her campaign, a newspaper describes her and Zain as "foreign-returned local brats who are both probably much more at home in the air-conditioned environs of big cities than in the dusty hearths of Pavit Pradesh. But . . . they seem to be in earnest. So is this the new, post-26/11 India? Genuinely concerned, young, educated people-like-us, coming to a head at the hustings?" (68). The promise that these young candidates represent, of a different kind of politics, begins to be fulfilled, as Jinni sees the flaws in her party, even though she respects her grandmother. For instance, she finds that promises were made during previous campaigns to important vote banks that were never kept: "Clearly, [my grandmother] didn't think that the people who'd voted her in, not once but *thrice*, had claim to her time. After all, hadn't she told me back in Delhi that: 'Afterwards, you can go back to your job and make your keeda-makoda all day. Go to Parliament on the first day of every sessun. . . . And go to Bittora every Diwali'"

(242). As Jinni realizes, this self-serving politics from afar only exacerbates the divide between country and city. "There was no way I could get anything done without *living* here," she realizes. "Otherwise, the moment I left, things would get slack, the schools I commissioned would never be built, nor the roads or hospitals or anything else. Wells would be dug where the tribals couldn't access them. Or people in the middle would pocket the money and that would be it" (242–243). Chauhan structures the subplots of the novel so that a reconciliation of the romance—ostensibly the primary goal of chick lit—coincides with Jinni's accepting her political responsibility by permanently relocating to the Bittora she now represents. The new provincialism is thus reconciled with empowerment and individuality in a way that is premised on the radical possibilities of female desire.

The various elements that so many critics have decried in Bhagat's novels—a spirit of enterprise, flat characters, formulaic plots, and an aesthetics of empowerment or self-help—appear in Chauhan's novels as well, but they are inflected differently when seen as part of a larger conflict inherent to modern feminism. Both authors vernacularize what might be seen as universal chick lit or lad lit formulas to write a contemporaneity that presents India's provinces as a site of futurity. They reconfigure home not as a site of tradition and nostalgia but as an imaginative chronotope that has to be actively constructed; home is not merely where you are born, but where you envision your future to be. Against the melancholic aesthetics of the Indian novel in English, this chronotope appears counterintuitive. These novels' immense popularity with Indian readers and the overall skepticism with which they are met by critics underline the disjuncture between the Indian contemporary and literary criticism, engendered by the openness of the text to the ongoing world. It is through this openness that these works offer a surprisingly simple antidote to India's postcolonial predicament. The contemporary, they suggest, is right here.

2

Writing the City Now

How does one represent the contemporaneity of the Indian city? The gleaming airports in Mumbai, Delhi, and Bangalore and the swanky highways leading there (Fernandes 2014), in addition to the recent growth of leisure spaces such as high-end restaurants, cafés, and malls, might give the impression that the city is where India's capitalist transformation has realized itself. At the same time, in global media and among critics of this rapid development, the Indian city is constantly asserted as a space of poverty, infrastructural failure, and bare life (R. Varma 2004, 77). The communal violence that has occurred all too frequently since independence only underscores this sense of urban decline and crisis. The persistence of these dystopic features next to the city's purported global emergence has resulted in a common progressive narrative that critiques the Indian city as one "of extreme contrasts" (Patel 2003, 21).[1]

Narratives of both the city's globality and its decline read the city in terms of larger political economic shifts, as a crucible of change, or as a symptom of the transformation of the nation as a whole. The city is thus an indicator of something else, whose real importance is somewhere else, legible according to a narrative whose end point is known in advance. But where in these formulations is the possibility for the contemporaneity of the Indian city outside the various narratives that seek to contain it? Where is the city as a space of daily life, the everyday, and the unspectacular? Where are the underworlds that remain largely untouched by spectacular events, the parallel economies, the small-time aspirations? Where is the *experience* of living in the city, with its repeated and banal commutes, its humble freedoms, its un-accounted-for moments, and its hidden alleyways as potential loci of desire?

This chapter argues that in recent years, we have seen a significant number of texts, especially nonfiction prose texts, that attempt to represent the city's contemporaneity outside the narratives of decline and emergence. In doing so, they present the city in other ways: as a radically variegated space, an underworld, a series of fragmentary stories, a visual landscape, a fun and queer space, and a space of freedom from narrative itself. I argue that these writings constitute a new genre in which the city features not merely as a backdrop or a microcosm but as an entity in itself. These city writings, like all the contemporary texts discussed in this book, mobilize a range of formal structures to carve out a space for the representation of the city on its own terms, outside preexisting and politically overdetermined narratives that tie it to the past or the future.[2]

The range of forms within the emergent genre of prose city writings suggests that the contemporaneity of the city, like the Indian contemporary more broadly, is not self-evident but must be actively asserted against dominant understandings of urban India. As I maintain throughout this book, texts are not inert recorders of contemporaneity; rather, the meaning of the contemporary is battled out in texts themselves, emerging at times in counterintuitive or surprising forms. Thus, individual works within this new genre of city writings range widely, demonstrating a variety of formal experiments that attempt to tell the story of the city anew. Some texts are long and excessive, attempting to mirror the city's vast heterogeneity. These books attempt to write the city outside a standard historical time line, seeking out parallel, synchronous, or nonnarrative spaces that cannot be understood merely through the lens of historical change. Others are short and present fragmentary alternatives to a historical interpretation of the city by offering glimpses of sensibilities that lie beyond the temporality of narrative itself. All these texts ask us to think outside allegorical narratives to consider the city not as representative of a larger trend but as a rich space of overlapping temporalities that offers, like the new provincialism, a rethinking of place in contemporary India.[3]

Representations of the Indian city must negotiate two narratives that structure today's urban imaginaries: a nostalgic lament for a lost cosmopolitan past and a celebratory plunge into the capitalist, globalized future. In the first, the city is seen as in decline, from—in the case of Mumbai—its cosmopolitan colonial history in the nineteenth century to the rise of Hindu chauvinism and rampant capitalist development in the 1990s, culminating in the Shiv Sena–influenced decision to change the name of the city in 1995 (Baweja 2015, 13), an event that, as Kelly Minerva writes, is "portrayed in nearly every Bombay novel" (2017, 243). This is supplemented by the narrative of Mumbai's transformation from a working-class city of factories to an elite city of unfettered capitalism, symbolized by the redevelopment of the old textile mill district, beginning in the 1990s, into elite spaces of consumption (Patel 2003, 9–13). Amit Chaudhuri sums up this narrative: "While 'Bombay' invoked the world of the colonial and the British-influenced, liberal, post-colonial middle class ... 'Mumbai' signifies the Post-Modern, contradictory city in which xenophobia, globalisation, extreme right-wing politics and capitalism come together" (quoted in Minerva 2017, 245).[4] In Delhi, the decline narrative is similar but includes the 1984 anti-Sikh riots and increasingly wears an environmental aspect in which the 2010 Commonwealth Games, the development of satellite towns such as Gurgaon (Srivastava 2016), and the city's perpetual battle with air pollution have contributed to a "feeling of crisis and constant breakdown" (Sundaram 2010, 247).[5]

At its most extreme, the narrative of decline results in an inability to represent the city's present except through the lens of loss. For instance, Abbas Tyrewala's "Chachu at Dusk," intended to be a short story, ends up being an angry rant about the loss of the Bombay the narrator once knew: "Frightening place, this city now. A city of law-abiding folk. The night belongs to their expensive, million-PMPO car stereos and the screaming bikes of hyperpubescent idiots. Fuck the day the Mumbai evening dimmed into a night that was no longer Bombay" (2012, 75). The narrator remembers a city where movie tickets were cheap and cinemas were not air-conditioned (79); where young people grew up fast, unlike the spoiled, "soul-sterile" teenagers of today (80); and before gentrification killed the city's "juice," "that thing that once flowed through the narrow, street-lit veins of the city, keeping her alive, sexy, alluring, dangerous, juicy, safe" (84). But his rant is so pervasive that what is supposed to be the retrospective musings of an aging gangster becomes an extended lament on the loss of the city, and every element of its present is read through the lens of this loss, presenting a completely dystopic urban landscape that has little resemblance to the lived city.[6]

At the other extreme, the Indian megacity is seen as on its way to being completely transformed by capitalism into a global metropolitan center. This is the discourse we might see in magazines such as *India Today* or the *Economist* or in the writings of free-market economists and journalists (Bhagwati and Panagariya 2014). This is a discourse that, as Manu Goswami (2012) writes, "sound[s] the drama of a brave new India, one bathed ... in a continuous present, forever arriving, shining, and booming. This [is] a distinct mode of writing India, a new neoliberal genre of emergence." There are several recent books that present this narrative, selling India's globality assertively, claiming India's futurity to a world that has long denied it. For instance, in Palash Krishna Mehrotra's *The Butterfly Generation: A Personal Journey into the Passions and Follies of India's Technicolor Youth*, which is set in postliberalization Delhi, the author charts the changes India has undergone in the past two decades in energetic, at times breathless, prose:

> The old walls are crumbling, and for the first time new ones are not taking their place. Globalization has given the Indian underground a new energy. In China, globalization's sharp edge is blunted by censorship. For the inward-looking West, globalization is more of a threat than an exciting new force—our jobs are being taken away. But an unfettered and liberal India is breathlessly absorbing everything, all the influences the world has to offer. Young India is in gobble mode. (2012, 243)

I argue that because of their dominance, representations of the Indian city must necessarily negotiate these two narratives. Both claim to represent the city as it is now, but neither captures its contemporaneity, which resides between and outside these two narratives, in the time of heterogeneity and the everyday rather than of prophecy or crisis. This contemporary is elusive because almost always, these two narratives are perceived as diametrically opposed and thus mutually exclusive. Anyone skeptical of capitalism's transformative potential is necessarily nostalgic; those who refuse nostalgia must be fully in favor of capitalism. Together, then, these narratives set limits on the possibilities for representing the city, appropriating the heterogeneity of the present into their predetermined logic and making it difficult to imagine alternatives. This chapter traces representations of the city that negotiate these limits in a variety of ways, disrupting the divide between the "bleak mood" (G. Prakash 2010a, 1) of urban dystopia and the adrenalin rush of utopic futurity.

That the limitations on alternative imaginations of the city might be a feature intrinsic to narrative itself is a possibility I present in this chapter to show how various texts find ways to respond to it. In Sudhir Patwardhan's painting *Lower Parel* (2001), the artist juxtaposes different times onto one surface, making use of the visual synchronicity enabled by the medium (Figure 2.1). The neighborhood of Lower Parel is the center of the formerly working-class mill district of Mumbai that has now become the site of luxury homes and retail spaces. When speaking on "Five Ways to Conceive a Painting" at a 2015 event in Mumbai, Patwardhan described how he places multiple viewpoints on the canvas, united by the invisible figure of the artist. This multiplanar technique allows him to present the story of the transformation of Parel "from mills to malls" not as a transition in time but as a state

Figure 2.1 *Lower Parel,* by Sudhir Patwardhan, 2001. Image courtesy of Jamshyd Sethna.

of metamorphosis in which both versions can be viewed as part of the same image.[7]

While this painting is often understood as a criticism of Mumbai's gentrification and the demise of mill culture (G. Prakash 2010b, 12), in fact the canvas offers a way for the present and past to coexist in the mind. As Ranjit Hoskote writes,

> "Lower Parel" gathers in evidence of all these phases of the district's recent history, to function as a palimpsest: we see, simultaneously, a bridge and its attendant system of pedestrian staircases giving access to a crowded marketplace, the buildings and chimney of a closed mill, and a skyscraper under construction. While fitting together into an integrated composition, each architectural element preserves its distinct identity, in terms of colour, amount of lighting, and evocation of surface. (2010, 35)

Hoskote notes that the very gallery in which *Lower Parel* was first displayed was housed in the now gentrified space of an abandoned Mumbai mill (35), which underlines this sense of the multilayered experience of urban life. Likewise, it undercuts any nostalgia by mediating the practice of viewing through the facticity of the gentrified present. Can narrative forms ever do the same thing? The new city writings suggest that they can but not necessarily in a straightforward or self-evident way; the power of narrative's progressive temporality is too charismatic to be merely wished away. Thus, representing the contemporary city will require new and ambitious forms.[8]

The Big Fat City Book

One of the forms that has emerged in recent city writing is the long, extended nonfictional book that presents the city as something sprawling and excessive—uncontainable, it suggests, in the space of a conventional monograph.[9] These works cross the boundaries between first and third person, between fiction and exposé, and between journalism and sensationalism, and their length is a testament to their broad ambition to tell *all* the stories without privileging one, to show multiple sides of the city, and to refuse moralism or closure. This gesture toward magnitude suggests a subject whose reality is constantly exceeding attempts to document it. These big, sprawling books mirror in form the "polyphony and multiplicity" of the city at large (Kabir 2015, 128): Sam Miller's *Delhi: Adventures in a Megacity* (2009) is 304 pages long; Gyan Prakash's *Mumbai Fables* (2010), 348 pages; Rana Dasgupta's *Capital: The Eruption of Delhi* (2014), 448;[10] Suketu Mehta's *Maximum City: Bombay Lost and Found* (2004), almost 600; Vikram Chandra's novel *Sacred Games* (2006), 992; and Gregory David Roberts's novel *Shantaram* (2003), 944. In their excess, these works challenge simple ideas of the city as a space of contrasts or as a symptom of a larger trend. They represent the complexity of the city on its own terms, alternating between describing its vast and variegated surfaces (neighborhoods, markets, the heterogeneity of people and professions) and probing what lies beneath (the underworld, crony capitalism, violence, sex). In embracing the city's simultaneity, their intent is manifestly contemporary.

Of these big fat city books, Rana Dasgupta's *Capital* seems most uncertain about the relationship between its excessive form and its contemporaneity. Dasgupta tells the story of Delhi as a series of successive upheavals, undergirded by intermittent violence that he reads as constitutive of the present-day city. In particular, he argues that the unresolved melancholy of the 1947 Partition hovers over Delhi, producing in its privileged citizens a sense of entitlement and an ability to condone a brutally violent and ruthless socioeconomic system. Most of the book involves Dasgupta driving around the city and interviewing wealthy Delhiites and members of the new middle class. He seems, at times, as enchanted with the new India as Mehrotra was in *The Butterfly Generation*. He presents the rise of BPOs and start-ups in Gurgaon, for instance, as changing the lives of those he interviews; for Raman, one of his informants, "entrepreneurialism . . . is the world's most powerful redeeming force" (68). Siddhartha's life was also changed by a BPO, and Manish now has the freedom to work in fashion design: "One has the sense, looking at Manish's clothes, that they are the product of a mind that is pre-ternaturally free" (85). These stories convey the exciting sense that, as Alex Tickell describes, "in cities like Delhi, there is no longer a sense that India is configured differently to a culture of late modernity or has to 'catch up' with a more technologically advanced West" (2015, 239). The Indian city, for Dasgupta, has arrived.

However, Dasgupta also knows that the new city's luxuries are not available to everyone. Thus, he veers across the chapters between interviews with those who have benefited from economic liberalization and naturalistic and at times gruesome descriptions of the continuing hardships many regular Delhiites have to face. We get, then, another narrative of contradiction in which the rich live in gated communities and the poor are increasingly rendered irrelevant as "human detritus" (276). He describes the failure of corporate hospitals, new stresses put on the family, the rise in the number of rapes in Delhi, farmer suicides, and other new and continuing problems. Yet at the same time, he is constantly seduced by the opulence he finds around him. He interviews a successful businessman at an exclusive Delhi golf club, chats with young men who say things like, "I have a friend who's a multibillionaire" (359), and visits a Lamborghini dealership in Delhi, only to point out the absurdity of owning such a vehicle in India ("I ask the philistine's question: what's the point of spending 30 million rupees on a car that can do over 300 kilometres per hour in a city where the traffic doesn't move?" [374]).

Like many other books in this genre, Dasgupta's narrative begins with his arrival in India from abroad. Dasgupta never lived in India as a child but was the son of immigrants, so his return lacks the sense of personal loss that we see in Suketu Mehta's *Maximum City*, as discussed later in the chapter. This means that at first, he is able to encounter Delhi anew, without the limitations of personal history, as "a vortex of prophecy and possibility" (36) in which "the old was dying, the new was in preparation, and we were living in the in-between" (39). Yet once he arrives, the narratives of decline and emergence both take an equal hold on his imagination, overrunning the contemporary embedded in the "in-between." As Ragini Srinivasan (2014) writes, "[*Capital*] fails to develop a new critical perspective. . . . Reading Dasgupta, we learn that Delhi's poor cannot afford Metro tickets and often live prohibitively far from bus routes, while among the glitterati, '*everyone*' owns a jet. But where do we—where does India—go from there? Such questions are left unanswered." The text thus ends at an impasse, an incomplete modernity rather than contemporaneity: another "city of contrasts."

This impasse inheres in the book's title, *Capital*, which carries several meanings. Most obviously, it refers to Delhi, the nation's capital, but it puns that with the word's second meaning, here specifically the vast amount of money, some legitimate but mostly black, that sustains Delhi's oligarchy: the capital of capitalism. But there is also a third sense, which signifies most clearly at the level of form, capital as the superlative, as in "capital importance" or "capital error" (Bal 2014). This sense of a text exceeding its limits is also conveyed in the book's subtitle, *The Eruption of Delhi*, in which the eruption refers to the city and, simultaneously and metafictionally, back to the text itself. This drive toward excess explains the multiplicity of settings, interviews, interlocutors, images, descriptions, and scenes that constitutes the energy and breadth of the long book. But at the same time, Dasgupta seems constantly drawn to the more straightforward meaning of capital as wealth, which he uses as a metaphor to unify the city thematically against its centrifugal tendencies. This limited sense of capital contains the multiplicity of those interviews within the overarching contradictions of wealth versus poverty and the haves versus the have-nots, which reinstantiates the narrative of the city of contrasts that its form is poised to contest.

Suketu Mehta's *Maximum City* even more obviously registers excess in its title, conveying the capaciousness of both the city—"too crowded" (111), "reaching its own extremity" (538)—and the book itself. And indeed, the "crowded" book wanders through a range of Mumbai locales in an attempt to find the heartbeat of the contemporary Indian metropolis outside Mehta's own sense of loss, having left the city as a child: "I have another purpose for this stay: to update my India, so that my work should not be just an endless evocation of childhood, of loss, of a remembered India. I want to deal with the India of the present" (38). This stated attempt to avoid the narrative of decline common in many diasporic writings takes Mehta to parts of the city that most middle-class Mumbaikars know little about, to the crevices of the city where the capital of postliberalization capitalism fails to penetrate, such as the underworld and the sex trade. Here Mehta finds people with relationships to money that are not merely ones of wealth or poverty. His interest in urban outcasts, for instance, individuals who are "not always . . . victims or revolutionaries, but . . . negotiators and strategists of these complex cityscapes" (M. Chakraborty 2017, 5), allows him to offer an alternative to both dominant narratives of the city. These figures cut through the assumed connection between agency and wealth in urban studies, revealing a kind of insight or freedom in those who have little else. Thus, while Mehta interviews some conventional subjects of new India narratives, such as Sunil, an entrepreneur who "is idealistic about the nation and utterly pragmatic about the opportunities for personal enrichment that politics offers . . . an exemplar of the capitalist success story" (2004, 75), the book spends much more time investigating the complex positionalities of a range of people *outside* the mainstream economy: from Chotta Shakeel, a local don; to Eishaan, an aspiring movie star; Monalisa, a bar dancer; and Babbanji, a homeless poet from Bihar. While the book has been criticized for sensationalizing the city

(Bird 2015, 388)—Mehta, who comes from a wealthy Mumbai family, enjoys shocking his dinner-party companions with stories of the seedy and the sordid—we might see these outcasts as part of an alternative urban epistemology, wherein the contemporary city lies in those underground realms that most representations conventionally do not reach.

There are moments when Mehta is unable to do what he promises—to read the city outside his own nostalgic lens; and the full title of the book, *Maximum City: Bombay Lost and Found*, hinges on what turns out to be a precarious colon that sutures together the excess of the maximum city with the author's own narrower sense of the loss of home. The word "Bombay," the centerpiece of the title, is simultaneously the topic of the book and an expression of this loss, as Mehta deliberately refuses to use the city's new name, Mumbai, in the book.[11] Reminiscent at times of "Chachu at Dusk," his dislike of the name changes that have swept the city occasionally morphs into a myopic, self-obsessed anger:

> I grew up on Nepean Sea Road, which is now Lady Laxmibai Jagmo-handas Marg. I have no idea who Sir Ernest Nepean was nor do I know who Lady Laxmibai Jagmohandas was, but I am attached to the original name and see no reason why it should change. . . . I got used to the sound of it. It is incorporated into my address, into my dream life. I can come back to Nepean Sea Road; if some municipal functionary bent on exacting revenge on history changes it to Lady Laxmibai Jagmohandas Marg, he is doing a disservice to my memory. (129–130)

This sense of personal affront intensifies when he discusses the city's name change, which has come to stand in for the death of cosmopolitanism in Mumbai at large:

> To change a name, for a person or a road or a city, there had better be a very good reason. And there was no good reason to change the name of Bombay. It is nonsense to say that Mumbai was the original name. Bombay was created by the Portuguese and the British from a cluster of malarial islands, and to them should go the baptismal rights. The Gujaratis and Maharashtrians always called it Mumbai when speaking Gujarati or Marathi, and Bombay when speaking English. There was no need to choose. In 1995, the Sena demanded that we choose, in all our languages, Mumbai. This is how the ghatis took revenge on us. They renamed everything after their politicians, and finally they renamed even the city. If they couldn't afford to live on our roads, they could at least occupy the road signs. (130)

Here, Mehta's anger turns away from the contemporaneity of the maximum city to find refuge in the narrative of its decline. The passage is slightly misleading, as it conflates Nepean Sea Road's name change with that of the city as a whole, even though the former took place in the 1960s, several decades before the latter, and was not necessarily part of a right-wing project. In addition, most people navigate Mumbai orally rather than through printed maps, so despite official name changes, streets are often known by their former names for decades (when Mehta grew up there in the late 1960s and 1970s, presumably the street name had *already* been officially changed, but he still knew it as Nepean Sea Road). Mehta's irrational anger at these changes and their impact on his memories lead him to use a racial epithet to describe the agents of the new Mumbai: "ghati" is a derogatory word used to refer to Marathi speakers from the countryside, with the insinuation that they are uneducated and uncultured.[12] He also displays a snide elitism ("If they couldn't afford to live on our roads"); indeed, Nepean Sea Road houses some of the most expensive real estate in Mumbai. This is not the tone Mehta takes in the rest of the book. It is as if his anger and frustration overwhelm his writing at this moment, allowing the decline narrative to rear its head even in the midst of an otherwise sprawling text.

Here, anger is the expression of an impasse between the heterogeneous reality of the city and the narrator's personal sense of loss. As Ragini Srinivasan writes about many new city writers, including Mehta, "If the exile in an earlier model of postcolonial literary criticism was a figure predominantly preoccupied with the vantage afforded by departure, then the outcast return-writer seeks to reclaim the Indian life he might have lived, in addition to the Indian subject he might have become. In each work of return-writing, there is a tacit self-critique of having left India in the first place, as well as a humbling awareness that the nation, India, is capable of functioning, thriving, and arriving into the future *without* the diasporic subject's presence" (2017, 109). Thus, the diasporic writer finds herself unable to acknowledge the city's contemporaneity because it marks a threat to her sense of self. Unwilling to bear this threat, Mehta insists on a linguistic resistance against not only the Shiv Sena and their politics but also against historical change writ large. Like Chachu's bluster in "Chachu at Dusk," the constant use of the term "Bombay," which begins as a refusal of Hindu chauvinism, ends up being a refusal of contemporaneity itself.

Aware of the charisma of the decline narrative, historian Gyan Prakash begins his nonfiction book *Mumbai Fables* from the premise that "the narratives of change from Bombay to Mumbai and the rise and fall of the city are deeply flawed" (22). He situates his book as being written at a time when "the images of the cosmopolitan city lie shattered," not as a condition merely to lament but one that allows "a new historical understanding of the past [to] become . . . possible" (24). From the outset then, Prakash takes the death of an older narrative of Mumbai's cosmopolitanism as a call to develop a new perspective on the city. He recognizes the importance of the city's history, beginning with Partition and followed by the rise of the Shiv Sena in the 1970s, the "destruction of working-class politics" thereafter (206), the 1983 textile strike and the rise of the Muslim underworld (298). But he does not want to reduce his story to these events. Thus, rather than merely offer an alternative narrative, he presents fragments and images that never quite cohere. The idea of Mumbai *fables* conveys the sense that at times, certain stories capture the imagination, but even so, they should still be recognized as fictions; indeed, the narrative of Mumbai's radical transformation itself might be "a fable" (23).

Prakash refuses the narrative of Mumbai's decline by exploring a range of genres and media: the paintings of Sudhir Patwardhan, the cartoons of Mario Miranda, the popular detective fiction of Naoroji Dumasia, the short stories of Saadat Hasan Manto and Ismat Chughtai, the films of Raj Kapoor, tabloid stories, Doga comics, and others. He juxtaposes historical events such as Partition, the textile strike, and bomb blasts with cultural histories of the Nanavati scandal, the various reclamations that expanded the physical space of the city, and thriving neighborhoods such as Dharavi and Chor Bazaar. Rather than rely on a single through line, these represent synchronous reflections on lived experience made possible in different ways by different genres. In crime fiction and revenge fantasies, for instance, we see stories that emerge from the dark undersides of urban life. In the scandalous, we see a world of desire that is not reducible to political economy. In art, we see not only alternative images of the city but also images themselves as alternatives to historical periodizing. Like Mehta's underworld, these reveal parallel formations that cannot be contained by the terms "capitalism" or "contrast," those big narratives that conventionally structure our understanding of the city. In the last lines of the book, Prakash reiterates this point: "Mumbai's everyday practice rejects history written as a linear story and presents it instead as a tapestry of different, overlapping, and contradictory experiences, imaginations, and desires. It is in such a historical survival that I find the living imagination of the city *as* modern society" (348).

These three texts offer different relationships between the city and the narratives that claim to understand it. While the various stories in *Capital* cannot quite free themselves from the eponymous narrative of wealth, and Mehta's investment in the parallel lives of the city's underworld is at times is broken by his own melancholy, Prakash's focus on stories and overlapping fragments offers a more open consideration of the contemporary city. His desire to move away from simple narratives is further evinced in his interest in nonprose genres such as comic books and paintings, which in their presentation of synchronicity offer to the city a new relationship between story and the unfolding of time.

We seem to have made a full circle, then, to Sudhir Patwardhan's *Lower Parel*, in which the story of the city is presented as a layering of successive images on a single plane. Prakash gestures toward what Patwardhan does as well, which is to illuminate the potential contradiction between contemporaneity and narrative itself. Paul Ricoeur defines narrativity as "the language structure that has temporality as its ultimate referent" (1980, 169), so that the "reciprocity between narrativity and temporality" (170) means that one cannot exist without the other. Thus "when someone, whether storyteller or historian, starts recounting, everything is already spread out in time" (175). The imprint of temporality in the heart of narrative is something confirmed, in different ways, by the three big fat city books. They raise the question of what forms of city writing lie beyond narrative and how an account of the contemporary city might require pushing even harder at the limits of narrativity itself.

The remainder of the chapter focuses on a series of shorter books that present alternatives to narrative itself, thus refusing the temporalities of decline and emergence in even more deliberate ways. These texts present this refusal as productive rather than only negative, finding alternative ways of inhabiting the city and envisioning new futures that are neither triumphant nor abject. I have termed these alternatives "freedom," "fun," and "Bomgay"—the last one referring to the contemporary queering of the city as an alternative to the death of cosmopolitanism. These texts put pressure on narrative to illuminate the city's contemporaneity as located in the everyday spaces where people live, desire, and imagine new possibilities.

Freedom

What is freedom, and how might it offer an alternative to both the narratives of decline and emergence and to narrative itself? In the language of capitalism, freedom is used to conflate the open market with an expansion of individual liberty. As Milton Friedman stated, "Economic freedom is an end in itself. In the second place, economic freedom is also an indispensable means towards the achievement of political freedom" (2012, 8). But the free market does not have a monopoly on freedom. One alternative is the concept of *jugaad*, a Hindi term that in its colloquial form refers to a spirit of improvisation and "qualities of resourcefulness and recombination" (Jauregui 2014, 77) that are a necessary response to the failure of the state to provide jobs, social services, and basic infrastructure to its citizens. Jugaad is a way for "creative solutions . . . [to] enable one to fulfil one's aspirations in contexts of scarce resources" (Mankekar 2013, 28). In this sense, jugaad sits uneasily in relation to narratives of both decline and emergence. For the former, jugaad suggests a resilience in the urban poor that refuses to be pitied, saved, or even advocated for, and it highlights what Parmesh Shahani (2015) calls "the immense creative energy that gets released when one has to be frugal." However, while some capitalists have attempted to harness the idea of jugaad toward a more neoliberal idea of "innovation" (Radjou, Prabhu, and Ahuja 2012), most believe that such localized and ad hoc practices only hurt India's innovative potential (Birtchnell 2011). In this way, jugaad signifies both freedom based in individual improvisation and freedom from the narratives commonly used to describe the city.

Thus, Dharavi, considered the largest slum in Asia, can be reinterpreted as a site of innovation and enterprise rather than urban dystopia (J. Anjaria 2016, 162). Gyan Prakash, in *Mumbai Fables*, describes Dharavi as one of the spaces where the contemporary thrives, "a cosmopolitan mix brought together by *dhandha*—business deals, clean and shady. Dharavi is pure Mumbai" (339). This sense of Dharavi's exceptionality is in part based on the way its residents mobilize jugaad: not a formal workforce in any sense of the term, their enterprise culture is based in small-scale industries and micro-workspaces that include men, women, and children (Echanove and Srivastava 2009). This side of Dharavi is represented in Danny Boyle's 2008 film *Slumdog Millionaire* as well. In the fantastic space of the film, Jamal's ability to navigate the city, undervalued in the real world in relation to formal education, turns out to be valuable knowledge, so the jugaad that is central to the lives of Dharavi residents becomes a profitable asset in mainstream India (Anjaria and Anjaria 2013b, 63).[13]

We see glimpses of jugaad-as-freedom in *Maximum City* as well. Several of Mehta's characters advance a concept of "freedom" (538) that is not the freedom of capitalist consumerism but still offers an alternative to the abjection with which the poor are often represented. The outcast characters Mehta describes are distinguished by their decision to opt out of both the capitalist and the progressive narratives that claim to know them. This is the freedom, for instance, of Monalisa, a young woman who dances in a bar, to *choose* that profession over others and to refuse a married life even when she could have it. It is the freedom of Mohsin, a young man who channels his feelings of discontent and masculine angst by working as an assassin for an underworld don who promises him protection for life. And it is the freedom to choose, as Babbanji the poet does, not to have a job, even if that means sleeping on the sidewalk: "How does he like the footpath life? I ask him. 'I like it very much. I have no problems. I don't want a home; I am more free on the foot-path'" (482). All three characters refuse the decline narrative that would understand their situations as symptoms of postcolonial failure. Yet they are hardly neoliberal subjects in a new enterprising landscape either. The conventional markers of subaltern misery—sex work, violence, and homelessness—are here subtly recast as forms of agentive, eccentric freedom.[14]

Freedom is the central premise of Aman Sethi's *A Free Man* (2011). The short nonfiction text follows Muhammad Ashraf, a freelance *safediwallah* (housepainter) in Bara Tooti, Delhi. Sethi is a journalist, but there is no "story" to speak of; the author lets Ashraf be his guide as he tries to understand his worldview. The background of the book is the lead-up to the 2010 Commonwealth Games in Delhi, now known across India as a time of replete government corruption and slum demolition, a time when the city was being "beautified" for the international media at the expense of its poorest citizens (Baviskar 2011). But Sethi does not cling to that decline narrative; the story he tells drifts, just as its protagonist does. And drifting is a form of freedom. Indeed, Ashraf works freelance not because he cannot find a formal job but because he finds it freeing to work when he wants and to spend the rest of his time drinking and hanging out with his friends: "'The ideal job,' Ashraf once said, as if elucidating a complex mathematical function, 'has the perfect balance of kamai [earnings] and azadi [freedom]'" (19).

Ashraf resists both the normativity of the formal workforce and Sethi's attempts to fit his story into a conventional narrative form. While Sethi repeatedly asks Ashraf for a time line so that he can put the different events of his life in order, Ashraf constantly ducks these questions. Thus, freedom is not only, as Ashraf wryly puts it, "the freedom to tell the maalik [boss] to fuck off when you want to" (19)—the freedom of being freelance—but also the freedom to not be narrativized in the first place.

Sethi begins by detailing how he initially met Ashraf while researching an article on health insurance for construction workers; Ashraf had refused even then to answer his questions, to fit into a story that, Sethi admits, "for all purposes, I had already written" (6). This representation of the encounter between journalist and informant, in which the informant exposes the journalist for his preconstructed narrative, becomes a parable for the deception that is at the heart of many city writings—a sociological impulse that claims to want to represent the heterogeneous reality of city life but in fact already knows what it is going to say. Even authors who try to understand the elusive nature of the contemporary city find it difficult to avoid the well-trod narratives that claim to represent it. Ashraf explicitly challenges this convention. "Arre, at least tell me the basic facts," Sethi reproaches Ashraf, to which Ashraf responds: "You take the mazaa [fun] out of every story" (75). Here narrative is opposed to *mazaa*, suggesting that pleasure is a key element of a nonliberal understanding of freedom, a perhaps overlooked element of jugaad. Another version of this dialogue appears later in a less subtle form: "I can't build a proper timeline, if you don't tell me things." "Fuck your timeline" (93).

This imperative to abandon the time line is what allows Sethi to write the city as contemporary. The time line represents narrative, order, and—even if unstated—some sense of progress or decline; fucking the time line is an interjection that lies outside narrative time. The book proposes that freedom lies here, where Ashraf's informal labor is neither romanticized (many terrible things happen to him, including being diagnosed with drug-resistant TB) nor consumed by a decline narrative that reads it as a symbol for a larger or more general phenomenon of neoliberalism.

In the final chapter of *A Free Man*, Sethi is able to present a time line, at first suggesting that after months of digging and putting together the disparate pieces, he was able to place the events of Ashraf's life in some discernible order. But looking closely at the time line reveals that temporality continues to be partial and unfinished: 1987 is marked as the year when "Ashraf marries for the first and only time. Worried that I might track his wife down, he still refuses to give me her name"; 1990 is the year that "Aslam [Ashraf's brother] stabs someone"; and 1999 is the year that Ashraf "works as a mazdoor [worker] in Surat, but hates it" (216). The time line format is thus a sort of ruse that capitulates to the expectation of narrative coherence but in fact offers no progressive or even legible history. Likewise, in the epilogue, contrary to the reader's expectations that this is the chapter that describes Ashraf's death, Sethi fails to disclose the end of Ashraf's story. Rather, the book ends on the author's hope that Ashraf will one day get in touch, and this imagined encounter is described as if it has already happened. This is not utopic—no one doubts that Ashraf will reach a difficult death sooner rather than later—but it refuses to allow the narrative to be plagued by his imminent death. Sethi ends the text as it began, as the story of "a free man."[15]

Fun

With the exception of Monalisa, the free subjects in *A Free Man*, *Slumdog Millionaire*, and *Maximum City* are all male, and a certain kind of freedom—the freedom to wander, to work when one feels like it, and to socialize with friends—tends to be more available to men. Shilpa Phadke, Sameera Khan, and Shilpa Ranade's book *Why Loiter: Women and Risk on Mumbai Streets* (2011) offers an alternative to the narratives of urban decline and emergence, as well as to the implicit normativity of the free male, thus rethinking the city's contemporaneity from a gendered perspective.

Why Loiter? is a Mumbai book, for sure, but it is not sprawling; it is surprisingly compact and straddles the divide between sociological study (the authors are a sociologist, a journalist, and an architect, respectively) and feminist treatise or even, at times, manifesto. This generic transgression complements the book's interest in transgression more broadly. Its thesis is elegant and provocative: in a context of unequal access to public space as in Mumbai, in a culture that views women's presence in public with suspicion and at times downright hostility, and in an urban context in which the lower-class male is pitted against the middle-class female as a source of threat and contamination, the act of *loitering* by women in particular, but really by everyone, becomes a way to reclaim citizenship and the public commons for men and women across social class.

The book is structured in four parts; the first three describe the myriad restrictions put on women's access to public space, with some attention given to describing how women negotiate these restrictions in daily life to lay claim to the city. But, the authors argue, these surreptitious strategies of finding freedom—"They negotiate where they can go and when. They cover up spaghetti tops with jackets and halters with scarves and travel in groups" (169)—belie the importance of claiming equal rights over public space, which requires better design of streets, parks, and other public spaces and an end to the moral policing of women who are the victims of violence (blaming her for being out so late or for what she was wearing). It should also involve the more subtle but, the authors argue, equally important task of rethinking the ideal of public space itself; rather than present a modernist version in which space exists only to move through, they advocate a new idea of public space that encourages loitering rather than censures it.

There are moments when the decline narrative appears in *Why Loiter?*; there are several references to the communalization of the city and, as in *Capital*, to the increasing attempts of the rich to retreat into private enclaves as social inequality increases. The book argues that seemingly public spaces like coffee shops and malls offer women an amount of freedom but ultimately distract from attempts to revitalize public space because they are private spaces masquerading as public ones. The decline narrative gives the book some of its urgency, as the authors exhort their readers to participate in the movement to reenvision an ideal city before it is too late. But I read this decline narrative as a prelude—ironically, perhaps, because it takes up most of the book—to the book's core, and most provocative, thesis, which in its fourth part offers not a vision of a dystopic city but a feminist utopia, where pleasure is included as a priority and freedom is laid claim to equally by men and women. The content of this utopia emerges from the difficulties women face in contemporary urban India, but it finds its outlet neither in merely lamenting those difficulties nor in finding a false freedom in capitalist spaces such as coffee shops and malls. Thus, the freedom the authors imagine—a utopic future of equal access to public space—like Sethi's, refuses both narratives of consumer capitalist utopia and of inevitable decline.

But why *loitering*? On one level, loitering is an act of reclaiming the streets and public commons, akin to Take Back the Night protests seen in other parts of the world. But loitering is more than that: it is a carving out of a particular kind of time, a time "without purpose" (Phadke, Khan, and Ranade 2011, 188), "a different temporality" (Ramberg 2016, 227), which is irreducible to the various narratives of the city. It is a literalization of what Lucinda Ramberg calls "temporizing": "to learn to dwell in time in such a way as to linger over its multiplicity and its movements and to delay its fixing in the teleologies that have come to be so self-evident" (227). The purposeless nontime of loitering is central to the authors' notion of a freedom founded in pleasure and fun, which is not just the freedom from violence so central to feminist discourse but freedom from time itself.

The book's feminist utopia is founded in loitering's radical, extratemporal value. Loitering, after all, is potentially frivolous. Frivolity has a certain specificity here, referring not only to an action's lack of value in and of itself but also to its seeming irrelevance, its triviality, in contrast to the gravitas of "politics" writ large. Literally, loitering is doing nothing; it is carving out a space in between other acts of importance and/or necessity, from work to child care to shopping to nourishing oneself, but also from protesting, agitating, or engaging in other forms of what is usually conceived as political action. Loitering is thus distinguished from purposeful or useful activity. It has, from a utilitarian standpoint, negative value. But, the authors say, it is precisely this lack of purpose that gives loitering its significance: "Loitering by diverse groups . . . has the capacity to decisively disrupt this taken-for-granted segregation of people into categories and makes these divisions not just redundant, but also ridiculous." Loitering is carving out a space of transgression qua transgression, a "space of ambiguity" that unravels the premises of patriarchy, capitalism, and modernist urban planning, as well as of politics itself (179).

It is for this reason that the idea of loitering as feminist praxis unsettles many feminists, committed as they are to political action and to reducing rather than embracing risk. Phadke, Khan, and Ranade are aware of these critiques of loitering's frivolity, its elitism, and its distance from real or pressing, "serious" political issues. From their perspective, loitering exposes feminism for its own potential prudishness, with its emphasis on risk management rather than female pleasure. By presenting loitering as a kind of nonproductive time, born in the ephemeral moment when a body occupies space it should not occupy, the book foregrounds pleasure itself as a site of feminist resistance.

Loitering is, like freedom, another nonliberal site of resistance, in part because it exceeds what Lee Edelman calls "reproductive futurism" (2007, 2). As the authors write in *Why Loiter?*, respectability in the context of urban India means "to be a young, able-bodied, Hindu, upper-caste, heterosexual, married or marriageable woman" (23). These markers of normativity link productive time with reproductive futurism—for the family and for the nation. Loitering is thus nonproductive time and a kind of queer time as well, which refuses advancement toward the goal of marriage and procreation. Moreover, the act of loitering itself might potentially hinder one's marriage prospects, as it calls into question the social respectability of the loiterer.

In all these ways, *Why Loiter?* advances a space of freedom and fun outside both emergence and decline. It offers a glimpse of the city's contemporaneity without either bleakness or unthinking celebration. As a sociological text, more pages might be devoted to decline than alternatives, but as a feminist manifesto, the text can be read not as comprising chapters of equal significance but as a piece of rhetoric: collecting evidence, mounting an argument, and building up slowly to its grand conclusion. In such rhetoric, the impact is most often at the end (a rousing finish) rather than, as in academic writing, at the beginning (a thesis statement). The book crosses genres to make both claims at once: we need to rethink our ideal of the city before it is too late (the decline narrative), and loitering offers not only a solution to the problem posed by the decline narrative but a language to think outside that narrative altogether (the contemporary).

Loitering thus serves as an alternative to many things: capitalist values of productive labor, patriarchy, mainstream feminist politics, and the antiutopic nature of sociology, which is invested in exposing structural violence rather than imagining new futures. If Sethi's word of choice is "freedom," which pervades his text through the title and in Ashraf's pithy rejoinders, this book's might well be "fun," a word that consistently punctuates the text. In fact, in part 3, "In Search of Pleasure," each of the thirteen chapters includes "fun" in the title, so scrolling down the table of contents becomes an experience saturated with this word:

This insistent use of the word "fun" offers new political futures beyond the pale, as it were, not merely envisioning an ideal society but offering a new understanding of what constitutes an ideal society in the first place. As the authors write, the loss of interest in feminism by India's young women has occurred in part because of traditional feminists' refusal to acknowledge pleasure and fun as part of women's experience, focusing instead on violence and legal redressal. In response, *Why Loiter?*'s repetition of the word "fun" disrupts this political reason.[16] The table of contents thus serves as an epistemological intervention as well as a playful paratext by promising affective entanglements that, because they are purposeless and unproductive, stand outside empty, homogeneous time.

Bomgay

Thus far, we have spoken of queering the city as a metaphor for thinking outside teleological narratives of emergence and decline. The metaphor is useful for helping us go beyond heteronormative and reproductive futures of the city that have been co-opted by those who celebrate the radical potential of global capitalism to transform Indian cities completely so that the only opposition to those futures seems to be a retreat to the past. Queer time is, in this sense, a form of dissonance or "asynchronicity" that allows us to view normative time askance and imagine alternative futures (Ramberg 2016, 223). But how does the *queer city* itself both queer time and offer alternative visions of contemporaneity that potentially encompass both the free man and the female loiterer? I look at two texts that present the city as a queer space, strewn with possibilities for pleasure and risk. These works advance a new geography of the city that allows us to further reconsider the relationship between place and temporality.

Parmesh Shahani's nonfiction book *Gay Bombay: Globalization, Love and (Be)Longing in Contemporary India* (2008) begins the project of queering Mumbai by offering alternative snapshots of the city. The book crosses a number of genres, from an academic thesis to an intimate coming-out narrative, to a diary/memoir to an activist piece. Like *Why Loiter?*, its crossing of conventional generic boundaries gives the book a productively excessive quality; but *Gay Bombay* moves between genres even within individual chapters or pages, which are dotted with narrative breaks, different fonts, and asides. This generic heterogeneity reflects both the subject Shahani is writing on, "Gay Bombay," and his own conflicted relationship to it.

Queering genre often implies telling stories along nonnormative or unexpected temporalities, and it is precisely this queering that allows alternative stories of Mumbai and Delhi to emerge that break from the widely disseminated time lines of their emergence or decline. This relationship between queer time and the city becomes literalized in Shahani's book, which uses its aesthetic of narrative breaks and bricolage to tell the story of the city as a queer space. The book is invested in synchronicity—the simultaneity of different kinds of queer lives—rather than historicity, such as tracing the origins of the gay movement in India; and synchronicity prefers the collage over the telos. Thus, the book cuts, sometimes jarringly, from long excerpts of Bollywood songs to footnoted academic writing to scenes of sexual intimacy. In a parallel fashion, the locales veer from Mumbai to Cambridge, Massachusetts, and back—with several liminal scenes in airports and airplanes as Shahani intersperses his personal story with that of the Gay Bombay group that is the subject of the book.

The title of the book has two referents. Most immediately, it refers to the online-offline platform that has been a "queer haven" (26) for gay men in the city since its founding in 1998. But Shahani makes use of the name's metonymic register to suggest that the book is about gay Bombay more broadly—the queer city that is his on-again, off-again home. By interspersing stories of his encounters with individuals and subgroups belonging to Gay Bombay with those of the larger city of which they are a part, the book interrogates the relationship of the part to the whole, initiating a new way of imagining the city outside the logic of time.

The decline narrative rears its head at times, but Shahani never lets it hijack the book. Shahani's personal story of leaving India is not the typical one of exile and loss; the text ends on his *return* to Mumbai, where he (although this took place after the book was completed) is currently the director of the Godrej India Culture Lab in northern Mumbai. His relationship to the United States is thus a constant back and forth rather than a one-way immigration—a movement that, as we saw with Jinni in *Battle for Bittora*, is more representative of the contemporary moment than the old exilic imaginaries of a Rushdie, a Desai, a Ghosh, or, indeed, a Suketu Mehta, where Bombay (never Mumbai) is *only* the city left behind, and any return, always temporary, must at its heart be a grappling with that loss.

It is, in fact, the cliché of loss—so central to representations of the city in India—that Shahani is more interested in, an oft-repeated narrative that, he suggests, mediates the experience of the city. In a scene where he lands in the Mumbai airport, for instance, he writes: "I have made this descent into Bombay airport so many times in the past, but this time when the plane taxies to a halt on the shantytown hugged runway, my emotions begin to swell" (142). Even readers who have never been to Mumbai will recognize this moment, so embedded in accounts of returning home in Indian writing in English. Yet Shahani immediately draws attention to the overrepresentation of this moment of arrival in his collagelike use of quotations from several books, including *Maximum City* and R. Raj Rao's *The Boyfriend*. These quotations have no clear diegetic justification; he never says that he was reading the books or explains why these quotes come to him at this particular time. They are set off from the narrative in italics and have only a metonymic relationship with Shahani's story. The result, therefore, is neither a criticism nor an endorsement of these earlier writings. Rather, they point to the experience of the city as itself textually mediated.

This inclusion of various and occasionally random quotations from other texts inscribes an oversignified city that can be encountered only through previous representations (see also Amitava Kumar 2012, 17). Yet at the same time, by wrenching these quotes out of their context, Shahani simultaneously shows that although these previous representations sit side by side in the brain, so to speak, they do so only as fragments or parts, not as totalizing narratives. These decontextualized quotes are already snapshots of the city and in being taken out of context are themselves queered.

The two quotations Shahani uses from *Maximum City* are especially telling in this regard, as they encapsulate Mehta's simultaneous love and disavowal of Mumbai. The first contrasts Mumbai from the air with the real Mumbai: "From the air, you get a sense of its possibilities. On the ground, it is different" (142). The second is a description of the city's overpopulation: "Some parts of central Bombay have a population density of 1 million people per square mile. This is the highest number of individuals massed together at any spot on the world" (145). Shahani quotes these truisms in a context that refuses their abstracting potential: as we later read, it is in fact "on the ground" that his emotional tie to the city reveals itself, and the overcrowded Andheri Station, with all its density of people, is the site of his first meeting with the Gay Bombay group as a researcher—the very seed of the book. The contrast between Mehta's depersonalized view of the city and Shahani's queering of it—revaluing population density as a site of sexual frisson, for example—dismantles conventional tropes of the city and rearranges them to produce new meanings, a move that in expressing itself spatially, by fragments juxtaposed on a page, writes the city as *synchronous* and grounded in experience rather than as a site merely where historical transformation, time, unfolds.

We see a similar gesture in the way the book deals with the city's name change. Shahani mentions the change of name in the context of the Gay Bombay group:

Bombay was renamed Mumbai in November 1995 by the BJP-Shiv Sena coalition government in power. Gay Bombay was established three years later. However, the founders of Gay Bombay still chose to call themselves "Gay Bombay"—not "Gay Mumbai," aligning themselves with the notion of the city that was "dynamic, intensely commercial, heterogeneous, chaotic, and yet spontaneously tolerant and open minded . . . the Bombay of ethnic and religious mixing, of opportunities, of-rags-to-riches success stories, of class solidarity, of artistic modernism and hybridized energies . . ." (Hansen, 2001). This mixing and matching and appropriating a variety of foreign influences to make them one's own is still the imagined inherent nature of *Bombay* and as I have observed during my study, of Gay Bombay as well. I have addressed the city as Bombay throughout this book to honour this vision of the city, even though I realize that it is and in fact, always was, quite frayed at its edges. (66–67; ellipses and parenthetical citation in original)

Formally, it is a somewhat unusual passage, as Shahani explains the group's decision to retain the name "Gay Bombay" using a quotation from another text rather than the words of the group themselves—here, from a book by Thomas Blom Hansen, an anthropologist whose *Wages of Violence: Naming and Identity in Postcolonial Bombay* (2001) begins with an introduction on the city's name change as a sign of the demise of cosmopolitanism in the city. Yet in another article that came out the same year as *Gay Bombay*, Shahani offers a different interpretation of the city's name change, through a reading of Riyad Wadia's film *BOMgAY*, considered to be "the country's first 'gay' film" (Shahani 2008b, 146), and based on a poem by queer writer and activist R. Raj Rao. Here, Shahani argues that the use of "Bombay" rather than "Mumbai" represents a queering of the name: "Insisting on Bombay, but queering it with a bold pink 'g' and the pink triangle gay icon below it was Wadia's way of reclaiming a recently lost heritage as well as mapping an emerging new space" (151). This repurposing of the old name is markedly different from the insistent use of "Bombay" in a book like *Maximum City*, in which the term stands as a concerted resistance against the contemporary; here, the term references the past and the future. Thus, whereas "Gay Bombay" is, at least as Shahani explains it, a form of resistance against the decline of cosmopolitanism, "BOMgAY" is an attempt to map out a more inclusive future by queering an antiquated name. Shahani's own awareness that this past vision "is and . . . always was, quite frayed at its edges" registers his own unease at the appellation, even though he continues to use the term "Bombay" in the book.

Can the heterogeneity of queer Bombay/Mumbai distinguish itself from a nostalgic perspective on cosmopolitan Bombay? In some sense, it must, because despite the seeming decline of cosmopolitanism, the spaces for queer inclusion in the metropolitan centers have increased dramatically in the last several decades as issues of gay and lesbian rights have gained more visibility (Bhan 2005, 40). We might say, then, that a queer perspective *necessarily* calls into question a straightforward narrative of decline.

The works of professor, novelist, and poet R. Raj Rao, including the film *BOMgAY*, go even further to merge a queering of the text with writing the city as a space of queer desire. Rao's 2003 novel *The Boyfriend* is a significant work in the queer Indian canon and offers a representation of contemporary Mumbai that pointedly refuses a narrative of either decline or emergence, representing instead the affective intensity—both pleasure and debasement—that characterizes the experience of the queer city. The novel follows its protagonist, Yudi, a middle-class journalist, as he makes his way around the city in search of sex and companionship. It traces his relationship with Milind Mahadik, the eponymous boyfriend, a young Dalit man whom Yudi meets one morning in the bathrooms of Mumbai's Churchgate Station. Their affair is characterized by intense pleasure but also miscommunication and frustration, and in the end, Milind agrees to a marriage with a woman arranged by his parents. However, the two still meet from time to time, and the novel ends on a somewhat optimistic note.

The Boyfriend is a quintessentially Mumbai novel in its investment in specific locations, but it offers a largely different rendering of those locations from what we see in other city writings. It rewrites several iconic Mumbai spaces as spaces of queer desire. The novel begins in the bathrooms of Churchgate Station, a site of gay cruising. Churchgate is the main commuting station in Mumbai; by representing Churchgate as a space of queer sexuality, Rao unsettles dominant narratives of the city as one of productivity and heteronormativity. The iconic Mumbai trains are also the site for sexual frisson (F. King 2012, 38), and Azad Maidan, Mumbai's centrally located cricket ground, is represented as the site of illicit sexuality and cruising after dusk (29–30, 47–49). Frederick King argues that Rao's spaces are not inherently queer but emerge as queer only as bodies move through them. He quotes Aaron Betsky to show that these spaces "will just appear exactly at the moment where they are least expected—or wanted. These spaces, moreover, have a sudden sensuality that belies the anonymous emptiness of the modern city" (39). In this way, "sexuality is literally on the move" (41). We see this not only on the Mumbai trains but in daytime public spaces as well. For instance, when Yudi in *The Boyfriend* takes potential partners to his home, "most men . . . disengaged their hands after the first few minutes, saying, 'People are watching.' To this [Yudi] would respond by reminding them that they were in India, not America; it was all right for grown men to hold hands as a sign of friendship" (8–9). This temporary unsettling of conventional hierarchies of homophobia—with Mumbai briefly *less* hostile to queer desire than American cities—rewrites what is usually considered a heteronormative public space into one shot through with the possibility for queer desire.

This representation of the city is noticeably free of many of the tropes we see in other city writings, such as poverty, terrorism, communalism, or personal nostalgia and loss. Space here—physical space—is given a thickness, offering an alternative to the hegemony of time in understanding the city. Yudi, for instance, lives in Nala Sopara, on the very far outskirts of Mumbai, two hours by train from his office. Much of the novel involves Yudi crossing the city on long train rides (e.g., 18–23), asserting the centrality of this commute to his everyday life. This crossing of space takes on particular significance in relation to Mumbai's decline narrative. In the last four decades, as the city has expanded northward, the center itself has shifted so that neighborhoods in South Mumbai—the historic center—are increasingly the city's peripheries. Thus, while the city's south, with its monumental colonial-era architecture, represents its past, its sprawling, unassuming northern suburbs embody its present. Or, more precisely, as *The Boyfriend* suggests, the tedious, daily crisscrossing of densely crowded space *is* the contemporary experience of Mumbai. The fact that Yudi makes this commute both for work and for sexual pleasure reinscribes the contemporaneity of the city—via the vast commute—as itself queer.

The queer city also offers a new perspective on the decline of cosmopolitanism. Set in the aftermath of the 1992–1993 riots but before the city was renamed Mumbai, the novel refuses the typical narrative of the loss of India's cosmopolitan culture. Furthermore, taking place ten years before it was published, it straddles the first decade of economic liberalization and thus is situated to offer unique reflections on the interrelationships among capitalism, pleasure, and freedom. It advocates not only queer identity as an unacknowledged subjectivity but also queer love as an alternative to the various disillusioned accounts of the Indian present. For instance, while the 1992 Babri Masjid riots feature in the novel, they are represented without the gravitas typical of most city writing, where they are the centerpiece for the loss of Mumbai's cosmopolitan culture. Yudi sees the destruction caused by the riots firsthand one day when he ventures into Mahim, where he goes on a futile search for Milind: "Mahim was a badly shattered neighbourhood. Muslims lived here in large numbers. As Yudi got off his train, crossed the tracks and began his expedition to Citylight Cinema, he saw gutted buildings everywhere. . . . Had he arrived for a walk in Mahim a few weeks earlier, he might have seen limbless corpses strewn on the sidewalks" (41).

However, for Yudi, witnessing horrific violence does not lead to any revelation or transformation. Instead, Yudi is single-minded in his pursuit of
his elusive lover, and everything else registers only dimly in his vision. He is
more bothered by his inability to locate Milind than the evidence of the riots:
"So he had been conned yet another time" (41). He tries to wait around to see
if Milind will pass by, but ends up leaving without seeing him: "It was late
afternoon when Yudi finally decided to abandon his mission and began trek-
king to the railway station. He was certain the Maha-dick chapter was over
even before it had begun. Life had fluttered into his hands, and then slipped
away for ever. Such things happened in Bombay every day" (42). Here what
sounds like a contemplation of daily violence in the city is actually a lamentation on the daily quelling of desire and the disappointment that are an
inescapable part of Yudi's queer life. When he later discusses the riots with
Milind, he hears that Milind had witnessed the murder of a group of Muslims by a Hindu mob and, as a boy, had briefly joined the Rashtriya Sevak
Sangh (RSS). Again, Yudi's reaction is unexpected: "Yudi forgot what he
wanted to say. The image of Milind doing the RSS salute in khaki knickers
was too funny for words. Guffawing, he closed his eyes and tried to picture
his boy-lover there, at Shivaji Park" (80).

In both the walk through Mahim and this imaginary picture of Milind in
khaki shorts, the question of chauvinism gets subsumed to the emotional-
sexual feelings Yudi has about himself, mingled with his feelings of desire for
Milind. Milind's body becomes the focus of both scenes, overshadowing the
liberal, secular feeling of fear or outrage at communal violence and the damage it does to India's secular fabric, as seen in a novel like Amitav Ghosh's *The
Shadow Lines* (1988). Whereas in books by Chetan Bhagat, Anuja Chauhan,
and other commercial writers, the disillusionment with Nehruvian secularism stems partially from a frustration with its elitism and outdatedness, here
it emerges from Yudi's queerness: "Homos are no different from Bhangis.
Both are Untouchables. . . . I am a homosexual. Gay by caste, Gay by religion"
(81). This recalls Toral Gajarawala's argument that momentous historical
events like Partition are reduced in epistemic stature when viewed from a
Dalit perspective, which sees the continuity of daily violence where Brahmins and other elites might see radical rupture (2013, 179). Here as well, the
queer perspective sheds new light on the postcolonial politics of religion and
caste.

Thus, while a critic such as Oliver Ross reads *The Boyfriend* as "a cynical
exposé of the power struggles engendered by the imbrications of a gay or
homosexual identity and other longer-standing identifications in India"
(2014, 110), I argue that such a reading is itself a residue of the decline narrative. Ross's interpretation seeks a fraught, melancholic subject as the true

inheritor of the postcolonial legacy and finds the desiring, at times politically indifferent protagonist to be an unsavory figure who needs to be redeemed in a language other than his own. But Yudi refuses such a reading. For instance, when he joins a Dalit procession to Chaitya Bhoomi with Milind's parents, he is overcome by a feeling of disgust: "If there was one thing that repelled Yudi, it was the odour that came from the crowd. Almost all of them stank. Didn't they bathe regularly? Hadn't they heard of soap, talcum powder and deodorant?" (173). This racialist disgust is complicated by Yudi's pursuit of working-class and low-caste men as lovers. Disgust is thus presented as the flip side of desire. It should be clear how different this sentiment is from Suketu Mehta's comment about the revenge of the ghatis quoted earlier. For Mehta, the poor are an undifferentiated mass, worth acknowledging only when their political mobilization disrupts the continuity between himself and his past. In contrast, here disgust comes from proximity, immediate bodily contact, of being in and of the crowd.

The erotic ambivalence of bodily smell is reminiscent of Saadat Hasan Manto's 1941 Urdu short story, "Bu" (Odor), which also describes a sexual encounter between a middle-class man and a tribal woman figured through the trope of her smell, which is "both unpleasant and pleasant [jo bek waqt khushboo aur badboo thi]" (2012, 97). The smell of the woman remains with the man even after they have parted and offers an eroticized contrast to his more conventional, domestic life, living with "his new bride, the daughter of a magistrate, a graduate," whose "milky body" (100), perfumed and powdered, fails to arouse him. Here, eroticism is tied up with class and caste transgression and figured as an intense sensory experience, so the woman's eponymous smell is experienced as "the swaying pepal trees bathing in the rain" (98), a "twanging" (99), and "a strange glow" (99). This surreal space of the erotic eludes the idea of class or caste prejudice as it is conventionally represented in postcolonial theory.

In Rao as well, we see new kinds of minglings between bodies that register difference not through the cumulative secularism of Nehruvian nationalism—in which, in the words of the 1977 film *Amar Akbar Anthony*, "Hindu, Muslim, Sikh, Isaai, sabhi to hai bhai-bhai [Hindus, Muslims, Sikhs, Christians, one and all are brothers]"—but through the simultaneous interplay of pleasure and disgust that marks a new, inhabited geography of the city. Thus, the Churchgate bathrooms, with their mixing of fecal odors and sexual smells, present the urban cartography as born of a queer, "excremental ethics" (Foltz 2008, 45), in which, as in the works of American writer Samuel Delany, waste returns to "threaten . . . the fantasy of a stable subject" (46). In his poem "Underground," Rao makes the link more directly between desire and excrement:

But goo has its uses.
Consider the ripe harvest
along the railway lines opposite Dharavi
fertilized by defecating humans,
and goo, strong on smell,
has the power of ammunition
to trigger off memories
of a long forgotten lover
met in an underground urinal. (1999, 97)

The smell of feces as generating memories of an old lover rewrites the city's underside as one not only of urban dystopia but of pleasure and desire, in which bodily waste is not a sign of abjection but an incipient "ethic . . . [that] calls for the late capitalist consumer to turn to the landfill, to eat of the leftovers, to enter the anus, and to do something different with shit" (Foltz 2008, 43). The imagery cuts through the decline narrative to offer not pity for the poor who, for instance, have no toilets, but an alternative vision of urban futurity born in the excesses of queer pleasure.[17]

The novel's contemporaneity lies in this ability to see the city askance. I disagree with Ross's assessment that the memory of the Mumbai riots "haunts the novel, just as the demolition of the Masjid has plagued the national imagination for almost two decades" (2014, 116). *The Boyfriend* in fact refuses to be haunted in this typical way. Rao is not envisioning "a secular, democratic, pan-Indian ideal" (Ross 2014, 118) but rather offering the legitimacy of queer desire to interrupt that ideal to imagine new temporalities outside the shadow of history. Space—queer space—allows Rao to write a novel that strains narrative conventions and thus to tell anew the story of the Indian city.

All these texts contest the narratives of decline and emergence that undergird so many city writings by disrupting narrative itself as a structuring principle. They put pressure on the temporality embedded in narrative to invoke other genres and other means of writing the city. They offer unfinished images of another city that cannot be understood through a predetermined politics, doomsday visions, or jubilant fantasies of transformation. They offer flashes of the *city now* as an experience, shot through with desire, a time outside time itself.

PART II

Publics

In Pursuit of the Common Man

Whereas the previous two chapters show how contemporary texts inscribe new cartographies of the present, Chapters 3 and 4 consider how the popular Hindi visual media of cinema and television engage with contemporary political debates to imagine new publics for an India in transition. Popular Hindi cinema—colloquially known as Bollywood—might seem an unlikely site of the Indian contemporary, characterized as it is by formulaic generic qualities that render it melodramatic and unrealistic, an epic morality centered on a charismatic star presence, and a distance from the pressing and unfinished questions of the present. For a long time the genre has been known as escapist—precisely the opposite of the contemporary—a form that takes its viewer *away* from the messiness of reality into a simpler world where black-and-white morality reigns. But this chapter argues that it is precisely Hindi cinema's formulaic quality, in particular its reliance on a charismatic star, and its use of genre—the way it invokes and reconfigures generic paradigms (Anjaria and Anjaria 2008, 129) rather than puts a premium on originality (Braudy 1999, 614)—that renders it able to present contemporary questions in unique ways.

I argue that we can see the emergence of a new trend in popular Hindi cinema in recent years that uses the formulaic qualities of Bollywood to address the contemporary question of who might constitute a new political collective in India, transcending older demographic categories founded on religion, class, and caste. Recent films engage this issue by raising the seemingly simple question of who is the common man, a question that reflects a desire for a new political subject and simultaneously an uncertainty about whether such a subject can ever exist, whether its universality can contain India's baggy heterogeneity, and whether it could ever make a legitimate political claim. The term "common man," *aam aadmi* in Hindi,[1] was made famous by R. K. Laxman in his widely popular *Common Man* comic strip beginning in the 1950s.[2] But over the last two decades, the term has become increasingly politicized as many have called for replacing the situated interests—known as "vote banks"—that have structured electoral politics in the postcolonial era with a new "universal" category of citizens. This new constituency would potentially unite different groups all impacted (albeit in different ways) by problems such as government corruption, a bloated bureaucracy, and police indifference outside the limited idiom of electoral politics (Viswanathan 2012, 110). To critics, this attempt to politicize the unmarked citizen reflects a larger neoliberalization of society (Chatterjee 2012, 118–119) and the hegemony of the elitist aspirations of the new middle class, which replaces the situated politics of the poor and marginalized and precludes restorative policies such as caste-based reservations of government jobs and higher education for the historically marginalized (N. Chandra 2010, 119). In this way, the question of the common man has become emblematic for the contested question of what politics will look like and who will be its agents in India's immediate future.

From the outset, Hindi popular cinema would seem to have little to say regarding these questions, born as a populist form in a context of widespread illiteracy and eschewing the bourgeois aesthetics of realism in favor of the spectacular theatrics of melodrama to offer what Ashis Nandy (2002) famously called a "slum's eye view of politics." But in the past several decades, Bollywood has undergone a gradual transformation, and many critics have noted that the genre's melodramatic and populist characteristics seem to have given way to an embourgeoisement of the form. These critics aver that since the 1990s and the rise of the multiplex cinema (Gopal 2012; Viswanath 2007, 3291), we have seen shifts in Bollywood's intended audience, visible in the increasing use of English, lighter and more frivolous stories, more branding and high-end settings like coffee shops and malls, an erasure of the poor and working people from the plots (P. Joshi 2010, 254), and less attention to questions of social justice, supported formally by shorter running times, a decreased centrality around the cult of personality of the star, and more realist characterization, among others. To most critics, this marks a decline of the genre's pre-1980 political sensibilities (Bhaumik 2004, 3; Kaur and Hansen 2016, 271). Pankaj Mishra (2014), for instance, writes: "Popular Hindi cinema degenerated alarmingly in the 1980s. Slicker now, and craftily aware of its non-resident Indian audience, it has become an expression of consumer nationalism and middle-class self-regard." Sudhavna Deshpande agrees: today's "new, liberalised [film] hero is neither angry nor is he particularly anti-establishment. He is, on the other hand, rich and conformist in his social attitudes" (2005, 187). In today's "de-politicized and consumerist blockbusters," writes Satish Poduval, "the 'anger' associated with the 1970s masala-Social films has largely dissipated" so that "the major stars of today (including the once-angry young man) function as relays in a libidinal economy of middle-class consumerism and depoliticized aspiration" (2012, 46, 47). This transformation in cinema, the loss of social consciousness in favor of a more frothy escapism, is seen as a symptom of a larger shift to a neoliberal and antipoor ethic in society as a whole.

However, contrary to this apparent trend, the new "common man" genre seems to return to political concerns, though not precisely in the same way as the earlier decades. For example, these films bring back the vigilante plot as a means of critiquing the ineffectual state and imagining a fantasy world where individuals can sidestep the corrupt bureaucracy to enact justice on their own. The vigilante has always been a part of Bombay cinema (Kulkarni 2017), from the avenging goddess subgenre (Sukanya Gupta 2015, 108) to the iconic *Mother India* (1957), which ends with the eponymous Radha fatally shooting her wayward son to protect the honor of the village's women. In the 1970s, the vigilante got a new avatar as the "angry young man" played by Amitabh Bachchan, who was frustrated with the limitations of the legal system in punishing criminality. But the more recent vigilante plots, while building on both these traditions, are more narrowly directed against an incompetent state and a corrupt police and bureaucracy and are buoyed by a new rhetoric of overcoming the long-standing political apathy of the middle class in the name not of vested interests but of a new collective, often specifically named as the common man. Recent films that might be included in this category include *Ek Haseena Thi* (2004), *Viruddh* (2005), *Rang De Basanti* (2006), *Lage Raho Munnabhai* (2006), *A Wednesday* (2008), *Dabangg* (2010), *No One Killed Jessica* (2011), *Kahaani* (2012), *Mardaani* (2014), *Gulaab Gang* (2014), *Ungli* (2014), *Jai Ho* (2014), *Gabbar Is Back* (2015), *Angry Indian Goddesses* (2015), *Madaari* (2016), *Pink* (2016), *Maatr* (2017), *Mom* (2017), and *Anarkali of Arrah* (2017). These films, while on the surface quite different, all express a pervasive sense of outrage against the corrupt system through characters who demand accountability from the state and are willing to take action if they do not receive it.

Although these films are political rather than escapist, they have been criticized for advancing not a progressive politics but one that is neoliberal and potentially reactionary. Indeed, critics show that such films feature "self-congratulatory" protagonists and "a shift from a 'popular' public to a recognizably educated and affluent public" (N. Chandra 2010, 121, 132). Justice becomes narrowly defined as a middle-class interest even if the language of citizenship and commonality promises a certain universality. Moreover, the fantasy of vigilante justice is a specific kind of political empowerment, one that absolves the state of its responsibility and locates justice in individual citizens rather than a wholesale reform of the police or judiciary. It also celebrates a mobocratic tendency already evident in India, as seen in the recent attacks on Muslims and those suspected of eating beef (Sarin 2016). As one commentator writes, "To advocate taking a life without fair trial, or by those who are not a legal authority, is by definition vigilantism. . . . Vigilantism turns democracies into mobocracies. . . . Far too many movies normalise the idea of the hero or heroine as more powerful than the law" (Shah 2017).

This potential of vigilantism to turn into a fascist anarchism is represented, in extreme form, in Neeraj Pandey's *A Wednesday*. Here, the vigilante protagonist, a self-named "common man," threatens to detonate a bomb if the police fail to release four suspected terrorists, all of whom are Muslim, from the Mumbai jails where they are being held. While initially the police think the common man is a fellow terrorist, it turns out that he wants the men released so that he can kill them himself in protest of the slow workings of the Indian judicial system that, he argues, in the long lag between the arrest and indictment of suspects, allows time for other criminals to organize hostage or other situations to free their comrades (R. Mukherjee 2010, 245). This scenario, which pits the self-named common man against the Muslim minority always already suspected of undermining the nation, explicitly envisions a world in which the citizen is majoritarian and unmarked and thus legitimizes execution-style violence against the nation's minority communities (Mazumdar 2007, 161; Khatun 2016, 53).

But *A Wednesday* is an extreme example. Most films in this new genre take a more nuanced approach to the question of how we imagine political action in the context of a lethargic bureaucracy and a corrupt state, in which the police are either incompetent, corrupt, or simply antagonistic to the people. The films rarely present as concrete an enemy as "the terrorist" or as simplistic a rendering of the nation's "others," instead outlining a more vague problem of governmental inefficacy and corruption caused by elite businessmen, the police, the judicial system, and easily bought-off individuals, whether witnesses, bystanders, or others, who will sacrifice justice for a price. In such a context, these films ask, What is the role of the citizen to act, and on whose behalf—in whose collective interest—might her action be taken? What new constituencies might be formed in the course of this action, and how might they challenge existing political demographics? Might these new constituencies actually portend a new political future for India?

The critique of recent Bollywood cinema as merely reflecting a new neoliberal ethos overlooks how these films make use of the elusive but imaginatively rich category of the "common man" to rethink the nature of the public in contemporary India and the role of popular culture in shaping it. These films are characterized by an insistent experimentation with one of Indian popular cinema's most notable formal features, the charismatic star: the core of the Bollywood film, the center of its libidinal energy, and the focal point around which all other aspects—plot, minor characters, even setting—revolve. In a classic Bollywood film, everything that occurs and all the other characters matter only insofar as they reflect back on the star. In this sense, Bollywood's treatment of the star resembles that of the epic poem: "The individual in the high distanced genres is an individual of the absolute past and of the distanced image. As such he is a fully finished and completed being. . . . He is all there, from beginning to end he coincides with himself, he is absolutely equal to himself" (Bakhtin 1981, 34). The fact that stars have larger-than-life presences offscreen only intensifies their charisma within the space of the text. By experimenting with different arrangements of the "character system" of the popular cinema (Woloch 2003), playing with various scenarios in which the conventional charisma of the star cedes to the presence of minor characters, experimenting with the relationship between film and television as media with very different interpretations of the star, and at times simply depleting the star's charisma or *commonizing* him or her, the new genre of vigilante films is able to ask new questions about the individual's role in the collective and what it means for one person to represent many.

I use the term "genre" here in its most active sense, as a mode of engagement with contemporary conditions rather than a passive set of formulas or aesthetics. As Caren Irr writes, following the work of Fredric Jameson:

> Literary genre [is] the imaginary resolution to certain concrete social issues of a particular moment, a resolution that can be sustained past the moment of its origin and updated to meet new needs. At certain moments, however, . . . the old resolutions must strain too hard to incorporate new conditions or to crossbreed with alternative literary traditions. In these instances, the imaginary solution that successfully responded to earlier conditions begins to break down, and a new genre—one that imagines a new ideological framework for social concerns—begins to emerge. These exciting moments at the crossroads of literary and social history reveal the specific work that genre performs as an institutional and social mediation. (2014, 13–14)

This allows us to "understand . . . genre as a historically mutable negotiation between social needs and literary history" (Irr 2014, 14), along with identifying emerging genres as particularly salient sites of the contemporary. It helps us see that, as documentary filmmaker Paromita Vohra (2016h) writes, "popular cinema is often the place where new, still-forming ideas are re-flected, emotionally managed and normalised."

This chapter argues that attention to the emergent genre that includes new vigilante films but can more broadly be defined as "in pursuit of the common man" illuminates how Bollywood manages complex reorientations of the popular and reaches toward new possible formations of the public outside the older colonial/postcolonial categories of caste, class, and religion. Genre allows us to see individual films in relation to one another and to read them not for their in-built ideology but as part of a collective working through of pressing political and social concerns. For example, far from merely a representation of the hegemony of the middle class, these films show how the very question of who is the middle class is up for debate. In this light, the films read more like questions than answers. They thus coun-terintuitively carry on the tradition of the social film in Bollywood, which Ravi Vasudevan defines as "the genre which the industry understood to ad-dress the issues of modern life" (1996, 65). Not always a single-issue or di-dactic text, the social film addresses larger-scale or more abstract questions facing society and includes a "mixture of codes, generic and sensational ele-ments" (70). From this more formal rather than solely thematic or ideo-logical understanding of the social film, we can see the recent common-man films as addressing the question of new political formations *through* the use of generic formulas rather than despite them.

A Prehistory of the Common Man

Whereas the production of common-man films has intensified in the last fifteen years, I argue that the predecessor to this genre might be found slightly earlier, in the 1989 film *Main Azaad Hoon*. The film, whose title is translated as *I Am Azaad* or *I Am Free*, tells the story of Subhashini, a news-paper reporter who is fired as part of a market-driven overhaul to sell more papers announced by the new, business-minded owner. As her last column, Subhashini writes a letter to the editor from a fictional identity, "Azaad," who criticizes the wealthy and the corrupt and promises to commit suicide on Republic Day by jumping from the top of the unfinished (*adhoori*) Suchita Hospital, "the tallest tower of corruption in this country [jo is desh ki cor-ruption ka sab se uncha minar hai]" as a protest. The letter increases paper sales, and Subhashini gets her job back, plotting with the new owner to con-tinue writing letters on different issues every day, all signed by the same, fictional "Azaad." When one targeted sugar mill owner accuses the paper of inventing Azaad, they quickly need a face to go with the name. Subhashini finds a homeless man from out of town, played by 1970s Bollywood superstar

Amitabh Bachchan, and asks him to pose as Azaad to earn some money. He does so, at first for the money, but as he learns about the problems people are facing, he starts to actually advocate for them. Eventually, his popularity becomes too dangerous to the politicians and mill owners, and they expose him as a fraud, causing the people, once his devoted fans, to turn against him. It is only when he actually jumps off the roof of Suchita Hospital on Republic Day that people begin to understand that although he was not literally Azaad, he embodied the promise enshrined in the fiction. They discover that Azaad is an idea rather than an actual person.

The fact that we know nothing about the man who plays the role of Azaad is significant and marks a departure from the 1970s films in which the hero had an identity often fixed in the working class—a dock worker (*Deewaar*, 1975), a porter (*Coolie*, 1983), a coal miner (*Kaala Patthar*, 1979), or a servant (*Muqaddar ka Sikandar*, 1978)—and whose anger came from hardships faced because of that identity (A. Sharma 2016, 15). In contrast, Azaad has no identity, so his real name, religion, and regional or caste background—in India all easily legible in a person's name—remain unavailable to us. Moreover, we know nothing about his past; we know that he is down and out but not why; we do not know who he is or what his grievances against the system are—in fact, we do not know whether he has any grievances at all, except for his somewhat mysterious relationship with a political protest song that becomes the refrain of the film, implying some political action in his past. Thus, Azaad becomes less a character who has experienced some injustice that needs to be avenged and more a *formal* concept around which to rally people in the present. Confirming this, most of the actual plot of the film involves the machinations of the various interested parties—factory owners, government officials, newspaper editors, and so on—to exploit the figure of Azaad for their own interests. However, his commitment to justice remains unwavering, and he refuses to be co-opted, working instead on behalf of the various people who genuinely need his help, from students to mill workers to farmers who bring sugarcane from the countryside. The film therefore shifts the question of the cause of anger—why Azaad is so angry at the system—to how a person can come to represent a political constituency. Since Azaad has no past and no identity, he can create political alliances based only on the commonalities he activates in the present. Thus, *what he says* becomes more important than who he is, and who he represents is constantly shifting based on the issues at hand. By constantly referring to the people who support him as a collective constituency, he engenders the constituency rather than merely describes a preexisting one.

We see this in the terminology Azaad uses to describe the people he speaks for, alternatively *mamooli insaan* (regular human) and *aam aadmi* (common man). The terms "aam" and "mamooli" generally tend to mean people outside the corridors of power; however, Azaad's somewhat loose usage of these terms anticipates what happens a few decades later, when these baggy political categories become useful for political mobilization precisely because they can be stretched or contained as needed (i.e., the common man as potentially every man). And indeed, Azaad defines the aam/mamooli aadmi broadly, as, for instance, "the man who travels on foot or on countless bikes or stands on a bus, who stands in line for rations or kerosene, who sells his labor for dirt cheap on footpaths, in markets or in offices [footpathon, bazaaron, daftaron mein]." Here *aam* is defined more expansively, as not only the conventional subaltern but as potentially including middle-class individuals such as office workers—or, as we see later, university students. Thus, the term becomes tentatively expanded to include everyone who suffers because of the corruption of the wealthy and the government—which is, as we see, a broader demographic swath than the category "workers."

The fact that it is Amitabh Bachchan, Hindi cinema's foremost star, playing Azaad is also significant.[3] Best known for his roles as the angry young man in 1970s vigilante films such as *Zanjeer* (1973), *Deewaar*, and *Sholay* (1975), which "offered a kind of articulation of the general sense of despair in India" in the lead-up to the declaration of the Emergency in 1975 (A. Sharma 2016, 15), Bachchan's career had begun to slump by the mid-1980s, at which point he entered politics and took a break from films. The 1989 film *Main Azaad Hoon* was made as he was trying to reestablish his career after this break and stars a visibly middle-aged Bachchan. Given that the body of the star is central to generating charisma and the power of the vigilante, the fact that Bachchan's body has, in *Main Azaad Hoon*, lost some of the libidinal qualities that had made him so popular in the 1970s is significant. The charismatic star attracts the gaze and the energies of the camera to his body so that it is very difficult not to sympathize with his vigilante actions; but the aging star puts pressure on the equation between charisma and action, and indeed *Main Azaad Hoon*'s premise lies precisely in the disruption of this equation, leading to a centrifugal gaze whereby energy is displaced away from Bachchan's body out to the mass of citizenry that his political protest increasingly represents. Whenever Azaad speaks, the camera alternates between representing him and showing the reactions of different anonymous members of the crowd to his words. The conventional relationship between the star and the other bodies and subjectivities in the film is recalibrated, as Bachchan's body itself can no longer sustain an entire film.

Thus, Azaad the man is not as much the hero of this film as Azaad the idea, which ironically can live on only if the man dies. Because the crowd has turned against him after he has been exposed—shouting "You are not

Azaad!"—the only way Azaad can prove that his whole act was not a lie is by committing suicide as his first letter had promised. His final speech, played to the crowd on a screen after his death, confirms this:

> I am nothing. I am no one. . . . But Azaad is someone. I have died, but Azaad is alive. . . . That Azaad who was just a piece of false news, he whom Gokuldas [the newspaper owner] wanted to make into a hand puppet . . . that Azaad is not some man's name but the name of a wish, a hope, a dream. A dream that there is no more hunger, poverty, sickness, or hatred in the world. And whoever has that dream, he is Azaad [wahi Azaad hai].

Then, pointing to various people in the audience from the screen, he names each of them Azaad: "You are Azaad [Tum Azaad ho]. You are Azaad. And you, you are Azaad. . . . They want to kill the Azaad in each of you, but you shouldn't let them. No. Say it, shout it: 'I am Azaad!' . . . and show them that killing one person won't kill Azaad. . . . You should forget me but remember Azaad." Here, and in a pattern we see throughout the common-man films, when Azaad dies, he does so not as a charismatic center, as in *Deewaar* or *Sholay*, but as a means of *transferring his charisma to the crowd*, effacing himself to birth many more common men in the process. This new formal relationship between the star and minor or peripheral characters parallels the question in the plot of the film of how an individual comes to represent a larger interest, of how one person can collect a variety of demographics into a politicized constituency. I argue that it is in this unlikely film, largely ignored in Hindi film criticism, that this question is most presciently raised, anticipating the central questions that come to occupy the popular cinema in the forthcoming decades.

The Death of the Star

Bachchan's declining charisma—and the declining charisma of the star more generally—becomes the defining formal quality of the common-man genre, as it allows for, and arguably necessitates, the emergence of other subject positions that compete for relevance in the plot and for the audience's emotional attachment. This formal tension also distinguishes this new genre of films from what we might call the classic vigilante film, which maintains its charismatic focal point in the body of the star by involving the enacting of *personal* vengeance for something that happened directly to the protagonist rather than an act of vigilante justice on behalf of society. The classic vigilante rarely represents an interest other than his or her own or of someone close.[4] Even in *Deewaar*, which many critics consider a progressive film because Bachchan plays a dock worker, Bachchan's Vijay refuses to take up the cause of the workers even when he naturally emerges as their leader, and he chooses to join a smugglers' gang instead. His sense of vengeance against the world is solved through the amassing of personal wealth rather than any action on behalf of other marginalized workers. He chooses this route in part because of his own disillusionment with union politics, after his father's dishonorable ejection from a mine workers' union during Vijay's youth—the start of the family's travails. In *Zanjeer* as well, Vijay's vigilante actions are meant to avenge the murder of his parents, and the film suggests that once he has done so, he can finally shed his anger and move on to a domestic life. Bachchan remains the center of both films from beginning to end. Even after he dies at the end of *Deewaar*, his mother and brother continue to live under the shadow of his memory.

However, in the contemporary common-man films, the charisma of the star must be mitigated for the protagonist's vengeance to take place on behalf of a larger constituency. If in classic epic melodrama the star is so charismatic that, formally and in the plot, all the characters exist only to strengthen and reflect back on him, then the waning charisma of the star creates the possibility for other competing energies to be unleashed. We see this, for instance, in *Viruddh*, a film that marked a further stage in the casting of the now significantly aged Amitabh Bachchan. If Bachchan's charisma as the "angry" hero began to wane in the 1980s, his popularity only reemerged in the 2000s under a new avatar, a wizened patriarch (A. Sharma 2016, 19). In *Mohabbatein* (2000) and *Kabhi Khushi Kabhie Gham* (2001), two films central to this reinvention, Bachchan plays a stern elder figure, as he does in *Sarkar* (2005). In all these films with multiple stars, Bachchan's waning charisma gives space for other stars of the newer generation to make their imprint, even as he retains his patriarchal authority.[5] Following Bachchan's success in these films, he has taken on further roles that rely less on his uniqueness and more on his replaceability as a sort of generic, good-hearted grandfather. Here the angry young man and patriarch of the earlier movies have been further domesticated into a gentle and kind old man who is loving to his wife and children and perhaps a bit naïve about how the world works, as in *Baghban* (2003), *Viruddh*, and *Baabul* (2006).

It is precisely this new persona that allows for what we might call a *commonization* of the vigilante, from a lone individual acting to avenge his traumatic past to a replaceable figure acting on behalf of a potentially larger group, a transition that I see not as "a massive shift" but as a gradual process (A. Sharma 2016, 22). In *Viruddh*, Bachchan plays Vidyadhar (Vidya) Patwardhan, a jovial, elderly man who shares a close relationship with his wife,

Sumitra, and their adult son, Amar, who is studying in England. The first half of the film depicts the closeness of the family and their loving acceptance of Amar's fiancée, Jenny, whom he brings to India to meet his parents. In this half, the scenes take place mostly within the domestic space, with the exception of the joggers' park where Vidya goes to exercise and chat with his friends. When Amar returns with Jenny, just before the intermission, the family unit is complete. The film's center is a surprise birthday party that Vidya, Sumitra, and Jenny are planning to throw for Amar; but before Amar can arrive at the party, he is fatally shot outside a pub by Harsh Kadam, a young man with political connections who attacked Amar when he tried to intervene in an argument between Harsh and his girlfriend. The second half of the film depicts the parents' grief and their futile attempts to get justice for their son's death. Everywhere they turn, they meet corruption, deceit, and incompetence. The police plant cocaine in Amar's belongings and frame a former gangster for the crime in an attempt to prove Harsh innocent. All the witnesses to the shooting are also paid off by Harsh's family. Vidya and Sumitra wait patiently for justice, but each day in the courtroom proves more frustrating than the last, until finally even Amar's best friend testifies that he did not actually see the shooting, so in the end, Harsh is acquitted. At that point, the lawyer tells the couple that they have lost the case and should move on with their lives. In growing anger and frustration, Vidya finally goes to Harsh's office himself and secretly records his confession. But when Harsh discovers the recorder and tries to stop him, Vidya pulls out a gun and kills him. He is jailed and goes to trial, ending his not-guilty plea with a speech about the failures of the justice system at large:

> When the whole system [poore system] doesn't carry out its responsibility [apni zimmedari], then one common man [ek aam aadmi], in order to prove his son innocent, bore that responsibility. If everyone had fulfilled their duty, then a life would have been saved. . . . So who is responsible for his [Harsh's] death? Am I? Because I wanted to prove my son's innocence? Or is it this system, which compelled me to do such a thing? I don't want to say anything here to save myself; you are the ones who need saving, Your Honor. Because I want to know: What reason do you have for this failure [laparvahi]?

Following this shaming, the embarrassed judge acquits him and apologizes on behalf of the entire legal system.

It is easy to criticize this use of the term "aam aadmi" as being misleading, as it pretends to speak for all citizens but actually represents a personal interest, here specifically a middle-class family's grief. But my point is that the meaning of this term is being contested in the film itself rather than being imported from the outside already predefined. The question of who constitutes the common man—more specifically, *whom Vidya represents* in this vigilante action—is precisely the question asked by the film. In shooting Harsh Kadam, Vidya gets a kind of justice for himself and his family. But in making this final speech and shaming the court, he transfers that sense of personal justice to a larger collective, who would also benefit if the justice system were less corrupt. Insofar as he takes the vigilante action, Vidya is the star of the film. But the transfer to the collective can occur only because he relinquishes that formal centrality, because he is not Amitabh Bachchan the Bollywood superstar but just an elderly actor playing an elderly role who *could be anyone*. This dynamic plays out in the final speech, when Vidya relinquishes responsibility for the shooting, suggesting that he did it not out of his own heroism but precisely the opposite: he was compelled to do it by the system's failure. He is marked by not heroic agency but a kind of anticharismatic replaceability: If I don't, someone else will. The passivity of Bachchan's character is emphasized from the beginning of the film: for instance, when Ali, a gruff mechanic, starts up his shop next to their house and makes loud noises throughout the day, Vidya is unable to stand up to him. Even after Amar's death and what is clearly a police cover-up, Vidya remains silent, continuing to maintain that he has faith in the legal system. It is only after facing one injustice after another that, the film suggests, he is pushed over the edge, almost despite himself. In fact, it is not until around fifteen minutes from the end of this almost three-hour film that Vidya decides to take his revenge. This goes radically against the logic of the charismatic star. Whereas in Bachchan's earlier career, it is implied that whoever he plays is destined to have something special about him, here we see the inverse. There is nothing ingrained in Vidya's character that makes him different from anyone else. His action is merely a product of circumstance. And it is precisely this weakness of character—this lack of charisma—that makes Bachchan now able to receive and play out the disillusioned catharsis of contemporary society as a whole.

We see a similar dynamic between the charismatic star and his commonization in *Lage Raho Munnabhai*, which followed the very successful 2003 film *Munnabhai MBBS*. The first film featured its title character as a *tapori*, a man of the people, a marginal but powerful gangster figure on the sidelines of India's economic boom, characterized by his slangy, vulgar Hindi and his darkly comedic worldview (Dwyer 2011, 351). In the first film, Munna pretends to be a doctor to please his parents, even though he is really a gangster. He usually puts on this act when they visit him, but when they discover the truth, he decides to go to medical school to make up for lying.

But he cannot abide by the strict rules that doctors must follow and bonds with his patients on a human level instead. The joke of the film is that Munna becomes a "better" doctor than the real doctors because he has compassion rather than medical training. He is the vernacular hero, unschooled in modern ways but actually better off for it. This is comically conveyed by Bollywood superstar Sanjay Dutt, who plays Munna and whose past action roles and his own associations with underworld activity in Mumbai (Rajagopal 2009a, 306n11) give him a tough-guy aura that makes the comedy even more funny. Indeed, Dutt's personality and charisma carry the first film. Thus, it is striking that the second requires the significant depletion of precisely those traits. While returning to the plot of pretending to be someone he is not—this time a professor rather than a doctor—in the second film Dutt actually transforms into that person, allowing for the emergence of new collectivities formed around contemporary political concerns.

In *Lage Raho Munnabhai*, Munna's desire to become respectable is motivated by his infatuation with Janvi, an English-speaking radio DJ. To impress her, Munna pretends he is a history professor who is an expert on Gandhi. As in the first film, the humor in some of the early scenes emerges out of the disjuncture between the real tapori Munna and this new, feigned identity—such as a scene in which Munna's lackeys hold several college professors hostage at gunpoint so they can provide him answers to a quiz show on Gandhi that Janvi is hosting. But soon Munna realizes that he will have to actually learn something about Gandhi if he wants to continue courting Janvi, so he begins to study, meeting Gandhi's ghost in the process. The ghost schools Munna on Gandhian philosophy, extolling values such as being honest and forgiving and turning the other cheek. He gradually teaches Munna what it means to protest injustice and to act in nonviolent and truthful ways, values that Munna the gangster did not previously have.

But unlike in the first film, in which Munna shows up the medical establishment with his own brand of street-tough love, here, even when Janvi finds out the truth about him, Munna still remains his new, transformed self. He actually *becomes* an earnest Gandhian and therefore loses much of the appeal he had in the first film, so the second is less reliant on Dutt's thuggish charisma. As in *Viruddh*, however, this deflection of filmic energies away from the star allows the emergence of a new set of characters, not differentiated characters but those grouped together in what we might call a constituency. As Dutt/Munna loses his charismatic authority within the filmic space, his figure can take on a wide representative role, merging class interests that are conventionally thought of as distinct and forging a new collectivity bound by the daily struggles of everyday life. Indeed, as Munna becomes better versed in Gandhian ideas of resistance, he merges his *gundagiri* (thuggish behavior) with doing good for others (an amalgam wittily dubbed *Gandhi-giri*) and thus extends the impact of his actions beyond himself. For instance, when the residents of the senior center run by Janvi's grandfather are being evicted by a greedy developer, Munna starts a protest campaign outside the developer's house during which the senior citizens do private things, such as shaving, bathing, and cooking, in public, as a form of *satyagraha* (Gandhian truth struggle), "until [the developer] realizes that what he is doing is wrong." Munna also hosts a radio talk show where he gives people advice on how to deal with bad neighbors, how to tell one's parents bad news, and how to identify whether someone would make a good husband after only one date. In the process of these actions, he creates a constituency around a range of contemporary problems:

> We have taps but no water. We have bulbs but not electricity. On the roads there are fewer cars and more potholes. You can't even walk on the footpaths because of the hawkers standing there. There are trains, but your name is on the waiting list. If your ticket gets confirmed, the train gets canceled. You go to the hospital, but there are no empty beds. If you get a bed, you don't get a doctor. If you complain, no one will listen. If you go to the politician, he sends you to a clerk. When you go to the clerk, he's in a meeting. If you call him at home, he's in the bathroom. When you finally meet him, he tells you to fill out an application, and that too in duplicate. Then the application keeps going round and round, round and round. . . . Ugh!

This list of hardships is wide in scope, and that is precisely the point. It brings together concerns of the poor with middle-class issues, defining a new, capacious aam aadmi in the process. While critics might argue that this conflation of class perspectives obscures issues specific to the poor and overlooks how these shared issues affect the poor and rich in different ways, the film's point is precisely to bring together these perspectives, even if unevenly. Thus, instead of a filmic gaze figuratively circling around a charismatic center, we have a diffusion of that gaze to accommodate a larger "crowd" of people, in this case, the diverse, anonymous (i.e., not characters in the film) listeners as they call in to Munna's radio show and as they listen to his advice to others, expressing shared emotions in the process. By cutting from one image of an empathetic face to another, and crossing various conventional boundaries of gender, age, and class (showing barbers and their customers, policemen, lawyers, and retirees all smiling and crying as they listen to callers' lives being changed by Munna's advice), the film advances a new demographic unit born in this collective experience of finding commonalities across a range of concerns. The figurative death of Munnabhai himself in the process—the charismatic tapori reborn as a somewhat boring professor—is a necessary price to pay to imagine the birth of this collectivity.

The Birth of the Public

The figurative death of the star is the condition of possibility for the emergence of a new protagonist/subject in popular cinema, a subject that through his or her very replaceability and commonality offers a vision, albeit unformed, of a new political collective that defies the demographic categories along which Indian politics have long been conceived. If in *Main Azaad Hoon* and *Viruddh* the common man is a concept that emerges in the speeches of their protagonists, in *Lage Raho Munnabhai* we start to see the visual representation of diverse, anonymous citizens who are not differentiated as characters but who exist en masse, collectively gesturing toward an idea of a people with shared frustrations around questions of corruption and systemic failure. In *Rang De Basanti*, another film in this genre, we have what I believe is the first Bollywood representation of a candlelight vigil, following the death of a young air force pilot due to faulty airplane parts substituted for sound ones by a corrupt defense minister. In that film, starring another Bollywood superstar, Aamir Khan, the candlelight vigil becomes a formal rejoinder to the charismatic star, offering the representation of thousands of collective grievances as an alternative to the wounded psyche of one man. In this case, the protagonist's personal grief around the death of his friend becomes relayed into a collective sense of frustration with government corruption and impunity.

Recent films take this further with representations of anonymous crowds and an intensified, productive tension between the star and the physical crowd. The crowd has a particular significance in the Indian context, hinging on the distinction between citizens and the "public." As Meera Ashar writes, "'The public' in India is not synonymous with 'the people,' but represents a large proportion of the people who do not fit easily under the category 'citizen'" (2017, 385). The public is *outside* the bounds of civil society and potentially threatening to it because of the ever-present threat of mob violence and the potential to "riot and destroy public property" (386). The crowd thus tends to figure in Indian liberalism as a menace. This subset of common-man films, however, represents crowds in new ways to imagine spatially a collective with the potential for social action.

This is evident in the film *Kahaani*, which begins when a pregnant woman walks into a Kolkata police station and asks to file a missing persons report. She tells the policeman that she is looking for her husband, a software engineer who disappeared two weeks earlier. The police begin an investigation that leads to a rogue intelligence officer who Vidya is sure has kidnapped her husband in exchange for some information. They collect the information and put it onto a flash drive. Vidya is sent to meet the intelligence officer on the day of the Durga Puja festival, and the police hope to catch him during the meeting. But when they meet, Vidya refuses to hand him the files, instead revealing her pregnancy to be fake and stabbing him in the foot and the neck with her hairpin. Finally, she shoots him and disappears into the puja crowd. The police quickly realize that Vidya's entire performance had been an act, the eponymous "kahaani [story]." Her husband was not in fact missing but had died in a terrorist act on the metro, and she had used the police to access the intelligence bureau to find the terrorist responsible for his death. Once the police had arranged the meeting for her, she could avenge her husband's death herself. As her friend, a disgruntled government employee, tells her after the shooting, "Today you were able to accomplish what none of us were able to do."

Also led by a big-name actor, Vidya Balan, *Kahaani*, like the other films, further experiments with the relationship between charismatic star and crowd. At the beginning, the protagonist introduces herself as Vidya Bagchi, but only later do we learn that it is not her real name. In fact, the appeal of the name Vidya Bagchi is precisely that it is a common name ("common *naam*," as the policeman tells her) in West Bengal, and thus even initially the film sets up a tension between the exceptionality of the star and the commonality/replaceability of her character. Unlike many other Bollywood films, the costume design and sets are highly realistic, so Balan, already known for her unconventional roles (Sukanya Gupta 2015, 116), is dressed in a plain sari and moves through realistic urban contexts, emphasizing her commonality. The climax of the film is set during Durga Puja, when many Bengali women wear a white and red sari. Vidya is dressed in the same way when she stabs the intelligence officer, and when he asks her, "Who are you?" she answers, "What difference does it make? [Kya fark padta hai?]." Then she turns around and swiftly blends into the throbbing crowd. When the police realize what she has done, they try to chase her, looking for a woman "wearing a white sari." But as they look over the crowd, they see a sea of women in white saris, and Vidya has merged into them. In addition to the idea of anonymity and replaceability—*what difference does it make who I am?*—this particular representation of a massive crowd in the midst of a *puja* presents a public even more threatening to the ideal of civil society because of its nonsecular nature while also invoking Durga as an avenging goddess.

The image of Vidya turning away and blending into the crowd becomes, I suggest, a paradigmatic gesture of this genre, conveying that the act of vengeance, which was initially for herself, is in fact ultimately on behalf of the collective. This is confirmed in the film's ending a short time later at a candlelight vigil, when a voice-over reports, "Now, two years later, the families of those killed in the metro attack finally have an answer." Vidya's action thus brings closure for all the victims' relatives and potentially all those who suffer because of government recalcitrance. Vidya is not even present at this candlelight vigil, implying that once her role is complete, she is no longer the film's center. She has, for all intents and purposes, disappeared, just like the goddess Durga, who, the voice-over tells us, comes "every year . . . , eliminates all evil, and goes back home, so that we can all live, without fear, happily and peacefully."

Like *Kahaani, Gabbar Is Back* experiments with the anonymity and genericity of its protagonist to imagine the crowd anew. The film is about a college professor, Aditya, who moonlights as a vigilante who conducts public lynchings of corrupt government officials. As we soon discover, Gabbar's anger stems from the memory of his wife, who died in the collapse of a building constructed out of inferior materials because of government corruption. Although at the time he had gathered evidence of the shoddy construction, the government officials to whom he made his appeal were indifferent to his pleas for justice. In fact, the builder tried to pay him off and eventually to kill him. In response, he decides to become Gabbar, the avenger of the aam aadmi. When he sees an injustice around him, in a government office or among the police, he announces his intention via an audio recording and then murders the official responsible with the help of some of his like-minded students.

The name Gabbar refers to the iconic Hindi vigilante film *Sholay*, but with a twist. Whereas *Sholay*'s Gabbar Singh is known to be one of the most evil villains in Hindi cinematic history, here Gabbar becomes a question—specifically, the question of what morality is and who gets to define it. Gabbar Singh was a cold-blooded murderer who killed policemen, women, and small children. This Gabbar kills also but supposedly to rid society of corruption. Is this morally justified? This is something debated within the film, in which discussions among people in the streets and in their offices—from joggers at the park to students to *dabbawallas* (tiffin carriers)—and newspaper and television headlines collectively debate the morality of Gabbar's vigilante actions. One newspaper headline reads, "Is he a hero or a villain? [Nayak ya khalnayak?]," and one television newscaster asks, "After all, what is his aim? Who is this Gabbar?" Through Gabbar's actions, the morality of vigilante justice becomes a topic of daily conversation, contrasting with what is presented as a generalized apathy in society at large, because of which, as Gabbar laments, "reality shows get more votes than elections."

Naming himself Gabbar thus raises the question, played out in the fictive public sphere of the film's world, of what it means to be a hero in the first place and how we might need to redefine morality for the changing times. As Gabbar proclaims, "I am neither sarkari, nor gher qanuni. Na neta hoon, na koi terrorist. Kaam se hero, naam se villain. Main Gabbar [I am neither legal nor illegal. I am not a leader or some terrorist. My work makes me a hero, but my name makes me a villain. I am Gabbar]."

Starring Akshay Kumar, another Bollywood superstar, this film also works to manage the star's charisma in relation to the crowd. Although he initially becomes Gabbar to avenge his wife, as in the other films the action quickly becomes a collective one. In almost every scene Aditya's dress is understated, jeans and a hoodie, and the brief mention of his wife aside, there is little of the romance or romantic songs conventionally associated with Bollywood heroism. He undertakes a brief flirtation with Shruti, a woman whose pregnant friend he helps get to the hospital, but their relationship never materializes, again denying Aditya the conventional role of the sexualized, male hero. The only exceptions are the fight scenes, for which Kumar is known, and where he gets to display his heroic physicality. These do not lead to his impunity, however. At the end of the film, Gabbar turns himself in at the police station, saying, "I take full responsibility for these murders. I did them with full knowledge [soch-samajhke]." This scene is followed by a montage of different public debates, on the street and in the media, along with images of public protests and candlelight vigils, in which people are holding up signs saying "Free Gabbar," "Gabbar is not the culprit," and "Main Gabbar Hoon. Mujhe pakdo [I am Gabbar. Arrest me]." When he is being taken to the courthouse, a huge crowd, mostly students, gathers behind the police van and there is almost a riot. The policeman asks him to quiet the crowd, which occupies a huge swath of the city streets. This is not an aestheticized crowd as we saw in the Durga Puja scene in *Kahaani* but nevertheless is marked by its sheer mass, underlined by overhead and crane shots that highlight its dimensions. To this crowd, which is agitating for Gabbar's acquittal and freedom, Gabbar explains that his actions had never been merely about himself: "After my death, don't burn cars. Continue to fight corruption," he tells them, warning them not to make a fetish out of his death. "Gabbar is every man who sees something bad and says something," he continues. "Aap mein se Gabbar kaun hai? [Who among you is Gabbar?]," he asks the crowd, and all raise their hands. Here, as in the similar scene at the end of *Main Azaad Hoon*, Gabbar transfers the energy of his own vigilante role to the collective, redirecting the affect surrounding his martyrdom back to the waiting crowd.

Unlike what occurs in *Viruddh*, *Kahaani*, and *A Wednesday*, here Gabbar is punished for his vigilante actions, something that rarely happens to

Bollywood heroes and that further emphasizes his diminished centrality. The last scene is of his death by hanging, with some influence from the cinematic martyrdom of nationalist heroes such as Bhagat Singh. However, the point of the hanging is less to convey an ethos of sacrifice than, once again, to unhitch Gabbar's actions from his charismatic body. As Vidya's blending into the crowd was in *Kahaani*, Gabbar's death is little more than a performative relinquishing of his centrality so that it can be taken up by the civic body as a whole. So his last line, a twist on Gabbar Singh's famous line in *Sholay*, is "Main toh mar jaunga. Tera kya hoga Kaaliya? [I for one am going to die. What's going to happen to you, Kaaliya?]," proclaiming that even after his own death, the struggle must go on.

In both *Kahaani* and *Gabbar Is Back*, the protagonists go by pseudonyms, suggesting, as in *Main Azaad Hoon*, that more important than who they are (religion, caste, etc.) or where they come from are the actions they take in the present—a kind of extreme formulation of contemporaneity. Such anonymity presents a liberation from identity, the past, and personal trauma. In *Madaari* we have another anonymous protagonist, known as Anaam or Nameless (i.e., John Doe) and on his Facebook page as Ek Pita (a Father). Early in the film, Anaam kidnaps the young son of the home minister, saying he will release the boy only when the home minister tells him who is responsible for the death of his own son. Anaam had lost his son in a recent bridge collapse and wants to find out which government official was responsible for it. His anonymity is, as in the other films, based on the fact that what has happened to him is not unique but has happened to many others. Nor is it a product of history or identity but a feature of the contemporary Indian landscape—one marked by corruption—that affects everyone. Indeed, deaths caused by bridge and building collapses are all too common in contemporary India, and by choosing this topic, the film underlines its own contemporaneity, further evinced by the initial credits appearing over a montage that includes what seem like actual images from recent news of floods, fatal infrastructure collapses, farmer suicides, corruption scandals, train derailments, and protests against high gasoline and vegetable prices. Thus, Anaam's vigilante actions come not from a space of exceptionalism but from what has become an entirely common experience. Aware of this, he makes a virtue out of his replaceability. When the police threaten to hunt him down, he responds, "I look and dress like the other 1.25 billion. You'll never find me." When the police try to trace his accent on the phone, they find that it could be from anywhere (*neutral accent hai*). The fact that the protagonist is played by Irrfan Khan, an actor known more for his everyman roles rather than as an action or romantic hero, only underlines this sense of replaceability.

Even more than the other films, *Madaari* is saturated with images of crowds and groups of anonymous people discussing current events both in person and virtually in English, Urdu, and Hindi newspapers; on newscasts; in barbershops; inside homes and cars; through tweets and texts; and on the streets. As news of the kidnapping goes public, newscasts and headlines flash on the screen, and we see anonymous people discussing and debating whether it is true or a rumor, whether Anaam is justified, and so on. Later, we see images of people—not characters, just random people—listening to a video message posted by the kidnapped boy's mother on Facebook. As the kidnapper's request for information regarding his dead son is publicized, the roadside conversations intensify, with some questioning Anaam's methods but many supporting him. Here, the film gives us visual representations of social media networking that show dozens of conversations occurring simultaneously as cars are stopped in traffic and as people text on a busy street. This use of text bubbles to represent simultaneous conversations marks a break in the narrative time of the film, via still shots that convey an enriched synchronous contemporaneity that becomes a spatial representation of a public sphere in which individuals debate the protagonist's actions. In these images we have mostly expressions of support—"He's decided to give it back this one time!" and "A tiger like this may not come around for ages"—as well as some dissenting voices who question Anaam's methods (such as "Baccha uthaana galat hai [It is wrong to kidnap a child]"). We have an English public sphere as well as one in Hindi and Urdu (Figure 3.1), which includes radical slogans such as "Inquilab! [Revolution!]," religious messages such as "Allah aapke saath hai [Allah is with you]," and others such as "Desh ko lalkaara hai Anaam ne [Anaam has challenged the nation]" and "Anaam Kumar ke liye insaaf [Justice for Anaam]." This use of both English and the bhashas, texted by car commuters as well as pedestrians, again suggests a public sphere that crosses conventional class and religious divides. More than suggests—it *represents* that commonality, it mobilizes an intermedia exchange between film and social media, and thus it envisions a public sphere that does not homogenize differences of language and class but, at least temporarily, transcends them to imagine an end to the impunity of corrupt officials, something that affects a range of class positions.

These three films reclaim the crowd from its association with incivility and mobocracy and imagine different ways in which its energy might unsettle earlier demographic arrangements. In all three cases, the protagonists' vigilante actions mediate the tension between the charisma of the star, which threatens at times to become the focal point of the film, and the democratic potential of the crowd, which threatens to efface the star altogether.

Figure 3.1 A texting public in *Madaari*. © Dore Films.

The Multi-starrer

Whereas the films discussed thus far offer different means of reconciling the tension between the star and the crowd, another group of common-man films have eschewed the star altogether, structured instead around multiple minor characters with roughly equivalent charisma and screen time. This is analogous to what Sangita Gopal describes as the "multiplot" film, in which several stories are told in interlocking fashion: "Just as the multiplex affords a *multiplicity* of events to occur within its domain, the multiplot allows for the simultaneous representation of multiple character types who together signify the middle class as a differentiated collective. The total field of the multiplot is constituted as a network—even though characters are situated on a common plane of interaction, they in fact connect with each other quite randomly" (2012, 141). While the multi-starrer presents characters who, unlike the multiplot, are part of the same cohesive narrative, nevertheless the group dynamic and the impossibility of collecting the viewer's affective energy in only one of the characters have very much the same effect as Gopal describes, by which institutional and formal shifts generate new modes of political imagination.

We see this structure in two recent vigilante films, *Ungli* and *Angry Indian Goddesses*. *Ungli* is about a group of friends who are told, after a recent case of police corruption, that "in this country, the common man cannot fight against this corrupt system, and if they do, then they cannot win [is desh mein aam aadmi is corrupt system se nahin lad sakte hain . . . aur agar ladte hain, toh jeet nahin sakte hain]." In defiance of that belief, they form the Ungli Gang to anonymously punish corrupt government employees.

They are pursued by a policeman who is himself a sort of rogue figure; although initially dispatched to identify and arrest the gang, he ends up joining them. Except for Kangana Ranaut, who plays the only female gang member, and Emraan Hashmi, who plays the cop, the other actors are less well known, and the ethos is of collective participation in this gang rather than any individual charisma or leadership. Thus, the energy within the film is less characteristic of Bollywood melodrama and more of a realist, buddy drama. This allows for a more seamless portrayal of collective action than in the films starring big-name leads, as the very possibility of one character generating all the film's affective energy is effectively precluded from the outset. This film is able to flirt more with the idea of an uncivil public; the *ungli* in the film's title refers to the image of a hand with its middle finger raised, which is the gang's symbol, and there is also something nihilistic and almost farcical about the forms of their protest, such as postering a minister's house with middle-finger images and making a corrupt driver's license officer ride in a car driven by a blind man who had managed to get a license through bribery. This nihilistic edge opens up the category of the common man to young and other kinds of nonnormative civil subjects. However, through its absurdity and willing defiance of sense, it presents a middle finger not only to the political gravitas of the other films but also to politics, signaling one potential end point of the genre.

On the other side of the emotional spectrum is *Angry Indian Goddesses*, which similarly offers a collective vision of revenge and vigilantism outside the charisma of the individual star. From the opening montage, which introduces the six protagonists in their different contexts, the world presented is one in which women face sexism, from the microaggressive to the explicit, in almost every aspect of their daily lives. The six women deal with these aggressions differently, from Freida and Nargis, who are planning their wedding despite the homophobia they face, to Suranjana, who tries to be ruthless in her business career to show she is no less than a man. When they come together in Goa to celebrate Freida and Nargis's engagement, these differences emerge and cause occasional flare-ups. But when Jo is raped and killed, the women unite. The policeman in charge of the case insinuates that the assault might have been invited by the women's clothing and the fact that they were out late at night. In the face of the policeman's mistrust and the growing sense that there will be no justice in this case, Suranjana finds a gun and goes out to shoot Jo's killers herself.

Suranjana's action is presented as a response both to Jo's assault and death and to all the accumulated aggressions that women in general have to face. This sense of avenging a collective crime rather than an individual one becomes further evident in the final scene at Jo's funeral. In the middle of the service, the policeman comes to the church to arrest the men's murderer, whom he knows to be one of the women. In a dramatic scene, he asks the murderer to stand up and show herself. The first person to stand up is Nargis, who is not the killer and who had always been critical of Suranjana's high-strung nature. Suranjana is the next to stand up, and then the other protagonists, one by one. Here the five women present a united front, claiming to have acted in unison and thus shifting the responsibility from Suranjana to the group. But then, random people in the church begin to stand up, and soon the whole church is standing, men, women, and children, presenting sexual violence and revenge as not solely the purview of their immediate victims but of society at large. The collectivity of the protagonists is extended to that of society as a whole. Suddenly understanding this, the policeman looks at the ground, ashamed. And the movie ends right there.

Once again, we have an ad hoc collective formed around what appears to be an individual crime but is at this moment registered as having collective significance. Gender here is especially salient because the issue of sexual violence is often seen as a woman's problem and, at its most extreme (as in the policeman's insinuations), the fault of women themselves. Released in 2015, *Angry Indian Goddesses* speaks to a pressing contemporary concern in India not only for the safety of women but also around the state's failure to respond to incidents of rape and sexual violence and a culture of victim blaming. Thus, in this final scene, by inflecting the question of the common man with the perspective of gender, the film opens up the gendered heart of that term to allow for other subjectivities. Yet it does so not by citing the exclusions of the term but by writing a new collectivity that keeps intact its universality but reframes it from a gendered perspective so that the violent rape and murder of Jo becomes a question for the commons, and one woman's vigilante action against the culprits becomes a common action. This film's pursuit of the common man thus presents a world in which sexism and misogyny are universal, rather than situated, concerns.

Domesticating the Commons

The example of *Madaari* suggests that to represent the public, popular Hindi cinema—with its formal reliance on the charismatic star at its center—might need to gesture beyond film to other genres such as social media. In Chapter 4, we see how television makes use of the charismatic potential of film to create affective publics. But here, we can also see how cinema resignifies the domesticated medium of television to raise particular kinds of political questions that are simultaneously questions of form: Who is the public, and who can represent it? We saw in *Madaari* that individuals driving in their cars and traversing the city on foot were able to form ad hoc publics through their use of social media to discuss and comment on issues of contemporary importance. In several of the films, newspaper and television headlines, and in particular images of people consuming those headlines, offer a new commons centered around the news media. These all demonstrate how common-man films are using the domesticated possibilities of nonfilm media to construct spaces of commonality and community even within a historically epical genre.

Fittingly, then, a figure who appears in many common-man films is that of the intrepid journalist who has rogue tendencies, breaking rules and refusing to take no for an answer in pursuit of the truth. We might see this figure as a nonviolent equivalent to the vigilante. The figure appears in films as early as *Main Azaad Hoon*, but also in 1980s and 1990s vigilante films such as *Mr. India* (1987) and *Mohra* (1994)—but in all these tends to be a minor character who works alongside the vigilante in his quest to enact justice (there are similar characters in *Ungli* and *A Wednesday*). But recently we have an increasing number of films featuring journalists as protagonists rather than as sidekicks. These films present the pursuit of truth as itself a sort of vigilante or rogue action in the face of a corrupt police and judicial system, and they present the contemporary medium of television as a key site for its dissemination, underscoring that "television pretends to actuality, to immediacy; the television image in many transmissions (news, current affairs, chat shows, announcements) behaves as though it were live and uses the techniques of direct address." Likewise, unlike the film star who is always distant and unattainable, "the television performer exists very much more in the same space as the television audience, as a known and familiar person" (Ellis 2015, 106).

In Raj Kumar Gupta's *No One Killed Jessica*, the journalist is the film's hero. The film is based on the real-life murder of model Jessica Lal, following which the social elite's narcissistic drive for self-preservation, together with the politically connected murderer's ability to bend justice and the incompetence, even if not the explicit corruption, of the judiciary and police, resulted in the young man's acquittal. Afterward, there arose significant social outcry and large protests took place across Indian cities (P. Varma 1998, xxix). In the film, the cause of justice for Jessica is taken up by Meera, an intrepid journalist, who makes it her mission to expose the true culprits of the crime. Meera is played by Bollywood superstar Rani Mukerji, who eschews the sexualized unidimensionality of many female roles and plays a ruthless, hard-nosed journalist determined to use the television news to bring the murderer to justice.

Indeed, while the first half of the film shows the murder of Jessica and its aftermath, much of the second half represents Meera on television, as she offers one revelation after another, exposing the true culprits and the nature of the cover-up. As she presents this evidence, the film shows different individuals and families watching her newscast on television from their kitchens and living rooms. We have seen this trope of anonymous viewers/listeners/texters in the earlier films, but here it is repeated and intensified, occupying most of the second half of the film with its iterative rhythm. By showing various anonymous individuals doing the same thing together and in the same way, the film builds a community unified around this injustice. And as Meera incites people to be outraged, and as we see viewers become increasingly animated, texting the station to show their support and texting their friends to join them in a candlelight vigil to support justice for Jessica, we see not only the formation of a community but also its politicization.

While the medium of television offers community building by means of a common experience that is received in private, individuated spaces, the representation of television *in film* works to republicize those experiences by remediating them through the large screen. Here the star's body retains its charismatic potential and refocalizes the disparate energy generated in the private sphere to reanimate the collective. In *No One Killed Jessica*, this is represented when the same faces we had seen watching television or texting now reappear as participants in the candlelight vigil, thus representing a continuity between the private and the public—as we saw in *Madaari* as well—rather than what is commonly perceived as their irreconcilability. This politicization, the film suggests, could not happen in one medium alone but needs the productive intermedia space between film and television to mobilize the various energies of the private individual in service of a broader public.

Therefore, even more than the other films, *No One Killed Jessica* is as much about the formal question of who the public is as about the particular incident of Jessica Lal's murder. Indeed, the intermedia formation of the commons is presented so insistently in the second half of the film that at times it exceeds the stated content of the political protest, "Justice for Jessica." In her newscast, Meera makes the case for justice (*insaaf*) and asks anyone who agrees to text his or her support to the station. Yet alongside this assertion of content (justice as opposed to injustice), the camera's movement indicates that what is at stake is form itself, the very process of rallying this diverse viewership into one social group and of registering that unity through the collective action of the text message. This is underscored by the insistent language of solidarity, such as "In Jessica's place, it could have been me," "it could have been my daughter," "it could have been my friend," and so on. In addition, we hear "We are with you Jessica," and "Jessica, Jessica," all of which suggest a syntagmatic mode of protest that is based not on Jessica's exceptionality but her replaceability and the commonality of her experience. As we have seen, the candlelight vigil as political practice works in a similar way; drawing an invisible continuity between the family's personal feelings of injustice and a larger, anonymous society, its own performative significance draws focus away from the specific issue being protested to the community formed in protest. Moreover, in *No One Killed Jessica*, the idea of having a vigil in the first place comes from an anonymous woman (not one of our characters) who has the idea after watching another film—which happens to be *Rang De Basanti*—underlining the metonymic significance of the action as well as demonstrating the metafictional incorporation of the common-man genre into the films themselves. In this way, the film interpellates its fictional viewers into a new constituency, and the film's viewers as well, mobilizing us together as a collective and converting us to caring about Jessica's cause. Whereas in the other common-man films we sit back and watch the protagonists become part of the collectivity, here we also become the protagonists, expanding the common man beyond the diegetic space of the film and into society at large.[6]

While a sole focus on the message of the film might lead a viewer to read *No One Killed Jessica* as closed and normalizing, insisting on a kind of politics-lite centered on the television-watching middle class (P. Varma 1998, xxix–xxx), I argue that the transactions that take place here, between film and television, and between charisma and the collective, offer a more nuanced picture of the political landscape and what is needed to reanimate it. At any moment, the solidarity represented here threatens to dissolve into an individualized politics, just as, formally speaking, cinema has the potential to cede its authority to the private space of the drawing room. This is constantly hinted at, as the repetition of solidarity comes close to becoming the cause, the form to becoming the content, and consciousness of the social to becoming the entirety of social consciousness. This is a danger that the film is aware of, even as it tries to build a commons nonetheless. More than the other films, therefore, *No One Kills Jessica*, in its excess, in its registering of the precarity of the enterprise, reasserts the open and unfinished imagination of the public in contemporary India.

"Mango Man"

Literary critics sometimes view "genre" as a term that signifies limitations on artistic freedom and a fundamentally conservative outlook with regard to originality and innovation. But genre is better thought of as a critical orientation that allows us to see precisely the opposite: to foreground innovation as central to how popular literature produces meaning, by repeating tropes of previous texts but with a difference and by adjusting and rearranging recognizable formal features in ways that open doors to new kinds of stories and new possibilities for grasping the present. It is through, not despite, generic conventions of melodrama and star charisma that Bollywood films reimagine contemporary political communities.

In this way, genres are not closed, finite receptacles of meaning but often portend their own limits. We can see this in the joke registered in this section's title, where the aam aadmi is humorously mistranslated as the "mango man," as in *Love Aaj Kal* (2009), referencing a second meaning of the Hindi word *aam* as "mango." Or in Rahul's farcical repetition of the line, in the comedy *Chennai Express* (2013), "Never underestimate the power of the common man!" even as he gets himself deeper and deeper into trouble. Even in *Gabbar Is Back*, there is a humorous scene in which two filmmakers are talking about Gabbar and one says, "I am Gabbar!" and then pauses and continues, "We should make a film with this title, Mr. Producer." And in *Rann* (2010), veteran newscaster Vijay Malik asks his channel executive, "What about that show we were planning, 'The Common Man?,'" to which she replies, with a sigh, "Headlines 24 [the competing channel] just started a new show, 'Aam Aadmi.'" All these examples gesture toward the possibility that the common man might at any moment cease being a meaningful category, having been too often repeated or commodified to such an extent that it has lost all its significance.

I suggest that these plays on the term "aam aadmi" and on the common man genre as a whole do not lie outside the genre but constitute it from the inside. They not only remind us that these films present the common man as a pursuit rather than an actual demographic category but also mark the limits of the genre itself, in which, as in *No One Killed Jessica*, the incessant repetition of the term is always on the verge of evacuating it of meaning. Seeing this as part of the pursuit of the common man rather than its negation contests a purely sociological reading, which would try to label the common man in terms of demographic presence—Who is the common man? What is its class and gender? What are its exclusions? Rather, the genre is defined by pursuit, by striving, by reaching beyond currently configured demographics and vote banks to think about potentially new formations that might emerge, even briefly, in the imagination. It is in this sense that the genre is contemporary.

As potential end points to the genre, therefore, these moments suggest that in the space between the common man as an idea and the common man as an actual demographic category or descriptor, there is significant likelihood for its distortion or corruption. This is not undermining the common man as an idea as much as noting that its potential might lie *in it as an idea*, in that moment before it takes form to become a "real" grouping of people—

something that did happen, for instance, with the foundation of the Aam Aadmi political party in 2012 and the passage of the Jan Lokpal bill in 2013.[7] This is an important rejoinder to criticisms of the common-man films that see them as heavy-handed in their representation of new constituencies. As Raymond Williams writes, "The mistake, as so often, is in taking terms of analysis as terms of substance. Thus we speak of a world-view or of a prevailing ideology or of a class outlook, often with adequate evidence, but in this regular slide towards a past tense and a fixed form suppose . . . that these exist and are lived specifically and definitively, in singular and developing forms" (2009, 129). In line with Williams's analysis, the common man too is a concept in formation rather than precisely delineated or concrete. As these films show, it is not so much the achievement of the common man but its pursuit that is significant.

4

Melodrama and the Open Edge of Politics

hapter 3 illustrates how cinematic representations of television might engender a commonality of experience that potentially activates new political formations. This chapter looks at the inverse: how television—in particular, Bollywood superstar Aamir Khan's (2012–2014) popular reality-based Hindi talk show *Satyamev Jayate*[1]—harnesses the affective energies of popular cinema to engage audiences in new ways. I argue that Aamir Khan is a significant figure in Indian popular culture because his work attempts to cross the deep-seated divides between film and television, mass culture and literature, politics and entertainment, realism and melodrama, and the epic and the everyday. In *Satyamev Jayate*, he seeks to raise awareness of social problems that continue to plague the country. The show is, like so much cultural production in contemporary India, vastly heterogeneous, covering hot topics like caste, sexual violence, queer rights, and female feticide; long-standing and pervasive problems such as the treatment of people with disabilities and the elderly and medical malpractice; and more general issues such as the role of sports in society and pesticides in food. Khan's approach is also heterogeneous, sometimes offering deep political insight, sometimes remaining on the surface of an issue, and sometimes tracking back and forth in the course of a single episode. Meanwhile, the show has been criticized for its formulaic aesthetics, commercialism, simplistic politics (Salgaocar 2012), and emotionally manipulative, staged performativity.[2] I argue, however, that these features situate the show where several worlds meet: where the epic world of Bollywood meets the contemporary, where entertainment meets politics, and where melodrama meets the world. Buoyed by gestures such as Khan wiping away his tears, repeatedly expressing shock, or ending a particularly poignant interview with a hug, the popular show stages a version of civil society that is scripted and self-consciously mediated, thus lying outside what we conventionally consider the domain of the political. I argue that by presenting a range of social issues in this melodramatic format, *Satyamev Jayate* gestures toward a new public, one potentially open to surprising alliances and to accommodating new political subjects whose characteristics and transformative potential are not yet determined.

This chapter continues the discussion of new political constituencies in India. Rather than abide by the old sedimented frameworks of either socialist dissent, which found form in progressive realism, or cosmopolitan postcolonialism, in which the experience of exile highlights the exclusions of nationalism, contemporary popular culture is less rooted in a fixed, alternative form, instead gesturing to multiple possibilities for morally just futures that might not fit into predetermined ideas of progressivism or even of the political. Melodrama, with its apparent distance from the real world, its heightened emotion, and its epic, Manichean morality, is not political in any obvious sense. But insofar as it registers new subjectivities rooted in emotive and non-Cartesian understandings of the self and the social, melodrama represents an "open edge" of politics in India today, not able to be subsumed within civil society but containing an unruly excess (Mazzarella 2013, 78). This means that not only has Aamir Khan "managed to 'reach the Indian mainstream by using Bollywood tropes in the service of larger causes'" (quoted in Chakravartty and Sarkar 2013, 67), but his melodramatic imagination is reframing commonplace understandings of the political via the idiom of popular cinema to mobilize new relationships between self and world.[3]

This is in opposition to understanding contemporary cultural production as merely neoliberal, marked by an increasing privatization of state industries, a transfer of responsibility from the state to the market or the individual citizen (Chakravartty and Sarkar 2013, 61; D. Gupta 2013), and an increased faith in philanthropy and in taking politics "into one's own hand." *Satyamev Jayate* invites such a critique because of its corporate sponsorship and encouragement to its audience to call or text in support of particular causes and to sign petitions as a means of political participation. These forms of what has been disparagingly dubbed "India Shining middle-class activism" (Sitapati 2011, 42) or "clicktivism" (Harindranath and Khorana 2014, 68) are seen to reflect, like the discourse of the common man, a neoliberal shift whereby the once apathetic middle class gets "empowered" to fight for its own rights under the banner of universal citizenship, uninflected by caste, ethnicity, or religion, using tools imbricated in consumer culture.

Khan's show, supported by corporations such as Airtel, AquaGuard, Coca-Cola, and Johnson and Johnson (Chakravartty and Sarkar 2013, 67), seems to reflect this new, consumer-oriented, politics-lite.

However, as the preceding chapters demonstrate, reading literature and cultural production merely as a reflection of the political economy flattens their heterogeneity and ignores any countertrends or possibilities that inhere within them. Anthropologist James Ferguson writes in the context of poverty-reduction programs in South Africa that neoliberalism cannot become a blanket category that stands in for antiprogressivism or "evil" (2015, 123). He argues instead that parts of neoliberalism—for instance, the market, the discourse of individual empowerment, or the ideal of abstract citizenship—can be "repurposed" for potentially progressive ends (174). Ferguson calls on progressive thinkers to evaluate *individual* cases of programs or initiatives that seem neoliberal, to take apart their different features, to see whether they are in fact evil rather than dismiss them in advance simply because of their tie to neoliberal formations such as the market. He suggests that scholars on the left need to approach these new initiatives with creativity rather than dogma. As Craig Hight similarly asserts about seemingly neoliberal forms such as reality television, "New theoretical tools need to be developed in order to properly understand and critique the significance of these new forms" (quoted in Holmes and Jermyn 2011, 17).

Indeed, by closely exploring *Satyamev Jayate*'s rhetoric and how it works as a form of representation, we can see it as a complex text. By foregrounding its mixed format, ambivalence, heterogeneous registers, and how it tracks between a straightforward call for political engagement and a more affective register grounded in the popular cinema's long association with unreason, we can reimagine engagement in terms outside what is conventionally considered the realm of civil society. This, combined with Aamir Khan's own oscillation between realism and melodrama throughout his career and the affective energy his body carries over from Hindi cinema, results in a form of representation that is surprisingly open and unformed. Khan's show seeks to birth new subjectivities in relation to real social issues—many of which are otherwise invisible to those enchanted by a consumerist lifestyle—via the medium of his own star's body. The question of whether it solves the social issues is less my focus than the new modes of collective affect generated in these spaces, whose political consequences are not yet known.

Cinema and Unreason

The relationship between cinema and liberal citizenship in India is a conflicted one that goes back to colonial times. Although much about popular cinema has changed since the early twentieth century, this tension remains—

and it has to do with the particular generic qualities of the popular cinema that seem to constitute a rejection of the reasoned individual subject. By privileging its affective register over its plot, by presenting a Manichean world structured around a good-evil binary, and by centering around a star who is the locus of charismatic desire, popular cinema seems to reject liberal reason. Moreover, Indian melodramatic film uses song and dance not in service of a story or a message but as a mode of bodily and erotic engagement. It is a genre seemingly oriented toward mobocracy rather than republicanism, anarchy rather than reason; it is visceral rather than cerebral and populist rather than progressive.

In India, the danger posed by cinema to the status quo was evident in discussions over censorship during colonial rule. As William Mazzarella observes, colonial officials met popular film with a certain "ambivalence" because of its "vital[ity]," "visceral[ity]" (2009, 66), and "sensual[ity]" (68). Cinema's "effectiveness . . . was understood first of all to reside in its appeal to the senses rather than to the intellect" (68) and in "the corporeal appeal of theatrical and ritual performance" (69). As Lawrence Liang writes, "For Habermas the idea of mass culture and the public sphere are contradictory, which means that the audience of cinema always remain a 'non-public'" (2005, 369–370). But what precipitates colonial fear around the cinema is precisely the fact that the public emerged "after being emotionally galvanized" (368). In the postcolonial period as well, "there is a definite sense . . . [that] the political elite considered the commercial cinema to be an inadequate place to nurture a culture of citizenship" (Vasudevan 2001, 60).

In contrast, Ravi Vasudevan's (2011) compelling idea of the "melodramatic public" shows how new forms of subjectivity and citizenship might emerge *through* the affective energies of the popular cinema in India. Countering the globally dominant form of the "classic Hollywood style," which implies, as Linda Williams summarizes, "efficient action-centered, goal-oriented linear narratives driven by the desire of a single protagonist, involving one or two lines of action, and leading to definitive closure" (1991, 3), Indian popular cinema makes use of a variety of aesthetic and formal techniques that create new subjects in their active incitement of spectators' affective and libidinal energies and new publics comprising such subjects. From this perspective, desire does not lie outside the political sphere but is integral to it. The collective experience of emotion, what one recent Bollywood film summarized as "kabhi khushi kabhi gham [whether happiness, whether tears]," produces a sense of affective citizenship—a collective identity bound up with powerful emotional responses to something viewed on-screen. As Christine Gledhill writes, "If realism presumes the adequacy of given linguistic and cultural codes for understanding and representing reality, and modernism embraces the infinite regress of meaning in the self-reflexive play of the signifier, melodrama's rootedness in the real world, its urgent ideological mission to motivate ordinary lives, leads it into an opposing stance. Faced with the decentred self, the evasiveness of language, melodrama answers with excessive personalisation, excessive expression" (1991, 218).

The Dualities of Aamir Khan

The political possibilities of melodrama are evident in the oeuvre of Aamir Khan, a top Bollywood star with a huge fan following and one who has wholeheartedly embraced the heterogeneous address of Indian popular culture at large. Khan is called "the thinking man's hero" for his choice of films and his progressive politics (East 2015), and as of 2018, he has starred in four of the ten highest-grossing Bollywood films of all time ("Top 20" 2018). He thus clearly understands audience appeal. Khan's filmic career is marked by a range of roles from actor to writer, producer, and director and a range of types of films from melodramas and nationalist epics to parallel and *hatke* (alternative) cinema. His first adult role was that of Raj in *Qayamat Se Qayamat Tak* (1988), and his success in that film led to leading roles in *Raakh* (1989), *Dil* (1990), *Dil Hai Ke Manta Nahin* (1991), *Jo Jeeta Wohi Sikandar* (1992), *Andaz Apna Apna* (1994), *Rangeela* (1995), *Akele Hum Akele Tum* (1995), *Raja Hindustani* (1996), *Ishq* (1997), *Ghulam* (1998), *Earth* (1999), and *Sarfarosh* (1999). These films were widely successful and led to a number of award nominations and wins for Khan, as did *Dil Chahta Hai* (2001), *Mangal Pandey: The Rising* (2005), *Rang De Basanti* (2006), *Ghajini* (2008), *3 Idiots* (2009), and *PK* (2014). In 1999, he started his own production company, Aamir Khan Productions (AKP), which has produced ten films as of 2018, including several that Khan himself starred in, such as *Lagaan* (2001), *Taare Zameen Par* (2007), *Dhobi Ghat* (2011), *Talaash* (2012), *Dangal* (2016), and *Secret Superstar* (2017). This range, while not atypical, makes Khan one of the more versatile figures in the industry today. Although certainly an actor first, his oeuvre is evidence that he wants to cross the boundaries that define his peers and the industry in general. This has been exhibited most evidently in his movement between conventional Bollywood cinema and alternative films, a movement that distinguishes him from others in the mainstream industry. He is seen by many, especially intellectuals and educated viewers, to stand apart because of his interest in realist films, films without songs, films with themes not usually addressed by popular cinema, films about women, political films, and so on.[4] This, combined with his commitment to method acting and authenticity—for instance, gaining more than sixty pounds for his role as a retired wrestler in *Dangal* and then losing it all at once (D. Goyal 2016)—his stated dislike of awards shows (Suggu 1999), his principled politics (Daniels 2012, 136–139),[5] and his decision to commit to shooting only one film at a time (Perry 2013), has associated his name with a certain dignity and restraint in the industry.

Yet understanding Khan's oeuvre as a teleology or a progressive move away from melodrama toward more "serious" art forms misses out on the modal hybridity that characterizes his work and the melodramatic publics of popular cinema more generally. Ashok Raj writes that Khan "has progressively refurbished his cine image from an upper-class teen hero to a street-smart *tapori* . . . and then to an important representative of realist cinema" and that "Aamir has undergone a complete transformation, indicating perhaps his permanent shift to serious and meaningful cinema" (2010, 246, 250). Yet this teleological account ignores that Khan's oeuvre has in fact spanned conventional categories of realism and melodrama, social cinema and entertainment—and continues to do so. As Christina Daniels writes, Khan is "both an icon and an iconoclast" (2012, 103). Moreover, his recent appearance on the small screen, at the same time as he continues to make films, means that he crosses media as well. From this perspective, his reality show *Satyamev Jayate*, which performs a scripted version of civil society to draw attention to various social problems plaguing contemporary India, might be seen as bringing together the various strands of his career. Both realist and melodramatic, social and entertaining, *Satyamev Jayate*, in its embrace of the mixed address, captures some of the possibilities and contradictions of the contemporary in India.

Indeed, a closer look at Khan's oeuvre shows it to be marked by a constitutive ambivalence rather than unidirectional transformation. For instance, two of his most critically acclaimed films to date were released in 1999, *Sarfarosh* and *Earth*, which are notably different from each another (Daniels 2012, 94). *Sarfarosh* is an action film that pits a policeman, played by Khan, against Pakistani terrorists who kidnapped his father and killed his brother. It was one of the first films that named Pakistan explicitly as an enemy state (Dwyer 2005, 279), which many see as a reflection of the nationalist sentiment unleashed by the Kargil War taking place at the time (Khatun 2016, 52). The film simplistically conflates the Muslim with the Pakistani terrorist and, like many Bollywood films, relies on a relatively straightforward idea of heroism and masculinity on one side and villainy on the other, in this case grafted onto binaristic, India-Pakistan, Hindu-Muslim divides.[6] By contrast, *Earth* is an independent film that for the most part refuses Bollywood melodramatic conventions and thus was seen as "a brave career choice" for a mainstream actor (A. Chopra 1999). Based on Bapsi Sidhwa's 1988 novel

Ice-Candy-Man (which was later reprinted as *Cracking India*), *Earth* was directed by Indian-Canadian filmmaker Deepa Mehta, known for her female-centered films such as the controversial *Fire*, released three years earlier. *Earth*, like the novel, takes a very different stance on Partition than *Sarfarosh* does; it is a lamentation of the violence of Partition in particular as it affected women (Neutill 2010, 74), and it mourns the damage wreaked by Partition on the subcontinent's heterogeneity. In this sense, it is specifically opposed to "nationalist histories that vilify one religious community for the sufferings of another or that emphasize the political heroes of independence while glossing over the attendant violence." Rather, "*Earth* constructs a multifaceted, transnational, and transcommunal popular memory of partition, asking its audience to view partition's traumatic and divisive history in a way that critiques the implicated forms of gendered and communal violence extending throughout the social fabric of 1947 India" (Herman 2005, 117). In addition to these thematic differences, the two films are different visually as well: while *Sarfarosh* uses the more theatrical, frontal shots typical of Bollywood melodramas, *Earth* offers a more intimate address, beginning with the first scene, a close-up of young Lenny's hands (Neutill 2010, 73). An interviewer at the time asked Aamir Khan about the seeming contradiction between *Earth* and *Sarfarosh*, one "offbeat" and the other "commercial," to which he replied, "I don't have any particular preference for an offbeat kind of a film or a popular film. I just like to do films" (Suggu 1999). Khan's response suggests that the ambivalence reflected in these two films poses little contradiction for the actor, even as it seems to for the critic; they are, for him, part of the same larger creative endeavor.

Even after the founding of AKP, we see a similar pattern of creative duality. The year 2001 saw the release of the blockbuster *Lagaan*, which Khan himself produced, along with *Dil Chahta Hai*. *Lagaan* had an epic quality to it, staging the coming together of communities, religions, and castes for the nationalist cause while "maintain[ing] the blend of action, comedy, melodrama, song-and-dance sequences, stereotypical pantomime villains and love triangles" common to Bollywood films (Stadtler 2005, 519). In contrast, *Dil Chahta Hai* was sparse and economical in its plot and visuals, paving the way for a new kind of Hindi cinema in the 2000s. In fact, *Dil Chahta Hai* might be seen as an explicit move away from long-held Bollywood aesthetics, with its "design catalog" style (Mazumdar 2007, 142), and from Bollywood generic conventions, with its representation of love as contingent rather than all-encompassing, the much-diminished role it gives to family, and its celebration of youth (Anjaria and Anjaria 2008, 132–133). While *Lagaan* makes use of vast, open rural landscapes to present a sweeping allegory for national integration, *Dil Chahta Hai*'s refrain was "We are new; why should our style be old? [Hum hain naye; andaaz kyon ho purana?]" and represented a younger generation disinterested in the past.

This duality intensifies in Khan's later works and compels us to read Khan's oeuvre as heterogeneous and experimental rather than progressively narrowing into a fixed political or aesthetic stance. In 2005 he starred in *Mangal Pandey*, a film about the 1857 Sepoy Rebellion, and, when asked by an interviewer whether he will "be working only in movies based on themes like freedom and patriotism," responded, "No, nothing of that sort" (S. Kumar, n.d.), again emphasizing his fluidity of roles against critics' attempts to pin him down. *Rang De Basanti* and *Fanaa*, which also diverge significantly in terms of explicit politics, were released in 2006. Like *Sarfarosh*, *Fanaa* was criticized for its stereotypical representation of Muslim characters—specifically the portrayal of Rehan, a Muslim terrorist, here played by Khan—and for its ending, which effectively forced the Indian Muslim Zooni to choose between her love for the terrorist and her patriotism (she chose the latter) (S. Khan 2009b, 129; Khatun 2016, 54). However, the film, set in the occupied region of Kashmir, also invokes a Sufi cosmology in its title to consider, as Bollywood films have long done, a pure love that exists right at the point of self-annihilation, captured in the film's refrain: "May my soul find refuge in your love. May my life find annihilation in my love for you [Tere pyar mein mere sansh ko panah mil jaye. Tere ishq mein mere jaan fanaa ho jaye]" (S. Khan 2009a, 87). On the surface, *Rang De Basanti* is a very different kind of film, featuring young protagonists who care little about the concerns of the nation. The visual style, too, is much closer to that of *Dil Chahta Hai* than *Fanaa*. But as these characters begin to change after the death of one of their friends caused by faulty airline parts, their own relationship to sacrifice also changes. Whereas in the beginning they think only about their own happiness, at the end they assassinate the defense minister responsible for the faulty parts, ultimately sacrificing their own lives for a larger cause. Thus, in a way, *Rang De Basanti* also experiments with the question of *fanaa* (annihilation), not in this case as a characteristic of romantic love but as a form of political protest. The connections between the two films suggest a mode of experimenting with the question of where the desire for self-annihilation is born, across apparent distinctions of form, genre, or politics.

Since 2006 Khan has continued to track between the melodramatic and the realist, the politically inclined and the entertainer. His directorial debut, *Taare Zameen Par*, in which he also starred, was released in 2007 and sought to raise awareness of and advocate educational reform for children with disabilities (N. Joshi 2012). In 2008 he starred in *Ghajini*, and in 2009, *3 Idiots*, both of which were "mainstream commercial" films that were hugely successful at the box office (Daniels 2012, 159); and in 2010 AKP released *Peepli*

Live, a quirky, low-budget "black comedy" (177) that sought to draw attention to the rise in farmer suicides in India. *Talaash* was another popular film, as was *Dhoom 3* (2013). In 2015 Khan starred in *PK*, which again proceeded to break box-office records, but with the explicit social project of criticizing institutionalized religion. His most recent films similarly merge politically empowering stories with emotion and melodrama: *Dangal* is a Bollywood epic based on the true story of Mahavir Phoghat, a wrestler from rural Haryana who trained two of his daughters to be gold-medal-winning wrestlers, and *Secret Superstar* is the story of a teenage girl who becomes a successful singer despite the constrictions of her family life.

Dhoom 3 and *PK* offer another productive contrast. *Dhoom 3* is the third film in the Dhoom (Noise) series, known for its over-the-top action sequences, adrenaline-pumping motorcycle chase scenes, and sleek image. As one reviewer wrote, "The film is powered by its action" ("Dhoom 3" 2016). *Dhoom 3* was, at the time of its release, the highest-budget film ever made in India. It can hardly be said to have a politics in any sense of the word, even though at its heart it is a revenge story of a poor man's son against an evil wealthy banker (named Warren Anderson, evocative for some Indian audiences of the CEO of Dow Chemicals at the time of the Bhopal chemical spill). Rather, it might be seen as intensely cinephilic, registering, as Ravi Vasudevan writes in another context, "an aesthetics of astonishment, where technology announces itself as a primary attraction" (2011, 329). Representation in such a film is less about conveying a reality than about intense affective engagement, the thrill of watching a chase, hearing a throbbing sound track, or experiencing "seemingly gratuitous excesses" (L. Williams 1991, 3). *PK*, by contrast, is a more intellectual film; as one film reviewer commented, "It has made people think" (quoted in Qadri and Mufti 2015, 5). The social satire pokes fun at institutionalized religion and critiques the false prophets who feed off poverty and alienation in contemporary India. Khan plays PK, an alien who comes to earth and is perplexed by the number of religious differences he sees, which seem to unnecessarily divide people. The film's subplot involves a romance between an Indian woman and a Pakistani man, who can finally be together at the end after PK has revealed the absurdity of communal mistrust. The film explicitly criticizes godmen and communalism in India as well as enmity with Pakistan, all pressing political issues at the time of its release. Showing that there is not only one formula that determines a film's success, both *Dhoom 3* and *PK* broke box-office records ("Aamir Khan" 2015), in part because of Khan's star persona but mostly because they were successful at what they did, even as what they did was significantly different: one engaged primarily at the level of the body, the other with the mind, and both found success with audiences on these terms.

Khan's movement between different modes of engagement should be understood as an extended experiment with representation itself and increasingly with the political meaning of cultural production. As Khan has said, "I want to give myself the freedom to do all kinds of cinema. I don't want to do just those kinds of films which make a social comment, or are very logical. Sometimes I too feel like doing something mushy, mad, crude, sentimental" (quoted in Daniels 2012, 155). Thus, he seems to ask, What does it mean to represent, and what does it mean to represent politically? What does it mean to engage an audience? What is the range of possibilities offered by popular cultural production? These questions are not unique to Khan but have underlain Hindi popular cinema from its inception, even though most critics simplistically describe Bollywood as a set of unchanging formulas and conventions. Early Bollywood filmmakers Nitin Bose and Bimal Roy, for instance, "aligned themselves with progressive causes and the representation of contemporary Indian reality without necessarily renouncing the more pleasurable aspects of the commercial cinema such as songs and dances. . . . While Bimal Roy's name . . . is associated with film realism, he has not gained admittance into the ranks of the 'greats' because he mixed modes which are perceived as fundamentally at odds with one another (realistic mise-en-scène with songs and dances)" (Sumita Chakravarty 1993, 88). We also see this mixing in individual actors such as Shashi Kapoor; Akbar S. Ahmed argues that because of the separation between art-house and popular film, Shashi Kapoor had to "come upon a workable solution" that would involve "giving excellent performances in serious films with limited appeal while also starring in the popular, multi-star films. It was as if there were two, distinct Shashis" (A. Ahmed 1992, 293). Actor and director Raj Kapoor, one of the most well-known names in Hindi cinema, also transgressed modes and styles in provocative ways. While his early films such as *Awaara* (1951) and *Shri 420* (1955) were critical of the corruption of the elite and the hardships faced by the poor, they were also "representative of the new drive to combine a social reform perspective with ornate spectacle" (Vasudevan 1995, 312) and "commerce with art" (quoted in Virdi 2004, 213).

Aamir Khan seems equally invested in teasing out this long-standing interest, within Bollywood itself, in experiment and modal hybridity, pursuing the questions of representation and political engagement from different perspectives. He has been criticized for this seeming inconsistency: by progressives for films such as *Fanaa* (S. Khan 2009a, 92–93) and by intellectuals for films such as *Dhoom 3*. However, seeing this oscillation as part of an alternative but overlooked trajectory within Bollywood itself reveals even melodramatic, formulaic popular cinema to be asking questions about the nature of representation and about the relationship between popular form and political engagement. Aamir Khan compels us to question the conventional wisdom that assumes that political filmmaking looks a certain way and, conversely, that melodrama is primarily a means of escape for its audiences, a gesture away from reality into a dream world.

Intermedia in the Age of Reality Television

Aamir Khan's experiments with the affective and political registers of Hindi cinema took a new turn in 2012 when he launched the first of three seasons of the television program *Satyamev Jayate* on Star Network, with himself as host. This reality-based program is centered around social and political topics in India today. In each episode, Khan introduces the day's topic and then invites a series of guests to the stage to discuss it. The guests include individuals who narrate their own stories and experts from the government, academia, or other professional fields. The explicit goals of the show are to raise awareness among its viewers about social injustices still present in India and to incite those viewers to do something about them.

Khan's move from cinema to television is not without precedent; the decades since the arrival of satellite television have seen several film actors grace the small screen (Mazumdar 2013; Mitra 2013). The first was Amitabh Bachchan, who was rebranded after his brief career slump into a television star as the host of *Kaun Banega Crorepati* (*KBC*) in 2000, which was a spectacular success (S. Rao 2005, 135), "transformed television" (136), and succeeded in restarting the actor's film career (Sadana 2012, 2). Shah Rukh Khan briefly took over from Bachchan as the host of *KBC* in 2007. *Bigg Boss* and the various talent competitions (*Indian Idol, Saregama*) also have celebrity hosts from the film industry. And in the last few years there has been a spate of new reality shows, some of which seem directly inspired by *Satyamev Jayate*. For instance, *Mission Sapne* (twenty episodes, 2014–2016) follows Bollywood stars and other celebrities as they take on everyday jobs (tea seller, vegetable vendor, etc.) for a few hours to raise money for a good cause.

On one level, and in line with the previous discussion of television, we can see this move from the big screen to the small as the domestication of the star, such that the distance and awe that characterize the cinematic star are replaced by a new, domesticated fantasy enabled by "television's rhetoric of familiarity and intimacy, the size of the screen, the perpetual presence of its everyday flow, and its domestic context of reception" (S. Holmes 2011, 116). By this token, the experience of desire previously unleashed in the public (or semipublic) domain of the cinema hall is now experienced in the privacy of the middle-class home, which "fundamentally alters the relationship between the star and the screen [from what] was seen in post-Nehruvian, pre-liberalisation India" (Akshaya Kumar 2014, 244). Indeed, the cinematic star moves to television precisely at the moment of the rapid growth of the middle class, potentially representing what Susan Sontag (1996) has identified, in another context, as "the decay of cinema."

However, presenting cinema and television as opposing media discounts the constant crisscrossing between different media in contemporary India—what Amit Rai calls "media assemblages"—not only between film and television but between both and new media, social media, pirated media, cell phones, iPods, and so on. For Rai, these assemblages mark a diffusion of the affective energy that was previously reserved for film into a variety of media rather than simply evince a one-way privatization of desire. Thus, contemporary affect is rearranged and reconfigured as media across public and private domains, resulting in "a stochastic or nonlinear experience of Bollywood" (2009, 2). This nuances accounts of television viewing in post-1990s India, which often focus on television as "a socio-technical apparatus" that enables the privatization of affect (Rajagopal 2009b, 3), especially surrounding the collective viewing of nationalist fantasies such as the Sunday-morning *Ramayana* (Mankekar 2000; Rajagopal 2009b, 25–26). This narrative has its present-day version in accounts such as Maitrayee Chaudhuri's, which argue that "the media plays a crucial ideological role in legitimising neo-liberal capitalism in contemporary India" (2010, 59). In this type of critique, television is seen as ideologically homogenizing and artistically simplistic. However, focusing on intermedia exchange suggests that television exists in "heteronomy," to use Adorno's word, to the market (N. Brown 2016, 184), one node in the complex circuits of affect and desire whose meaning cannot be considered apart from their constant crisscrossing of multiple domains.

The work of the media assemblage is made only more "untimely" by the particularly hybrid and interactive form of reality television (Rai 2009, 2), which further unsettles the unidirectionality associated with popular culture. Reality television has been criticized for embodying neoliberal enterprise "by depicting ordinary people gaining extraordinary competitive success by dint of their own concerted drive and effort, as well as intensive and arduous cultivation of their merits, talents, and abilities" (Gooptu and Chakravarty 2013, 142–143). Its straddling of documentary and entertainment is also seen as suspect (S. Holmes 2011, 112; Gooptu and Chakravarty 2013, 143), "as if this mixing of traits is disingenuous or unethical in some way" (Holmes and Jermyn 2011, 10). "Thus one of the most recurrent features of the popular and critical reception of Reality TV has been comment on the ways in which it manipulates and constructs 'the real'" (Holmes and Jermyn 2011, 11). But it is precisely these characteristics that make it a potentially fruitful form in which to consider representation as experimental in relation to the world. Reality television is a reminder that terms such as "fact" and "fiction," "politics" and "entertainment," and "private" and "public" "are always under 'reconstruction' and negotiation" (11). Even in a star such as Oprah Winfrey in the United States we see "the intimate, the private, making it public but with intimate trappings, sending it back to the private realm of the home, further blurring those already fuzzy distinctions" (Haag 1993, 120).

Indeed, this transgressive quality of reality television has been recognized by some critics as generating new political vocabularies (Kraidy 2009; S. Holmes 2011; Pullen 2011). As Tania Lewis, Fran Martin, and Wanning Sun write about *Kaun Banega Crorepati*, India's first reality show, despite its seeming repetition of a rags-to-riches fantasy, it was often enjoyed by people from a range of class positions, revealing "a more complex and at times troubled sense of people's imagined relationship to . . . 'national' aspirations" (2016, 90). Aswin Punathambekar similarly argues that "reality television, combined with mobile media technologies and practices, has enabled new modes of cultural and political expression"; in particular, he shows that "participatory cultures surrounding television create possibilities for the renewal of everyday forms of interaction in public settings" (2010, 241). Using the example of the 2007 season of *Indian Idol*, Punathambekar argues that in Shillong, "texting and casting a vote for one's favorite contestant did signal a new way of being at home and in the world" (251). Rather than always assume that new technologies are closing off avenues of democratic participation—thus "compressing the wider story of Indian television into a single-stranded narrative" (Lewis, Martin, and Sun 2016, 103)—Punathambekar shows that new avenues are also being opened up. He argues that, even in the context of neoliberalism, there are "possibilities for mobilization that are not wholly anticipated and controlled by media corporations and other vested interests" (2010, 252).

For all its claim to be a straightforward show to raise political awareness, *Satyamev Jayate* actively negotiates this arena, muddying the contradictions between a cluster of concepts: fact and fiction, the film star and the domestication of desire, the time of epic and the time of the everyday, iconicity and intimacy, the affective and the reasoned. These contradictions play out in the course of individual episodes and the show as a whole and complicate the otherwise seemingly self-evident distinctions that commentators across the board want to draw between progressive politics and entertainment, realism and melodrama, and civil society and emotion. In this way, even though the show claims to engage with particular political problems, its innovation is as much in how it stages a series of scenarios in which cinematic affect seeps into political discourse to build new melodramatic publics built around topics of "common" concern as in the solutions it provides. It is thus not a fixed form of representation with stable values but, as Su Holmes and Deborah Jermyn write of reality television more generally, "a space for experimentation and exploration . . . which we perhaps shouldn't be too eager to resolve or close down" (2011, 18).

"The Truth Shall Prevail"

Epic melodrama, with its black-and-white morality, does not seem conducive to addressing contemporary issues. Melodrama works by relegating lived contradictions to a space outside the everyday and registering them on a distanced plane so that they feel like universal struggles rather than those born of the present. But Aamir Khan seems to recognize the uses of the epic in his presentation of *Satyamev Jayate*.

The title of the show, translated as "the truth shall prevail," is the national motto of India and a line from the *Mahabharata*, where it is part of the couplet "Satyameva jayate nanrtam / Satyena pantha vitato devayanah [Truth alone triumphs, not falsehood / Through truth the divine path is spread out]." This epic ring makes it seem initially like an inappropriate title for a show that seeks to illuminate complex political issues. In interviews, Satyajit Bhatkal, the show's director, has talked about other possible titles for the show, including *Maa Tujhe Salaam* (I bow to you, Mother) and *Hum Honge Kamyab* (We shall overcome), which was his personal preference. The first has an explicitly nationalist ring to it; the second is associated with global progressive activism. But, Aamir Khan relates, the name *We Shall Overcome* made him slightly depressed, because "when you say we shall overcome, you also mean that you haven't yet overcome" ("Making" 2017). And indeed, as globally, the song is associated with a particular kind of anticonsumerist activism, which in India has associations with *khadi* (homespun cloth), hunger strikes, and other Gandhian practices that many consider outdated. Clearly, those values are very different from the sleek, packaged, corporate image of this show. In contrast, the title *Satyamev Jayate* offers a more self-assured stance, one inflected by an idiom of cultural confidence in which a position is asserted rather than feebly wished for in the near future (Chakravartty and Sarkar 2013, 66).

But in its centering of "truth," the phrase "Satyamev Jayate" also references the world of Hindi cinema and its own conflicted relationship with the epics. Like other melodramatic forms, Bollywood abides by an epical rationality of good versus evil (Rosie Thomas 1998, 163). *Satya*, or truth, is a concept that circulates throughout many Hindi films, both explicitly and implicitly. Despite these epic ambitions, however, Bollywood characters are often plagued with uncertainty about how such a grand notion of truth should play out in their daily lives. For instance, in *Deewaar*, Ravi is a policeman who struggles to decide whether he should pursue his criminal brother Vijay, admitting that he is not sure if he can do what Arjun did in the *Mahabharata*, when he declared war on his brothers for the sake of a higher moral truth. Ravi is, instead, conflicted. As he tells his girlfriend, "Veera, sometimes there is a time in life when one doesn't understand what is true and what is false. . . . Everything I'm doing, is it right, is it good? [Veera, kabhi kabhi zindagi mein aisa waqt bhi aata hai ki samajh mein nahin aata ki kya sahi hai, kya galat hai. . . . Jo kuch main kar raha hoon, kya woh sahi hai, kya woh thik?]." When Veera reminds him of Krishna's advice to Arjun, to pursue moral truth at all costs, Ravi responds, "I know, Veera, I know. But the person who heard that response was none other than Arjun. But I'm not Arjun. I'm not Arjun, Veera." The anxiety that emerges in the space between the epic and the everyday plays out in the film as a whole, which betrays a profound moral uncertainty prompted by the failures of the ideals of independence that culminated in Indira Gandhi's declaration of the Emergency in 1975. This shattered postindependence idealism finds expression in films precisely where the universal idea of satya meets the contemporary moment.

Truth, then, despite Bollywood's epical ambitions, is not an external value that films passively accept but can also be a site of loss in the face of contemporary reality. In *Deewaar*, even though Ravi does end up taking the supposedly moral path, engaging in a war with his brother, the film presents this decision with ambivalence. We see a similar ambivalence in Ram Gopal Varma's film *Satya* (1998), which inaugurated a Bollywood subgenre of noir in the 2000s that represented the Mumbai underworld and its "alternative ethical world" saturated with everyday violence (Mazumdar 2007, 180). Despite being named for truth, *Satya* and other films like it represent a landscape that has been so distorted by violence that the parameters of high morality no longer obtain, and the title asks to be read with irony.

Satyamev Jayate is not melancholic or dark, as these two films are, but it similarly writes the contemporary as a point of contact between an epical ideal of satya and the present world—where, we might say, truth meets reality. The words *satya* and *sachaai* (also meaning "truth") abound in the production team's interviews about the show, but in the show itself, we are presented with multiple points of view on the topics at hand. Although the show's title and these interviews promise a certain commitment to truth, the show is in fact a series of questions about what truth actually is. When Khan offers an opinion, it is not presented as a universal truth but a perspective born in the present. At the end of the episode on untouchability, for instance, Khan asks members of the audience to reflect on what they learned during the episode: "Aap ke kya kya vichar hain? Kya mehsoos ho raha hai aap ko? [What are your thoughts? What are your feelings?]." One woman responds that she never thought about caste before, because she was immersed in her own sachaai born in her privilege. Now she realizes that "everyone has their own truth" based on their own "world [duniya]" and to make change, we have to accept others' truths as true. The acknowledgment of the contingency of truth is evident in Khan's own statements as well, such as in the prologue to the first episode of the series, when he says his goal is "har sach ko bahar nikaalna chahta hoon [to bring to light every truth]." He talks at once about finding the truth but then presents many truths. Even the title song that starts each episode, whose refrain is "Satyamev Jayate," ends with the line "Saccha hai pyaar mera [my love is true]," referencing an internal, rather than solely external, foundation for truth.

Therefore, I disagree with critics who read the show's title as necessarily moralistic and overdetermined. The show tempers the title's epical ambitions with the everyday realities it pursues. It is not grassroots; nor is it advocating a sole higher truth. It might better be described as a space that, as John Ellis writes of the star image itself, is "at once ordinary and extraordinary" (2015, 91), thus marking a certain openness of the epical imagination.

Subject/Object

The potential contingency of truth opens up *Satyamev Jayate*'s political project beyond the limited discourses of political uplift (where an activist works on behalf of the subaltern) and self-improvement (associated with a new neoliberal regimen). As mentioned previously, the show attempts both to remind its viewers of continuing political and social issues and also to awaken a complacent citizenry. The oscillation between these two endeavors is important, because it simultaneously recognizes that the middle class as only the subject of activism (with the poor and subaltern as the object) can lead to a paternalism or objectification of the poor, even while it acknowledges the potential but as-yet-untapped power of the middle class to effect change. This play of subject and object is negotiated throughout the different episodes, constituting a complex political imaginary across the show. In the first episode, for instance, Khan introduces the show by asking, "'*Mujhe kya fark padta hai?*' ('What does it matter to me?') that society is troubled by so many ills?" and then answering that "it matters . . . because 'I am also a part of this society'" (quoted in Akshaya Kumar 2014, 243). This idea of being both commentator on society and part of society appears throughout the show. In the first episode of season 2, "Fighting Rape," Khan introduces the episode by discussing the nationally known Nirbhaya rape case that took place in December 2012 and the immense protests that followed: "This incident changed something in our country. People, and especially young people, did not remain silent. They were tired of being patient." Footage of the protests is then shown in a two-minute segment on a screen, with a voice-over: "Thousands of people took to the streets, demanding justice for Nirbhaya." Images of police using their lathis and water cannons against young protesters are also shown, as well as a candlelight vigil. The segment ends with the line, "This struggle [sangarsh] has brought us hope. . . . Might Nirbhaya's story hearken a new dawn for India? [Nirbhaya ki yeh daastan kya Hindustan ke liye ek nayi subah ko roshan karegi?]."

Even as the episode schematically details the various obstacles rape survivors face in obtaining justice—from the disinterest of the police, the recalcitrance of hospitals to do a physical exam, the trauma of the exam itself when done, and the dysfunctional courts—it frames those stories within the contemporary question of political awakening, of a new political subject who is no longer content to dismiss such events as merely a part of Indian life. In fact, before Khan brings in rape victims or experts, he interviews a group of young people in Delhi who talk about how this case opened their eyes to the condition of women in the country. The interviews with the guests and experts, therefore, are constantly mediated by the outrage of the regular citizen, not only *on behalf of* the victims but in relation to her own historical apathy. Khan ends the show by saying that you can tell a country's status based on how much a citizenry demands change from the system: "The question is, do we accept the situation as it is today? [Saval yeh hai, ki aaj ka haalat kya humein manzoor hai?]." Thus, the show is as much about citizens' empowerment as it is about rape.[7]

This episode embodies a pattern of alternating between the register of awakening and empowerment—what we might gloss (cynically, perhaps) as "entertainment"—and its commitment to social issues, or "politics." Presenting the two as part of one broader enterprise potentially dilutes the purity of the politics but also opens up the political imaginary beyond what is conventionally understood as activism by muddying the subject-object binary. To put it simply, the audience is asked to reflect on itself as much as to learn about injustices that poor or otherwise marginalized Indians face. Sometimes, the two projects are intertwined. Early in "Female Foeticide," for instance, Khan shows a video of his team asking people to describe where they think female feticide is most prevalent, and they predictably respond that it happens most in India's villages [gaon mein zyaada hota hai] or in small towns [chote sheheron mein, of course], and mostly among the poor and illiterate [gharib log; lower income wale; unpad log]. But this question is then revealed as a setup, as Khan proceeds to debunk these myths: "The truth is exactly the opposite [Sacchai bilkul alag hai]." He projects data that show that female feticide began in big cities rather than in villages, not by the poor and illiterate but by the well-off and educated. To drive in the point further, he interviews a doctor who lives in a "posh colony" in Delhi and whose mother-in-law had tried to kill one of her twin daughters at birth. When prompted by Khan, the doctor reveals that her husband is an orthopedic surgeon; her father-in-law, a history professor at Delhi University; and her mother-in-law, the vice principal at a school. A social worker confirms that as he was trying to figure out who it is that practices female feticide, "I also thought it must be people from the village, but when I tried to really understand, I realized I didn't need to go anywhere; these people are the people around me; they are right here among us [hum hi mein se hain]." Khan then interviews a gynecologist who works in a small village in Rajasthan, who says that among Adivasis there are very low rates of female feticide. Khan says, "We have so much to learn from Adivasis."

In such episodes, Khan disputes middle-class assumptions about "the poor" or "villagers" or others who live out there in a different India—even as in other episodes they might become the objects of pity or reformist uplift. Across the show, pity is repeatedly disrupted by self-reflection, and potential self-involvement is repeatedly disrupted by a call for empathy. In the untouchability episode, Khan plays a video of nine interviewees reflecting on whether untouchability and caste-based discrimination still exist in India today. All nine confidently maintain that they do not. As it does with female feticide, the episode becomes a rejoinder to that mistaken belief. Khan's first guest, activist and filmmaker Stalin K., asserts that untouchability still exists in both the cities and villages. A Sanskrit professor reveals her experiences of discrimination in campus housing while at Jawaharlal Nehru University, India's most well-known university. Thus, caste is presented as something not elsewhere but right at home. The *surprising* nature of this fact for privileged viewers and audience members means that in addition to hearing from those suffering under caste prejudice, the gaze also turns back to the self, who is exposed as ignorant. At the end of that episode, one audience member reflects: "Today in order to judge our development status, we say, a city is developed because in it there are this many malls, multiplexes; there is a metro. But our actual development checkpoints should be, here there is no caste; here there is no discrimination" ("Untouchability" 2012). The show has compelled her to look differently at "progress," a term thrown around by the state and the elite to celebrate India's economic aspirations. Likewise, the fact that Adivasis perform female feticide less than other groups upturns the nation-state's conventional modernist hierarchy whereby the tribal is backward and must catch up to the rest of the population. Both moments, however brief, preclude the professed separation of the viewer from the problems of India, a stance that the corporate form of the show might otherwise be seen to encourage. This is a repeated gesture. In the "Toxic Food" (2012) episode, Khan brings together the plight of farmers who have to use pesticides with the dangers urban consumers have to face from consuming these pesticides, thus linking the fates of these seemingly distinct populations. And in the "Water" (2012) episode, Khan reflects, "I didn't know [where the water in my house comes from]. I learned about it as I was researching the show." In an interview he elaborates: "I had no idea till we began our research. Now I know it comes from a place . . . 100 kilometres away and that people living there do not have water because of me. . . . I feel I've come to understand—actually understand is the wrong word because I'm still grappling to try and understand it, but I have come to know so much more" (quoted in Akshaya Kumar 2014, 252).

It is in this context of rethinking the subject/object of political activism that we can understand the participatory aspect of the show, whereby viewers are asked to send a text to support various initiatives or to participate in audience polls. This aspect has been criticized by progressive commentators, who see it as a simplification of real political problems by offering easy "solutions" (Chakravartty and Sarkar 2013, 69). For instance, at the end of the female feticide episode, Khan makes an appeal to the television audience to write a letter to the chief minister of Rajasthan to fast-track two cases against doctors who practiced female feticide, as it has been seven years since their arrest and they have not been tried. As the seasons go on, Khan adds more breaks during the show when people can text their responses, which he calls "Badlav ke liye vote [Vote for change]." This act links *Satyamev Jayate* with other reality shows such as singing and talent competitions, which create an idea of "the ordinary public" by having "public votes decide the winner" (M. Chaudhuri 2010, 62, 60). In addition, Maitrayee Chaudhuri writes, "most channels also have a current issue on which the audience can [e-]mail their opinions. Newspapers too have regular opinion polls" (59–60). These types of participation tend to be very popular: "*Kaun Banega Crorepati-II* received over 130 million and *Fame Gurukul* received 50 million responses through SMSs" (60).

But to read this as a sincere belief in participatory democracy through texting misses how participation is in fact staged in *Satyamev Jayate*. As Christine Gledhill writes, "If melodrama sentimentalises ethics, at the same time it constructs a new form of audience participation with an appeal to its sympathetic emotions in the working out of poetic justice" (1991, 225). A closer look at Khan's polls reveals that rather than an opinion survey, many of the questions Khan asks his audience actually have only one "right" answer. For instance, in the episode on alcohol, Khan's question is "Should the law against drunken driving be made more stringent and stronger action be taken against those who drink and drive?" ("Alcohol Abuse" 2012). Likewise, in the episode on untouchability, his question is, "Do you wish to see the immediate end to manual scavenging or not?" ("Untouchability" 2012). And in the water episode, "Will you make an effort to start harvesting rainwater from today?" ("Water" 2012). This way of asking a question with only one obvious answer underlines the performative nature of these questions, presenting the act of participation as potentially more important than its content. The point is clearly not to hear what people think but rather to perform a sense of community or consensus around a given issue. This is a *melodramatic* public; just as a melodramatic film works as "a form of theatricality" (Brooks 1976, 13) that gathers a universal consensus around one side in a Manichean moral universe, here political participation is recast as an act of collective affect. It is akin to what Lauren Berlant has called, in the U.S. context, an "intimate public," which by "expressing the sensational, embodied experience of living as a certain kind of being in the world, it promises also to provide a better experience of social belonging" (2008, viii). For Berlant, this public is not pure; it is not apart from commodity culture but often relies on it:[8] "It is a place of recognition and reflection. . . . It flourishes as a porous, affective scene of identification among strangers that promises a certain experience of belonging and provides a complex of consolation, confirmation, discipline, and discussion" (viii). Sentimentality is a key mode that bonds the intimate public.

In this way, the show that is ostensibly about political problems "out there" doubles back to direct the gaze of political activism at least partially on the complacent middle class itself, who is asked to consider itself as a unit, bound through affective ties born of a shared realization of collective ignorance, followed by a performed investment in India's betterment. In a context of a rapidly expanding middle class ostensibly enamored with the discourse of progress, the intimacy of this self-reflection is significant. It does not come from preexisting political ideologies but is a call to rethink what politics is and who is its legitimate subject/object.

Impersonation and Desire

What is interesting about [stars] is not the character they have constructed . . . but rather the business of constructing/performing/being . . . a "character."
—RICHARD DYER, *Stars*

The presentation of political engagement as a kind of performance is made possible by Khan's star persona, which carries traces of the cinema onto the small screen. Even though the star is now in the viewer's own domestic space rather than in the public cinema hall, is interacting with people "just like you" in his "real" voice (rather than acting), and is chatting in what appears to be informal speech (even if it is in fact highly scripted), the star cannot be completely detached from the filmi world where he was born. This residual filminess charges the televisual encounter with Khan with a certain excess. S. V. Srinivas argues that this excess, which he also sees in fan practices in South India, has the potential to awaken new political subjectivities: "Not only do these stars address spectators in rather direct ways (including by looking at the camera) but seem to perform according to 'our' demands" (quoted in Punathambekar 2010, 250), asking us, Punathambekar writes, "to re-think what constitutes the 'political' beyond the narrow sense of the term" (250).

The opening sequence of *Satyamev Jayate* stages this excess. Here we see a presentation of the transition between Khan's cinematic identity and a voice that directly addresses his television viewers in every episode that follows as "Doston" (friends) or "Darshakon" (viewers). The opening of each episode shows Khan walking on a beach, traveling to different parts of India, and interacting with a range of people, and then as the sequence fades, Khan looks squarely at the camera and the talk-show portion begins, forging "an . . . *intimate* relationship between participant and viewer" characteristic of reality television (S. Holmes 2011, 117). This movement constructs a bridge between two kinds of viewing positions: from that of Hindi cinema, in which the viewer is accustomed to gazing on the body of the star but gets no gaze in return, to a viewpoint where the star turns to face the camera in an intimate address. Because this second type of viewership is constantly linked to the first through their repetition in sequence, it carries traces of the other form, so the direct gaze elicits a thrill particular to the cinematic medium. Thus, the star's "extraordinariness" is preserved even in the presentation of his "ordinariness"; "the star is tantalisingly close and similar, yet at the same time remote and dissimilar" (Ellis 2015, 97–98). This tension distinguishes *Satyamev Jayate* from other star-hosted television shows such as *Kaun Banega Crorepati*, in which from the outset we see Amitabh Bachchan or Shah Rukh Khan in his television incarnation, looking straight into the camera (A. Sharma 2016, 21). In contrast, here the productive tension between film and television is constantly reasserted in the particular form of this opening sequence. And because of the expressly political nature of the show, here the thrill trace Khan brings from cinema gains a particular interpellative meaning, calling on his audience to consider the topic presented by the show as an *emotionally* meaningful topic. Simultaneously, it serves as a metagesture that bridges the informative with the entertaining. It creates a particular kind of melodramatic intimacy, heightened with affective resonance as it carries the traces of the unreasoned publics imagined by Hindi popular cinema.

Who, then, is the Aamir Khan who stars on the show? Is he the actor, or is it simply another role? In an interview, Khan claimed that he is uncomfortable showing his emotion on-screen because people are not used to it; they see only a certain version of him in films, which is not the "real" him. He was initially "embarrassed" to expose his real self in front of so many people ("Making" 2017). But for most viewers, Khan's presentation of what he calls his real self is yet another of the many roles he plays in the course of the show. His audience encounters the star as an accretion or "composite" of his various roles (Gledhill 1991, 214). Impersonation, central to the Hindi popular cinema, becomes not an act of falsity but a key site of empathetic identification.[9]

Indeed, impersonation has always been central to the Bollywood imagination; as Sumita Chakravarty writes, the term contains

> notions of changeability and metamorphosis, tension and contradiction, recognition and alienation, surface and depth. . . . Indian cinema . . . has made the drama of impersonation its distinctive signature. This is more than a matter of reinforcing the truisms that films impersonate life; characters impersonate real men and women; the film-viewing experience impersonates dream. Impersonation subsumes a process of externalization, the play of/on surfaces, the disavowal of fixed notions of identity. But it also encompasses the contrary movement of accretion, the piling up of identities, the transgression of social codes and boundaries. (1993, 4)

Impersonation occurs at different levels of *Satyamev Jayate* and its reception. The fact that the show was aired at 11:00 A.M., "the slot previously reserved for the state broadcast of Hindu epic dramas *The Ramayana* and *The Mahabharata* in the late-1980s," led one critic to dismissively say that "Aamir Khan is Rama and Yudhishira, slaying Evil, vouching Truth, all this without cumbersome props" (Sumana Roy 2012; also quoted in Chakravartty and Sarkar 2013, 66). The criticism aside, however, this comment accurately reveals an underlying trope of the show: mobilizing diverse heroic archetypes as part of a new, melodramatic public. As Akshaya Kumar writes, "Stars like Khan derive their appeal from their roles as heroes in cinematic narratives. . . . On screen, they might rebel as lovers against conservative norms, fight injustice, oppose poor policies or challenge moral corruption. In so doing, they become inherently associated with righteous politics" (2014, 243).

We can see the use of impersonation as early as the first episode of *Satyamev Jayate*, which Khan begins by saying:

I work in films. I play different sorts of characters; I live different sorts of lives [alag-alag kirdaar nibhata hoon, alag-alag zindagion ko jeeta hoon]. But between all those, I have my own life as well. . . . A lot of things come to my mind. On one hand, the country is progressing, reaching new heights, which makes me very happy; I am very proud to be Indian. But on the other hand, there are also some bitter truths in our society, which we don't want to see. When I look at those, I get worried, and I get sad. . . . Today if Gandhi, Tilak, Bose, Nehru, and Maulana Azad were alive, what answer would we give them? In fighting for independence, did our ancestors dream of such an India? ("Female Foeticide" 2012)

While speaking to India's failures, Khan also names himself as an actor of roles, a liver of many lives, presenting the political *through* the language of impersonation. So the tension between his roles and his real self offers a certain access into the other tensions he describes, between progress and bitter truths, the past and the present. This opening thus registers the productive "incoherence" not only of "the star image," as Neepa Majumdar (2010) writes, but of the show as a whole.[10]

Indeed, impersonation exists outside the model of liberal civil society, as it contradicts the idea of an individual with a stable identity irrespective of context. Impersonation suggests that identity is ever shifting, a series of masks, and something that emerges in performance. In the star system of Hindi popular cinema, impersonation exposes an excess of meaning that arises as an actor becomes a character. This has appeared in Bollywood in a number of ways, such as in the convention whereby one actor plays a series of characters with the same name across different films. Amitabh Bachchan did this with Vijay, his name in more than twenty films (Maity 2015), and, more recently, Shah Rukh Khan did this with Rahul and Raj (N. Chopra 2015). It also appears in the way actors occasionally impersonate their characters even outside the film, such as in a 2017 episode of the singing talent show *Saregama*, when Shah Rukh Khan, who was a guest judge, was asked by audience members to repeat lines and reenact his dance moves from several of his films.

These examples demonstrate a porosity in the seemingly discrete categories of actor and roles. The sense that a role can actually change the actor who plays it becomes central to the plot of *Rang De Basanti*, a film about political awakening through impersonation. Aamir Khan plays DJ, the carefree protagonist who, along with his friends, learns about the Indian independence movement as he reluctantly agrees to act in a film about Bhagat Singh made by Sue, a British filmmaker. The footage from Sue's project is integrated into the film in sepia tones, so Khan ends up playing a second role as well, the role that DJ is playing: of freedom fighter Chandrashekhar Azad. The two films, *Rang De Basanti* and Sue's reenactment film, are linked both thematically and formally: the various characters of *Rang De Basanti* learn new things about political action as they play their roles, and toward the end, the film moves seamlessly between the two stories. By linking the two films, *Rang De Basanti* presents *playing a role*—DJ playing Chandrashekhar Azad, and his friends in the roles of Bhagat Singh, Rajguru, Ashfaqullah Khan, and Ram Prasad Bismil—as actually having the potential to transform one's self. DJ and his friends begin as entirely unconcerned about politics or the nation; the first time they read Sue's script, they burst out laughing at what appear to be stilted and outdated lines about revolution and self-sacrifice. But as they begin to act in the roles of these freedom fighters, something in them changes. It is not merely that they learn to appreciate the past; rather, there is a certain excess born in radical impersonation—an excess that, the film suggests, might actually generate political inquiry. In an early scene, Karan tells Sue that he cannot connect with his character, Bhagat Singh; Sue tells him, "Stop trying to understand. . . . Just try to feel it [Bus ab samajhna chhodo. . . . Ek baar feel karke dekho]." And that works. By mouthing their lines and wearing their clothes, the students are able to gain a new understanding of the revolutionaries of the past, but it is an understanding premised primarily on affective identification rather than reasoning or consciousness. This changes their view on the present as well. As their impersonation becomes more intense, as they start to *feel* the roles, they begin to see the present not just as offering a space of fun and youth but as bearing its own injustices, which they feel empowered to protest. Thus, the contemporary appears right in the space between their lives, who they are, and the lives of the characters they are impersonating, and this is the space where "politics" is birthed as an idea and a practice.

This is also a cinephilic space. The viewer gets pleasure in seeing an actor such as Aamir Khan play not one but two roles. Here, the classic "double role" (N. Majumdar 2010, 159–169), the cinephilic trope par excellence, has a thematic thickness, as Khan's first character, DJ, cannot seamlessly act as Azad but only in a fraught and troubled way because, at least at first, he finds Azad unrelatable. The carefree DJ struggles to step out of his own skin and take on an entirely different role, that of a politically driven young martyr, literalizing the duality of Aamir Khan's entire oeuvre, encompassing both entertainment and politics. Cinephilia marks a time outside narrative time—in this case the viewer's knowledge of the existence of an "Aamir Khan" figure that transcends *both* DJ and Chandrashekhar Azad, who here appears in the space between the two characters. This cinephilia is captured in a frame near the end where we see DJ and Azad together (Figure 4.1). Both

Figure 4.1 Cinephilia in *Rang De Basanti*. © UTV Motion Pictures.

characters, in their respective scenes, are surrounded by soldiers on all sides and have been shot. Their deaths are imminent. But in an uncanny image, DJ seems to be looking over at Azad for guidance on what he should do next, and Azad returns the gaze. They both half-smile at each other, sharing this final and inevitable end that comes from national self-sacrifice. As Neepa Majumdar writes, "When a star is acting as a character who is acting, the audience gets a privileged view of both identities" (2010, 165), and that is precisely what happens here. This is the moment when the edges of the actor's self merge into those of the character, when new possibilities for political action in the contemporary world are opened up. Thus, ironically, cinephilia becomes the prerequisite for the political.

Satyamev Jayate mobilizes this potential of impersonation to birth new political subjects in its periodic assertions of *identification*, a form of impersonation that includes not only the star and his roles but also the fan. As Jackie Stacey writes, "Identification involves recognising desirable qualities in the ideal and wanting to move towards it," through pretending, resembling, imitating, and/or copying (2003, 151, 153–156). These are not pathological or signs of an immature consciousness but "involve processes of transformation and the production of new identities" (160). For example, in the season 2 episode on the police, discussing the reasons why the police are so mistrusted, Khan interviews Bipin Gopalakrishna, the director-general of police from Karnataka, who discusses the history of the police in India ("Police" 2014). He traces the current system to 1857, in the wake of the rebellion, when the British instituted an armylike police to keep the Indian populace under its control: "Basically yeh jo police system bana hai, woh bana tha 1857 ke baad—aap Mangal Pandey reh chuke hain—toh 1857 ke baad British sarkar ne took over the administration [Basically the police system that was instituted, it was instituted after (the rebellion of) 1857—you played Mangal Pandey (so you understand)—the British government took over the administration after 1857]." In this parenthetical phrase, Gopal-akrishna draws a link between understanding how a historical system like the police works and playing a historical character, in this case Khan playing Mangal Pandey, one of the initiators of the 1857 rebellion, in his film *Mangal Pandey*. In a season 1 episode on people with disabilities, one of the guests tells Khan, "First I wanted to tell you that I'm a big fan of your movies, especially *Rang De Basanti*. In that film there's the Bhagat Singh character who says, 'Those who are hard of hearing need a big bang'" ("Persons with Disabilities" 2012). Aside from referencing the Bhagat Singh *character* rather than the historical figure, this interruption in the story of his disability folds in this cinematic reference—and specifically from one of Khan's own films—as part of his own representation of his life as a disabled man. Likewise, in the season 2 episode "The Criminalization of Politics" (2014), a former election commissioner describes the fake weddings sometimes held by corrupt politicians to essentially buy votes by saying, "We might consider ourselves clever for discovering a bogus wedding, but next time they might even hire a bride and groom! That's no problem for them. . . . You must have played a groom several times in films. . . . They could do it the same way." Here, the invocation of Khan's own roles as part of the commissioner's testimony makes the political critique (in this case, of corruption) legible on and through the charismatic body of the star, who grins in self-recognition, along with the audience, who laughs as well. In all these examples, *understanding* is relayed through the body of the star, indicating, as in *Rang De Basanti*, a space of potentiality where the two domains merge and the counterintuitive possibility that impersonation can give birth to understanding.

The political potentiality of identification was expressed most forcefully in season 1, in the episode called "Big Fat Indian Wedding" (2012). Khan is interviewing several members of the Tanzeem Khuddam-e-Millat, a nongovernmental organization (NGO) that has worked to end the practice of elaborate and expensive weddings in various small towns. All of a sudden, without being asked, one of the Tanzeem men interrupts the discussion to say to Khan: "I hope that you take this message to all of India. And the sacrifice you will make is in your destiny, because I know that your blood is the blood of Maulana Abul Kalam Azad's family [aapka khoon jo hai, woh Maulana Abul Kalam Azad ke khandan ka khoon hai]! Because of that, the sacrifice that your family made for India, you need to make that sacrifice and you are making that sacrifice! I pay my respects to you and I thank you!" Khan is indeed the great-grandnephew of Maulana Azad, one of the leaders of the nationalist movement. But the Tanzeem member's eruption registers that blood line through a moment of excess, which is the only possible moment when Khan's personal lineage could be invoked in this fashion to present Khan as a nationalist hero. This moment captures, in the language of impersonation and identification, the way the audience interprets Khan's body as an accretion of different characters, so that the line between who he is and who he has played becomes blurred.

This abundance of discourse created about and around Khan's body is perhaps most evident in the episodes on contemporary political issues surrounding sexuality and sexual freedom, such as the season 3 episodes "Accepting Alternative Sexualities" (2014) and "When Masculinity Harms Men" (2014). In these two episodes, Khan uses his position as both a male host and a potential object of desire to engender a reconsideration of entrenched social beliefs, such as, in these cases, homophobia and misogyny. For instance, in a scene in "Accepting Alternative Sexualities," he is discussing the genetic basis of homosexuality with a psychiatrist, who tells him that it is impossible to change the reality of whether an individual is gay or straight. As an example, she asks him, "If I told you that from today onwards you had to not look at women but think of men sexually, could you do it?" Without missing a beat, Khan responds, "No, I couldn't do that." "Then if you couldn't do it how could we imagine that a [gay] man or woman could do it?" In this dialogue, Khan uses the supposedly self-evident fact of his own heterosexuality—a fact that positions him as a *legitimate* desiring subject—to counter the prevalent myth that homosexuality can be "cured" and thus to open up a space for the acceptance of what has long been considered *illegitimate* desire. In the episode "Domestic Violence" (2012), Kamla Bhasin, a feminist activist, explains that domestic violence in part arises because of misguided ideas about masculinity, for instance, the idea that real men don't cry. Khan interjects to say, "I cry a lot [Main bahut rota hoon]," and she quips in response, "So then you are not a real man, my friend; you'll have to do something about it [Toh aap poore mard nahin ho, miya; aap ko kuch karna padega]," which is greeted by laughter from Khan and the audience. Here again, we see Khan's self-evident masculinity put to the use of debunking a myth about "real" men. And at the beginning of the masculinity episode, Khan asks the men's side of the audience what it means to be a man: "Ek asli mard ki kya paribhasha?" They propose some adjectives—*rakshak* (protective), *bahadur* (brave), *mehnati* (hardworking), *madaddar* (helpful), *nek* (virtuous)—which he writes on a board and which the women's side proceeds to refute one by one, the point of the show being that women's conceptions of men do not correspond with men's own self-image. When they reach the last adjective, *balwaan*, Khan asks the women what they think: Are all men strong? The women shake their heads, and he responds, as if pleading, "At least give us that one!," in response to which both the men and women laugh. After crossing out *balwaan*, Khan concludes the segment by saying, "So it seems clear that how we men see ourselves, that's not how women see us." Here again, Khan interrupts his role as host and pedagogue to present himself as a "man"—even one of the men—to channel his critique of toxic masculinity through the fact of his own body.

In these instances, we see a purposeful use of desire in building affective communities around newly visible political issues relating to gender and sexuality. Through the focal point of his body, which elicits the libidinal desires of his viewers, Khan attempts to convey the dangers of homophobia and patriarchy and delineate a space from which new political positions might be formed that do not fall along previously established party lines. These are the most complex episodes because Khan's filminess corresponds with an expanding politics of desire in India at large. In contrast, in the episodes in which he advances more ascetic positions, the excess of his body jars with his stated intent. For instance, in the episode on alcoholism, Khan takes a staunch Gandhian position that maintains that even a drop of alcohol has the potential to be corrupting ("Alcohol Abuse" 2012). This kind of paternalistic monitoring of especially poor bodies invokes a very different relationship between politics and desire than we see in the sexuality and masculinity episodes. Indeed, Gandhi despised both alcohol and Hindi cinema for the same reason: as "distractions and temptations, capable of diverting people from the national quest for freedom and reformation" (R. Jeffrey 2008, 19). In this episode, too, Khan ends up effacing his own body for an affectless political stance. The ineffectualness of this episode in comparison to the others highlights how central desire and excess are to the show's melodramatic imagination.

The Uses of Glycerine

Actors both do and pretend, sometimes at one and the
same moment—hence the potentially scandalous nature
of their work.
—JAMES NAREMORE, quoted in Neepa Majumdar, *Wanted
Cultured Ladies Only!*

Khan's emotion in the show—the fact that he often sighs, exclaims, and bursts into tears—is something many critics point to as part of its manipulative register and its emotional exploitation (Sen 2014). However, I suggest that as in melodramas, which are characterized by "hyperbolic emotions, extravagant gesture, high-flown sentiments, declamatory speech, spectacular settings and so on" (Gledhill 1991, 212), emotion here is not meant to be believable or authentic but a mode of affective engagement that potentially gives rise to new political imaginaries. Here, excessive emotion is condensed into a series of repeated gestures, such as Khan wiping his teary eyes with the back of his hand and often looking into the camera when doing so. His wet eyes are also visible at other points, and he sometimes takes a moment, after a particularly heartfelt speech by a guest or a sad film clip, for the audience to register his visible emotion. He often exclaims to himself, offering expressions such as "Wah!" or "Kya baat hai" (both of which roughly translate to "Amazing!") after an insightful comment by one of his guests, sometimes looking straight at the camera when doing so. The show frequently elicits tears from its guests and audience as well (Chakravartty and Sarkar 2013, 68). Sohini Ghosh discusses how the show operates on "a number of 'affective tropes'" such as "cathartic revelations, shocking testimonies, interviews with experts, cutaways of shocked or tearful studio audiences and a host who is both emotive and emotional," along with "poignant background music and studio performances" (quoted in Chakravartty and Sarkar 2013, 67), with each episode ending on an original song performed onstage. These set pieces can easily be seen as presenting contrived emotion; from a realist perspective, they are meaningless because they are staged and hyperbolic.

In a special, forty-five-minute segment on the making of *Satyamev Jayate*, the show's creators discuss Khan's emotions on the show. Satyajit Bhatkal, the director, refutes the accusation that Khan's emotions are fake: "Aamir's tears came easily. Some people have suggested that we've manipulated that but it's actually the opposite. Many times we actually had to stop the shooting because he's become so overcome with emotions that he couldn't control himself." Khan addresses this as well:

> I knew all their [the guests'] stories from the research . . . but now, this time, they were sitting in front of me . . . a few feet away, telling their stories. That time I felt very sad. I found it very difficult. I am very emotional anyway. Anyway, I think we laugh out loud so we should cry in the open as well. If you feel sad why should you stop yourself? But it was the first time my audience saw me this way, because they don't know much about my real life. . . . I didn't like that the whole country was seeing me this way, but then I thought if I were not this emotional or sensitive maybe I wouldn't be doing this show in the first place. ("Making" 2017)

Meanwhile, commentators in the media and on Twitter make jokes about Khan's use of glycerine, a trick allegedly rife in Indian cinema as a way to make actors and actresses look like they are crying ("Why Is Aamir" 2015; Beer and Biryani 2015). The discussion of glycerine is an index for the critical sense, especially among more educated viewers, that Hindi cinema is nothing more than a repertoire of hyperbolic, fake, and staged emotions, most notably melodramatic sadness or despair.[11] Glycerine stands for the lengths the industry will go to to deliver manufactured emotions to its audiences. Khan's alleged use of glycerine in this show is a way of saying not only how filmi the show is but how fake as well.

I argue, however, that the debate over fake or real tears misses the point. In Hindi cinema, as well as on *Satyamev Jayate*, tears appear as surface-level indicators of emotion. Melodramatic films work through such surface indicators—"in gesture, dress and above all in action" (Gledhill 1991, 210)—rather than through a more realist representation of psychological interiority. These indicators should not be judged on whether or not they represent real emotion; rather, they signify in the act of performance, which binds the viewer to the actor and to fellow viewers. For instance, as Linda Williams writes of the women's "weepie," there is a release in seeing "the spectacle of a body caught in the grip of intense sensation or emotion" (1991, 4). Neepa Majumdar similarly records audience reactions to the thrillers of Fearless Nadia as generating "a visceral and bodily engagement with the physicality of [her] stunts" along with "emotional release" (2010, 110), so by the end, as one fan writes, "We were completely drained and exhausted. But at the same time there was a magnificent relief, a catharsis" (quoted in N. Majumdar 2010, 109). This release and its potential to incite its audience serve as a means of creating and binding an affective community. The tears serve as an expression of collective catharsis that affects the different participants in that moment, temporarily trumping previous emotional commitments and imbuing the issue at hand with an ethical valence. In short, "gesture becomes a major link between ethical forces and personal desires" (Gledhill 1991, 210). This is an affective community akin to the laughing clubs that exist around India, in which laughter *produces* a sense of joy rather than, as a more realist understanding of emotions would have it, the other way around (Strubbe 2003).

Khan's tears thus make the show *entertaining* in the sense of engaging the body. As discussed earlier in relation to his filmography, it would be a mistake to see *Satyamev Jayate*, because of its political content, as simply a turn toward more serious forms of cultural production; rather, it is part of Khan's extended experiment to rethink the relationship between knowledge and entertainment in the first place. Khan's provision to Star TV that the show be aired on Sunday mornings rather than in a prime-time television slot partly reflected his insecurity about whether the show would do well. But, as he says in an interview, he did not want the show to replace people's normal entertainment—their *naach-gaana* (song and dance)—but to supplement it. The gestured tears, which mark the line between filmi emotional entertainment and sympathy, pity and awareness, mark out this intermediary space of political affect.

This is the collective endeavor in which Khan's show explicitly participates. As one of its taglines announces, "Dil pe lagegi tabhi baat banegi" (Only when you feel it in your heart will things change). Such lines question the conventional distinction between entertainment and information. Thus, the show overtly—proudly—appeals to its viewers' emotions. Knowledge about the conditions most Indians face is important, not as a sterile, joyless endeavor but one birthed by emotion. This explicitly counters the reasoned public sphere of civil society. Like the Hindi film, the community forged in the collective shedding of tears becomes as important as the particular event for which the tears were shed.

Despite the show's seamless scripting, there are moments when this affective community is disrupted, revealing potential limits to the melodramatic public. In the episode "Untouchability" (2012) in season 1, for instance, Bezwada Wilson, an activist working to end manual scavenging in India, completes his extended account of the inhumanity of the practice by criticizing those who pity the situation of untouchables or see it as merely sad. In response, he explains, his voice slightly raised: "Mujhe aapka aansu nahin chahiye! Aapka daya nahin chahiye! Aapka ghussa chahiye yeh vyavastha ke upar. Aapka ghussa hai toh bilkul yeh badal ho jayega. [I don't want your tears! I don't want your pity! I want your anger about this state of affairs. If you are angry, then the situation will definitely change.]" The message here is clear: tears and pity, even Khan's, will do little to further the cause of Dalit empowerment. Wilson's challenge has particular significance in the context of caste, an issue in which the appropriation of Dalit sentiment by high-caste saviors has a long history that goes back to the Gandhi-Ambedkar debates and continues today (Ambedkar 2002). Dalit politics, increasingly a politics of "rage and fury," has symbolically rejected the tears that represent paternalistic Hindu charity (Nagaraj 1993, 18). Dalit poetics has also rejected tears as an obfuscating trope that romanticizes the brutal hardships of the Dalit experience (Gajarawala 2012, 342).[12] By calling the liberal audience members out—and even, by inference, Khan himself—on the shedding of empty, pitying tears, Wilson temporarily disrupts the collective premise of the show from a caste perspective. He exposes tears for their metaphorical register and pity for its savarna politics. In his critical response to the episode in *Outlook* magazine, S. Anand (2012) similarly criticized its reliance on tears as a vehicle of transformation: "Khan obviously thinks we can flush away middle class shit with tears."[13]

Another moment of disruption of the melodramatic register of the show appears in the season 2 episode on corruption ("Kings Every Day" 2014). *Satyamev Jayate* uses a fairly standard format of collective laughter common to many studio-audience shows. But in this episode, Khan comes close to criticizing the audience—and Indian viewers in general—for laughing at stories of corruption rather than taking them seriously. He begins the episode with the parable of a man whose servants gradually stole all his milk, leaving him with nothing except a smear of cream on his upper lip, which the thieves put there at night, making him think that he had drunk the milk. As Khan tells the story, allegorical for the theft of government money by corrupt officials, the audience laughs at the various stages of the man's naïveté. Khan then introduces a guest who explains to the audience that even if they think they are not paying income tax—because they are students, for instance, or below the income threshold—all Indians are still paying taxes on everything they buy. Thus, the money that is being stolen by corrupt officials is in fact their own. Khan then says,

> I am often surprised, friends, that whenever we hear news of a [corruption] scandal, I've noticed that people talk about it with a sense of humor [bada mazaa lekar]; they even laugh [hanste bhi hain], saying, one guy stole ten thousand crore rupees, another guy twenty thousand crore. This time when you read news of a scandal, read it knowing that someone has stolen the earnings from our daily work.

In this speech, Khan assumes that knowing that the money stolen through corruption is *their* money will make people approach the issue with more seriousness and less *mazaa*. Despite this advice, the audience continues to laugh at the various corruption stories that ensue from his guests over the rest of the episode. This rare disjuncture between Khan and his studio audience results, I suggest, from his *misreading* of the role of collective affect in his own enterprise. As Indian novelists such as Srilal Shukla and Upamanyu Chatterjee have long realized, corruption is ripe for satire (U. Anjaria 2006). This is not to render the problem of corruption unimportant but to register and process its absurdity from the perspective of collective life (Khanduri 2012, 318). Laughter is in this episode what crying is in the show as a whole: a way of establishing a collective community from a shared affective engagement. In this case, laughter registers a collective sense of impotence and frustration in the face of the state's failure. It is not meant to be taken literally (as in, something is funny) but performatively, as a collective eruption of the absurd, merely the flip side of tears. Yet in his surprise at the audience's laughter, which Khan interprets as their not taking the issue seriously enough, Khan momentarily retreats from the show's overall experiments with the political potential of staged emotion.

These moments mark the limits of the melodramatic public, where it runs up against a historically specific relationship to a particular emotion in the first case and a deeply ingrained commitment to reasoned political debate in the second. Rather than unravel the entire enterprise, however, these moments stand as further reminders of the show's engagement with an *open edge* of politics rather than with the creation of a new political ideology. Clearly, the question of whether a melodramatic public can be a force for change has yet to be answered. As Arvind Rajagopal writes, "If electronic media work by mobilizing desire and creating new forms of association, there is surely no guarantee that desires, once stimulated, will flow in obedient fashion" (2009b, 11). This is part of the ongoing work of the contemporary. Indeed, for a form (reality television) that is otherwise so scripted and closed and for a mode (melodrama) whose morality has seemingly been worked out in advance, *Satyamev Jayate* is striking for how open it is to unformed and excessive affective impulses that mark out a place where the old political vocabulary has broken down and a new vocabulary, new categories, and institutions have yet to take its place. Thus, rather than ask, as many have, "Is *Satyamev Jayate* going to *change* anything?" (Akshaya Kumar 2014, 248), we might see the show as engaging with the question of what an ideal society is in the first place, mobilizing impulses of impersonation and desire that offer an alternative to the restrained reason of what is commonly imagined as politics. By foregrounding mediation and by staging political debate as a particularly filmi practice, *Satyamev Jayate* becomes the somewhat ironic "exemplary text" of the contemporary, flaws and all (S. Holmes 2011, 130).

PART III

Representations

5

Literature beyond the Pale

The story . . . [is] not something that took place once upon a
time, long, long ago. The story is, in fact, just a fraction of a
larger narrative that is still taking place, even today. It's a
work in progress, a tale that's under construction, a report
of what just happened one second ago in a life very much
still being lived.[1]

—UDAY PRAKASH, *The Girl with the Golden Parasol*

As the previous chapters show, the contemporary is marked by a persistent restlessness or dissatisfaction around existing forms of representation. Nowhere is this more evident than in the literary novel
of the post-2000s, which is considered to mark a contrast to the internationally recognized Indian English novels of the 1980s and 1990s. With the spec-
ter of these texts looming behind them, recent works often take pains to
represent *differently*, to breach the parameters of literary fiction as established by these predecessors. Just as postcolonial writers interrogated how
representation might serve as an act of dissent against the consolidation of
nationalist hegemony (Sunder Rajan 2011, 203), today's writers are also
thinking about representation in complex and often counterintuitive ways,
but this time to offer alternatives to postcoloniality itself. Their texts ask not
only: What does it mean to represent the contemporary in India? They ask,
even more broadly: How does one write something new? What does it mean
to move beyond older concerns? What new forms are required for literature
to be other than what it has previously been? These are not merely questions
about literature's temporality but, as this chapter shows, about its epistemology as well. If a text represents differently, then it might well require new
modes of reading to access its meaning. Is our interpretively minded literary
criticism still the best way to read? Where exactly does meaning lie in an
open, unfinished, contemporary text?

This chapter focuses on several recent works—mainly novels—by three
writers, Aravind Adiga, Uday Prakash, and Manu Joseph. These texts, which

are mostly set in the present, offer a complex reworking of the legibility of the postcolonial novel to pose new questions about the nature of representation that reflect what I see as in part an exhaustion with postcolonial literary forms—in particular with the presumption of what counts as political writing. In doing so, these works envision new possibilities for the novel. They present meaning not as lying deep in a text but as awakened through acts of perception and reading and as always on the verge of erupting into the world of the reader. They thus stake a claim on politics not as a preexisting belief but as something born in the act of reading. Their works transform novelistic conceptions of time, rethink the conventions by which tropes become meaningful in the novel, question the centrality of allegory to postcolonial reading, and consider what representation looks like beyond the limits of language. In doing so, they participate in a global trend in contemporary literature to rethink what it means for fiction to be political. As Mitchum Huehls and Rachel Smith write:

> Authors of [recent] literary fiction have been . . . producing texts that challenge readers to imagine what it would mean to mean differently, for meaning and value to derive not from referential acts of representation but from being's relation to other beings. . . . Much of this work seems on its face to be post-racial and/or post-political. But that diagnosis misses the fact that these authors are also trying to think about politics immanently, biopolitically, and nondialectically. . . . [These] texts and authors . . . recognize the potential obsolescence of earlier forms of representation and critique and struggle in various ways to develop new literary modes that acknowledge that condition without succumbing to the neoliberal totality that produced it in the first place. (2017, 10–11)

While *Midnight's Children* in its own way used language to go beyond the pale, now, almost forty years later, its playfulness, multiplicity, and self-referentiality have coalesced to structure expectations brought by both readers and critics to the global novel. Part of the challenge that contemporary literature faces is to invent new forms to contain the new stories it wants to tell, a project that requires rethinking what it means to mean in the first place.

Thus, insofar as many new Indian novels are set in the present and are no longer handcuffed to history, they ask: How can a text be open to the present? Is it just a shift in setting, or does it require a metafictional assertion of its own difference? How does temporality move from background to foreground? These transformations are not intuitive but require rethinking some of the most fundamental characteristics of postcolonial literary fiction. Largely rejecting the formal integrity and metaphorical register of the Indian novel in English from *Midnight's Children* to *The God of Small Things*, contemporary works are significantly less cohesive, leading some commentators to lament the death of the great Indian novel (U. Anjaria 2016a). Although *The White Tiger* won the Booker Prize in 2008, many critics noted that it failed to offer the literary satisfaction of its predecessors (Shingavi 2014, 2; Gajarawala 2009, 21). I suggest that these new works deliberately break with the formal and aesthetic conventions of the postcolonial novel to activate sites of meaning making in the interface between reader and author and to offer new accounts of human action that are not solely historical or political. Thus, they assert the contemporaneity of not only the stories they tell but also the novel form itself.

Interruptions

Intrusions of the present are a pervasive form of interruption in the contemporary novel. According to Roland Barthes, a certain rationality of time is assumed in literary realism, through what he calls the preterite, the temporal vantage point of realism, which "calls for a sequence of events, that is, for an intelligible Narrative" and which "presupposes a world which is constructed, elaborated, self-sufficient, reduced to significant lines, and not one which has been sent sprawling before us, for us to take or leave" (1967, 30). For Barthes, the preterite ensures that "reality is neither mysterious nor absurd; it is clear, almost familiar, repeatedly gathered up and contained in the hand of a creator" (31). Many recent Indian novels suggest that representing the contemporary requires rupturing the preterite. These works use visceral forms such as the rant to break apart the formal integrity of the text in order to present a contemporary reality whose full meaning is not yet known. They disrupt the free indirect style that is inherent to realism, what Jeffrey Staiger calls, paraphrasing James Wood, "the fertile tension that results between the character's perceptions and the author's. . . . 'Free indirect style' is inherently ironic, and how an author balances this necessary irony with sympathy is the chief occasion for the exercise of his artistry in realistic fiction" (2008, 637).

Hindi writer Uday Prakash, for instance, constantly interrupts his novella *Mohan Das* with a series of rants that situate what otherwise might be read as a classic tale of village India in the contemporary moment:

> (Let's stop here for a minute. I bet you're thinking that I'm taking advantage of the one hundred and twenty fifth anniversary of the birth of Premchand, the King of Hindi Fiction, to spin you some hundred-and-twenty-five-year-old story dressed up as a tale of today. But the truth is that the account I am putting before you, in its old and backward style, manner, and language, is a tale of a time right

after 9/11, in the aftermath of the collapse of the World Trade Center in New York; a time when two sovereign Asian nations were reduced to ash and rubble. It's a tale of a time when anybody worshipping any gods other than the god of the US and Europe were called fascists, terrorists, religious fanatics. Gas and oil, water, markets, profit, plunder: to get all of this, companies, governments, and armies were killing innocent people every day all over the world.) (2012, 67–68)

The novella's discussion of tuberculosis, debt, caste, and a rural family scraping by invokes a long tradition of village-based social realism, most notably the writings of the iconic Hindi author Premchand (1880–1936),[2] but this apparent literary historical continuity is broken by these assertive interjections that refuse to relegate Prakash's story to a time apart. There are at least eight such one- to two-paragraph rants throughout *Mohan Das*. The lists of contemporary global incidents—the World Trade Center attacks, the Monica Lewinsky scandal, the Narmada Dam protests, the Kargil War, India's nuclear tests, the Abu Ghraib torture revelations—are both expressions of rage at present-day violence and disruptive interjections that assert the pressing, lived presentness of the world the novella describes by breaking the carefully constructed diegesis of literary fiction. Moreover, they contemporize Hindi, a language often associated with rural life and national literary heroes such as Premchand rather than with globality or the present day. They do this not through a polite assertion of Hindi as a contemporary language but by violent "interruptions" into the novel form (Gopalan 2002).

We see a similar aesthetic in Aravind Adiga's novel *The White Tiger* (2008), whose epistolary form allows Adiga to present temporality as immanent and open rather than as an inert setting or backdrop (U. Anjaria 2017b). The novel is structured over eight letters written by its protagonist, Balram Halwai, to Wen Jiabao, the Chinese premier, who is "visiting [India] this week" (2) and to whom Balram wants to explain the real India before he arrives. This sense of a pressing motivation pervades the whole novel, in which Balram constantly breaks from his narration to assert the presentness of his narrative: "That was at 11:37 P.M. Five minutes ago" (3); "It is a little before midnight now, Mr. Jiabao. A good time for me to talk" (5); and "11:52 P.M.—and it really *is* time to start" (7). Many of the chapters end on similar instantiations of present time: "But that will have to wait for tomorrow, Your Excellency. It's 2:44 A.M." (78); "That is all for tonight, Mr. Premier. It's not yet three A.M., but I've got to end here, sir" (145); and "Alas: I'll have to stop this story for a while. It's only 1:32 in the morning, but we'll have to break off here. Something has come up, sir—an emergency. I'll be back, trust me" (166).

While *Midnight's Children* also employs the temporality of the count-down, with Saleem rushing to complete his story before he cracks "into (ap-proximately) six hundred and thirty million particles of anonymous, and necessarily oblivious, dust" (Rushdie 1981, 36), in *The White Tiger* the effect is intensified, as it demands a constant readerly vigilance, generating an im-mediacy not only to the storytelling but in the world of the reader as well. Balram's rendering of time as hours and minutes on a clock and as opportu-nities to begin and end his story interpellate the reader as part of the story's temporality. This affects the politics of the novel as well: while narrating the story of Balram, a man who begins as a servant, robs and murders his boss, and uses the money to build his own business, it simultaneously indexes the possible unfolding of subaltern insurrection at the very moment of being read, so the middle-class reader imagines her own servants potentially plan-ning the same thing. This eliciting of the reader's terror becomes inextricably tied to the meaning of Balram's story (Dhillon 2008). Time here moves from being background to an affective mode, and like the excessive description Fredric Jameson identifies in the novels of Émile Zola, this affective mode "becomes autonomous, that is to say, it begins to have enough weight of its own to counterbalance the plot" (2013, 50).

In his third novel, *Last Man in Tower* (2011), Adiga pushes the openness of time even further to gesture toward the limits of the novel form in repre-senting the contemporary. *Last Man in Tower* tells the story of the residents of a crumbling middle-class housing society who receive a buyout offer from a redeveloper at higher than market value but with the provision that all the residents must agree to sell by the deadline for the deal to go through. Most of the residents are thrilled, but three or four hesitate, attached to the build-ing for sentimental reasons. One by one, the dissenters change their minds under pressure from the builder, until there is one last man standing, a re-tired schoolteacher and widower, Yogesh Murthy, known as Masterji, who feels connected to the building because he had lived there with his daughter and his wife, Purnima, before their untimely deaths. Oblivious to these ties to the past, the society's occupants go to increasingly desperate lengths to compel Masterji to sell, sending him threatening phone calls, hiring thugs to attack him, and smearing excrement on his door. Finally, the residents' greed and their fantasies of a better life lead them to undertake "The Simplest of Things" (351), Adiga's ironic name for the residents' murder of Masterji, which ensures that the buyout takes place.

This critique of the dark underside of development inflects the linear time of the novel with a sense of naturalist inevitability, in which we witness the progressive deterioration of neighborly sociality from the moment the residents receive the buyout offer to the final violent event, marked by an impending countdown: "Every day I can hear [the deadline] coming closer. Can you hear it too?" (146). The novel is structured as a countdown, with each chapter marked by a successive date closer to the deadline, so that, seemingly, the overdetermined futurist temporality of redevelopment reins in the possibility of multiple meanings. This is the decline narrative, the temporality of capitalism—what Fredric Jameson invokes when he characterizes the "immense international division of labor, which has certainly been anticipated at certain moments of the past," as *now universal and irreversible*" (2008, 375; emphasis added).

But at the same time, the novel suggests that the experience of the present cannot be captured in a countdown format and that time also has, after Henri Bergson, the "capacity to surprise, to fork in ways that diverge from those expected" (N. Khan 2012, 6). Thus, the progressive countdown of capitalism is undercut by the peculiar section titles, most of which are in the present tense and thus exceed the linear temporality of the novel's plot through their synchronicity and contemporaneity: "Book One: How the Offer Was Made," "Book Two: Mr Shah Explains His Proposal," "Book Three: Four or Five Seconds of Feeling like a Millionaire," "Book Four: The Rains Begin." These titular articulations of the present suggest that against the single-minded countdown of the plot, the present offers some space unaccounted for by the progressive march of time. Reading this way offers a different version of the story: rather than a story of the gradual demise of human sociality in the face of greed, it becomes one of myriad unknown possibilities.

The potential openness of time is captured by the alternative temporality of journalism, which, unlike the novel, can move easily between the preterite and the present. Thus, we have the book's title, *Last Man in Tower*, which is not the more typically novelistic *The Last Man in the Tower* and instead seems to belong to a newspaper headline such as the one discussed in the novel, "Last Man in Tower Fights Builder" (296). In journalistic time, the story of Masterji remains perennially unfinished, always open to the possibility of taking a surprising new turn the following day. Adiga, Uday Prakash, and Manu Joseph were all at one point (or still are) journalists (Moss 2017; Brouillette 2014, 40), whereas most of the postcolonial novelists of the earlier generation are associated with more literary forms: Vikram Seth, for instance, likes to be known as a poet first and a novelist second, and a poetic aesthetic, an intense sensitivity to the economy of form, pervades even his lengthy fictions. Amitav Ghosh earned a doctorate in social anthropology at Oxford before turning full-time to literature, and again the influence of academic writing, a form characterized by its protracted temporality and distanced reflection, is clear across his novels. In contrast, the novels of Adiga, Prakash, and Joseph are receptive, in different ways, to the continuing passage of time. It is not that their novels are journalistic but rather that journalistic time interrupts their works to question the inevitability of both progressive and capitalist time. Time is taken from its hallowed position in the postcolonial novel—from its status as History with a capital H—and repositioned as an interjection, an excess, an enriched synchronic moment, a pressure on the divide between text and world. These works thus demand a reorientation of the relationship between reader and text and a depletion of the conventional distance that has marked the postcolonial literary.

The Elusive Trope

We would not think [butterflies] so beautiful if they did not
fly, or if they flew straight and briskly like bees, or if they
stung, or above all if they did not enact the perturbing
mystery of metamorphosis: the latter assumes in our eyes
the value of . . . a symbol and a sign.
—Primo Levi, quoted in Palash Krishna Mehrotra,
    The Butterfly Generation

The presentation of time as perennially unfinished elicits a model of reading premised not on depth but on surface, unsettling dominant modes of meaning making in the postcolonial novel. Metaphor, too, is subject to such reassessment, from being perhaps the most significant literary figure in the postcolonial novel to a red herring or false promise in the contemporary one. Whereas for early Indian writing metaphor allowed authors to "escape referential boundaries" (Gajarawala 2012, 335) and imagine worlds beyond their immediate purview, in the 1980s and 1990s metaphor became the Indian English novel's central form-giving feature. For instance, in Amitav Ghosh's *The Shadow Lines*, there is a partitioned house that represents the partition of Bengal (Anjali Roy 2000, 38), and the eponymous shadow lines become "a metaphor for the pathos of nationhood" (Almond 2004, 93). Many book titles from these decades express the form's dependence on evocative metaphor: *The God of Small Things, The Inheritance of Loss, River of Smoke*, and even *Midnight's Children*. As a figure, Jaina C. Sanga writes, "metaphors prompt us to create alternate perceptions, implicitly forcing us to look beyond literal meanings" (2001, 2). Thus, the use of metaphor in the postcolonial novel demands a specific reading practice in which thematic through lines are unearthed to relate different parts of the text together in service of a formal whole.

What, then, do we make of the elusive trope of the white tiger in Aravind Adiga's novel by the same name? And the mysterious golden parasol (*peeli chhatri*) of Uday Prakash's 2001 *Peeli chhatri wali ladki* (*The Girl with the Golden Parasol* [2008])? In both cases, I suggest, what seem like structuring metaphors refuse to signify as expected. Even as they promise to link the different elements of the novel, they ultimately fail to do so, directing readerly investment away from formal closure or legible politics and into a space of indeterminacy and openness.

As we have seen, *The White Tiger* is the story of Balram Halwai, a low-caste boy who rises from an unschooled villager to an entrepreneur in India's new globalized economy. Balram narrates the story of his humble beginnings working in a village tea shop to his gradual social advancement, acquiring by means of his wiles and intelligence a job as "number two driver" for a corrupt village leader and then ultimately being promoted and transferred to Delhi. There, facing abuse and humiliation from his employers and being exposed to the gross juxtapositions along which poor and rich live in Indian cities, Balram's desire to rebel grows. Finally, in an act of ironic entrepreneurship, Balram takes control over his life by murdering his boss, stealing a large sum of money intended for a government bribe, and escaping to Bangalore where he opens a taxi service for late-night call center workers. Along with its irruptive temporality, the novel registers the contemporary through its use of discourses of enterprise and self-empowerment characteristic of the new India (Shingavi 2014, 7). The quintessential Hindu-Muslim conflict, towered over by the event of Partition (as seen in *A Suitable Boy*, *The Shadow Lines*, *Ice-Candy-Man*, *Midnight's Children*, and so many other English-language novels from the subcontinent), has in this text been replaced by the more indeterminate questions of class, caste, aspiration, and social mobility.

Thus, the novel strains legibility from the outset, pushing beyond the recognized features of the postcolonial novel. Its open temporality advances a contemporary that threatens the safe diegetic distance between world and text. The narration too is jarring and unsentimental. Balram begins the novel by saying to the Chinese premier: "Sir. Neither you nor I speak English, but there are some things that can be said only in English" (1). By presenting the supposed communication between Balram and Wen Jiabao in this space of the conundrum, Balram mocks the India-China connection praised by business elites and the state and also satirizes the centrality of the metaphor of translation in postcolonial writing (Sanga 2001, 6)—embodied, for instance, in the figure of Neel in Amitav Ghosh's Ibis trilogy. Balram continues: "Out of respect for the love of liberty shown by the Chinese people, and also in the belief that the future of the world lies with the yellow man and the brown man now that our erstwhile master, the white-skinned man, has wasted himself through buggery, cell phone usage, and drug abuse, I offer to tell you, free of charge, the truth about Bangalore" (3–4). Far from the shared cosmopolitanism of postcolonial literature, or "the gradually unfolding, slowly revelatory description of place, the laboured realist detail that characterises the writing of Anita Desai or Amitav Ghosh" (Gajarawala 2009, 22), Balram advances a mode of connection founded in human debasement and reliant on conspiracy, homophobia, and racialist slang. As Snehal Shingavi writes, "Despite his claims to be able to show the real India, Balram also confesses he cannot be trusted" (2014, 8). The nihilistic tone of the novel is epitomized by Balram's oft-repeated adage, which lies at the limits of language itself: "*What a fucking joke*" (5; emphasis in original).

This pressure on conventional novelistic legibility extends to the trope of the white tiger, which at first blush seems to be an image of subaltern awakening. Critics and readers have generally understood the tiger as a metaphor for Balram's uniqueness, as "the rarest of animals—the creature that comes along once in a generation" (30). From this perspective, the novel works as a Bildungsroman, in which Balram, the white tiger, is marked by his distinction from others around him and realizes that distinction through his successful act of rebellion (Buckley 1974, 17). However, the tiger has several other possible referents: a caged beast (150) or, "given that the tiger is a symbol of power and might, the title . . . also alludes to India's rise as a tiger economy" (Mendes 2010, 276). The tiger is also "exotic" (Mendes 2010, 276), and on a more general level, it is an animal in a dehumanizing world (Suneetha 2012, 166). The latter is supported by the fact that the novel is dotted with indeterminate animal imagery, including the narrator's reflections that at independence "the cages had been let open; and the animals had attacked and ripped each other apart and jungle law replaced zoo law" (54).

The lack of clarity around the meaning of the white tiger is confirmed when Balram actually encounters the animal on a trip to the Delhi zoo:

> I watched him walk behind the bamboo bars. Black stripes and sunlit white fur flashed through the slits in the dark bamboo; it was like watching the slowed-down reels of an old black-and-white film. He was walking in the same line, again and again—from one end of the bamboo bars to the other, then turning around and repeating it over, at exactly the same pace, like a thing under a spell.
>
> He was hypnotizing himself by walking like this—that was the only way he could tolerate this cage.
>
> Then the thing behind the bamboo bars stopped moving. It turned its face to my face. The tiger's eyes met my eyes, like my master's eyes have met mine so often in the mirror of the car.
>
> All at once, the tiger vanished. (237)

Although ostensibly an encounter with the tiger, the passage presents the tiger as elusive; although Balram is "watching" the tiger, what he sees is never translated into text. Instead, the text registers the tiger as a series of fragments: snippets of stripes and fur, face and eyes, its path, and a disembodied "thing behind the bamboo bars." At the moment when these fragments might cohere into a legible image, Balram faints ("the tiger vanished"), signifying a failure or lapse instead of consciousness or understanding. Far from clarifying the text's operative image, this passage presents a missed chance. Although this is the moment when Balram comes to understand the extent of his disempowerment—the moment when he decides to murder his boss, realizing, "I can't live the rest of my life in a cage" (239)—that revelation is founded in an image that in fact eludes the text's representation. The white tiger is not a figure for the legibility of subaltern rebellion but an elusive trope that doubles back to question the conventional hermeneutics of postcolonial metaphor.[3]

This presentation of meaning as elusive and centrifugal is even more striking in Uday Prakash's Hindi novel *Peeli chhatri wali ladki*. *Peeli chhatri* is the story of Rahul, a master's student who changes his discipline from anthropology to Hindi when he falls in love with Anjali, a Brahmin classmate at the university. Their love flourishes, even as Rahul experiences the corruption of the university leadership and of campus student groups connected to political parties who harass and steal money from the students. He and his friends become increasingly empowered against these college goons, and in the end, Rahul and Anjali run away together against her parents' wishes. But *Peeli chhatri* refuses the standard trope of cross-caste love as a metaphor for national unity. Even while it offers a searing critique of globalization, capitalism, Hindu nationalism, and Brahmin hegemony, the novel is strikingly whimsical in its description of Rahul and Anjali's love, centered not on its allegorical function but on the elusive—alternative—logic of metonymy:

> As Rahul emerged from the classroom into the corridor, someone snuck up from behind and bumped into him. Rahul turned around to look—it was Anjali, with her laugh [Woh Anjali thi. Apni hansi ke saath].
>
> In the library, Rahul was hunched over a desk, taking some notes, when suddenly someone blew into his ear—*pffffff!*—so intense it sent shivers up his spine. It was Anjali [Anjali hi thi].
>
> Rahul was taking a walk when a cold, pointy thing jabbed him in the neck. He turned around. Anjali was standing there, laughing, holding the closed parasol, the tip pointed at him—en garde!—trying to frighten him.

Back in the library, looking at books in the narrow space between the shelves, someone's shoulder gave him a little shove. It was Anjali's [woh kandha Anjali ka hi tha]. (108–109)

Here, Anjali is conveyed in fragments: her laugh, her breath, her body, her umbrella. Symbol is deliberately deferred to represent love as a bodily presence rather than as something that has the power, as it were, to break down caste division and become meaningful as national allegory. The umbrella, the "cold, pointy thing [ek thandi, nukili cheez]," characterizes this impulse; Anjali is carrying it the first time they meet and almost every time thereafter, and several times, it is the umbrella (*chhatri*)—or, even more synecdochally, the umbrella's yellow color (*peeli*)—that indexes Anjali's arrival: "Just then, Rahul saw a spot of yellow [ek peele rang ke dhabbe] far away by the residential area slowly making its way along the road. The yellow glowed beautifully in the morning light. There was something different about this particular yellow [dusre peelon se bilkul alag]. This one entered through his eyes, dissolved in his blood, and went straight to his heart" (43–44). Anjali is represented as a function of the umbrella rather than the other way around: "There was no doubt: it was the yellow parasol. . . . It must be her underneath [iske neeche woh hogi], the one I saw that day" (44). By characterizing the umbrella through its color, and Anjali through the umbrella, the text inverts the traditional hierarchy of human and object and the whole and the part, even in so potentially politically charged a relationship as Rahul's and Anjali's. Like the image of the white tiger, the yellow umbrella takes on a materiality of its own that asks to be read not for what it symbolizes but for where it leads.

Thus, the meaning of the umbrella emerges not via excavation but in the highly contingent act of perception. Rahul watches the yellow spot from his hostel room, through a window where he has hung a poster of Hindi film actress Madhuri Dixit: "His eyes remained wide open. A few moments passed like this until, in a blink of an eye, Madhuri Dixit eclipsed the yellow parasol [dekhte dekhte Madhuri Dixit ne us peeli chhatri ko dhank liya]" (44). In this inverted description, told from the point of view of the perceiver, the still image of Madhuri Dixit appears to be the moving image, as it blocks Rahul's view of the yellow parasol for a moment as he remains still. Rahul responds to this eclipse not with action (moving to gain a better spot) but with an irruption of futile interjection: "Shit! Shit! It was unbearable. For the first time ever Rahul felt uncontrollable anger toward Madhuri Dixit and her pretty back. This isn't some film, this is real life, madam. It's not merely an image. This is reality. Understand?" (44). The detaching of agent from action reflects a larger, surrealist impulse in the novel as a whole, which constantly subjects reality to the distorting lens of perception. Objects are not imbued with meaning, as metaphors, but rather reflect back on the viewer/reader, directing meaning away from their symbolic qualities and resulting in a disorientation of the reading experience. It is no surprise that Rahul's frustration culminates in an expletive; like "What a fucking joke" in *The White Tiger*, the use of "Shit! Shit"—specifically the English expletive transcribed into Devanagari (शिट् . . . ! शिट् . . . !)—marks a limit in the hermeneutic enterprise, as the significance of the expletive is not something that must be unearthed but lies in the very utterance of the word itself.

The novel thus offers a very different perspective on cross-caste love. Although caste threatens to break Rahul and Anjali apart, and the college campus they inhabit is marked by brutal violence, their love lives partially apart from these narratives, in a world of its own, where signs do not signify as expected. Rahul, for instance, is often described as inhabiting a "state of unconsciousness [in which] a yellow parasol quietly fluttered like a butterfly coming up the hills from the valley below" (67). Later the parasol actually becomes a butterfly (93, 102). This butterfly makes Rahul smile, even when the situation in the college is terrible (105). When things get worse, the parasol-butterfly appears to offer the two of them respite: "Anjali and Rahul had become invisible. All that remained was Anjali's yellow parasol. That too was shut closed, hidden under a lentina bush. And what about the other parasol? That was a butterfly, which had one day transformed its very form, playing a trick on the whole world. In front of everyone's eyes and in broad daylight" (164). Here the image works like Madhuri Dixit's poster earlier, eclipsing the reader's view of Anjali and Rahul and allowing them a moment of invisibility, a space of privacy to enact their love outside the narrative of their historical transgression. Its function, therefore, is not symbolic but metonymic; its significance lies in its position rather than its meaning. The temporary invisibility afforded by this image suggests a mode of reading not premised on illuminating or bringing unrecorded voices to light but conversely on the possibility of privacy, what Ramón Saldívar refers to in discussing the contemporary fiction of Salvador Plascencia as a means of combating the "commodification of sadness" (2011, 578), which the postcolonial novel, and its insistence on the violence of nation building, has been implicated in as well.

Metonymy is not always utopian here; fragmentation is at times represented as a violent consequence of the present. For instance, a disturbing image in the novel are the sandals of Sapam, a student from Manipur who commits suicide after being harassed and robbed by local goons. When Rahul and Hemant go to see the well into which Sapam jumped, they catch sight of one of his sandals floating on the water. Here the sandal, wrenched from the body to which it belongs, represents a broken system: "What awful irony. This plastic, inanimate, 40-rupee sandal that had come into being in Sapam's life a short two months ago still exists, floating on the surface, while a real life was no more. Vanished in the shimmering water" (80). Campus violence is also presented in this way: "Regionalism, casteism, and the muck of cheap petty powers were suddenly seeping out, laying waste to all the great metaphors [maha-rupak] and federal myths this country had so far constructed" (57).

Yet the text does not put its hope in the reassembling of these fragments or the reconstitution of the great metaphors. Rather, in the yellow parasol, which is profoundly free of convention or paradigm, we see the potential for metonymy to offer an alternative to totality itself. The constant potential transformation of the parasol into a fluttering butterfly indicates not only a metonymic chain of signification but also the promise of the elusiveness of the sign itself: the metaphor metamorphizing into metonymy and fluttering away in the breeze.

The elusiveness of the parasol allows the Rahul-Anjali love story to not be represented in the heavy, tragedic tone that Arundhati Roy, for instance, represents the Ammu-Velutha affair in *The God of Small Things*. There is little historically significant about their transgression. Caste is slippery, problematic, and, like the yellow parasol, at times also a product of perception rather than a historical distinction: "Do you think he—might there have been any confusion about you?" Rahul's Brahmin friend Gopal asks Rahul after he has been accepted into the Hindi master's program. "'What do you mean?' Rahul didn't understand. 'Nothing. I'll take care of it. What I meant was confusion about caste,' Gopal said lightly" (51). Unlike in Roy, caste in Prakash is at times a fixed thing and at other times a mode of confusion: "O bastard offspring of Ravana, cackling through the centuries, seizer of socioeconomic power, head of the caste system, I truly don't know whether I love you or hate you!" (130).[4]

This ambivalence extends to language as well. Postcolonial literary studies often poses English in contradistinction to the bhashas, as evident in Amitava Kumar's comment, reproduced on the back cover of the English translation of *Peeli chhatri*, that "*The Girl with the Golden Parasol* brings news from a world that the English novel doesn't even know existed." Kumar's comment reads the fact that the novel was originally written in Hindi as an indicator of its authenticity, which is often how bhasha writing is portrayed in contrast to Indian English. But this is not quite Prakash's view in the novel. At one point Rahul asks, "Am I working toward an MA in Hindi literature or Brahmin literature?" (162), mocking Hindi's pretensions as well as noting the potential slippage between language and caste domination.

Moreover, the Hindi department is described as uncanny rather than insurgent: "They didn't look like they were living in today's world. From the clothes they wore to the way they walked and talked, they were completely *other* [sab se bhinn the]" (31). Thus, like the yellow parasol, the meaning of Hindi cannot be easily pinned down. In Rahul's first encounter with the Hindi department chair, the latter confuses the Indian English writer Arundhati Roy with the beauty pageant winner–turned Bollywood superstar Aishwarya Rai: "So! Even supermodels are writing modern novels these days, eh? I haven't read anything by her but I've seen that Arundhati on TV in her ad for Lux soap" (50). While satirizing the provincialism of the Hindi department and the celebrity status of many Indian English writers, this slippage also suggests a secondary logic of meaning that follows that of the yellow parasol: the logic of association, whereby meaning emerges syntactically rather than syntagmatically. Arundhati Roy in Hindi is spelled अरुंधती राय, with "Roy" transcribed as "Rai," so that the department chair's association is both absurd and strangely legitimate. Hindi is thus perennially *something else*: the language of caste hegemony, the language of homophony, and indeed, the elusiveness of meaning itself. When Rahul resolves to quit Hindi, his friend O. P. responds: "Right, you dumb bastard, why pull yourself out of that gutter? That's where your paracetamol is, where your parasol is, where your butterfly is, where your bird is. Everything's in Hindi [teri kroseen, teri chhatri, teri titli, teri chiriya—sab toh usi hindi mein hai]" (165). Here Hindi is slippery; meaning slips and slides down this sentence, where *kroseen* becomes *chhatri* becomes *titli* becomes *chiriya*, and Hindi becomes the paradigmatic language of metonymy and metamorphosis. We see this also in one of the department chair's speeches, in which he uses so many garbled words that "there was a dire need for [it] to be translated into Hindi from whatever language he was speaking" (143). Prakash presents Hindi not as righteous writing back to Anglophone hegemony but as corruption and confusion, as a mode of difference, the slipperiness of meaning.

Hindi is therefore not the language of subaltern authenticity but an index to another world that potentially lies beyond language itself. Even as he devotes himself to Hindi study, Rahul begins to realize the inadequacy of language in formulating dissent: "In order to get across his revolutionary message, Buddha had to abandon Sanskrit, seeking refuge in Pali. So now, must Hindi be dropped in favor of using some other language to formulate ideas to provoke change? . . . 'Oh, shit, shit, shit!' [ओह! शिट्! शिट्!]" (162). Hindi is not inherently the medium of radical thought (*parivartankari vichar*); rather, revolutionary thought lies beyond the pale of any one language, signified here by the moment in which communication collapses into expletive. As the narrator writes in *Mohan Das*, "I [am] writing this story in a language that imprisoned me inside just like Iraqis were imprisoned in Abu Ghraib! Or like Jews in 1943 were imprisoned inside a German gas chamber! [Us bhasha ke bheetar main Baghdad ke Abu Garib jail mein Iraqion ki tarah hoon! Ya 1943 ki Germany ke kisi gas chamber mein Yahudion ki tarah!]" (129). In both texts, Prakash suggests that language is not necessarily liberating but can become a prison in its own right. In *The White Tiger* as well, we saw how English elicits a fundamental paradox: "Sir. Neither you nor I speak English, but there are some things that can be said only in English" (1). In *Peeli chhatri*, Rahul's friend Hemant puts it another way: "*To hell with Hindi*" (165). Like the previous exclamations, this English line is transcribed in Devanagari—टू हेल विद हिंदी (126)—marking not only a frustration with the Brahmin politics of the Hindi department but also the limits of the Hindi language itself to represent its own futility. At the same time, Hindi is what makes this novel possible, just as Adiga's presupposes English. The text itself is thus subject to this performative utterance. To hell with the novel!

Both *The White Tiger* and *Peeli chhatri* use the slipperiness of trope and language to gesture beyond the conventional paradigms of literary fiction, offering a new epistemology of the contemporary that is elusive rather than fixed, always on the verge of transforming into something else. By reorienting reading from a process of unearthing meaning to one that is perennially redoubling back to the world of the reader, emphasizing the materiality of language and moments of invisibility or obscurity, these works reorient the conventional epistemology of the postcolonial novel to offer new possibilities for meaning in the contemporary world.

"I Am Not Mohandas": The Limits of Allegory

How can one man become another?[5]

—UDAY PRAKASH, *Mohan Das*

Uday Prakash's novella *Mohan Das* takes up the question of allegory in Indian literature, long debated within postcolonial literary criticism (Ahmad 1992), to call into question assumptions about how we make meaning and how a story becomes meaningful. The novella tells the story of Mohan Das, a man who struggles to find work, despite holding a college degree, because he lacks the "criminal, illegal connections and back-door deals, nepotism and nefariousness, bribes and rewards [sors-sifarish, jod-tod, rishwat-sampark, jaalsaaji vagaira]" necessary to get a government position (51). He becomes increasingly frustrated; "a dark pessimism began to grow inside [ek gehre avsaad aur niraasha ne uske bheetar dera daalna shuru kar diya]" (52). Finally he is offered an office job at a coal mine, but he never receives the promised contract in the mail. Four years later, he discovers that the job had been stolen by Bisnath, a high-caste villager who claimed to be named Mohan Das to take the job and is now living under Mohan Das's identity. Disturbed by this revelation, Mohan Das goes to the mining town where Bisnath is living as Mohan Das. He struggles to prove that he is the real Mohan Das, but he becomes more and more frustrated when people do not believe him. Meanwhile, Bisnath convinces everyone that he is the real Mohan Das, and through bribery and manipulation he manages to refute an official inquiry and later a court case. The loss of his name and identity raises doubts in Mohan Das's mind about the reality of the world: "The names people went by, was that who they really were? Or had they committed fraud and assumed the identity of others? [Ve kya vaastav mein wahi log hain, jis naam aur pehchaan se ve jaane jaate hain, ya ve asal mein koi aur hain aur unhonein jaalsaaji kar ke kisi aur ka mukhauta laga rakha hai]" (93). He gets a glimmer of hope when a judge invokes special judicial powers to have Bisnath arrested, but that judge soon dies and Bisnath begins to act with impunity, committing petty crimes for which the real Mohan Das is arrested and beaten. The novella ends when Mohan Das finally gives up his fight for his identity: "I take your hands and beg," he tells the narrator, "please find a way to get me out of this. I am ready to go to any court and swear that I am not Mohandas. . . . Whoever wants to be Mohandas, let him be Mohandas. I am not Mohandas [Jise banna ho ban jaye Mohan Das. Main nahin hoon Mohan Das]" (127–128).

As we see in the previous discussion of *Mohan Das's* rants, this satirical novella is a biting critique of corruption, poverty, the bureaucratic state, and continuing caste and class hierarchies, and it refuses the impulse that would relegate those ills to a space apart from the present. But it is also critical of the allegorical impulse central to postcolonial reading in its use of Mohan Das as its central figure. An allegorical reading might interpret the reference to Gandhi in the protagonist's first name as a reflection on the loss of Gandhian values in the present day or a disillusionment with nationalism (Brueck 2017, 87). But this novella actively plays with its reader's allegorical expectations. For example, the Gandhian allegory is *over*written; not only is the novella's protagonist named Mohan Das, but his wife is Kasturubai; his mother, Putlibai; and his son, Devdas (the real Gandhi's wife, mother, and son were Kasturba, Putlibai, and Devdas). They live in a village called Purbanra (Gandhi's birthplace was Porbandar). The associations with Gandhi's family and birth village are so copious that the text invites an allegorical reading while simultaneously satirizing it. In yet another aside, the narrator breaks from the story to explicitly address this issue:

(Please stop for a moment and tell the truth: did you begin to get the feeling that I'd gone and started telling you some kind of encoded, symbol-laden tale [koi prateekvadi kutkatha]? The main character [mukhyapatra] of the story is called Mohandas, the wife is Kasturi-bai, the mother is Putlibai and the son's name is Devdas . . . ?

Kasturibai reminds you [yaad dilaata hai] of Kasturba—and, well, Mohandas couldn't be more clear [ekdum saaf hai]. If you read Mahatma Gandhi's autobiography . . . you'll discover that his father, Karamchand, was also called Kaba. And His mother was Putlibai . . . and who doesn't know the tale of his son, Devdas? Look at Mohan-das, his build, and the state he's in: he shares the same history as the Mahatma. The difference is that Mohandas looks the way he does not because of Porbandar—the place where Gandhi was born—or Kathi-awar, Rajkot, England, South Africa, or Birla House, but as a result of the hunger and heat, sweat and sickness, insult and injustice in the fields and pastures, caverns and caves, jungles and marshes, of Chhattisgarh and Vindhya Pradesh. Otherwise, all the rest is the same.

I'd also like to stop the story right here and now to solemnly af-firm that the similarity of names is honestly and truly just a coinci-dence [ek sanyog hi hai]. When I sat down to write this, I had no idea these sorts of echoes could possibly be hidden in the story of Mohan-das and his family from the village [mujhe khud pata nahin tha ki hamare gaaon ke Mohan Das aur uske parivar ke sadasyon ke byau-ron mein itihas ki koi aisi anugunj bhi chhipa ho sakti hai].

You'll have to take my word, and don't read too much into it [aisa kuch bhi nahin hai]. It isn't some symbolic story or allegory or coded fable [Yeh koi prateek katha, rupak ya kutakhyaan nahin hai]. It's totally on the level [Yeh to ek bilkul sapaat sa kissa hai]. . . .) (48)

The narrator anticipates that the reader will understand the story of Mohan Das as the story of Gandhi, allegorically linking text and nation. However, the narrator says, this is the story of the present, "on the level [sapaat sa]," *not* a nationalist allegory and *not* a story whose meaning lies under its surface (Brueck 2017, 85). Yet, the narrator acknowledges, even against his warnings, the reader is inclined to "read too much into it." Combined with the rants discussed earlier, we can see the text's attempt to disrupt the reader's as-sumptions about what constitutes Hindi literature, rural literature, and the Indian novel as a whole. What are the limitations of an allegorical reading of Mohan Das as a Gandhi figure, and how might it obscure reading for the contemporary? What might be lost in this allegorical reading, and what al-ternatives are possible? How might refusing to read Mohan Das as a coded version of Gandhi compel a reading that is free of the looming shadow of history or the nation?

We see a similar questioning of the seemingly inherent connections between things in *Last Man in Tower*, a novel that is also skeptical of allegorical associations and romanticized collectivities. At one point, Masterji says of his increasingly aggressive neighbors, "*They treat me like they would treat an untouchable in the old days . . .* : even at the thought of his shadow falling on them, his neighbours cringed and withdrew" (217; emphasis in original). Later, when Masterji tries to rally the justice system in support of his cause, he imagines himself momentarily linked to a laborer sitting next to him at a cheap restaurant: "Until now he had only been conscious of fighting *against* someone: that builder. Now he sensed he was fighting *for* someone" (301). Both these associations offer a fleeting sense of solidarity. For a moment, "the straining coolies" he encounters on the street become "symbols" of a new collective, a thought that leads him to "fe[el]—for the first time since his wife had died—that he was not alone in the world" (302). This feeling appears once again when Masterji links himself with "people, men of various races, standing in white shirts, close together . . . the commuters on the suburban train" (341). In *The White Tiger*, as Sarah Brouillette writes, Balram sees that "the construction workers who built the upscale apartment building left traces of their work . . . which might encourage him to identify with their labour," but "his fixation on emblems is a symptom of a ghostly solidarity that is ultimately fruitless: he feels it but cannot articulate it or act upon it" (2014, 45). For Masterji as well, these possible collectives dissolve the moment he imagines them. In all these cases, the potential connections fail to signify; individual stories remain untouched by meaning beyond themselves.

These texts present allegory not as an assumed structure of the novel but as a problem of reading. In *Mohan Das*, the narrator insists that the story of Mohan Das is only the story of Mohan Das, that it has no greater significance than that. This claim seems, at first, tongue in cheek because the allegory is so overwritten. But the theft of Mohan Das's identity is central to the story's plot. So while the reader watches Bisnath make his wretched moves, stealing Mohan Das's identity and driving him to insanity, we also, in looking for a greater significance in Mohan Das's story, participate in a kind of identity theft.

Thus, Mohan Das's frustrating journey to reclaim his identity causes him to reflect on the problem of allegory at large: "How can one man become another?" (70). What are the implications of this for the world as we know it? He "began to feel as if the officers and the hakims and the wealthy and the party members were so powerful, they could turn anything into anything: a dog into an ox, a pig into a lion, a ditch into a mountain, a thief into a gentleman" (70). Where does it end? While there is an element of the absurd here, for instance, in Mohan Das's observation on "how totally ludicrous [it was] that in order to find out where Bisnath's flat was, he'd have to ask for his own name [apna hi naam lena pad raha tha]" (76), these thoughts compel Mohan Das to question the very reality he sees before him: "Then Mohandas began to ask himself who, after all, he himself was? [Mohan Das ko swayam apne upar sandeh hone lagta ki aakhir woh khud kaun hai?].... Did it happen like this to everyone? [Kya sabhi ke saath aisa hi hota hai?]" (93). This madness is in part a consequence of making too many connections, of too eagerly linking the part and the whole, so that the past, the nation, and the authentic take over everyday reality. These visions are so powerful that Mohan Das has to give up his own identity to free himself from them, and thus he finally admits: "I am not Mohandas." However, it might be too late. The narrator writes, near the end:

> I looked up; Mohandas was approaching, limping heavily. He was not wearing the washed-out, patched up pants and torn checked shirt, but only a loin-cloth. His hair had fallen out, and he wore cheap round eyeglasses. He walked slowly, using a walking stick, shuffling along like an old man [kisi bimar budhe ki tarah chal raha tha]. (127)

Mohan Das has no inherent connection to Gandhi; here the likeness is born in the narrator's perception. His poverty and the repeated beatings at the hands of the police have left Mohan Das a poor and wounded man, so he wears a loin cloth, has a shaved head, and carries a walking stick. Even while the narrator describes these attributes, the reader cannot help, once again, cohering these observations into an image of the Mahatma, even after finishing a story that is clearly not about Gandhi. Once again, the readers reach for significance that takes us away from the fact of corruption and Mohandas's brutalized self, as we ask, What is its larger meaning? But like the Madhuri Dixit eclipse in *Peeli chhatri wali ladki*, this image of Gandhi is in fact a trick of the eye rather than something that is actually there. We believe the trick because we want—perhaps even need—the story to have a larger meaning. But in its refusal to cohere around an allegorical reading, the text asks us to put aside the image for the reality it presents to us: the broken body and soul of *this* Mohan Das.

Beyond Language

The texts discussed thus far put pressure on conventional forms of meaning making in the Indian novel, suggesting new possibilities for the novel's relationship to the world. Such works refuse the hermeneutics of postcolonial reading and demand that we attend to meaning born in perception or otherwise on the surface of the text. Mohan Das's self-questioning—his doubts about whether he exists at all—suggests a larger ontological turn in contemporary Indian literature that runs against the grain of the linguistic play of novels like Rushdie's or the materialist historicism of Amitav Ghosh. It allows texts to probe philosophical questions that the postcolonial novel has long avoided, such as what the meaning of life is, how we understand reality, and what lies beyond the known world. The political exists in these texts but is no longer the fulcrum of meaning, as we see in regard to caste in *Peeli chhatri* or subaltern revolution in *The White Tiger*. The prologue, the rant, the irruption of time, the elusive trope, and *Mohan Das's* meta-allegorical structure: these all contribute to thickening the interface at which the reader encounters the work, refusing the formal integrity of "the text" as it is often conceived in postcolonial criticism and offering an array of points at which meaning can emerge.

Manu Joseph's *The Illicit Happiness of Other People* (2012) is perhaps most experimental in this enterprise, rejecting the aesthetics and politics of the classic postcolonial novel to probe the limits of language in representing human thought and the limits of history and society in explaining human action. In its philosophical questioning and political nihilism, it refuses to be read through the lens of postcolonial criticism. It is not allegorical and has no reference to the nation, no interest in history, and no obvious politics. It presents language as not a vehicle for knowledge but, as in Uday Prakash, potentially an impediment; as one character explains, "Language was created by nature to guard its secrets, not to reveal them. We are trapped in language" (216). In this way, it enables a contemporary imagination that lies beyond language, thus rethinking the role of the novel itself in political resistance.

The Illicit Happiness of Other People is structured over the unsolved question of the suicide of seventeen-year-old Unni, cartoonist and son of Ousep and Mariamma Chacko. Even though Unni's suicide took place three years ago, Ousep is convinced he can find the key to his son's death in the sixty-three cartoons Unni left behind. However, the cartoons take Ousep and his family deeper into Unni's world of mystery and silence. This work's interest in the expansiveness of the human mind continues some of the themes of Joseph's first novel, *Serious Men* (2010), the story of Ayyan Mani, personal assistant to the director of the Institute for Theory and Research in Mumbai, who attempts to advance his family's social status by convincing the world that his son Aditya is a genius. He steals exam answers and pulls other tricks in a game that he hopes will make a small headway in defeating "three thousand years" of Brahmin hegemony (22): "At the end of those cursed centuries, the new Brahmins arrived in their new vegetarian worlds, wrote books, spoke in English, built bridges, preached socialism and erected a big unattainable world. I arrived as another hopeless Dalit in a one-room home as the son of a sweeper. And they expect me to crawl out of my hole, gape at what they have achieved, and look at them in awe. What geniuses" (22). Like *Peeli chhatri* and *The White Tiger*, *Serious Men* is a political novel but not in the same way that characterized Dalit protest literature in the late twentieth century or social realism more generally. It renders revolt individual, sporadic, and even arbitrary and envisions no revolution of the social structure (Gajarawala 2015, 381, 374). Rather, its investment in political futurity is tied up with its radical epistemology—in this case, its consideration of the philosophical status of unanswered questions—which, it suggests, might help us rethink what politics is in the first place. These questions constitute an alternative to the sociohistorical epistemology of the Indian novel in English, an alternative that is taken up more directly in *Illicit Happiness*.

The world in which *Illicit Happiness* takes place is nihilistic and banal.[6] Anything that smacks of traditional politics is subject to satire or deadpan humor, such as hunger strikers who sneak bananas into their flashlights so they can eat them on the sly (66) or the characterization of socialists as "noble conservationists, working hard to preserve [abject poverty . . . as historical evidence]" (71). As Ousep is waiting at a bus stop, he sees a small girl playing a game where she pats her mother on the backside, runs away, and then comes back to do the same thing again. The mother ignores her. When the girl is distracted, a random man starts to pat the woman's backside, seeing if she will begin to notice:

> She thinks it is her daughter, so she stands there without any expression. The man pats her again and looks away. He pats her at short intervals, and finally he lets his hand stay on her. Ousep stares at the scene without opinion, without outrage. A man's hand on a woman's arse and the woman, yawning now, looking at the world go by. (14)

Countering the dominant affect of the political novel, Joseph's is a world "without outrage" or "without any expression" at all—suggesting what Huehls and Smith call a "post-ideological mode of existence" (2017, 12). The act of yawning exhibits boredom, but it is not boredom as a "response to the perceived fracture of colonial modernity," as in some strands of literary modernism (S. Majumdar 2015b, 75), but the entirely uninterpretable boredom of a petty world emptied of meaning, like the toothpaste tube in the Chacko residence, whose "life . . . is squeezed out of it until it is a flat strip of thin tortured metal. Then it is violated by toothbrushes and even index fingers for several days" (58). Neither the man's action nor this daily violation is meant to be read as social critique. "It is a moment that has no meaning" (14), the novel continues. "It is as if the tired charade of human life with its great pursuits and history and wounds and deep convictions has collapsed, and the world has been suddenly revealed as a place that has no point, that does not need the hypothesis of meaning to explain its existence" (14).

There is something naturalist about such a world, with its lack of point. It is a stagnant world punctuated only by shortsighted scheming; it offers very little redeeming about the human condition. But this is not naturalism, in Émile Zola's sense, as political critique of a dehumanized system. Rather, it is naturalism as a positive mode, one that seeks to create a *new* epistemology as a response to what are presented as the anachronistic ethics of the postcolonial novel. As Pieter Vermeulen writes, "Stories in which nothing happens . . . or in which a character refuses to be transformed, constitute massive challenges to the meaning-making mandate of the novel; alternatively, they generate creative spaces for imagining life and affect differently" (2015, 6). Here, too, Joseph asks us to think beyond progress and telos. Thus, in *Serious Men* we have infinite repetition: despite Ayyan having told his son, after each successful ruse where they had passed him off as a genius, that "this is the last time. The very last time we do something like this. OK?" (326), the novel ends as the two are planning yet another deception. In *Illicit Happiness*, time is even more bleak, as Ousep's nightly drunkenness is presented as "an inevitability that masquerades as a decision" (161).

The only alternatives to such a world lie, in *Illicit Happiness*, beyond the knowable universe. The novel presents suicide—and death more generally—as one means of accessing these alternatives. By centering the story around death, the novel finds meaning not in the conventional structures of human making, such as history or society (where the Indian English novel might previously have located it), but in an entirely other world, beyond human understanding. Indeed, death hovers over *Illicit Happiness*. Along with Unni's suicide, we have Ousep's repeated staging of his own suicide every night when he comes home drunk, as well as the character of Somen Pillai, a victim of the Cotard Delusion, who "feel[s] as if he were a living corpse, that he was rotting inside, that he was actually dead and so eternal" (287). There is also Unni's longest comic work, *The Album of the Dead*, a series of drawings of his family and friends in coffins (123), and his comment to his mother that if she were to die, he would use her skull as a pen holder (124). There is a proliferation of discourse surrounding death, suggesting a kind of productivity of death rather than a finality.

Representations and enactments of death thus furnish the novel's present, in a way similar to what anthropologist Jocelyn Chua (2016) describes in her study of contemporary Thiruvananthapuram as a world structured around the potentiality of suicide. Chua disputes accounts that argue that such a world is necessarily an apocalyptic one, presenting discussion, fear, anticipation, warnings, and other elements of suicide discourse as constructing an apparatus whereby living individuals can reimagine their own lives and the possibilities for their own futures. Chua discerns the existence of this suicide sensibility, as it were, not in language but in the crevices of the linguistic, in the space between words. And we see that in Joseph as well. Despite the melancholy that affects all the characters in the wake of Unni's suicide, his death fills the crevices of their otherwise meaningless lives, where they find a whole world beyond language. Thoma, Unni's brother, considers that "the hurting sweetness of memory, it has no name in Tamil or Malayalam" (90), and in Mariamma's partial translation of *One Hundred Years of Solitude* into Malayalam, "some objects in Marquez's story remain blank gaping spaces in her prose" (204). The existence of worlds beyond language, as in *Peeli chhatri*, offers an alternative to the naturalist flatness of daily life: "I know it does not mean anything. Such an ordinary thing, actually. I don't know how useful something like this is to you" (74), one of Unni's friends tells Ousep, and another speaks in strange speech patterns: "slowly, carefully, with an inarticulate superiority, as if his thoughts were too complex for words" (85). And Thoma tells his mother, "I know everything. I just don't tell" (88).

This constant gesturing to a space beyond language contests the historical and political ethos of the Indian novel in English, in which language registers knowability and becomes the prerequisite for political futurity. Joseph has been critical in his journalistic writings of what he calls an elite leftism whose proponents explain current events through the lens of historical or systemic injustice. For instance, in an editorial following the much-publicized 2015 suicide of Rohit Vemula, a Dalit student in Hyderabad, which became an emblem of the struggles Dalit students face on university campuses, Joseph (2016) wrote a scathing critique of "the archipelagos of liberal activism" who blame Vemula's suicide on his experiences as a Dalit student rather than on mental illness or other cerebral factors. He also maintained that the recent spate of farmer suicides in India should be understood as "a depression story, not an economics story." In a more recent article on the suicides allegedly caused by the Blue Whale Challenge, Joseph (2017) similarly argues that suicide cannot be explained by factors that "reside . . . outside the person who has committed suicide," despite the "ideologues" who say otherwise. While both editorials are somewhat simplistic and seem more interested in criticizing progressives than in understanding why people commit suicide, we might see *Illicit Happiness* as engaging with the question of suicide in similar but ultimately more complex ways. The novel suggests that suicide might not necessarily or always reflect the burdens of identity or circumstance; there might be other explanations that lie in the human mind.

Suicide, for Joseph, becomes analogous to the contemporary novel, both of which offer an unconventional means of imagining life beyond the articulable domains of history and political reason. As Ousep digs deeper into the reasons for Unni's suicide, the novel follows the strange worlds he encounters, for instance, one in which a nun has taken a vow of silence and thus communicates only in writing. To represent her, the narrative is forced to describe her writing as part of what she actually says—her form as content: "She writes on her notebook in good Malayalam, and in a beautiful miserly hand. She writes that she will go to a far corner and write down everything she remembers" (82). This strange form of ekphrasis, where one medium is describing its own medium as medium, signals a doubling where writing gestures to itself to draw attention to the materiality of representation. Suicide offers a transgression of both the world and the word that allows the novel to illuminate these new possibilities.

Ousep's struggle to decipher Unni's comics therefore becomes generalized in the novel's own struggle to represent the nonlinguistic. Unni's comics serve as the only physical reminder of his life, and Ousep is convinced they will provide the key to unlock the mystery of his suicide, but most are barely legible. Some lack the prose that would make their story apparent (127), others are untitled (171), and others have blank dialogue boxes, as if the prose would have been filled in later—which, as we later learn, is how Unni worked: "The only thing Unni hated about cartooning was filling up the dialogue bubbles with text. He found it tedious, probably the reason why he usually devised stories that did not need prose" (224). Unni's final comic, the one he mailed to his friend Sai on the day of his suicide, is aptly titled "How to Name It," and Ousep and Mariamma try hard to read it as a suicide note. But this comic is impossible to read, at least according to the limited logic of social or historical explanation. Its meaning lies beyond the pale: "Does the absence of an explanation contain within its baffling emptiness a simple message that Unni presumed his parents would be smart enough to see?" (127).

By juxtaposing various media and using writing to reflect on itself and its own limitations, *Illicit Happiness* develops an ekphrastic imaginary that marks, as Timothy Bewes writes, an "ontological" turn in contemporary literature more broadly (2012, 160). Unni's own search for meaning beyond language is redoubled in the text in the thirteen ekphrastic passages that occur throughout the novel, in which the narrative describes Unni's comics. While varied in length, these passages make up a protracted struggle to represent that which lies at the edges of language. The single-panel comics are perhaps easiest represented in language, as the spatial register is diminished in importance. But in the novel's descriptions of the long-panel narratives, such as "How to Name It," we see the struggle to represent the spatiality that characterizes the form. The narrative uses words like "now" and "still" to denote the progression of the story from one panel to another (62), as well as spatial designations such as "the next panel" (63). Once again, this form of ekphrasis necessarily privileges readerly perception in the generating of meaning: "Something strange happens next. There is the image of a giant bra as a suspension bridge that spans a wide river, linking two mountains. The comic then returns to the amiable middle-aged woman" (63). This image, we later find out, refers to Unni's thought that a woman's bra could be used as a suspension bridge (235). Here, ekphrasis is used as its own kind of bridge between perception and reality, represented here in the space between narrative temporality and graphic synchronicity. In *Serious Men* we read, "If you stare long enough at serious people they will begin to appear comical" (4), which similarly presents ontological change as born through the power of perception. In *Illicit Happiness*, the pause in translating one form of representation to another or, more precisely, the elongation of perception so that it does not merely identify what is on the page but actually generates new visions marks the new imaginary of this text. It is fitting, then, that Joseph has described himself as a "cartoonist who can't draw" (Singh 2012), highlighting the possibilities and limitations of different media as central to his representational practice.

Joseph's criticism of liberal understandings of suicide thus might also be seen as a negation of postcolonial reason in an attempt to generate new interpretive possibilities for the contemporary world. Rather than approach every issue with a predetermined lens, the novel suggests that some realities might lie beyond understanding, in a space beyond the parameters of the known world. When seen as part of an overall interest, by other writers such as Adiga and Prakash, in rethinking the way the global novel is read, we can locate Joseph's provocative politics not only as a symptom of a right-wing shift but also as an epistemological intervention into postcolonial thought.

All these works represent the contemporary not merely as the time of the present but as a disruption to the conventions of the Indian English novel. They show how representing the contemporary requires asserting difference in the face of these long-held conventions, which at times results in a jarring aesthetics or a violent rejection of political sureties. In different ways, they all gesture outward—toward the reader, toward the world—offering new models of reading that are open to the uncertainties of the contemporary. As the range of ideological positions and kinds of texts show, this is less a unified movement than a persistent dissatisfaction with what literature has been for so long.

6

Inside and Out

This book advances the idea of representation not as a fixed, closed field that can only reflect dominant power systems but as an open, creative practice offering new future possibilities. Language not only is the site for the consolidation of power but also allows writers and practitioners to think outside prescribed political positions so that even formulaic and commercial genres like pulp fiction or popular cinema can compel us to see the world anew. However, to glimpse these futures, we need to read in new ways, employing a literary criticism that reads not from a critical distance of skepticism and mistrust but from a place of intimacy. The previous five chapters try to delineate what this might look like, reading not to disarm power but to see how texts themselves create interpretive possibilities. This will clear the way for an expansive account of the Indian contemporary.

This chapter both advances this project and reflects on its stakes through a study of the multigenre and multimedia oeuvre of filmmaker, critic, curator, and cultural practitioner Paromita Vohra. She began her career as a documentary filmmaker and has since worked in a range of media, including screenplays, television, a comic book (Mantri 2016), and a multimedia web platform. Vohra is also a cultural critic, writing weekly columns in two daily newspapers and periodic publications in other venues and appearing as a frequent panelist and commentator in literary and film festivals and contemporary cultural spaces such as the Godrej India Culture Lab in Mumbai. Her work as a feminist documentary filmmaker and increasingly as a commentator on questions of love, desire, and sex in contemporary India constitute trailblazing articulations of new and emergent sensibilities in ways that actively refuse the assumptions of the traditional left, mainstream feminism, and postcolonial theory. Moreover, her refusal to be contained within one medium or genre and her fluidity in moving inside and outside the text imagine a new space of the contemporary in which the hierarchies between practitioner and critic are called into question and in which writing, art, and criticism never remain fully external to the objects they represent. Vohra's work thus offers a way of rethinking not only recent literary and cultural production but my book itself as also contemporary. Rather than view literary criticism as a distanced methodology of analyzing texts from the outside, this chapter suggests that a literary criticism of the contemporary also has to become contemporary itself.

Vohra's work also allows for a rethinking of the conventional lines along which we conceive of political art and politics more generally. Like the other authors and practitioners discussed so far, she locates her own experimental work as having emerged in India's postliberalization era, which, besides inaugurating a consumer-oriented economy, marked a shift in "the world of organization left politics . . . [during which] feminists broke away from Marxist groups, Dalit feminists challenged the feminist movement on its non-reflexivity vis-à-vis caste or religion, and sexuality movements challenged other movements on account of heteronormativity and prudery" (Vohra 2011, 49–50). As Vohra recounts, this breakdown of a unitary leftist politics gave new impetus to documentary filmmakers previously restricted by a narrow definition of political filmmaking. Vohra thus finds an opening in what in much commentary is conceived of as a lamentable fragmentation of the left and as the decline of art and culture through their commercialization. In the perspective of commentators such as Pankaj Mishra, liberalization heralded a decline in political integrity and counterculture. But Vohra's perspective claims that while some possibilities have been closed down in the new India, others have been opened up. Her works compel us to do away with a unitary definition of political progressivism rooted in fixed categories like the worker, the woman, or the outcaste and instead think through "the nature of the political" and art and culture's continuing relationship to it (Vohra, quoted in Kishore 2017, 168).

In these various endeavors, Vohra's work as it crosses conventional boundaries both models and reflects on the unfinished contemporary with which this book is concerned. While innovating within particular media—her open-ended, experimental documentary style, for instance, her weekly newspaper columns, or her website on issues surrounding sex in contemporary India—her work is marked by a persistent frustration with preexisting categories and subject positions such as "liberal," "feminist," "activist," and "critic." She envisions art as enabling "a public discourse that is comfortable with ambiguity and able to comprehend difference without alarm" (Vohra

2010). Yet far from a marginal outlier or an artist for the elite, Vohra has become more mainstream over the past fifteen years, even as her generic experimentations have intensified. Thus, Vohra's work, for all its precarity and dissatisfaction with prevailing norms, can render visible new outlines of the contemporary in India at large.

"Films for a Purpose"

I see feminism as anti-fixity and about looking at the
outside and the inside in tandem.

—PAROMITA VOHRA, quoted in Shweta Kishore, "Interview with
   Paromita Vohra"

Vohra began her career in documentary film, but she has insistently rejected the dominant style of political documentary and the Griersonian tradition in general, with its "sobriety" (Nichols 1991, 3), "authoritative aesthetic" (Rajagopal and Vohra 2012, 13), and inherently oppositional stance, what K. P. Jayashankar and Anjali Monteiro (2016) call the position of being "a fly in the curry."[1] Vohra's films are playful and experimental, using formal innovations such as fiction interspersed with documentary, animation, faux advertisements, and personal cameos, combining "*epistephilia*, the desire to know" with "*scopophilia*, pleasure in looking" (Kishore 2013, 742), which are conventionally held distinct in documentary. These innovations constitute a deliberate move away from the Films Division (FD) documentary tradition, in which documentary was invested in a certain political bottom line and displayed "a strongly objectivist tendency, uncomfortable with intuitive observation and ambiguous responses" (Vohra 2008, 420); and in which, "given their ambitions to give 'voice to the voiceless,' it was a widely shared assumption that the filmmakers themselves would not be the protagonists" (Gadihoke 2012, 145). As Anuja Jain writes, the original mandate of the FD, established after independence, gave documentary film a "utilitarian purpose . . . that of propaganda" for the new nation, with its concomitant aesthetics of "didactic, nonstory, nondialogue documentary with a 'voice of God' narrative" (2013, 17, 21). In contrast, "a concern with aesthetics and form" was seen to weaken "the documentary's *raison d'etre*—[which was] social upliftment" (Rajagopal and Vohra 2012, 9).

Although there were debates during Indian documentary's formative period between "experimental documentaries" and "films for a purpose" (quoted in A. Jain 2013, 20),[2] the latter trajectory grew prominent in the 1970s and 1980s, as Anand Patwardhan became the leading figure in activist documentary filmmaking (Wolf 2013, 366). Patwardhan's films concern "everyday and extraordinary cases of injustice and profound problems with

Indian democracy. His films have been among the most important depictions of issues crucial to recent Indian history, including the rise of violent Hindu nationalism, militarism, and exploitation of the indigenous and disenfranchised by corporate and developmental interests"; his self-described style is "guerilla filmmaking," which is meant "to illustrate the injustice of the system in order to produce social change" (Matzner 2014, 128). As Deborah Matzner writes, "Guerilla filmmakers eschew aesthetics, associated with the escapism of commercial cinema, in favor of a 'whatever-is-necessary approach to what was hitherto a carefully upholstered, meticulously protected medium'" (129). Patwardhan's work is thus "self-avowedly polemical, instrumental and interventionist. . . . His preoccupations are essentially political with little commitment to what he terms superfluous formal elements" (Jayashankar and Monteiro 2016, 21).[3]

Vohra worked as an assistant on Patwardhan's set for three years at the start of her career (Nathan 2015), but her own vision of documentary grew very much out of the limitations of his.[4] As Vohra has criticized, "The documentary's purpose is most clearly identifiable when related to a list of predetermined progressive topics, rather than through a political approach open to self-criticism" (Rajagopal and Vohra 2012, 10). And elsewhere: "I find Western ideas of documentary reality that push toward notions of a seemingly essential real as equivalent to truth, while emphasizing the unflinching attitude of the filmmaker, as oppressively literal minded. . . . I find this to be an antierotic, ascetic principle—the masculine warrior over the erotic feminine" (quoted in Kishore 2017, 171).[5] Thus, her documentaries are interested in representation as a form of open questioning of the materiality of the world rather than merely a representation of the world, experimenting, for instance, with "practices which are interested in treating the invisible creatively, as much as or more than, practices interested in connecting visible evidence" (Rajagopal and Vohra 2012, 14). She opens up the relationship between camera and object to account for "not the explicit world of proof, but the implicit world of sense and how we understand the world through what we can feel underneath the world" (Vohra, n.d.). This involves widening our sense of art's relationship to politics: "I have a deep and abiding belief in art as a thing that makes us better people. Not by lecturing us or by posturing as our savior, but with its sensory strength and emotional core art unfolds the truths hidden in our hearts" (Vohra 2014c). She elaborates:

The belief in the visual as the bright shining light of truth and thus, the automatic harbinger of justice severely undermines our discussions today. It replaces showing with exposing. Showing, which considers the storyteller's particularity, believes in light and shade, considers many facets, some visible, some invisible, invites tentativeness and doubt, and reflection. So, it helps us learn about the world and ourselves. "Exposing" implies revealing an unvarnished, uncontestable truth, leaving nothing hidden, nothing unknown, obscuring all greys, imbuing the exposer with not only nobility but with authority. (Vohra 2015g)

This investment in showing rather than exposing is apparent in *Unlimited Girls* (2002), Vohra's first feature-length documentary. Rather than advance a feminist agenda by, for instance, exposing patriarchal social structures or "hav[ing] poor women speaking to power on screen" (quoted in Wolf 2013, 367), *Unlimited Girls* is structured as a question: What does it mean to be a feminist? It begins with the uncertain musings of its fictionalized narrator, Fearless (named after the popular 1940s Bollywood star known as Fearless Nadia), played by Vohra herself. Fearless logs on to a chat room in which various women are discussing what they understand feminism to be. These discussions pique Fearless's interest, leading her to learn more about the history of Indian feminism by interviewing young people as well as established feminists such as Veena Mazumdar, Urvashi Butalia, and Sonal Shukla. She talks with antidowry activists, Mumbai's first female taxi driver, and men and women of various ages. She comes at the question of feminism from the position of questioning: how the history of feminism matters in the present, whether labels such as "feminist" might limit women's freedom, what role sex and pleasure play in feminism, and whether feminism is primarily a negation of patriarchy or a positive imaginary of a better world. Never extracting a moral or even a common thread, *Unlimited Girls* is "a film untidy with both doubt and certitude, moody with questions" (Vohra 2008, 421).

By broaching these questions through the fictionalized space of the chat room, Vohra foregrounds the idea of feminism as emerging in conversations, as resolutely processual. The chat-room scenes are supplemented by other conversations, among women and men, in classrooms, in public fora, and outside in public space—conversations that are full of questions and disagreements. The sensibility here is one of multiple voices constituting multiple feminisms born in dialogue and exchange rather than a fixed political movement that one can either subscribe to or reject. This is a feminism beyond the pale—a feminism that is *unlimited*. Vohra takes this idea of the "unlimited" from one of the male college students she interviews, who believes that women should advance only up to a certain limit ("limit tak aayen toh thik hai"), and beyond that, when they become "un-limited," something goes wrong ("unlimited hoti toh uske saath galat hota hai"). But Vohra goes beyond a straightforward critique of such sexist views, as she suggests that it is not only men who seek to limit women. In a chat-room conversation about sexual harassment, Fearless asks, "Can we just talk about the girls who want to say yes?" and is met with surprise from the other participants. "I don't mean yes to sexual harassment," Fearless hastily explains. "Whenever we talk about sex and women, it's about rape, assault. If we only teach women to fear sex, then how are we supposed to feel good and free about it?" One responder, with the screen name Marxistusha, writes back, "It's ok for western women to talk about sexual liberation. In our country there are so many other problems to solve." And Fearless retorts sarcastically, "Ya ya, no sex please, we are Indian." This conversation reveals another set of limits on women's freedom, yet one set by progressive feminists themselves, in this case around pleasure and desire. As Fearless asks the other chat-room participants, "Has sisterhood become an excuse for doing the same old things? You were women who broke away from families, husbands, jobs for what you believed in. But did you do it only to take refuge in another kind of structure? And do you hesitate to question it?"

"Un-limited" thus becomes the film's utopic wish, a feminism that always exceeds its prescribed limits, even those prescribed by feminists themselves. This sense of the unlimited is replicated in the film's form. Structuring a documentary over a scripted chat-room conversation, with interviews occupying the margins, pushes the limits of what is considered a documentary, unsettling what filmmaker Madhushree Datta calls the "triangle: of the filmmaker who collates and presents the facts, the protagonist who is the fact, and the audience who receives the fact" (quoted in Jayashankar and Monteiro 2016, 62). The camera's focus on the computer screen and on the faceless Fearless's hands typing on her keyboard refuses the positivism generally associated with political documentary and reinforces the film's desire to unsettle assumptions and unearth doubts rather than to advance a political agenda based on an established documentary format. But these doubts and questioning are, for Vohra, precisely the prerequisite for a reengagement with feminism. As Fearless asks at the end, "Do you think feminism is something we pointed to and chose? Or was it something that grew a little more each time our minds were not closed and our hearts were open?"

Unlimited Girls presents a feminism that refuses certainty in a film form that refuses "purpose"; thus, both represent new formations of the contemporary. "How do we find," Vohra asks, "a new complex language rich with ideas and questions, as opposed to clarifying a prescribed understanding?" (2008, 421). Art can take us there, not art as a fixed means of advancing an agenda but as "a constant reconsideration and refining of politics. It is a spontaneous form of politics but also vulnerable because of its openness" (422). By presenting these reflections in the technologized space of the chat room, Vohra widens the scope of feminism to include those idioms partially complicit with capitalism. In part this reflects what Jayashankar and Monteiro describe as today's "consumerist context, where buying becomes the mode of expressing the right to choose." Indeed, infinite choice means that "contemporary feminisms need to rethink notions such as agency and access to public space, desire and pleasure" (2016, 107). Rather than dilute feminism, however, these new realms of possibility offer another kind of freedom.[6] This freedom is not devoid of risk—several of the chat-room scenes are interrupted by men cruising for sex—but is a space where new, experimental collectivities might be formed. Thus, in the last lines of the film, Chamkigirl tells Fearless that she sounds "like a true feminist" after all, and Fearless is able to respond, "Thank you for the compliment."

"Sandra from Bandra"

Vohra continues to pursue a feminism at the limits of feminist politics in her later films, specifically asking the question, raised in *Unlimited Girls*, of the role of frivolity, fun, and desire in feminism. At the same time, she continues to unsettle the assumed politics of the documentary form. Her short film *Where's Sandra?* (2006) is almost not a documentary at all. It is an eighteen-minute film structured around its eponymous question, which refers to a phrase, "Sandra from Bandra," used to describe a certain kind of carefree or sexually liberated woman. Bandra is a well-known Mumbai neighborhood with an old and significant Catholic population (hence the name Sandra). The religious reference embedded in the name and the stereotype, which pits supposedly freer Christian women against more conservative Hindus and Muslims, suggests at first that "Sandra from Bandra" is an ethnic epithet or insult against a supposedly promiscuous type. Yet in pursuing the question of where and who Sandra is, Vohra's film demonstrates that the phrase's meaning is in fact ambivalent. In the film, Vohra asks several people what they think the phrase means. Some reiterate the stereotype of Sandra as a "loose" or "chaalu" woman, a "good-time girl." Some of the interviewees whose real names are Sandra recall how they were taunted as children. However, that narrative of Mumbai's ethnic exclusivism—the decline narrative I discuss in Chapter 2—is not the direction the film takes. Rather, as Vohra persists in her questions, she finds that for many women, the phrase "Sandra from Bandra" stands as a locus of desire rather than an insult directed at one ethnic type. Some women, such as a Bandra resident named Lillete, actually claim the name, announcing, "I am a Sandra from Bandra." Another woman asserts that "Sandra has moved to Malad," referring to a newly built-up northern suburb of the city. In both cases, by delinking the two parts of the phrase, these women represent Sandra not as literally a Christian girl from Bandra but as a free-floating term to describe a certain kind of freedom in a world in which women's freedom and desire are seen as illegitimate. The terms used earlier—"chaalu," "good-time girl"—are revealed as inadequate not only because they rely on ethnic stereotypes but also because they refer to types fixed in the mind and already understood, when in reality, as Vohra said in a postscreening discussion of the film one evening in Mumbai, "Sandra" describes the huge space in between the two poles that exist for women, of heroine and vamp.[7]

So, Vohra's narration concludes, after meeting various Sandras, "Maybe Sandra isn't from Bandra anymore. But there's a little bit of Sandra in each of us. In the part of us that likes to throw our heads back and laugh, the part that runs to catch the train to work, the part that likes to swish our skirts when we dance. That's where Sandra is." Like *Unlimited Girls*, this documentary attempts to go beyond language to access the moments of freedom and pleasure that language can only partially capture. The "Sandra" that looks at first like a demeaning epithet thus becomes a word that papers over the gap in language, allowing a space where women can be free from preestablished roles. The film itself is named after a question, suggesting that what is being "documented" in the documentary is not the truth behind Sandra from Bandra but the complex subjectivities of women that can only partially be captured (hence, not naming the film *I've Found Sandra!*).

Moreover, the film rejects the premise that, as one critic writes, "the committed documentary has always been seriously asexual" (Gaines 1999, 90) by considering this question of freedom in the form of an entirely playful text, interspersed with film songs including a remade "Look at Me, I'm Sandra Dee" from *Grease*, filmed using Indian Catholic women. The result is a further questioning of "purpose," that key term for political documentary. Many of Vohra's questions to her interviewees are included in the final edit, and the film moves between song and story, dialogue and narration, rejecting "the dominant system of continuity editing prevalent in global media cultures [that] calls for the ethical spectator-subject to always be centered, keeping him/her spatially and temporally oriented by using seamless editing techniques that maintain the illusion of continuity" (Bandi 2016, 11). The songs in part invoke Bollywood, eliciting the viewer's scopophilia. But scopophilia sits outside the conventional limits of documentary, and thus the film continually defers the viewer's epistephilia or desire to *know*; rather than find truth only in reasoned argument, the film presents truth as residing in affect, turning scopophilia into a form of knowledge. Perhaps this is a mobilization of the disavowal that is at the center of all documentary, which incites "a desire for the real not as knowledge but as image, as spectacle" (Cowie 1999, 19). In film history, this possibility for spectacular incitement "was quickly disavowed. . . . Instead the pleasures of cinema have become defined as narrative and the standard account of film history is that the thrill of the spectacle of actuality in the new form of imaging gave way to the pleasures of narrative in the fiction film and its more successfully illusionistic world" (26). By bringing this repressed aspect of documentary back to the surface, Vohra reclaims as legitimate the potential "immorality" not only of her subjects but of the film medium itself (19).

Documenting Desire

These films show Vohra's persistent interest in the question of how documentary form can accommodate desire. Desire for the most part eludes sociology; as Lee Edelman writes, desire is marked by a "refusal of singularity . . . a resistance to whatever forces would separate the social or the political from the unexpected, and often 'incorrect,' mobilizations of those desires" (2007, 345). In Vohra's terms, desire cannot be "exposed" but only shown or sensed. Thus, Vohra's resistance to a purely sociological interpretation of women's issues in her films is a way of creating space for desire. The tension between documentary and desire appears in different ways throughout her oeuvre. Desire as elusive and potentially productive of new affective communities rubs against "the classical observational style or the juxtapositional activist/political style" of the political documentary (Vohra 2011, 43), in which the "personal, subjective voice" is removed from the frame. Even when representing the political agency and subjectivity of the marginalized subjects of documentary, the observational style privileges a reasoned rather than embodied response as a prerequisite to its political stance.

Vohra's 2007 film *Morality TV aur Loving Jehad: Ek Manohar Kahani* (Morality TV and loving jehad: A thrilling tale) centers around the police attacks on couples that took place in a public park in Meerut in 2005. In the thirty-minute film, Vohra interviews victims of the attacks as well as policemen, lawyers, and members of the media. The complex film works on at least three levels. Most obvious is a critique of the violence and culture of moral policing in which women in a public space are seen as a threat to morality and the public practice of romance is perceived as a threat to Indian/Hindu cultural values. But that level of critique has a light touch. Vohra lets her subjects—including policemen, RSS leaders, and the young women she interviews—speak long after they have or have not answered her questions, and in all of these extended monologues we see the emergence of contradictions,[8] which, when taken together, reveal a common, secondary theme of the film: the insufficiency of language in which to talk about romance, desire, love, and sex in the culture at large. How can we, the film asks, contest the regulation of romantic and sexual activity by society's moral police if we do not have a nuanced vocabulary in which to describe different shades of pleasure, sex, and desire? Third, the film is critical of the media's role in sensationalizing the police action: even as the individuals she interviews struggle to define their own sexual identities and their understanding of the role of sex in society, Vohra represents how the media swooped in to turn the story of the Meerut action into "ek manohar kahani" (a thrilling tale) that packages the whole incident into an object of titillation for the twenty-four-hour news shows' middle-class audiences.

These three critiques are sustained by the film's innovative form that breaks from the conventions of documentary. It refuses to become a blunt instrument of political dissent, which might merely wag its finger at the corporate news media, or another kind of moral policeman, tsk-tsking at the commodification of desire. Vohra intersperses a montage of newspaper headlines describing the Meerut attacks with brief images from a range of other titillating fictions, including film posters, magazine covers, and erotic novels. She thus cuts through the political message of the film by inciting the viewer's own desire. The narrator of the film also sounds like a romance fiction narrator, reveling in the salacious details of the story she is telling. One of the pulp magazines shown is the Hindi magazine *Manohar Kahaniyan* (Titillating tales), another referent of the film's subtitle. *Manohar Kahaniyan*, known for its provocative covers and tawdry crime stories, was founded in 1944 and has a large readership comprising mostly lower-middle-class men whose primary reading language is Hindi. As they circulate in Vohra's film, these images are not easily assimilable into the meaning of the documentary but constitute instead formal excess. As arousing images, moreover, they offer the possibility of pleasure to their viewers and serve as a formal and affective counterpoint to the dominant narrative of moral policing that the film critiques and potentially employs.

Manohar Kahaniyan represents a parallel popular culture largely ignored by the English media and the English-educated middle class. The magazine makes only rare appearances in the English-language news, for instance, in 2011 when it featured a photo of Bollywood star Vidya Balan on a cover as a promotion for her upcoming film *Dirty Picture*. The Bollywood Hungama website reported: "So while travelling in the train don't get surprised to see magazine cover [*sic*] on . . . stalls across India, sporting the picture of leading actress Vidya Balan on the cover of popular Hindi magazine Manohar Kahaniyan. As the magazine is known for 'raunchy' content, the cover only promises the truth behind the film" ("Check Out" 2011). The article's warning to its English-language readers not to be "surprised" to see a Bollywood star adorning this vernacular magazine, even while it acknowledges that the film is also "raunchy," exposes a distinction that is at the heart of the hypocrisy of moral policing: the desires and pleasures of the educated viewers of "good" cinema (which includes a section of quality Bollywood productions along with Hollywood and Indian art cinema) are more legitimate than the desires and pleasures of the mostly male, lower-middle-class Hindi readership of *Manohar Kahaniyan*.

By interspersing images of this particular magazine in her film, Vohra exposes this hypocrisy, the middle-class complicity in moral policing. Even while criticizing the Meerut action and the media's response to it, Vohra refuses to comply with a pious liberalism that would find the media response *distasteful* and thus close down the possibility of desire as a legitimate mode of public discourse. The problem with the media's response is not only that it turned the Meerut attacks into a manohar kahani but more fundamentally that it adjudicated on the question of who are the legitimate subjects of desire: in telling the story of the attack on the lovers in the park as a patronizingly titillating tale for their middle-class viewers, they displace the potential pleasure of the former with the supposedly more legitimate pleasure of the latter. The images from *Manohar Kahaniyan* have the double role of exposing this hypocrisy and, equally importantly, of themselves serving as possible sources of pleasure—as filmmaking that purposefully elicits bodily response in its viewers, enabled by, as Linda Williams writes, "an apparent lack of proper esthetic distance, a sense of over-involvement in sensation and emotion" (1991, 5). By using images from *Manohar Kahaniyan* in service of this bodily relation, Vohra relegitimizes the desire of both the lovers in the park and the readers of this pulp magazine with which they are linked—and in doing so links *her* middle-class viewers with this group through images of a potentially shared desire, creating a new affective community in the process.[9]

This film builds on *Unlimited Girls* and *Where's Sandra?* to represent the complex interplays between pleasure and citizenship in contemporary India. Again, to do so, Vohra must rupture documentary's "performance of a unitary being who had gathered knowledge and then processed it for our benefit into bite-sized bits. It implied, therefore, that the one who was speaking knew more than they were telling you and was somehow qualified to speak thus" (Vohra 2011, 46). By undercutting this style in her films, she reanimates a certain vulnerability of the political, which she sees opposed to the masculinist "pomposity" or "a paternalistic declamatoriness that is constantly employed to denote seriousness—and thereby dominate the political discourse, designing a disguised elitism." Instead, she "presents . . . intimacy or uncertainty" as a prerequisite for the political (51).

"Our Everyday Lives"

In the last several years, Vohra has supplemented these experiments in documentary film with explorations in a range of other media. As she said in an interview, once a particular idea "become[s] a thing, which you can easily settle into," that's the point where she begins to move away from it. "I don't want to be fixed into that thing. So I guess now I am also looking for another kind of language to do these same things but differently" (quoted in Jayashankar and Monteiro 2016, 109). In another interview, regarding her cross-media work, she has said, "The thing is I don't see myself as wearing many hats; it's not different professions for me. It's all born out of an interest in the same set of themes and wanting to talk about different aspects of certain things in the world. . . . Some things work better in film, some in writing. . . . I use whatever form is available to me" (Vohra, n.d.).[10]

This impulse toward formal transgression suggests that Vohra's interest lies in considering the nature of representation itself rather than in gaining expertise in one medium or topic. Her movement across forms gives representation a certain materiality that questions its assumed self-evident status. Representation thickens, in these experiments, from being a transparent vehicle that links intention with text to an act of world making, wherein new political possibilities emerge. Rather than "politics [as] defined and dispensed through an example of an event or a process," these texts show how "the political process exists in everything at all moments" (Vohra, quoted in Kishore 2017, 168). While a documentary such as *Unlimited Girls* played with the idea of alternative temporalities through its incorporation of the chat room, which was filmed in real time, Vohra's weekly newspaper column in *Mid-Day* (2010–present) and her sixty-four-episode reality television show *Connected Hum Tum* (You and I connected; 2013) both take this experiment with real time even further by experimenting with a dilated temporality that replicates the rhythm of the everyday. But these texts are not "merely" representations of everyday time. Rather, they are experiments with representation itself. By presenting a range of topics steadily across time, Vohra transforms the everyday from the undifferentiated time of daily life to a meaningful temporality, imbued with possibility. In this way, both the weekly column and the episodic, naturalistic television series present everyday time as an alternative to the spectacular time through which the Indian present is often understood.

Since 2010, Vohra has written a five hundred–word weekly column for the daily newspaper *Mid-Day* titled "Paro-normal Activity." By the end of

2016, she had published more than 330 columns, and as of late 2018, the column is still ongoing. In her five-year reflection on the project in an April 2015 column, Vohra admits that at first she had been worried she would not have enough to write about every week. But that ended up being far from the case: "I no longer wonder what to write about. I've developed the opposite problem of wanting to write about too many things each week" (Vohra 2015e). Vohra thus presents the formal expansiveness of the weekly column as generating content that is seemingly infinite rather than, as might be expected, progressively diminishing; content is birthed, here, *by form*. Indeed, in these columns Vohra has written about a vast range of topics. She has discussed issues of immediate political importance, such as the passage of the Right of Children to Free and Compulsory Education Act (2010) and the Sexual Assault Bill (2013b), the continuing prevalence of dowry deaths (2014d), and the various bans instituted by the government and right-wing groups. She reports on films she has seen or episodes of television shows— such as *Koffee with Karan*, a celebrity talk show, or *Bigg Boss*, a reality show— that have caught her eye. She offers her thoughts on holidays like Diwali and Women's Day. Sometimes she merely describes something without revealing her opinion on it, such as a column on the newly modernized Mumbai airport (2014f) and one on the cultural politics of the *salwar kameez* (2015a). At other times her viewpoint is clear, as in her column on the sexist rules for dress and behavior in girls' college hostels (2016f) and her criticism of the lynching of Mohammed Iqlakh in 2015 for the alleged crime of eating beef (2015f). The themes of love and sex are increasingly evident, as in her defense of pornography after the government's 2015 ban (2015d) and her criticism of feminists who police other women for not being modern/feminist enough (2015c). There are also topics seemingly unconnected to current events, such as personal experiences with friends or relatives (2017d) and a column on a Google crowdsource to find a dessert that starts with the letter "N" for its Android updates (2016c) (Vohra suggests neyappam, but nougat was chosen). Across these various topics—in their very range—the columns refuse a predetermined sense of what it means to be a progressive or feminist critic and, indeed, *what it means to be a critic at all*. In their variety, Vohra seems to ask: What is important, and what is not, and how does a critic choose? What is relevant, and what is mundane? What issues "count" as crucial questions of our time?

The regularized rhythm of newspaper writing offers what Alex Woloch calls, in the context of George Orwell's weekly column "As I Please," an "underlying temporality of disposability, transience, and contemporaneity," which is in stark contrast to what we might call the more spectacular forms of the novel, feature film, or academic monograph. The insistence of this form on a regularized time opens up the question of relevance to include a broad swath of daily experience and thus "resolutely resists monumentality" (2016, 200, 187). At the same time, this sense of daily experience is always verging on the infinite, the unfinished—on, as Vohra put it, "too many things" (2015e). This tension between the transient and the infinite offers a new relationship between world and text, especially in the context of Vohra's larger politico-representational ambitions. The heterogeneous topics promised by the weekly column refuse predetermined understandings of "relevance," and the columns as a whole go further to present knowledge—whether feminist insight or reflections on pleasure—as inseparable from the multiplicity of daily life; relevance is grounded in the heterogeneity of the world. As Vohra (2015e) wrote, "Writing this column . . . actually makes me feel young because it offers infinite opportunities to learn new things, and helps me be part of a rich ongoing conversation about the political and philosophical meaning of our everyday lives."[11]

We see a similar experiment with representation, politics, and everyday time in the Hindi-language television series *Connected Hum Tum*, which Vohra directed for Zee TV and which aired over three months in 2013. For the show, six Mumbai women were given handheld cameras and trained to use them to record their lives over the course of six months (Duggal 2013). Although called a reality show, *Connected Hum Tum* is striking for its naturalist aesthetics and its marked refusal of the sensationalism usually associated with reality television. While the show was edited, and the participants were advised on how to effectively film their lives, the aesthetic remains highly episodic, refusing a tight plot or narrative drama and interspersing moments in the six lives without overdetermining their meaning.

Hosted by film star Abhay Deol,[12] who opens and closes each episode and sometimes offers commentary, the show enters into the lives of the six women on what is presented as their own terms, in a sprawling set of episodic narratives shown in sixty-four twenty-minute episodes. The women, Preeti, Pallavi, Mahima, Sonal, Malishka, and Madhavi, narrate their own stories, which involve romance, family, profession, and the ups and downs of daily life. Preeti is married and has a young son; she tries to balance her career as a dentist, her love of dancing, and her family life, including a husband who is largely oblivious to her needs and a mother who is emotionally distant. Pallavi works in fashion retail and has just married for the second time; even though her husband means well, she struggles to prove to him that she can work and look after their home. Mahima has come to Mumbai from Meerut to try her luck in films, leaving behind a disappointed family. Sonal is a young, gay woman whose partner, Janooh, has to muster up the courage to come out to her parents. Malishka (the only one of the six who is a public figure) is a successful radio DJ debating whether she ever wants to get married. And Madhavi, the oldest participant, used to be a theater actor, has been divorced for twenty years, and is growing accustomed to living alone, even when her ex-husband gives her hints that he wants to get back together. As we can see, the show's choice of these six women refuses a sociological approach that might instead choose six "types" to represent the diversity of India. The show eschews big themes like class, caste, and religion; rather, there are small, mundane conflicts—Madhavi's ex-husband returns, Malishka breaks up with her boyfriend, and Pallavi decides to quit her job. But these "events" are not the show's focus. Rather, they serve as a sort of scaffolding on which the real matters of everyday life play out.[13]

Each episode has a unifying title and features three of the women whose lives loosely relate to it. Some themes are topical, like marriage or the family. In episode 11, for instance, "Gharwalon ke khatir [For the sake of your family]," Preeti struggles to reconcile her love of belly dancing with her husband's and parents' insistence that she focus more on advancing her dental career.[14] Mahima is thinking of marrying her boyfriend, Gaurav, but her parents think he lacks the status to be her husband. And Sonal worries that when her girlfriend, Janooh, goes home for a family wedding, she will not tell her parents about their relationship and instead will be pressured into getting engaged with a groom of her parents' choice. This episode presents family obligations as a problem for all three women, but in different ways. The connections between the stories are sometimes made by Deol and sometimes by a brief montage sequence at the end, but otherwise they are for the viewer to determine. There are also a few episodes that cover what might be considered more explicit or legible feminist issues, such as episode 12, "Azadi [Freedom]," in which Malishka, Madhavi, and Pallavi reflect on what it means to be free. Pallavi is hounded by her husband, who criticizes her for dressing inappropriately when she goes out, even though she insists that she likes looking nice. Malishka learns how to do more things for herself in her house so that she is less reliant on her mother. Madhavi, who now lives alone, reflects on freedom in positive ways: "I am a very romantic person. Getting wet in the rain, drinking hot tea in the winter. I like these things a lot. But to do these things, do we need a companion? Can't we do these pleasurable things alone? Of course we can. I enjoy it." Episode 16, "Bahu betiyan [Daughters and daughters-in-law]" focuses on relations with parents and in-laws as they are affected by gender, and episode 46, "Working ladies ki prem kahani [Working ladies' love stories]" focuses on the struggles working women undergo to find and manage romantic relationships. Episode 52, "Mera pati mahan [My husband the great]," concerns dealing with difficult husbands.

But these are largely exceptions; by far, most episodes are structured around an affect or attitude rather than an explicit topic or political issue, reflecting the show's investment in excavating the contours of women's everyday lives. Thus, we have episodes on loneliness ("Akeli [Alone]," episode 3), things taking a turn for the worse ("All is well . . . magar [but]," episode 8), traveling ("Happy journey," episode 10), thinking the grass is always greener ("Wah uski kya life hai [What a life she has]," episode 13), longing ("Dooriyan," episode 18), dashed dreams ("Umeedon ki khichdi," episode 22), healing old wounds ("Purana zakhm, naya malham [Old wounds, new ointment], episode 24), new beginnings ("Nayi shuruat," episode 30), trying ("Koshish," episode 35), anger ("Dimaag ki ghanti baj gayi," episode 39), doing things for the first time ("Pehli baar," episode 42), feeling trapped ("Hum phans gaye," episode 43), new intentions ("Naye irade," episode 51), and making decisions ("Faisle," episode 56). These episodes give form to what are ephemeral emotions or sensibilities rather than legible feminist issues. In episode 14, "Tayari [Getting ready]," Madhavi begins to plan for her pregnant daughter's visit, Preeti's son practices for his Annual Sports Day at school, Sonal waits for Janooh to come home from her parents' house, and Pallavi plans a birthday party for her father-in-law to prove she can balance her home and professional life. This episode is particularly interesting because "tayari" marks a nontime, a time of waiting and anticipation, rather than the time of an event itself. Moreover, as Deol says in one of the show's interludes, we the audience are waiting too—to see whether Preeti's son will win his race, whether Janooh will come out to her parents, and whether Pallavi's father-in-law will change his impression of her. The dilated time of the episode rises to the surface as the dominant affect of the show itself. In episode 15, "Koi jeeta, koi hara [Some win and some lose]," Mahima's sister Garima loses a martial arts match at the London Olympics, leading Deol to likewise reflect, "Unlike the Olympics which comes every four years, life's race continues every day [Olympics ki tarah char saal mein nahin, zindagi ki race roz jaari rahi]." Deliberately eschewing the temporality of the event, the show shifts focus to the much less spectacular time of "life's race."

This representation of everyday time is also apparent in episode 4, "Sunday ke funde [The deal with Sundays]," which registers Sunday as a day of rest among an otherwise chaotic week. In this episode, Sonal goes on an outing with her sister Rupa and spends the day wandering the city. Madhavi hosts her daughter, granddaughter, and ex-husband at home and then sits down to watch a movie by herself. Preeti has a plan for an ideal Sunday at home with her family, but her husband spends most of it on the phone and then proceeds to go to the office, leaving her depressed and alone. Sunday captures the tension evident in the show as a whole between the special and the mundane. Madhavi begins to describe her Sunday ritual by saying, "Today I am going to oil my hair [Aaj din bhar tel laga ke rakhaungi]." She continues, "On Sundays there are some special things [Sunday ke din kuch cheezein special hoti hain]" and describes a special kohl she uses on Sundays. But she finds little else to add to that list of what actually makes Sunday special and instead makes a cup of tea and sits on the balcony listening to the sound of the rain falling. Sunday is special, Madhavi's story suggests, *precisely because it is not special*; it is a day when the routine rituals of daily life, which are usually hidden in the folds of what are seen as more important events, fully constitute the day. We see this with Sonal and Rupa as well; they go to Marine Drive not to do anything particular but just to enjoy each other's company.

In this way, like Vohra's documentaries, *Connected Hum Tum* questions the distinctions between the important and the mundane and between women's connections with one another and their particularity. Each episode alternates multiple times between the different women's stories, the cuts sometimes simply occurring and sometimes mediated by Deol, who offers bits of analysis. To take any one woman's story out of this embedded form and trace it from the beginning to the end is possible but would run against the form of the show, which revels in the juxtapositions, sometimes seamless, sometimes jarring, between the different stories and the connections and contradictions they throw up. For instance, in episode 19, "Paisa [Money]," what could easily be a criticism of a new commodity culture becomes a subtle meditation on the relationship between money and women's freedom. Pallavi saves judiciously but is upset when she finds out some of the silverware given to her by her parents has gone missing. Madhavi has financial woes as well but is not sure whether she should take up a job, and she finds that most employers do not want to hire older women anyway. Malishka, by contrast, is doing well in her career and can afford to buy a new car. Rather than condemn commodity culture writ large, we can see how money affects these three women in different ways, suggesting that big questions like money are inextricable from particular circumstances.

The fact that it is the women who are filming their own lives further questions the distinction between the everyday and the special, as the apparent politics of this decision finds itself at odds with the unremarkable way it plays out over the episodes. Indeed, rather than the epistemic revolution that the viewer might expect through this trope of women having control over their own representations, throughout the episodes the six women in fact move in and out from the camera, alternating between being subject and object, character and critic. As Deol narrates in the opening credits, underlining this fluidity of roles, "In one hand they negotiate a camera; in another, their life [Ek haath se camera; doosre se life sambhale]." This suggests that far from the camera being wholeheartedly empowering, it is just one of the things the women have to negotiate. The show is less a reversal of the traditional subject-object binary associated with political documentary than a muddying of that line itself. The fact that the women control the camera, while essential to the story, is not fetishized, and stylistically there are scenes in which the women appear on the screen in a more traditional documentary style—because they have placed the camera on a tripod, on a selfie stick while they walk or drive, or on a table and are speaking directly to it as if it were a person in the room. In these scenes, in which the women represent themselves as object, it is possible to forget the premise of the show, in contrast to the various scenes when it is clear they are holding the camera, as in the case of handheld shots, selfie shots where the camera is being held at arm's range, very close and low-angle shots that suggest the camera is in a bag or otherwise close to the body, and mirror shots where we see a reflection of the character filming herself. This range of shots presents a routinization of the act of filming, refusing the idea that the reversal of the gaze *simply* overturns dominant power relations.

Vohra has written elsewhere about her frustration with the progressive documentarian's paradigm of simply handing cameras to subaltern or underrepresented people and making that the subject of a documentary:

> There is no denying the first surge of power that comes from being able to write, draw, take a picture, or record a voice. But can our process of change really be suspended forever in that poster moment? With due respect to the people who pioneered the placing of technology in the hands of the underprivileged, we have to move on. It is still surprisingly in vogue to hand cameras to women, children, and other underprivileged groups as if they were a tabula rasa, noble savages whose truth will automatically emerge. (2008, 422)

Connected Hum Tum reflects the skepticism of this "poster moment" supposedly born when a marginalized person gets access to a camera (Frota 1996).[15] Rather than a radical epistemic rupture, *Connected Hum Tum* gives us a continual movement, a blurring of subject-object and inside-outside through a constant crossing and recrossing between them. At times, a character feels empowered by holding the camera; she gets to author her own story. Yet at other times, she simply wants to be filmed; she wants her testimony and emotions recorded by this technology. The show's empowerment lies not just in control over the camera but in the characters' control over *this movement*, refusing a one-way teleology from object to subject or victim to agent. By the end of the thirty-two hours, little substantially has changed for the six women, and there is a moment when the viewer might ask, What was the point of it all? The series ends not with monumental change but with small adjustments, signaling a future of continuing adjustments. Malishka might have warmed to the idea of marriage, but it is not clear whether she is going to accept Kirti's proposal. Preeti seems determined to take charge of her own life, but it is not clear whether her husband, Sanju, will actually change. Mahima wants to stay and continue her career in Mumbai, but it is possible she might succumb to her parents' pressure and move back home. In none of these stories do we get dramatic change. Clearly, what has been televised is not a revolution in a person's life, in patriarchal social structures, or in dominant viewing practices. What has been televised are many small transgressions of form itself.

"How to Find Indian Love"

The text you write must prove to me *that it desires me.*
—ROLAND BARTHES, *The Pleasure of the Text*

Vohra's interest in various topics surrounding love and desire have coalesced in the last several years in a number of experiments with representing love beyond the documentary format. One of these is a weekly column in *Mumbai Mirror* called "How to Find Indian Love," in which she explores questions of love and desire in India today outside simplistic narratives that attribute increasing discussions of sexuality in India to the influence of the West. As in her films, throughout the columns we see a resistance to seeing love as a sociological phenomenon rather than an episteme in its own right.[16] She wants love to guide thought rather than be subsumed into a theoretical paradigm determined in advance. For instance, in her columns on the use of dating apps such as Tinder, which opened to the Indian market in 2013, she shows that there is no one-to-one connection between these new apps and new forms of love, and she pointedly refuses the commodification narrative that, as Chapter 2 discusses, is so often used to explain the contemporary Indian city: "People use dating apps in multiple ways. Some do it to kill time at traffic lights, others, to make friends. A few, even to network. Some are looking for love, some for an unending series of mini affairs, extramarital or regular, some for validation, some for someone with enough shoes to orgasm into and others for they don't quite know what" (Vohra 2017b). This heterogeneity of sexual practices is the formal impetus for Vohra's own formal heterogeneity; she looks at these different desires with a nonmoralistic, "loving eye" ("March on Women" 2016). This mode of engagement is explicitly different from *analysis*, which, she says, is more limited: "Perhaps it is only colonisers, who love anthropological catalogues, and corporates, who love excel sheets, who expect this [heterogeneity] to be otherwise. They prefer subjects and consumers to behave in homogenous and hence controllable ways. The world of sex and desire is radical precisely because it defies this, pulses with a polyphony and libidinal caprice, upends categories and alters norms" (Vohra 2017b).

Taking on these themes in yet another medium, in 2016 Vohra's production company Parodevi Pictures launched a multimedia web project called Agents of Ishq (Agents of love, http://agentsofishq.com). The website makes use of striking, colorful visuals and offers fiction, music, quizzes, poems, and news stories with the intention, in the words of the website, to "give sex a good name." As she did in 2002 in *Unlimited Girls*, Vohra identifies a problem in the way sex is always associated with violence against women and has since explained that in the wake of the infamous Nirbhaya rape case in 2012 that laudably turned the country's attention to the pervasiveness of sexual violence in India, this association of sex with risk and violence has only intensified, even among feminists. Thus, "giving sex a good name" is an attempt to begin a conversation on sexuality that offers a proliferation of positive stories about sexuality, not solely ones that elicit fear and highlight risk.

There is an educational element to Agents of Ishq, collected in a section called "Necessary Funde" and containing quizzes such as "Are You a Genital Genius? How Much Do You Know about Male Genital Organs?" and articles on sexual hygiene ("Gyaan [wisdom] from your Gynae") and how to find a good sex educator. But it would be misleading to say that the primary goal of the website is educational. Rather, the layout and overall playful design suggest that sex education cannot be seen apart from the worlds of pleasure and desire. Education means not only warnings about sexual health but also an expansion of the very vocabulary in which we talk about sexuality. This is central to the Agents of Ishq project, underlining the idea of representation as a generative process rather than only reflective of already existing realities. Features on the website such as "Is pyaar ko main kya naam doon! [What name should I give to this love!] Words people use for masturbation" (Agents of Ishq 2017); and the results of a penis survey that recorded "things that people call their penis" and included a wide assortment of terms in Hindi, English, and other Indian languages (Sen and Vohra 2017) are attempts to collect the wide vocabulary that people in India have to talk about practices that are not much discussed in the public domain, to give a representational thickness to these practices—both to legitimize them and to record the rich vernacular vocabulary already existing around them. Agents of Ishq has likewise constructed a "kiss map" in which the word for "kiss" in

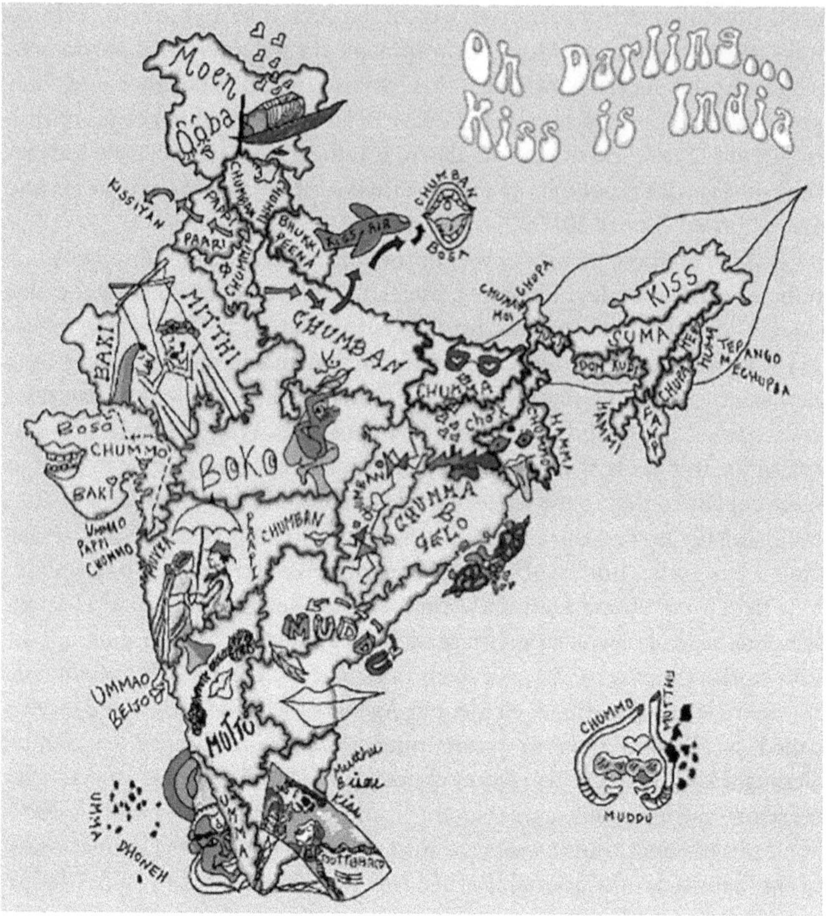

Figure 6.1 Kiss map, by Paroma Sadhana, curated by Paromita Vohra. © Agents of Ishq.

different Indian languages is represented visually (Figure 6.1). The masturbation, penis, and kiss vocabularies register an active attempt to collect, record, and indeed inspire a new vernacular of sex that emphasizes creativity and refuses the Indian tradition–Western influence binary. The contemporaneity of these projects lies in their inability to be contained within any existing category or form.

Agents of Ishq's interest in vernacular sexualities is evident in its choice of stories as well, which include coming-out narratives, experiments with practices such as sex toys and BDSM (bondage, dominance, and sadomasochism), queer explorations, and humorous testimonies about sex and sexual awakening. The orientation here is toward organic exploration and lack of judgment rather than the use of categories or already-established labels. Vohra (n.d.) recounts in an interview that one of her favorite pieces published on the site involves "a guy from a small town" who had little to no vocabulary to talk about his queer sexuality:

> The way he describes it is that he started having sex with men when he was quite young. He said every time I'd have sex with this one boy I would dream afterwards of a woman doing to me what that boy had done and I didn't know what this dream is, he didn't know what BDSM is, he'd never heard of it. And then he said I had a friend like a best girl friend who used to like mildly insult me and there was that zing but I didn't know what it was. And then one day we were playing dumb charades and I had to mime *Joru ka ghulaam* and I bent down in front of her and I suddenly felt this feeling fill me up, this is what I am.[17] When I read that I was like, oh my god this is like magic about how the mind shows you images of what you desire. I found it so powerful to discover how magical nature is.

What compels Vohra about this story is a queerness felt and practiced but not articulated in any predefined terms. This is opposed to concepts of ideal masculinity and femininity already fixed in language. For instance, Vohra (n.d.) feels that some Indian men are getting pushed into narrow definitions of masculinity based on models imported from global popular culture: "Straight men are not willing to talk about sex. I don't believe it was always like that, I think regular Indian men did engage in poetry and philosophy. . . . But now we are in the grip of one infantilised Americanised notion of what it is to be a man." In these antithetical cases, a restricted vocabulary around sexuality becomes an impediment to its flourishing, while a large, heteroglossic and multilingual vernacular around sexuality opposes that normativization.

The web interface is an ideal medium for representing this new expanding vocabulary for sex and sexuality, as it is never singular or fixed but continually shaped by new perspectives, stories, languages, and terminologies. As Jayashankar and Monteiro write regarding the recent "explosion of documentary-inspired, often collaborative media production on the web[,] the emergence of online interactive archives is an interesting development that redefines the role of the maker and the user, and the nature of the text" (2016, 226). In addition to content added by Vohra and her team, the orientation of the web interface is geared toward open fora such as a "Sexy Saturday Playlist" curated by different contributors and poems, illustrations, and stories by different authors and artists. Content changes regularly, so each time a user opens the site, she experiences a different set of stories and images. There is a multifariousness to this kind of representation of sexuality that plays a legitimizing function, steering deliberately clear of any moralizing or normativizing and offering multiplicity as the form of sexuality more broadly. It offers a utopic forum where people are free to talk about their sexuality and also a utopic instantiation of formal openness itself.

Consent is something Vohra has been interested in throughout her career, and on Agents of Ishq she takes up the concept more directly. Because consent is a key legal concept to adjudicate whether a sexual act counts as rape, mainstream feminism has worked to narrow the idea of consent to account for contexts such as marriage, where marital rape can occur even where consent is assumed (Santhya et al. 2007; S. Basu 2011, 201). Activists emphasize that it is often difficult to "distinguish genuine from coerced consent, particularly where coercion takes the form of subtle and implicit threats"; thus, "even if a woman says 'yes,' there remains the difficulty of determining whether the circumstances in which she expressed consent invalidated the consent. Coercion can take many forms" (Kazan 1998, 28, 41). In response to this narrowing of consent into an ever-smaller space by a well-intentioned feminist legal activism, Vohra attempts to open up the meaning of consent to thinking about female desire and pleasure in affirmative terms.

To this end, Vohra has directed a *lavni* video on consent for the Agents of Ishq site (Agents of Ishq 2016). Lavni is a genre of popular, erotic Marathi theater from the seventeenth century associated with female sexuality (Rege 2002, 1040). Vohra's video features well-known lavni performer Shakuntala Nagarkar and Marathi actor Megha Ghadge. Their performance complicates mainstream feminist discussions on consent by raising the question of women's sexual desire. Their dialogue expresses the difficulty women have conveying the complexity of consent to their partners, when no means no, but sometimes, also, yes means yes. The refrain of the lavni is "He didn't get my point!" referring to the significant potential for miscommunication in the giving of consent. Shakuntala begins by relating that she met a man and let him walk her home but then did not allow him to come into her house. The man interprets this as unfair and begins to stalk her, waiting outside her house to give her gifts. Megha then tells of an opposite experience: She shook off the advances made by her date, even though she secretly wanted him to continue. He stopped and she was disappointed. Shakuntala interrupts Megha to say, "What do you mean, he didn't get your point? You said no, right?" to which Megha responds, "Yes, but I meant yes in my heart. . . . If I'd said yes, he'd think I'm easy and cheap." Shakuntala then turns to the camera and says, "Say yes only when you mean yes. Say no and it means no." And for everything in between? "Then you say, 'Maybe!' . . . The guy who gets [maybe] is a hero. If he doesn't get it, then zero!"

The idea of *maybe* reveals a gap in mainstream discussions of consent, which hinge on the importance of no meaning no. Maybe opens up a space of possibility where female desire is allowed to flourish even in the face of risk and where female pleasure is rendered legitimate. As Vohra (2017e) explains elsewhere, "Consent isn't only about rape and assault but the entire universe of desire and a life of choice." Yet "the vast spectrum of pleasure and erotic activity that lies between the poles of marriage and rape, exists mostly at the far edges of our public discussion" (Vohra 2013b). The short video ends when Shakuntala meets a new man, to whom she says "Maybe" and who responds, "I can wait for you, baby." The healthy sexual relationship is thus found not in utter and total agreement about sex but in the precarious concept of "maybe," which, the film suggests, is a space of both safety and pleasure. Like the kiss map and the vocabulary around sex, the sexually open form of the lavni is another instance of Vohra's investment in vernacularizing conversations about sexuality, in this case by tracing lines of continuity between vernacular art forms and contemporary questions of women's choice.

Crossing the significant divide between sex education and pornography, Agents of Ishq presents a vernacular erotics that illuminates a set of contemporary issues around masculinity, sexuality, women's desire, and pleasure while never resorting to a sociological stance that remains outside the issues it unearths. The multifarious website, with its proliferation of authors, genres, terminologies, and perspectives, and its occasional investment in eliciting arousal, together constitute a new kind of textuality, one with its own "pleasure." Its erotics in part emerge from its embrace of contradiction and its "abrasions," which encourage the reader to "read on, . . . skip, . . . look up, . . . dip in again" (Barthes 2011, 12). Through this formal excess, it deliberately positions itself against a kind of dry sociological textuality that Roland Barthes finds in the "prattling text . . . [the] frigid text" (5), in which the reader is positioned as resolutely *outside* rather than as a potential object of "seduction" (6). In contrast, in Agents of Ishq the reader is constantly invited in to partake in the pleasures the text offers. Agents of Ishq thus stands as a supplement to the aesthetics of real time seen in *Connected Hum Tum* and the *Mid-Day* columns. Oscillating, doubling, expanding, breaking apart, and reconstituting—these form the basis of the creative practice that is at the heart of Vohra's sociology of the contemporary, which is a *contemporary sociology*, born of pleasure and shorn of the distance that constitutes a conventionally critical imaginary.[18]

The Critic and the Fan

Megha's date scene in the lavni was set in a movie theater where the couple was watching the 1994 Bollywood film *Kabhi Haan Kabhi Naa*, whose title translates as "Sometimes Yes, Sometimes No" and thus is a humorous way to link Bollywood with the question of consent. As the often filmi aesthetics of Vohra's documentaries demonstrate, along with her use of Bollywood songs as sound track in *Connected Hum Tum*, the countless film references on Agents of Ishq, and her extensive writings on film in her columns and interviews, Bollywood is for Vohra another vernacular form that is a key yet largely unacknowledged source of pleasure and desire in contemporary India. As earlier chapters show, post-1990s Bollywood is criticized by intellectuals and progressives for its melodramatic and populist politics and its heightened emotional and romantic register.[19] But it is precisely for its fervent faith in love that Vohra finds Bollywood so rich as a source of vernacular theorizations of desire, outside the narratives of traditional Indian prudishness—"Ya ya, no sex please, we are Indian"—and of Westernized sexual immorality. She is critical of many things about Bollywood, including its insider culture, sexism, and self-hype.[20] But she still finds it a promising alternative not only to a rational civil society but also to a frigid criticism. As she wrote in a 2017 *Mid-Day* column, "It's not as if I always enjoy each Hindi film I have seen. I frequently find some very badly made and even a little bizarre. Yet, there are elements and tropes, patterns and pleasures that popular films bring us which reveal something of the emotional life of our society, some implicitly [*sic*] or nascent rhythms, that I think are worth thinking about. Sometimes I also discover beauty and insight, in places we were conventionally told it does not exist" (Vohra 2017c).

This desire to unearth possibilities for pleasure and desire in unaccustomed places has led Vohra to offer a very different perspective on contemporary popular film than most critics. For instance, one recent trend has been for critics to praise films that move away from Bollywood conventions and are more realist and downplayed in their aesthetics and storytelling. The general sense is that these films are broadening Hindi cinema and moving it away from its tried-and-true formulas—hence the term *hatke* cinema, or something a little different (Dwyer 2012). However, Vohra is largely critical of this trend. For instance, *Dum Laga Ke Haisha* (2015) is a recent realist film about a couple brought together by an arranged marriage; the woman is obese, and the man first thinks he cannot love her for that reason but eventually does. This is the kind of story praised by critics for representing love more realistically than conventional Bollywood and also for including stories of nonnormative body types rather than an idealized female figure. Vohra is on board with these two features; however, she also criticizes the movie for "seem[ing] to promise something unconventional . . . [but] provid[ing] a peculiarly defeated answer to th[e] question" of "What is love?" Even when making a case for the couple's romance, she writes, "[the film] provides not even one image, leave alone scene, of these two people, which is sensual, sexy, romantic, lush, joyful, tender, intimate, fun or beautiful" (2015b). The film is *politically* committed to representing their nonnormative relationship but, in taking a strong political stance, ends up taking all the sensuality out of its representation. "This isn't just a failure of cinematic imagination. It's a lack of belief in love and sex as strong transformative forces in our lives" (Vohra 2015b). Thus, even when younger filmmakers try to do something different within Hindi cinema, they end up "taking [themselves] too seriously" and subscribing to "the manipulative pieties of the art/commerce and politics/entertainment divide" (Vohra 2014b).

In contrast, Vohra is full of praise for the 2017 hatke film *Anarkali of Arrah*, the story of an erotic dancer in Bihar who takes revenge on a policeman who sexually assaulted her. This is also a realistic, more gritty representation than what is conventionally found in Bollywood, but what Vohra (2017e) likes about it is that despite being realistic, it is also seductive, in the protagonist's "raunchy songs, her blingy cold-shoulder kameezes, her full-lipped, curvy hipped presence, her friends with benefits relationship with her manager, the fact that his wife runs off with the milkman—all of it is an evocation and affirmation of the naturalness of erotic life, seeing sex not as an exception, but as a part of life, and Indian culture, in myriad big and small ways." Even though the film is about sexual assault, it does not take a prudish tone but offers female desire as legitimate, even in a world overshadowed by sexual violence. This cultivation of pleasure is, for Vohra, even more important than the politics of the plot; it is the former that compels her as a critic: "I think I cried [after seeing it] because, as a woman, if I express dissatisfaction or critique of a so-called women's issue film, I am made to feel churlish and demanding, by acquaintances, friends and strangers. 'Arre, at least it did this' people will say. I think I cried because I realised somewhere I had begun to believe this was my lot—in movies, life and love—this kanjoos [stingy], male-appeasement version of consent, not a full-bodied, full-blooded celebration of pleasure and consent" (2017e). Anarkali "is preoccupied not with sexual trauma but living a life she loves. . . . I cried with relief that I didn't have to be cravenly grateful for a patriarch pinkly saying 'No Means No' (though sure, it's good). . . . At the end, as a woman who loves art and red lipstick and romance, as a woman who loves to live, I wanted to stand up and say Yes! Yes! A million times, on my own terms, Yes! That's also what we mean when we say consent" (2017e).[21]

In addition to rethinking consent, here we also have the expression of the critic's own emotional investment and desire in the film she is watching—something that, as we see in Agents of Ishq, infuses the text with its own erotics. But here, the erotics appears in criticism, which is the most frigid of the genres. The passage is not just a description of Vohra's emotional response to the film; it *is* her emotional response, complete with the climactic interjections of "Yes! Yes!" We have a doubling here, whereby the moment when the film invites the critic inside its world of desire (a moment that never occurs in *Dum Laga Ke Haisha*) becomes the very moment the critic invites her reader inside her world of desire, rupturing the standard distances between film and its object and criticism and its object.

We see this merging of the critic and the fan throughout Vohra's Bollywood writings, in which her perspective is always slightly at odds with prevailing critical opinion. For instance, she has defended Rakhi Sawant, a dancer, model, and Bollywood actor known for her sexy persona, outspoken views, and outrageous actions and largely looked down on by critics and middle-class audiences. When Sawant arrived at an event in a dress plastered with images of the prime minister, she was criticized as vulgar, but for Vohra (2016e), it is precisely her absurdity that makes her so interesting: "[Her] wholly artificial, exaggerated vulgar, ribald style, which has no moral or instructive aims . . . [and which] completely undermines pomposity and self-seriousness . . . through flamboyant theatricality . . . highlights the absurdity in reality. . . . If you take the absurdity in her show seriously, you are the one who looks ridiculous." Vohra (2016g) has also defended outspoken Bollywood star Kangana Ranaut, criticized by the press for the "untidiness of her private life" and for making "bad boyfriend choices." Stars for Vohra are neither the gods they are imagined by their fans nor the regular people often dismissed by critics; she does not seek to tame or rationalize the excess of the star. As she writes, "The marvellous thing about an artist is that even if she somehow represents the gestalt of the time, she is also so much more than that, suggesting through persona, a way to be. An actor's body, presence, the look in their eye function in an almost primeval way, affecting us physically, sensually, infusing us with the desire to be an emanation of the idea they represent" (Vohra 2014b). This embrace of their potential superhumanness completely explodes the secular rationality of most film criticism. For Vohra, this is what it means to be both fan and critic.

Nowhere is this clearer than in her expressed fandom of Bollywood superstar Shah Rukh Khan, known for his romantic roles and also derided by many critics and intellectuals for his formulaic and cheesy on-screen persona—unlike, for instance, the more serious demeanor of Aamir Khan (a star whom Vohra [2016b] deems appealing only "if you're vegan"). But it is precisely for this reason that Vohra prefers Shah Rukh Khan (often referred to by his initials, SRK). She argues that "to track the on-screen journey of SRK is to track the journey of a certain middle-class India, which has not partaken of Nehruvian India's structures for mobility . . . those who[se] . . . entrepreneurial energies, frustrated by older systems, took centre stage in the new regime of liberalisation." But that, she concedes, might be "too literal" an interpretation: "Perhaps, it is more fruitful to understand SRK as one does a dream—a mixture of the explicit, reflecting social and economic currents, and the implicit, a mix of unconscious feelings that infects our consciousness and transforms it." For a new generation of Indians

> [SRK] gave us someone to love . . . someone to love our way, someone to long for, someone to conceivably be. . . . The moral compass SRK provided was love. . . . This was not simply romantic love, but a concept that develops individual ethical frameworks, allowing us to look at the opposition with loving eyes, that takes others into consideration. . . . The characters SRK played find their better selves through love, using it to find new resolutions and solutions. (Vohra 2016k)

In this kind of masculinity, there is room for women beyond "be[ing] objectified or uplifted by men. . . . In this universe, a woman with ambitions is not weird, selfish or unfeminine, but natural and desirable. She is not domesticated by marriage but partnered through fun and sexual passion. . . . With this fantasy of a passionate yet light romance, SRK has pleasured and ruined a generation of women, while making them open to a whole other kind of man" (Vohra 2016k). When pressed in an interview on her love of SRK, Vohra responds: "SRK is like a catalysing *rasa* that exists in the world, that makes *you* feel sexy. . . . He is the mechanism that turns you on, not necessarily for him, for you, to experience desire. How many things in this fucking world are made for women to experience desire? You tell me. You can count them on one hand" (Vohra, n.d.).

Several scholars and journalists have written about fandom in Indian cinema (Dickey 2007; Srinivas 2002; Larkin 1997), but what distinguishes Vohra's take is how she writes herself simultaneously as fan rather than as a distanced sociologist of fandom in general. This is again apparent in an article on the Pakistani-born Bollywood star Fawad Khan. Vohra (2016b) begins the piece by affirming that she is still loyal to SRK, even though recently he "seems to have turned his gaze elsewhere. . . . But meanwhile, who is a woman to love if she wants to feel the pure pleasures of lust along with a feeling that she could actually talk to the object of lust if they were stuck on a desert island together? Enter Fawad Khan." According to her, Fawad Khan has many of the same qualities as SRK: "He is comfortable sharing space with women characters. . . . He seems comfortable being a character rather than replaying an archetype, which makes him feel accessible, touchable, real." But it's not just that:

> He's hot with those soft brown eyes and spiky eyelashes and slow smile. You might almost never notice His Hotness until you suddenly do and then you notice little else. . . . His eyes have both mystery and mischief and many other things you could spend a while observing. . . . His manner is composed, controlled as if he keeps his own counsel and is in no hurry to decide anything or show you what he's all about. Like he's in no hurry for you to decide and is totally secure giving you some space. If you matched with Fawad on Tinder, he would not ask you, what are you looking for on Tinder? He'll be perfectly capable of taking his time to figure it out with you. His delicate beauty lends vulnerability and at the same time he seems absolutely together, able to take care of himself, not asking you to be his mother or be like his mother, not blaming you for his broken heart, not trying to[o] hard to impress—in other words, he seems grown-up.

Most writings on Fawad Khan focus on the fact that he is a Pakistani actor in Bollywood and thus represents headway in overcoming the two nations' enmity, despite a recent politically motivated ban on Pakistani artists working in India ("Fawad Khan's Statement" 2016); but for Vohra, this is the *least* interesting fact about him. The first line of this article begins: "Let me just say this very simply, OK, without any culture studies costume and Aman ki Asha accessories" (Aman ki Asha is a left-leaning group that advocates for peace between India and Pakistan; Vohra 2016b). In this comment, preconceived ideas of both progressive politics and cultural analysis are discarded from the outset, clearing the way for a new kind of engagement with contemporary culture outside these dominating discourses, one predicated on not only female desire but also the *desiring critic*. As we see in Vohra's comments about *Dum Laga Ke Haisha*, for Vohra, political righteousness does not translate into the ability to represent love or desire; in fact, it might impede it. Here, too, the question of India-Pakistan peace is discarded for a more libidinal engagement across a different kind of border.

What does it mean for the critic to subject herself in this way in her writings? Criticism tends to operate on an established but rarely articulated distance between the writer and the object of her representation. We can see how in Barthes's terms, this distance is generative of a textual frigidity. But what if criticism were to come from and enter *inside* the object itself? It would dismantle, as Vohra's works so often do, the assumed hierarchies between writer and critic, and between object and observer, just as SRK and Fawad Khan open up space in their films for a multiplicity of desires. This is the general modality of Vohra's oeuvre as a whole. Her writings on Bollywood do not ask to be read as merely commentary but as a kind of submission or radical humility. By putting her own libidinal self on the line, as it were, she presents the object anew. Desire becomes the prerequisite for criticism rather than something criticism can merely explain.

Inside and Out

What does it mean to be both practitioner and critic, lover and writer? What borders are transgressed in this practice? To cross these divides is to inhabit what George Orwell called the "semi-sociological . . . half-in and half-out" (Woloch 2016, 159). Alex Woloch explains that Orwell's formulation refers to "criticism [that] is only reluctantly or intermittently 'sociological'" (145), thus asking, "What are the stakes of a *purely* sociological approach to literature, or of a 'literary criticism' that fails to be sociological altogether?" (146). It gestures to the broader question of the relationship of literature to the world, something I try to ask throughout this book. Woloch writes, "What form of writing can adequately comprehend history, and, in moments of political crisis and tumult, what purchase can writing have?" (146). Vohra's response is not a more rigorous sociology or an intensified drive to capture reality in language. Rather, she creates forms of representation whose relationships to their objects are always shifting—in Woloch's words, "fram[ing] the self that is both at stake and at work . . . as particularly fragile and insecure: someone staring across a boundary separating inside from outside, self from world" (156).

These questions underlie Vohra's oeuvre, which represents the world and is always on the verge of representing representation itself. At a presentation on Agents of Ishq in Mumbai in May 2016, Vohra spoke of the "space between high art and low art [as] 'just art.' You can't make a film and say, 'This is an art film.' It doesn't work like that" (Vohra 2016a). Refusing the logic of high versus low, Vohra also makes a claim about the relationship of critic to writer. While presenting her own creative work at this event, she also opens up a space of critical adjudication, where the critic is called on to determine a film's status in partnership with the filmmaker. Vohra is constantly interested in this space where artist meets critic, where the two overlap and interact, generating new relations and, potentially, new forms of critical art. In her reflections on five years of her *Mid-Day* column, she wrote,

> I agonised because when we set out on any creative enterprise people intone "insights" about what "readers," "audience" and "public" like/accept/want. It implies your [the critic's] thoughts are not sufficient. You should somehow know what others think and echo that. You should preferably say it in a grave, dadi-wala [bearded], authoritative way or people won't take you seriously. . . . Truth, though, is an ever-expanding understanding of that reality. By writing what I feel, without that venerable vibe, trying to do it as fairly and professionally as I can with as much respect for those I disagree with, as love for those I agree with, I've learned readers/people/audiences are not a frozen entity. Many different ways of thinking prosper in the world. (Vohra 2015c)

Here we see that Vohra's criticism is born from the world and refuses an authoritative stance over it. In another column about political change, she asks, "Maybe the question is not only how do we intervene in change, but can we simply intervene in change? Because this idea sometimes comes from an imagination in which we are outside the world, looking on it from above, in a position to change it. The inescapable truth though, is that we are part of this world, living and creating energies, words and thoughts that generate change" (Vohra 2014a).

This chapter brings us back to the question of the critic's relationship to the text she reads, one that arises throughout the book and in my own readings as well. Vohra's recent essay on Chetan Bhagat's novel *Half Girlfriend* takes us full circle, as it allows us to merge an analysis of the Indian contemporary with an analysis of literary criticism—or, as Woloch writes of Orwell, to shift "from an object outside of itself to writing that is analogous to itself" (2016, 174). Unlike most critics, Vohra does not set out to excoriate Bhagat but reads *Half Girlfriend* with a loving eye, even if she is generally critical of him. She reads him, in a way, as a fellow writer. There are things she likes about the novel, such as its title that seems to gesture to "those might-have-beens, those ambivalent, ambiguous, hesitant relationships that are there, yet not quite there" (Vohra 2017a). She likes the first part of the story with its "experience of uncertain love." But ultimately, she feels, Bhagat cannot follow through on these precarious sensibilities. Rather, the book ends up subscribing to rigid distinctions, between men and women, urban and rural, English and bhasha. Moreover, it is "earnest" and "sanctimonious." The novel teaches rather than engages; there is no ambiguity. Bhagat's openness to the contemporary, Vohra suggests, is largely a ruse, as it is quickly contained before it can become un-limited. He writes, in the end, from the outside, even when he claims to be invested in entering his characters' worlds.

In contrast, her approach to reading is open and unfinished, even in relation to a text like Bhagat's. Regarding her own process in writing this essay on *Half Girlfriend*, she reflects:

> I started writing a diary of reading a book [as I was reading it]. . . . I could see that [*Half Girlfriend*]'s written like a very dull three act structure that everyone adheres to, the orthodoxy of commercial script writing. I also wrote my diary in three acts. So it became in a sense a dance with Chetan Bhagat's book and I thought that was important to do because you know whatever my critique of it should happen on the terms of that work. There is no point of critiquing something because that thing is not like you. What's the point of that[,] right? (Vohra, n.d.)

In an interview, Vohra has spoken about her films in similar terms: "As I see it, my film is an invitation to dance. I lead and ask my audience to join me by following the rhythm I suggest. However, there is no foregone conclusion to this dance" (quoted in Kishore 2017, 173). Once again, Vohra's works consider what it means to represent the contemporary. The dance she describes offers a radically new imagination of engagement between critic and object of study that implies partnership and even desire: the intensity of two bodies joined in embrace. The dance does not have to come from perfect harmony with the object, as it is clear she does not necessarily like *Half Girlfriend*, but it does have to remain open to the possibility of love. What kind of criticism might emerge from this image of dance and the possibility of love? It is not solely a question for the Indian contemporary but also for literary criticism itself. What relations between critic and text are possible in our current state of critical culture? What energies attract us to our subjects, other than the ones of a potentially frigid critical theory? What bonds tie us to the worlds we study? Are we just analyzing those worlds from the outside, or do we also live in them? Can our criticism be more than just negative; can it involve the creation of new images, the imagining of new worlds?

Vohra's constant probing of the luminous insides of the objects of her study offers a model of criticism that presents the contemporary as a space of possibility, that also is itself contemporary, and that I attempt to take inspiration from as well. Rather than criticize, for instance, the representation of women as heroines or vamps or the prudishness around sexuality, from a position outside these representations, Vohra has spent her quarter-century-long career actually offering alternatives, using her art to participate in the collective effort of creative world making. What does it mean to critique, and what does it mean to *practice*, and why have we placed the two on opposing ends of our conceptual imaginaries? It is not only that the contemporary demands new critical categories, but, ideally, the contemporary must infuse those critical categories so that the relationship between criticism and its object is continually called into account. This is a criticism of dance rather than distance. As Vohra said in an interview, "I feel it is the job of an artist to recognize the rhythms around her, put them into a pattern, and make meaning out of it" (quoted in Kishore 2017, 169). This is not an art or a criticism that transcends the world but one that is *in* and *of* the world. Thus, it will continually transform itself as the world around it changes and will remain perennially unfinished. Rather than await its completion, we might embrace this quality and try to find in its unfinished nature glimpses of a better tomorrow.

Afterword

Contemporaneity's Futures

aromita Vohra's work as critic and practitioner raises the question of the continuing role of the critic in the Indian contemporary and in the future of literary criticism more generally. I end this book by briefly gesturing to three directions in which we might turn to follow through on the argument I lay out here. The first regards the political possibilities opened up by the Indian contemporary. Recent electoral victories around the world have shown us how sharply divided we are along political lines. But I hope this book might allow us to rethink the literary and cultural production of the present outside the simple rhetoric of the right-wing turn. Thus, seemingly apolitical practices and forms such as loitering (Chapter 2), social media and candlelight vigils (Chapter 3), love and desire (Chapters 1 and 6), and the novel's ontological turn (Chapter 5) might be understood as open questions about political futures rather than lamented as symptoms of decline. While some authors I discuss, such as Chetan Bhagat and Manu Joseph, have taken assertive, conservative stances on contemporary issues, seeing these figures in continuity with other more tentative forays beyond the preexisting frameworks of liberal thought emphasizes a larger cultural trend toward political experiment, in contrast to what some critics have labeled simply the demise of progressivism.

This has significance beyond India. The recent debate between Ta-Nehisi Coates and Cornel West (S. Sharma 2018) over the best vision for African American futurity demonstrates a similar culture war, with progressives largely split between standard, inherited paradigms of political struggle formed around abstract figures like the worker and the refugee and a new, what we might call *creative* progressivism, embodied by Coates, who is interested in crafting new imaginaries responding to new times rather than clinging to the old ones for fear of losing ground. The censuring of Coates by progressives seems an anticontemporary gesture similar to what I describe here, which reflects an interest in policing what counts as progressive thought that has the potential to inhibit the recognition of new, unfinished political imaginaries.

The second and related role of the critic has to do with our ability to tell alternative stories. Recently, the president of the United States deemed significant parts of the world "shithole countries." His comment garnered a good amount of criticism, but it simultaneously revealed how little vocabulary we have to develop counternarratives in which to describe the majority of the world that lies outside the West. While the Internet and media platforms such as Netflix and YouTube make it easier than ever to watch and engage with contemporary international media and cultural production, and it is possible to travel to many different countries and shop for books there, how many Americans or American academics are actually doing so? While the liberal arts are growing in other parts of the world and shrinking in the United States, how many of our graduate students actually envision careers for themselves abroad? There is an imperative, then, for us to create new accounts of the global contemporary, to imagine a vibrant, complex, and rich vocabulary for describing the present outside the chauvinism of the current White House. And where those accounts do exist, we need to be more attentive to them rather than, as in the case of the *New York Times* review of *Americanah* or most critics' dislike of Chetan Bhagat, dismissing them because they do not fit our preconceived understandings of what literature should look like.

The third direction relates to the role of academic writing in our current climate. The Internet and prevalence of social media have enabled the democratization of research and scholarship, but it is not yet clear exactly what forms that democratization will take. Print publishing is in crisis, as are the humanities. If we want our work to continue to be relevant, we have to do more to harness the possibility of publishing in more contemporary, nonprint forms. This is not a call to do away with the academic monograph but to consider different forms of publication in relation to different goals and different audiences. My experience writing about Indian literature for online magazines like *Scroll.in* and online book reviews like *Public Books* are just some of the ways I have tried to make my writing on the Indian contemporary itself contemporary. Not only can these publications be easily disseminated online and on social media, but the turnaround time for these articles and their freedom from the disciplinary protocols that continue to affect what gets published in peer-reviewed journals mean that a broader range of ideas can circulate in these virtual media. Of course, the printed book has a longevity that online writing does not; each form of writing and publication offers its own rewards. There are certainly practical reasons for publishing online relating to the changing profession and the digital landscape. But it is also a way that we, too, as literary critics, can become part of the transmedia landscape that I describe in this book, where we can also participate in re-thinking the traditional hierarchies between text and critic. Ideally, the more we publish, the less we remain at a critical distance from our texts, the less we can assume an antagonistic relationship to them, and the more we be-come constitutive parts of the textual worlds we are writing about. Publish-ing widely and often thus lessens the distance between the critic and the world she describes—a shift that, although it might diminish the stature of the critic, might paradoxically herald the rebirth of literary criticism in the twenty-first century.

Notes

INTRODUCTION

Parts of this chapter were previously published in Ulka Anjaria, "The Realist Impulse and the Future of Postcoloniality," *Novel* 49, no. 2 (2016): 278–294. Copyright 2016, Novel, Inc. All rights reserved. Republished by permission of the copyright holder and the present publisher, www.dukeupress.edu.

1. The Indian middle class is a vastly heterogeneous group made up of people with a variety of socioeconomic statuses, ranging from lower-middle-class shopkeepers or bank employees to well-off professionals and managers in the corporate sector. Some members of this group have little in common, beset by vast differences in education, access to English, and culture. What unites the group, then, is not shared characteristics as much as its demographic difference from the two other categories long used to understand Indian society, elite and subaltern. When, in the 1980s, the subaltern was defined by Gayatri Chakravorty Spivak as everyone who is not elite (1988, 284), those two terms became central to scholarship on modern India and together were taken to encompass all of society. But there was a rapid expansion of the middle class after economic liberalization in the 1990s, which makes such a dichotomy increasingly untenable. This issue is pursued more deeply in Chapter 3.

2. As discussed later, this book does not survey all contemporary literature. For that, see Dawson Varughese 2013, which is the most comprehensive overview of new fiction genres. Fantasy fiction is perhaps the most popular genre that I do not discuss here and one that deserves further study in relation to the Indian contemporary, especially since its revival of mythological Hindu characters might be seen as a further entrenchment of Hindu nationalism (Khair and Doubinsky 2015, 341).

3. Popular romance writer Durjoy Datta, for instance, published fifteen novels between 2008 and 2017, Ravinder Singh published seven between 2008 and 2017, and fantasy-fiction writer Amish published six novels between 2010 and 2018. Even a prolific postcolonial writer like Amitav Ghosh published eight novels over *thirty* years.

4. This is true in other parts of the global South as well. Cara Cilano argues that in recent Pakistani fiction, "other events and issues eclipse the relevance of Partition. . . . Critical expectations need to be altered, then, to allow for the range of topics this younger generation of writers present" (2009, 189). Njabulo Ndebele recognized this shift as early as 1994 in South Africa: "With the demise of grand apartheid now certain, what are South African writers now going to write about?" (1994, vii).

5. The applicability of the term "neoliberalism" is up for debate in the Indian context, and perhaps globally as well (Brouillette 2017). A useful survey of the use of the term in literary studies is provided by Huehls and Smith, but their focus is solely on the United States and United Kingdom (2017, 4).

6. Mishra continues: "I think we can safely say that what has largely defined India since the 80s is a highly individualistic culture of aspiration, one that has coincided with neoliberal globalisation, and the writing produced during this period—both high and low, literary or social-scientistic, Chetan Bhagat or Katherine Boo—is primarily concerned with this phenomenon of a society fragmented by the private pursuit of an urban, highly consumerist way of life. Everything has been reconfigured by it—from gender relations and mental health to the environment and electoral politics" (Mishra and Sethi 2015).

7. The increasing encroachment of religion on private life is evident in recent laws such as the bans on hundreds of pornography websites and on the consumption of beef, which are seen by many as an overreach of a nanny state (Majumder 2015).

8. There are clearly connections between the Indian case and others globally. As Pankaj Mishra writes in *Age of Anger*, the right-wing resurgence being witnessed in India has analogs in Russia, China, and Turkey (2017a, 164). We can expand this to say that many of these countries are also coming to terms with the various forms of capitalism that have transformed their societies over the last several decades. Across these contexts, the contemporary will take different forms in relation to the specificity of political and literary conditions (for a discussion of contemporary literary conditions in Russia, see Ivanova 2009; for conditions in China, see Lu 1997 and Huang 2007). There is a lot of fruitful comparative work that needs to be done to describe formations of the contemporary across these global contexts.

9. Here I differ from periodizations that designate the present based on either the seminal publication of *Midnight's Children* in 1981, or, less often, the economic reforms of 1991 (Tickell 2016, 38–41).

10. The relationship of postcolonial criticism to *bhasha*—Indian vernacular—fiction is complex, as the institutionalized version of postcolonial theory that emerged in the U.S. and U.K. academies focused mostly on English-language literature, leaving bhasha fiction largely by the wayside. More attention to bhasha literatures from the outset might well have transformed the vocabulary of postcolonial literary studies. For instance, beginning in the 1980s Indian English fiction has been characterized by its attention to history and its formal cohesiveness. In contrast, bhasha novels from their earliest examples in the late 1800s have generally been more episodic, formally open and focused on the present, from the intrusive satirical narrators of Fakir Mohan Senapati's *Six Acres and a Third* ([1899] 2006) and Shrilal Shukla's *Raag Darbari* (1968) to the nationalist-era novels of Premchand, Mulk Raj Anand, and Ahmed Ali (U. Anjaria 2012). The English translator of Bibhutibhushan Bandopadhyay's Bengali novel *Pather Panchali* ([1929] 1999) famously cut out whole sections, finding it too digressive to be called a novel (S. Mukherjee 1981, 89). Even more recent bhasha novels are generally more episodic and formally open than their English equivalents. For example,

Pakistani author Mushtaq Ahmed Yousufi's Urdu novel *Aab-e-gum* (*Mirages of the Mind*, [1990] 2015), despite being set in the past, has an entirely different form from what Ananya Jahanara Kabir calls the "big fat Partition novels" of the 1980s and 1990s. In fact, Yousufi's novel deflects Partition from an event of epistemic significance to one of a misplaced nostalgia (U. Anjaria 2016b). This is a markedly different sensibility from the dominant version of the South Asian English novel in the 1980s and 1990s.

11. There are, of course, some literary critics who do not share this secular cosmopolitanism or the imperative for social justice. This emerged during the Jawaharlal Nehru University (JNU) demonstrations against the arrest of student leader Kanhaiya Kumar in 2016. Makarand Paranjape, for instance, a well-known professor of English literature, was one of the few academics who was critical of the demonstrating students, calling JNU a "Left hegemonic space" ("JNU Prof" 2016). However, despite such exceptions, it is fair to say that the values of cosmopolitanism, democracy, and secularism are shared by a majority of scholars of Indian literature, both in and outside India.

12. Pedro Erber elaborates: "Th[e] burden of the past is heavy to the point of being detrimental to life. The untimeliness of this meditation consists precisely in going against the dominant and fashionable adoration of history. . . . Nietzsche's 'untimeliness,' his inadequacy to his own time, is intrinsically connected to his attempt at being timelier; that is, closer to the present and less burdened by the past and by historical consciousness" (2013, 40).

13. It is important to distinguish "postcolonial time" from notions of temporality advanced by postcolonial theory in the 1980s and 1990s. In *A Critique of Postcolonial Reason*, Gayatri Chakravorty Spivak does not present postcoloniality merely as a rejoinder to narratives of modernization but as a deconstructive gesture that has the possibility to expose the epistemological assumptions of those narratives. She seeks to "produc[e] a counternarrative that will make visible the foreclosure of the subject whose lack of access to the position of narrator is the condition of possibility of the consolidation of Kant's position" (1999, 9) and indeed of Western philosophy more generally. Here, postcolonial time has a *negative* ontology, so "time often emerges as an implicit Graph only miscaught by those immersed in the process of timing" (38). In contrast, postcolonial time as defined in this book refers to a specific (positive) temporality evident in the Indian novel in English, in which the present is marked as a degraded time due to the rise of capitalism and the decline of cosmopolitanism. We might see this as a simplification of time as it was theorized by postcolonial scholars like Spivak. However, a more recent article by Spivak, "Why Study the Past?," seems to follow along this trend, calling for a straightforward reassertion of the importance of the past as a bulwark against "the quick access provided by the silicon chip" (2012, 3).

14. Similar critiques have been made of contemporary fiction in other contexts; see, for instance, Carroll on the role of prizes in creating markets for contemporary fiction in the United Kingdom (2015, 21–23) and Mark McGurl (2011) on the role of university-based creative writing programs in constructing the category of contemporary fiction in the United States and, more recently, on the role of Amazon in changing literary tastes (McGurl 2016).

15. Hasan is both a critic and novelist, and her novels *Neti, Neti, Not This, Not This* (2009) and *The Cosmopolitans* (2015a) advance a skepticism of the market similar to what we see in her critical writings. However, the latter novel also recognizes the futility of finding refuge in the past, and its protagonist, Qayenaat, is constantly articulating her sense of frustration with both the idea of unceasing progress and a narrow nostalgia. This tension is part of what I anticipate will be a new impulse in the contemporary

Indian novel, which is to actually thematize the misfit between the postcolonial and the contemporary as part of the fictional project.

16. Another commentator writes, "There is a loss of reading culture, you can't deny it. . . . And our span has shrunk. People are writing short love stories, going to slam poetry. It's a popular cultural landscape where not just cricket has gone for a new format of IPL but also literature. What you see as a reading explosion is sustained by middle class neo-literates" (quoted in Dore 2018).

17. Thus, when Salman Rushdie tweeted in 2012 that meeting Chetan Bhagat was like meeting Dan Brown, the wildly popular American novelist, he meant it as an insult, but Bhagat famously took it as a compliment: "He's done me a huge favour. He's told the entire world—because his followers are worldwide—that Chetan is India's Dan Brown!" (S. Chakraborty 2012).

18. There is also a residual asceticism to these kinds of comments influenced by a traditional Brahminical prudishness around money as well as a Nehruvian skepticism of consumption, cultivated in the early postcolonial years as part of national responsibility. Mukul Kesavan (2016) writes about growing up middle class in preliberalization India: "It was a world where the absence of things—Wrigley's Juicy Fruit, Seiko watches, Parker Pens—was experienced not just as scarcity but as a superior form of austerity. Superior because the absence of this and that and the other, taken together added up to the republican project of self-reliance. Not consuming the world promiscuously was a form of civic sacrifice in the cause of economic independence without which the political freedom of 1947 was meaningless. Autarky, even if we didn't know the word, was the state of grace to which we collectively aspired. Scarcity was ideologically sexy because it was the price we paid for self-sufficiency and inconvenience was a hair shirt worn for the greater common good."

19. In this book on contemporary literature, Bill Ashcroft (1999) argues for the continued purchase of the term "post-colonial" for the project of documenting the legacy of colonialism in the present, and Mpalive Msiska's chapter shows how Wole Soyinka criticizes colonial knowledge through his use of history and myth in *A Dance of the Forests* (1999, 129). Referring to these two chapters, the editors note that "what has proved interesting is the way in which nearly all of the contributors to this part of the book [on colonial contexts] become engaged less in the immediacy of the contemporary moment than in an attempt to *excavate* the histories lying behind our current cultural forms" (Luckhurst and Marks 1999, 7).

20. There are exceptions to this, of course, including scholarship by Sangita Gopal (2015), Priya Joshi (2015), Toral Gajarawala (2015), Emma Dawson Varughese (2013), Mrinalini Chakravorty (2014), Sonali Perera (2015), Devapriya Roy (2016), and several others. Beyond literature, the work of Shiv Viswanathan stands out for going against the grain of expected political positions. For instance, in his analysis of the massive popular support for self-proclaimed godman Gurmeet Ram Rahim Singh even after his 2017 rape conviction, Viswanathan (2017) explains, "Democracy and modernisation have not delivered equality. The lower castes, the Other Backward Classes needed an imagination beyond the aridity of socialism and Marxism, the promises of equality that offer little. . . . As citizen social scientists today, we have to go beyond . . . knee-jerk celebrations and dismissals," even of groups or ideas we find disturbing or dangerous.

21. This section's heading adapts Faith Smith's pithy provocation, "Whose modern?" from "Strolling in the Ruins," a talk given at Brandeis University, February 4, 2015.

22. For instance, in a recent article in *Modern Language Quarterly*, James English (2016) schematizes various trends in what he calls "contemporary fiction studies," but his focus is mostly on the United States and the United Kingdom. In a recent special issue of *Contemporary Literature*, "Fiction since 2000: Postmillennial Commitments," most of the articles discuss Western literature. Many scholarly titles use the term "contemporary" without any specification, when in reality they are talking about mainly Western novels (e.g., Ganguly 2016; Eshel 2013; Greaney 2006; Karnicky 2007; Huehls and Smith 2017, 10). The scholarly journals *Contemporary Literature* and *Critique: Studies in Contemporary Fiction* both emphasize recent fiction, with the latter specifying "fiction after 1950 from any country." However, both journals' articles are predominantly on Western literature with the exception of a few internationally significant (but, I argue, resolutely *anticontemporary*) works such as Rushdie's *Midnight's Children* (1981), Kiran Desai's *The Inheritance of Loss* (2006), Jhumpa Lahiri's *The Namesake* (2003), and a couple of novels by V. S. Naipaul. Moreover, when non-Western texts are included in such contexts, it is most often because of their cosmopolitanism, thus presuming the content of the contemporary in advance and foreclosing its multiple possibilities. (Chapter 1 discusses, in contrast, how the Indian contemporary is in part constituted by a *refusal* of cosmopolitanism and a new interest in literary provincialism.) For example, Debjani Ganguly defines the global contemporary as the "'compulsion' to be world-oriented in the aftermath of the cold war and the geopolitics of violence that we have been witness to" (2016, 1).

23. As Amarteifio has said about the show, "I wanted something for African women, something for us and by us. I was tired of the sole narrative of the African woman being about poverty and disease. I wanted to see another narrative—one of beauty, glamor and intelligence" (quoted in Karimi 2016).

24. In this sense *Black-ish* is like other contemporary black writing, in which "race remains substantial; it affects and influences the world, but its value can never be known in advance. Its value is ontological rather than representational; its significance derives from the way it does or does not impact, connect to, link up with, and influence other things in the world. Race is, but it doesn't necessarily mean." This is "racial thinking shaped by, but also uniquely resistant to, neoliberalism's easy appropriation of racial representation," a "space beyond racial meaning and meaninglessness, beyond diversity and colorblindness" (Huehls 2016, 109, 126). Unsurprisingly, its negotiation between politics and everyday life has subjected *Black-ish* to some criticism (Waters 2014), which bears similarities to criticism of contemporary Indian cultural production in its narrow definition of what qualifies as political art. Similar criticisms of the African American contemporary's complicity with capitalism emerged in responses to Beyoncé's "Formation," such as in the critique by Dianca London (2016).

25. See also Chris Abani's *GraceLand* (2004) and A. Igoni Barrett's *Blackass* (2015) for formations of the African contemporary that similarly disrupt universalist ideas of the global novel.

26. Botswana-based author Siyanda Mohutsiwa (2016) satirizes the recent African novel's obsession with immigration in her web piece, "I'm Done with African Immigrant Literature." Here she uses "revolutionary" not as it might be used by the political left but as a way to characterize the implications of saying something that has been largely unthinkable before—in this case the idea that African literature might tell African stories. As Yogita Goyal points out, in critics' quickness to condemn Afropolitan aesthetics as merely celebrating elite leisure spaces in Africa, they lose "the value of an Afropolitan consciousness as a refusal to over-simplify and a willingness to

complicate existing portraits of Africa" (2014, xv). Goyal also writes that *Americanah* "challenges the conventions of the typical immigrant novel, where no alternative to life in America is entertained, as Ifemelu chooses to return home not under any kind of compulsion, but just because she wants to be in Lagos" (xii).

CHAPTER 1

Parts of this chapter were previously published in Ulka Anjaria, "Chetan Bhagat and the New Provincialism," *American Book Review*, September–October 2015, pp. 6–22; and Ulka Anjaria, "The Realist Impulse and the Future of Postcoloniality," *Novel* 49, no. 2 (2016): 278–294. Copyright 2016, Novel, Inc. All rights reserved. Republished by permission of the copyright holder and the present publisher, www.dukepress.edu.

1. This cosmopolitan imaginary had its source in earlier literature, beginning, perhaps, with Rabindranath Tagore (Bharucha 2006) and including figures such as Mulk Raj Anand, Raja Rao, and Ahmed Ali (U. Anjaria 2012). Indian nationalism was also spearheaded by a cosmopolitan generation. The image of Apu holding a globe in Satyajit Ray's *Aparajito* might be seen as emblematic for early twentieth-century cosmopolitanism (S. Majumdar 2015a, 3).

2. Arundhati Roy is an exception; she has always lived in India and has contrasted herself with other postcolonial writers for this reason: "If you read other Indian writers most of them are very urban: they don't have much interest in, you know, air or water. They all went from the Doon School to St. Stephen's and then on to Cambridge. Most of those who are called Indian writers don't even live here: Rushdie, Seth, Amitav Ghosh, Mistry: they're all abroad, while I've never lived anywhere except India" (quoted in Sunder Rajan 2011, 213).

3. For a long time, as Om Prakash Dwivedi and Lisa Lau remind us, "many major writers of IWE [were] settled abroad, either by choice or by birth, and, as a result of the opportunity to have work published and reviewed in the Global North and in world literary centres like London and New York, some enjoy[ed] the wide distribution necessary to achieve celebrity status. . . . It is the diasporic version of India on which the primary focus lies within Eurocentric scholarship and postcolonial studies" (2014, 2).

4. This is not to say that cosmopolitanism no longer features in India's contemporary; for instance, there are vernacular cosmopolitanisms (Werbner 2016; Luo 2013; Bhabha 1996), which underline how, as Tabish Khair points out, the provincial is not always provincial (2015, 5). There is also "provincial modernity," defined by Arunima Paul as the "*other* non-metropolitan trajectory of postcolonial and neo-liberal modernity . . . in which are intertwined the obscured histories of the developmental state, the postcolonial afterlives of caste and political power, the gradual 'democratization' of caste, and emergent neo-liberal notions of selfhood and forms of governmentality" (2013, 116). My intent is to mitigate the critical focus on cosmopolitanism in literature by pointing out that there might be other and even opposing tendencies at play. The September–October 2015 issue of *American Book Review* offers a series of useful essays on the possibilities of provincialism in Indian literature as a refreshing antidote to the valorization of cosmopolitanism in the field. As Saikat Majumdar writes in his introduction to the issue, "The vibrant, sometimes disturbing history of post-independence India can be re-imagined as the intriguing transformation of the cosmopolitan into the provincial, and the energization of the erstwhile provincial backwater into a new, vernacular cosmopolitanism" (2015a, 4). See also Tania Lewis, Fran Martin, and Wanning

Sun for a discussion of another kind of new provincialism in regional television programming in India (2016, 103–105).

5. As one commentator explains, "Back in the BC [Before Chetan] years, a book that sold 5,000 copies was an Indian bestseller. . . . Today, Bhagat's publishers, Rupa, are reviewing a drill that will take a couple of million copies of *Half Girlfriend* to bookshops for a countrywide release on October 1" (Kapoor 2014b). See also Pal 2012.

6. For instance, Nirpal Dhaliwal (2014) calls Bhagat's novels "Hornby-lite: schmaltzy, earnest and simplistic." Nilanjana Roy (2013) is also critical. Another reviewer writes, "Bhagat is the opposite of a thinker. He is our great 'unthinker.'. . . He wants to go shopping, like so many of us, and can't understand why India, that precarious project, keeps getting in the way. Bhagat likes to talk about 'innovation, imagination and creativity,' but he uses these words as the human resources department of an international corporation would, as synonyms for conformity. Bhagat is not interested in ideas, only in 'the good life' as conceived by the builders of Gurgaon apartment complexes. And so, as they do, he sells his readers a mirage, a cut-price American dream" (S. Dasgupta 2013).

7. For instance, Bhagat tweeted on Father's Day, "Mothers give birth, but ultimately, the coke belongs to the guy who puts the coin in the vending machine. Happy father's day ;)." Later, Bhagat apologized and said that he meant it as a joke (S. Chakraborty 2012).

8. The question of whether Bhagat is a realist writer is something I touch on elsewhere (U. Anjaria 2016c, 287–290). His refusal of literary devices such as metaphor and his disregard for the subtleties of language suggest that he represents a plain-style turn in Indian fiction. At the same time, his works are criticized for their formulaic qualities and their overdetermined, predictable plots. We might see the phenomenon of which Bhagat is a part as a *realist turn* rather than an embrace of literary realism as it is conventionally defined.

9. I am thinking specifically here of fellow romance writer Durjoy Datta, whose novels also feature young men struggling with romance but, relative to Bhagat's, are much less interested in problematizing the narrator or having him undergo any kind of self-transformation.

10. "Chick lit" has been variously defined, but the term is often used in distinction from romance, with the latter involving a grand love story and the former being more consumer oriented (Harzewski 2006), potentially "postfeminist" (Mazza 2006), and less tied to monogamy. Some scholars have criticized the infantilizing term "chick," which seems to denigrate the genre from the outset, but as Cris Mazza writes, defending the use of the term, "When we titled our anthology *Chick-Lit*, it was not to reduce the contributing authors into shopping-and-dieting airheads. It was a way of saying, 'Careful, if you think you know us.' . . . Men write about what's important; women write about what's important *to women*. So our title of *Chick-Lit* was meant to point out this delusion, this second-class differentiation; not pretend it isn't there" (2006, 27–28).

11. Ravinder Singh "proudly admits, 'I am not an avid reader. I must have read one or two books before I started writing'" (Mongia 2014, 142).

12. As Suman Gupta explains, "The international publishers in India are there to generate profits by entering the Indian reading market, not by opening up Indian commercial fiction to an international market. The great bulk of commercial fiction produced by Penguin India, Harper Collins India, Hachette India, and so on, is only distributed within India" (2012, 49). At the same time, these new texts have potential additional audiences in other parts of Asia. Bhagat has written about international

sales: "It's not been a focus for me. The millions and millions in India are, I think, enough (laughs)! You know, I might just make a little bit of an effort now. . . . Like I'll tell you, Five Point Someone has been a bestseller in Korea. My friends from my banking days wrote to me saying, 'You know what, your book is a bestseller here'! And you know why? Because they have a similar system. Like we have the IIT, they have the KIT . . . Korea Institute of Technology—same style. Intense competition, very engineering-driven society . . . so, they really liked FPS. Now how do I keep track of that? The book also did very well in China after 3 Idiots came out" (S. Chakraborty 2012).

13. The skepticism toward commercial writing exists beyond India. It is seen as shoring up a "middlebrow" reading culture, "reflect[ing] middle-class self-improvement and auto-didacticism, associated with institutions like book clubs, reading groups, literary festivals and ticking off lists such as '10 best films,' '100 best books' and 'films to see before you die'" (Dwyer 2016, 52). Even around U.S. minority writing, there is a critical skepticism of any writer who is too popular or inadequately nuanced in the representation of minority struggles. Rita Felski documents that although politically oriented literary criticism is frequently seen as a way to shore up minority struggles, it "often cast[s] a skeptical or jaundiced gaze at more popular forms of minority expression" so that "forms of ordinary self-understanding are often held to be laden with metaphysical residues and essentialist assumptions." Felski cites the scholar Sue-Im Lee, who describes how many in her field dismiss popular works in Asian American literature for their "pandering to middlebrow expectations and dominant US values. Popular novels by Maxine Hong Kingston, Amy Tan, and others are reproached for endorsing a 'vision of normative progress toward wholeness'; the very deployment of a language of Asian-American identity is seen as a sign of complicity vis-à-vis prevailing regimes of thought" (2015, 144).

14. Likewise, Meredith McGuire writes that young people's participation in self-help training should not be seen only as a reflection of a neoliberal ideology but also as a means "to produce new understandings of self and agency" in a changing India (2013, 110).

15. This is a different project from what I might call ironic self-help novels, such as Mohsin Hamid's How to Get Filthy Rich in Rising Asia (2013) or Tash Aw's Five Star Billionaire (2013), which mobilize the new proliferation of self-help guides and get-rich-quick advice to satirize the kind of aspiration born of global capitalism and new consumer cultures (Poon 2017).

16. This frustration with Indian writers' desire for international recognition has been repeated by a number of contemporary authors. For instance, graphic novelist Sarnath Banerjee has said, "Who gives a fuck about New York? What's great about being in one small section of the bookshop in the Strand? I don't think it makes me feel any culturally greater. I think that age has gone: of having my work understood in New York, or by an Anglophile Indian for that matter. It's not my intention to be understood. I will continue writing for a readership that is fundamentally local" (Asokan 2016). This is in contrast to someone like Amitav Ghosh, for whom writing for a global audience is a particular kind of "challenge" that he enjoys: "I have been writing for the New Yorker. The people who read it do not know anything about India. Literally nothing. They do not know where Calcutta is, they do not know where Delhi is, they do not know where Bombay is. . . . In this instance, what was really challenging for me was to discover exactly what was interesting, what was universal, what was communicable. The challenge was to write with a universal human interest" (quoted in Sunder Rajan 2011, 215).

17. Amitava Kumar (2012, 73–74) records how rare it was for Indian English novels of the 1980s and 1990s to be translated into Indian languages.

18. As Sangita Gopal writes, India's smaller towns are rapidly expanding; whereas in 2001, "a third of India's urban population lived in India's largest metropolitan areas . . . by the end of 2007 . . . that percentage had declined by 10 percent, while that of smaller cities and towns began to rise. The balance between the two has shifted quite radically; currently, 70 percent of the Rs. 74 trillion consumer market is located in key urban towns (KUTs) and the rest of urban India (ROUI). More important, most growth is now centered round this secondary sector. . . . These newly emerging urban areas will be the new drivers of consumption and present rich opportunities for businesses" (2012, 138–139).

19. Bhagat explicitly defends his "bad" writing: "I know that I am not the best writer in India, but I am the bestselling writer because I write for the people of my country. I write in the language they understand and converse with them through this" ("I'm Not the Best" 2014). Likewise, "I want to reach people. It's like, you know, condemning a newspaper for not using eloquent language. But I submit to that, my writing is not that eloquent. At the same time, it doesn't mean that my writing doesn't have any insight. Fact is, what I have said has struck a chord" (quoted in S. Chakraborty 2012).

CHAPTER 2

1. This idea of the Indian city as a land of contrasts can be seen, for instance, in the titles of several recent books: Siddharta Deb's *The Beautiful and the Damned: A Portrait of the New India* (2011), Katherine Boo's *Beyond the Beautiful Forevers: Life, Death and Hope in a Mumbai Undercity* (2012), and Sanjay Srivastava's *Entangled Urbanism: Slum, Gated Community and Shopping Mall in Delhi and Gurgaon* (2015).

2. Several critics have identified recent urban writings as constituting a new genre, including Srinivasan (2017, 95), Sunder Rajan (2011, 218), M. Goswami (2012), and Sandhu (2013). Mumbai and Delhi are not the only cities written about; however, they are the most commonly documented cities in this new genre. Kolkata has been extensively represented but rarely as a contemporary city, as Sandip Roy (2016) writes. But this might be changing, as evinced by the recent publications of *The Epic City: The World on the Streets of Calcutta*, by Kushanava Choudhury, in 2017 (Shankar 2017) and the novel *Kalkatta*, by Kunal Basu, in 2015. Choudhury is concerned with challenging some of the same narratives we see in the Mumbai and Delhi writings discussed later, inflecting the nostalgia that pervades bhadralok culture with "the possibility for being made anew" (2017, 234) that he brings as an American-educated returnee to the city he loves. In Basu's novel, contemporary Kolkata is represented as two cities, Kolkata/Calcutta, the Hindu Bengali city of the old middle class, and Kalkatta, a contemporary city of crime, sex, and refugees. The first is a world in which "everybody went to Presidency College or to Lady Brabourne, listened to Beethoven, rehearsed Rabindra Sangeet in the evenings and argued over art and culture" (Basu 2015, 216), and the second, a world of criminality and life on the streets. As the narrator reflects, "What would [Allah] find if He gazed down through the clouds into His creation? Would He draw a neat line between the sinners and the saints keeping all the illegals—heroin dealers, satta gamblers and malish-wallahs—on one side and the legals—office-going, poetry-writing, theory-loving true Kalkatta-wallahs—on the other?" (Basu 2015, 291). Kannada author Vivek Shanbag explains the paucity of city writings on Bengaluru: "Bangalore is still a relatively new city; there are things that are yet to become part of our experience. Bombay has certain unwritten rules that it throws at the outsider. There is no such thing in Bangalore. . . . A book like *Maximum City* can be written about

Bangalore, but then it will be about old Bangalore. Because new Bangalore is still settling down" (quoted in T. Gupta 2016). However, that seems to be changing as well, as Anna Guttman notes in her discussion of recent Bengaluru crime novels. For Guttman, new crime fictions distinguish themselves from postcolonial urban writings because they "all playfully deconstruct identity and demonstrate that the identities of the elite and the outcast alike are at least partly fictive and unfixed" (2017, 266).

3. This chapter is not a comprehensive study of all recent city writings on Mumbai and Delhi but focuses on recent nonfiction prose writings (with the exception of the novel *The Boyfriend*) that innovatively center the contemporaneity of the changing city. There is a much longer and broader tradition of city writings of Mumbai and Delhi that is not discussed here, such as the English and Marathi Bombay poetry that flourished from 1955 to 1980 (Nerlekar 2016, 7) and Dalit poetry that reads Bombay "as an ugly city" where "men eat men" (quoted in Bhagwat 1995, 119, 121). There is Mughal poetry marked by loss and the exile of Bahadur Shah from Delhi in 1857. More recently, there has been a spate of mysteries and crime fiction set in Mumbai and Delhi, such as Vikram Chandra's *Sacred Games* (2006), Ambai's *A Meeting on the Andheri Overbridge: Sudha Gupta Investigates* (2014), and Jerry Pinto's *A Murder in Mahim* (2017), all set in Mumbai; and Tarun Tejpal's *The Story of My Assassins* (2010) and Manish Dubey's *A Murder in Gurgaon* (2016), set in Delhi (Bhatt 2017). There have also been several collections of essays and fiction on both cities, such as *Bombay, Meri Jaan: Writings on Mumbai* (Pinto and Fernandes 2003), *Delhi Noir* (Sawhney 2009), *Mumbai Noir* (Altaf Tyrewala 2012), and others. The 2010 compilation *Bahurupiya Shehr* (translated by Shveta Sarda as *Trickster City: Writings from the Belly of the Metropolis*) stands out for its formal innovativeness, comprising three dozen vignettes written in Hindi by twenty different authors and originally published as a blog that Sarda would translate and post every evening. Although loosely centering around the demolition of the Nangla Machi settlement in Delhi in 2006, the episodes refrain from mounting a cohesive critique of urban politics and instead present a rich world of everyday life that constitutes the lived city (Sarda 2010).

4. "This thoroughly divided city," Rashmi Varma writes of Mumbai, "far from being a model for the secular Indian imagination, now seems to be emulating a different model of nationalism rooted in provincial and exclusionary identifications" (2004, 67).

5. For more such disaster narratives of the third-world city, see Saldanha 2016; Davis 2006. See Sundaram for a compelling account of the limitations of urban dystopic narratives. Sundaram locates the origin of the alarmist narrative of Delhi's decline in the 1990s, when, "focusing on infrastructural collapse, headline font size increased steadily over the decade, racing to keep pace with an expanding city. Papers reported road accidents caused by speeding buses, regular blackouts, and water shortages. This sense of a city out of control even affected international reporting from Delhi.... The prominence of crisis stories reflected a new form of writing and reporting about the city that emerged in the 1990s" (2010, 255).

6. Chachu quite inaccurately narrates present-day Mumbai as having undergone radical transformation from a city of the people to one of a domesticated, "law-abiding" bourgeois. For instance, "Few places remain where a man can still eat a meal cooked by human beings. Café Olympia. Holding out. For how long? Already citizens wait for tables, elbowing out taxi drivers" (Abbas Tyrewala 2012, 76). "Through the '90s, Citizens joined the nocturnal celebration that was Bombay. Discotheques, those mysterious places where exotic people went for erotic escapades, suddenly sprouted everywhere" (84).

7. K. P. Jayashankar and Anjali Monteiro similarly write: "Sudhir Patwardhan . . . talks of a sense of fragmentation with the demise in the 90s of any ideology of the left

that could provide an 'integrative grand narrative within which to frame the city and its people.' He describes the overpowering albeit exhilarating experience of the city crowds, as he travelled on the trains everyday, and of the conflict in his painting between two poles—the desire to 'allow the city to flood into [his] work' and the struggle to focus on the individual, the desire to find a way to bring the city and its people into a single frame. Patwardhan talks of how to grasp this life without imposing on it any overarching meaning, and the importance of capturing the emotional charge of the city on canvas, of how this mark on the canvas 'can't be a dead mark'" (2016, 169). This is also evident in Patwardhan's *Mumbai Proverbs* paintings. As Patwardhan explains, "These multiple fragments of experience have two narratives linking them together. . . . The seven panels chart a history of the city from its colonial beginnings to the Age of Information Technology. The other narrative linking the fragments is that of roaming the city in order to find what makes it one composite city. This 'finding' is also an act of naming it 'my city'" ("Seven Course Feast" 2015).

8. Certainly visual art is not the only nonnarrative medium with relevance here, the other primary one being poetry. As Anjali Nerlekar writes in her study of sattothari poetry in Bombay in the mid-twentieth century, "Poetry reveals a site that stages the inexpressible contemporaneity of Bombay" (2016, 15). This is especially true because of what she identifies as the materiality of sattothari poetry, which "requires the conceiving of a poem as a material construct and the writing of it as a craft rather than an art. The emphasis is on the 'making' of a poem" (21).

9. Ananya Jahanara Kabir describes "'the big fat Indian novels' of the 1980s onward" as those that "achieve narrative extent through complexly intertwined stories and a fascination with detail. [Their] obsessive recourse to the 'meanwhile'. . . projects polyphony and multiplicity as core characteristics of the Indian nation" (2015, 127–128). My twist on her term similarly highlights the way bigness of form is an attempt to mirror the vast heterogeneity of the Indian city.

10. *The Eruption of Delhi* is the subtitle of the book's international edition, but the subtitle of the original Indian edition was *A Portrait of Twenty-First Century Delhi*.

11. As discussed previously, the city's official name was changed from Bombay to Mumbai in 1995, and this name change has proven controversial because it was backed by the right-wing Shiv Sena as part of an overall localism that imagined Mumbai as a city primarily for Maharashtrians. Even before the change, Mumbaikars speaking in Hindi, Marathi, or Gujarati would already have been saying "Mumbai" (or the in-between "Bambai"). "Bombay" was a term primarily used in English, and many English speakers continue to use that term today in spoken language. In writing, however, people tend to use the official name, and thus Mehta's insistence on using "Bombay" can be read as a deliberate attempt to protest the name change.

12. Mehta explains the term "ghati" in another section of the book: "We lived in Bombay and never had much to do with Mumbai. Maharashtra to us was our servants, the banana lady downstairs, the textbooks we were force-fed in school. We had a term for them: ghatis—literally, the people from the ghats, or hills. It was also the word we used, generically, for 'servant.'" And then, again, this time more clearly ironically: "Many of the people on Nepean Sea Road were aghast not so much that the mobs were hunting out Muslims from the tall buildings but that they had dared to come to Nepean Sea Road at all. The arrogance of ghatis demanding to see the building directories!" (56).

13. *Slumdog Millionaire*, like so many contemporary representations of urban India discussed thus far, was subject to significant criticism by those who thought it

celebrated the entrepreneurialism of Dharavi residents instead of focusing on the social conditions of poverty. In these criticisms we see, once again, the way the decline narrative functions as an obstacle to grasping the contemporary. Without either romanticizing Dharavi or seeing it as an abject consequence of neoliberal capitalism, attention to sensibilities such as jugaad allows a nondeterminist understanding of present realities. For a longer discussion of this, see J. Anjaria 2016, 176–177.

14. Interestingly, Gyan Prakash seems to dislike this aspect of Mehta's book. In *Mumbai Fables*, Prakash describes the city Mehta conjures as "a place bursting with not just urban desires but also urban problems. Here and there, Mehta finds honest and straightforward characters, but his city is a cabinet of curiosities peopled by violent policemen, vicious killers, crazed communal rioters, brutal underworld foot soldiers, and troubled but kind hearted beer-bar dancers" (12). For Prakash, it seems the "cabinet of curiosities" is less able to capture the essence of the city than more "honest and straightforward characters" might. But, I argue, it is precisely in these "curious" characters that we see Mehta's most complex articulation of a theory of freedom.

15. The original title of Sethi's book was *A Free Man*, but the U.S. version, published two years later, added the subtitle *A True Story of Life and Death in Delhi*. As Sethi has said, "In a number of reviews, there seems to be an inability to look beyond Ashraf as an artifact. I find that kind of strange, because the book itself is consistently being reviewed as an exposé on poverty, which is fine. But for me, Ashraf is more of a philosopher than someone who should have another life. Ashraf, as a person, has a kind of crazy, well-thought-out view of the world. Ashraf is free, but Ashraf is poor. You can't really say they're oppositional things, because Ashraf has chosen a life of making do with poverty, which allows him a certain world of freedom. . . . The kind of book I did *not* want to write was the kind of book which is focused on the horror of poverty, the kind of book that would have introduced Ashraf as the victim, the kind of book that presents poverty as a kind of trap, which people have no way of getting out of. . . . And always this sense of pity for people—the working class, the victims. That's the kind of book I didn't want to write" (quoted in Sandhu 2013).

16. As Phadke (2017) has written elsewhere, "Fun is central to feminism. However, even within the feminist movement the claim for fun is often seen as 'asking for too much' or as being far less important than other more pressing concerns like education or healthcare. However, there is no contest. We can claim the right to purposeless fun even as we demand better and universal healthcare and education. Just as we have contested the claims that the feminist movement is 'West inspired' so also the feminist claim to fun is not a neo-liberal one. Nor is it an elite claim, for working-class women have as much desire and right to fun as middle-class women."

17. As Thomas Waugh confirms, "One of Rao's favorite themes, excremental eros is elaborated most fully in 'Underground,' where sexual fantasies, memories, and experiences are scented with the abjection of the underground toilet network. . . . Elsewhere in *Bomgay*, excretion symbolizes release from the constipation of urban life, a release triggered . . . by receptive anal intercourse, and thus acquiring a particular association with pleasure, desire, and sexual exchange" (2002, 198–199).

CHAPTER 3

1. As in English, the Hindi term "aam aadmi" is gendered masculine, signifying to many critics a conflation of its apparently universalist premise with a limited vision of who it actually represents. However, I argue that the films I discuss in this chapter

want to retain the universality of the term, even as they seek to expand who is included within it; the universality of the term is precisely its appeal.

2. The Common Man character allowed Laxman to "portray the realm of everyday life in India" based on "ordinary scenes" (Khanduri 2012, 305). He, too, was experimenting with universality, as in one anecdote in which he reportedly called himself "the universal man, neither Muslim nor Hindu" (306). As Khanduri writes, "Laxman notes that the Common Man was his technique for capturing the diversity of the Indian people and to save him the effort of portraying diverse communities through distinctive headgear or clothing" (309).

3. As Aparna Sharma writes, "Starring in over 180 films since his career began in the late 1960s, Amitabh Bachchan epitomises the quintessence of stardom in India. His domination of Hindi cinema from the 1970s to the 1990s and his extra-cinematic media undertakings since then have ensured that Bachchan is a persistent presence in India's public imagination. He is both a media participant—that is, a vehicle of media messages—and a subject of media attention, spanning news media and fanzines that have persistently followed his work as well as his political and personal life for decades. A vast and highly evolved fan culture exists around him, made up of the usual items, such as posters, T-shirts, calendars, and mugs with Bachchan motifs, but also the actor's memorabilia, and dedicated shrines where fans worship and perform rituals before iconic objects including photographs and the star's film costumes. This means that Amitabh Bachchan has a quite material and iconic presence across India" (2016, 11–12).

4. For instance, in *Mohra* (1994), Vishal's vigilante actions are a response to the brutal rape and murder of his wife. In *Ek Haseena Thi*, Sarika takes revenge on Karan for his betrayal of her. An exception to this is perhaps *Mr. India* (1987), where Mr. India's actions are on behalf of society as a whole.

5. A more conventional reading would simply lament Bachchan's waning charisma (see Dalvi 2017).

6. The representation of candlelight vigils in films such as *Rang De Basanti* did filter to real life; as Shiv Viswanathan documents regarding the Anna Hazare movement against government corruption, "The candlelight marches . . . conducted in over a dozen cities were reminiscent of Amir [sic] Khan's film *Rang de Basanti*" (2012, 106). See also R. Mehta 2012.

7. The Jan Lokpal bill requires a citizen's advisory group to monitor government corruption. It was passed with controversy following Anna Hazare's agitation in 2011 (Harindranath and Khorana 2014).

CHAPTER 4

1. The show was recorded and broadcast in Hindi but was aired simultaneously in Telugu, Tamil, Malayalam, and Marathi with dubbed dialogue.

2. There are similar critiques of celebrity culture in the United States (Monbiot 2016), as well as of U.S.-based reality television (McCarthy 2007).

3. Peter Brooks describes the melodramatic imagination of Henry James in the following way: "James's moral manichaeism is the basis of a vision of the social world as the scene of dramatic choice between heightened moral alternatives, where every gesture, however frivolous or insignificant it may seem, is charged with the conflict between light and darkness, salvation and damnation, and where people's destinies and choices of life seem finally to have little to do with the surface realities of a situation,

and much more to do with an intense inner drama in which consciousness must purge itself and assume the burden of moral sainthood" (1976, 5).

4. For instance, "Khan's star vehicles seem more substantial and reflective than the bulk of the Indian mainstream" (Hoad 2015).

5. For example, Khan is praised for his expressions of support for villagers displaced by the Narmada Dam (Daniels 2012, 136), which also earned him the criticism of Narendra Modi, then Gujarat chief minister, and led to the banning of his 2006 film *Fanaa* in Gujarat (S. Khan 2009a, 93).

6. Although, as Kavita Daiya points out, *Sarfarosh* also "problematizes the discrimination and minoritization of Muslims in contemporary India, through the representation of Sub Inspector Salim. Although Salim has an excellent network of informers and is working on the arms trafficking case, he is dismissed from it following his botched apprehension of a Pakistani suspect. The implication is that he deliberately failed to catch the suspect because they are both Muslim. . . . He voices . . . what he recognizes as the discriminatory implication that he is a disloyal, anti-national Muslim citizen in India" (2011, 596).

7. See Chandrashekhar 2013 for an assessment of the impact of the Nirbhaya case on political empowerment in India.

8. Berlant discusses the centrality of "commodified genres of intimacy, such as Oprah-esque chat shows and 'chick lit,' [which] circulate among strangers, enabling insider self-help talk such as 'girl talk' to flourish in an intimate public. These genres claim to reflect a kernel of common experience and provide frames for encountering the impacts of living as a woman in the world" (2008, x).

9. In contrast, normative acting theory "states that in playing any character, the 'real' personality of the actor should disappear into the part or, conversely, that if the range of the actor is limited to parts consonant with his or her personality then this constitutes 'poor' acting" (B. King 1991, 168). This belief is behind Anupama Chopra's praise of Aamir Khan's acting over that of fellow superstars Shah Rukh Khan and Salman Khan: "Shah Rukh may be the flashier actor and Salman, the boy toy, but Aamir's performances have rare depth. Shah Rukh, no matter what role he plays, is always Shah Rukh, but Aamir becomes Raghu in *Dil Hai Ke Manta Nahin* and Munna in *Rangeela*" (quoted in Daniels 2012, 101).

10. "The star image derives from a complex relation between multiple personae constructed through film texts and extra-filmic discourses; . . . the composite star 'text' thus produced is often incoherent" (N. Majumdar 2010, 7–8).

11. "Glycerine tears" is an epithet commonly used to make fun of Bollywood (see Bose 2006, 11). There are also articles on actors who supposedly can cry without glycerine, with the implication that they are more authentic (see "I Can Never" 2013).

12. Eleanor Zelliot documents how Marathi Dalit poet Daya Pawar gradually rid his poetry of romantic influences: "At first, after his move to the city, he wrote romantic poetry, and then when he realized that he was being untrue to both past and present, that he had no acquaintance with the 'holy gourd' he had used as an image, that his beloved slept on the ground and had no pillow to stain with tears, he stopped" (1978, 87).

13. This particular episode attracted significant criticism, as Khan was seen to ignore some of the more salient aspects of contemporary Dalit politics, such as the issue of caste-based reservations and the historical legacy of B. R. Ambedkar. These apparently were topics discussed in the various interviews but edited out of the final cut (S. Prakash 2012).

CHAPTER 5

Portions of this chapter were previously published in Ulka Anjaria, "Realist Hieroglyphics: Aravind Adiga and the New Social Novel," *Modern Fiction Studies* 61, no. 1 (2015): 114–137.

1. The original text reads: "Yeh kisi sudoor ateet mein ghat chuki ghatna ka iti-vrittaant nahin hai. Yeh us aakhyaan ka maatr ek ansh hai, jiski ghatnaaein abhi, aaj tak ghatati chali ja rahi hain. Yeh ek banti jaati, nirmit hoti, rachi jati kahaani, ya abhi, is pal tak jiye jaati jeevan ka thik is pal ke pehele tak ka bayaan hai" (U. Prakash 2001, 148).

2. *Mohan Das* was originally published in the Premchand anniversary issue of *Hans* literary magazine in 2005 (Consolaro 2011, 15).

3. Brouillette shows that "Balram is unable to settle upon a coherent message" (2014, 43). "It should be supremely difficult for readers to settle on interpretations of the signs and symbols we encounter in Balram's narrative. Are they really evidence of an incipient revolution, or manifestations of his troubled psyche, which has him project-ing his internal struggle on to the city streets, seeing symbols of class war everywhere?" (45–46). Gajarawala also notes that *The White Tiger* refuses an allegorical reading: "There is no easy linkage here between Balram Halwai, his village, his region and his nation" (2009, 22).

4. Toral Gajarawala similarly writes about Ajay Navaria's story "Chikh": "Most telling is that the final act of 'Chikh,' the murder of a man—the narrator? The land-lord's son? The jealous husband? The possessive mistress?—is left radically in doubt, its perpetrator unknown. The inability to properly name 'the other' is what justifies this epistemological uncertainty and clearly marks a kind of turn in casteist fiction. Contemporary writing on caste might be said to theorize precisely the inability of culture to do the work of protest—aesthetically, generically, and narratively—that it for so long has been able to do" (2015, 383). This suggests that "capitalist modernity has produced a confusion in the various forms of subjectivity, one that no longer allows for the neat delineation between the outcasted and the privileged" (376).

5. The original reads, "Koi bhi aadmi aakhir koi dusra aadmi kaise ban sakta hai?" (U. Prakash [2005] 2006, 31).

6. As Joseph himself has confirmed, "*The Illicit Happiness of Other People* . . . is not a political novel, not even a novel that aspires to be sociological or critical of the nation—unlike my first novel, *Serious Men*" (Mahboob 2013).

CHAPTER 6

1. A "fly in the curry" is not "a 'fly on the wall,' a neutral observer, but . . . an actor whose presence precipitates action" (Jayashankar and Monteiro 2016, 2).

2. As Anuja Jain shows, there was significant dissent even in the 1940s and 1950s on what political filmmaking should look like. J. S. Bhownagary, deputy chief producer of the Films Division from 1954 to 1957, "encouraged politically critical films and was strongly of the opinion that 'new ideas, new approaches had to be found, encouraged, and put to work.'" He "encouraged experiments with the language of film and the de-velopment of innovative techniques like the use of found footage, pixilation, and so on was prioritized" (A. Jain 2013, 18). K. A. Abbas, while agreeing that documentary had a "social purpose," also "disapprov[ed] of the heavy-handed didacticism and insist[ed] that 'it must make them laugh, make them cry, make them think'" (A. Jain 2013, 20).

And for Mrinal Sen, documentary "will always remain a medium of ever newer experience in form as well as content" (quoted in A. Jain 2013, 20).

3. Patwardhan's legacy is still strong in contemporary documentary in India, as evident in the work of current documentary filmmakers such as Sanjay Kak (P. Ghosh 2013).

4. As an alternative genealogy, Vohra has claimed finding inspiration in the more reflexive documentaries of Pramod Pati and S.N.S. Sastry, whose works are less well known than those of the more overt political filmmakers, in part because they eluded straightforward classification: "The names of Pramod Pati and S.N.S. Sastry, experimental, personal, open ended and exploratory in style, although political in concern, are much less recalled (generally) than a figure like S. Sukhdev, who worked in various forms, but is usually connected with a more realistic, political statement-driven film-making about issues more definably related to development and politics" (Rajagopal and Vohra 2012, 16). Vohra praises Sastry for this reason: "I absolutely love Sastry's films. He was a confident artist. As far as I know, Sastry is the first filmmaker in India to use the first pronoun both in the title and the content of a film. Take *I am 20* or *And I Make Short Films*. He uses 'I' to denote the nation, the people as well as himself. It is a radical thing to do—to say that the nation is not one and is in fact, fragmented. One can watch his films many times and each time they give you something new. Film viewing is the greatest form of travel afforded to us. It breaks the limits of one's body and is a transcendent experience" (Nathan 2015). For more on the self and subjectivity in Indian documentary, see Gadihoke 2012 and J. Kapur 2003. Wolf also describes the "discontent" that grew among many documentary filmmakers in the 1990s because of a culture in which "documentary film [was] being used as a vehicle to visualize an argument or set position and thus lacking open-minded inquiry and reflection" (2013, 368). For other critiques of Patwardhan, see Matzner 2014, 129–130.

5. Even feminist documentary, Vohra argues, has largely followed in the realist, masculine style: "Over the years women's media work has seen fewer new feminist approaches or narratives; a tendency to clarify a position has supplanted efforts to speak from it . . . a reiteration of known ideas, not a deepening or widening of the feminist discourse. . . . To suggest the need to engage with aesthetics or semiotics, to explore the implications of form, is often, at best, to be told by those who see themselves as media activists or political filmmakers, 'Well, this is not an arty film; it's an issue-based video,' or its variation, 'We are not artists; we are activists'" (2008, 419–420).

6. The openness of *Unlimited Girls* to a range of political positions has led some to criticize Vohra for her seeming lack of politics, for instance, calling the film "soft feminism" (Sen and Thakker 2011, 31). As Vohra recounts, "The film was rooted in various urban contexts, which were my contexts to an extent. More than once I was lectured about how I ought to be making films about rural and underprivileged women and told that by speaking of my own and allied contexts I was effectively silencing the women of rural India. One person even sent me a four-page academic article about how my film was elitist, as was my persona. Therefore, by implication, the film could not be a valuable political document because, after all, the 'real' India is in the villages and the rest consists of various vaguely elite, modern, deracinated phenomena and is definitely not an area of political importance or complexity" (2008, 420–421). This policing by feminists about what counts as "real" Indian women is something Vohra writes about in other contexts as well. In a *Mid-Day* column in response to feminist criticism of a Nike ad that featured female athletes—an ad some feminists found elitist—Vohra (2016d)

writes, "Are Indian women only 'authentic' and 'real Indian women' when they embody suffering, poverty and rurality? As soon as they progress do they become inauthentic?"

7. Paromita Vohra, postscreening discussion, The Hive, Mumbai, December 19, 2015.

8. Letting interviewees speak fully is a deliberate practice of Vohra's and one she has specifically defended: "I consider the desire to generate the real truth as minimizing people, reducing them to the filmmaker's notion of what they should represent. . . . How can we speak about others in ways that acknowledge their fullness rather than merely in terms that implicate them in our argument through ventriloquism?" (quoted in Kishore 2017, 174).

9. Contrast this to Rahul Roy's film *When Four Friends Meet* (2001), which, Jyotsna Kapur argues, is slightly derisive of its lower-middle-class interviewees, so "the filmmaker's own masculinity is not open to discussion" and "ignorance here becomes a phenomenon limited to young working-class men and therefore a problem to be solved" (2006, 338, 339). "This analytical, expert-centered structure forecloses the possibility of exploring the emotive and imaginative aspects of sexuality" (339). Moreover, "the overall film's didactic structure . . . is so driven by argument that it gets nervous if there is no narration interpreting the image. The reliance on realism and argument also closes the space for a more ambivalent and open expression of sexuality" (339).

10. In a *Mid-Day* column on the Marathi film *Fandry*, Vohra (2014g) praises its editor, Chandan Arora, who had previously worked as a director and editor on mainstream films: "That felt unusual and nice. Too often people function through a strange sense of status: now I have directed a film, I cannot edit one. Abhi [Now] I have worked on a big movie, so I can't do a small movie. These are stories not of success but enslavement, to the idea of hierarchy, not filmmaking, storytelling or art. What we make and how we work, both generate the worldview of the work. When we step out of this grid of hierarchy, we humanize others, and ourselves. We show respect for work and audiences and create works of love—whether arthouse or commercial—not arrogance."

11. The fact that Vohra's column appears in *Mid-Day*, a popular newspaper with a Mumbai circulation of two hundred thousand (Robin Thomas 2010), situates her representation of the everyday in the public culture of the city itself. Vohra's insistence on everyday life as the source of political engagement offers a different model of progressivism. The unfinished nature of the column—the expansiveness of the everyday born in this seemingly never-ending form—speaks to the unfinished nature of the political in the city at large.

12. Deol comes from a well-known Bollywood family but has made his name in alternative or hatke films (Dwyer 2012, 198).

13. As one critic writes, "By focusing on ordinary Mumbai women rather than celebrities . . . *Connected Hum Tum* lets viewers feel they are watching a version of their own lives" (Ramnath 2013). The title deliberately draws out that sense of commonality between the viewer and the characters.

14. All translations from *Connected Hum Tum* are my own.

15. The idea of putting cameras into the hands of the underprivileged continues to be a compelling one, as evidenced by the success of a film like *Born into Brothels* (2004). As one reviewer wrote, "Briski bought the kids cameras, taught them how to take pictures and in the process transformed the way they saw themselves, and the world. . . . Inevitably, they will be swept into prostitution and drugs themselves. But their photography brings them a shot at a different future, and Briski becomes determined to help

them escape their vicious environment. . . . It's an artful film about, among many other things, the power of art to transform lives" (Ansen 2004).

16. Vohra wanted this column to be different from the *Mid-Day* column because "for me the aim in each love column is that it should be like a Hindi film song. Each column should have that beauty, that idea. You know in a Hindi film song it's just one strong idea or emotion explored in two or three paragraphs with a really great hook. So that's what I am trying to achieve in a written form. In some senses I feel like the column itself communicates the feeling of love, that's why the Hindi film song which in essence is very ornamental, very *bhavuk*, you know it's very *ras bhara*. So if I can bring that much *ras* then the feeling of love is in the column but I may speak about politics, feminism, I may also speak about dating and trends and Tinder and what's going on. I think that these are interesting creative puzzles to solve, how do you bring in that feeling of interactivity which is there in live performance into the film or into writing" (Vohra, n.d.).

17. The phrase *joru ka ghulaam* refers to the husband of a dominant woman who is supposedly treated by her like a *ghulaam* (slave)—similar to the English "hen-pecked."

18. We also see this in a piece on sensory pleasures Vohra wrote for the Junoon theater blog. She begins the piece with a poem: "Who taught us to fear pleasure so much? / Too many people to count and name / Who were taught the same / So no one to blame / . . . To make sense of things / We need the senses." This play on sense and senses reinforces Vohra's view that a topic such as Indian love cannot be known simply through a distanced analysis but must be accessed through other forms of interactive engagement. The "prayer thali of cultural aphrodisiacs" that she presents in this piece portrays love as constituted through the senses, including a Bollywood song "all about the memory of touch and what touch means," an image of a luscious banquet calling on the brain's "pathways of pleasure at home with the abundance of taste," and the mogra (jasmine) as Bombay's "official flower of love" (Vohra 2016j).

19. As Vohra explains in an interview, "I found that people around me didn't watch Hindi films because they were considered regressive. In the world of documentary, pleasure is never considered to have political worth. But because I wasn't schooled in this rather austere, celibacy-tinted thinking, it was normal for me to integrate everything. At the same time, I was also consciously questioning this very hypocritical hierarchy of how, crudely put, a cinema committed to equality functioned" (quoted in Kishore 2017, 170).

20. See, for instance, her critique of sexism in Bollywood, her critique of the excessive hype around new releases, and her critique of the television show *Koffee with Karan* as being a humorless conversation among industry insiders (Vohra 2016g, 2016i, 2013c).

21. The comment about the patriarch is a reference to the Hindi film *Pink* (2016), which took on the issue of sexual violence against women through a courtroom drama in which the lawyer, played by veteran actor Amitabh Bachchan, defended a young woman vengefully accused of assaulting a man who had attacked her. The film was widely praised for addressing the issue of sexual violence, but Vohra found it mostly moralistic. In contrast, Vohra has praised the Hindi film *Queen* (2013), which follows a young woman to Europe on a solo honeymoon after her fiancé cancels their wedding: "For all kinds of women, it is a relief to see a film that is guided by its endearing and funny protagonist's desires rather than a lecturesome morality or manipulative filmmaking" (Vohra 2014e).

References

"Aamir Khan Beats Aamir Khan: 'PK' Goes Past 'Dhoom 3,' Becomes Highest Bolly-wood Grosser Ever." 2015. *Daily News and Analysis*, January 4. Available at http://www.dnaindia.com/entertainment/report-pk-goes-past-dhoom-3-to-become-highest-bollywood-grosser-ever-2049238.

Abani, Chris. 2004. *GraceLand*. New York: Farrar, Straus and Giroux.

"Accepting Alternative Sexualities." 2014. *Satyamev Jayate*, season 3, episode 3. Aired October 19. Star Plus.

Adichie, Chimamanda Ngozi. 2006. *Half of a Yellow Sun*. New York: Knopf.

———. 2013. *Americanah*. New York: Knopf.

Adiga, Aravind. 2008. *The White Tiger*. New York: Free Press.

———. 2011. *Last Man in Tower*. London: Atlantic.

Agents of Ishq. 2016. "A Lavni about Consent: The Amorous Adventures of Megha and Shakku." March 9. Available at http://agentsofishq.com/a-lavni-about-consent-the-amorous-adventures-of-megha-and-shakku.

———. 2017. "Is Pyaar Ko Main Kya Naam Doon! Words People Use for Masturbation." May 3. Available at http://agentsofishq.com/words-people-use-masturbation.

Ahmad, Aijaz. 1992. *In Theory: Classes, Nations, Literatures*. London: Verso.

Ahmed, Akbar S. 1992. "Bombay Films: The Cinema as Metaphor for Indian Society and Politics." *Modern Asian Studies* 26 (2): 289–320.

Ahmed, Firdaus. 2011. "Mr. Bhagat: Please Get off Our Backs, Will You!" *Milli Gazette*, September 25. Available at http://www.milligazette.com/news/2349-mr-chetan-bhagat-please-get-off-our-indian-muslims-backs-will-you.

Akbar, Prayaag. 2013. "Why Chetan Bhagat Shouldn't Speak for Indian Muslims." *Live Mint*, July 1. Available at http://www.livemint.com/Leisure/ttG5vmCqQ3ncenP77exXnK/Why-Chetan-Bhagat-shouldnt-speak-for-Indian-Muslims.html.

Akele Hum Akele Tum. 1995. Directed by Mansoor Khan. Digital Entertainment. DVD.

"Alcohol Abuse." 2012. *Satyamev Jayate*, season 1, episode 9. Aired July 1. Star Plus.

Almond, Ian. 2004. "Post-colonial Melancholy: An Examination of Sadness in Amitav Ghosh's *The Shadow Lines*." *Orbis Litterarum* 59:90–99.

Amar Akbar Anthony. 1977. Directed by Manmohan Desai. Digital Entertainment. DVD.

Amarteifio, Nicole, creator. 2014. *An African City.* Naa Amerley Productions. Television series.

Ambai. 2014. *A Meeting on the Andheri Overbridge: Sudha Gupta Investigates.* Translated by Gita Subramanian. New Delhi: Juggernaut.

Ambedkar, B. R. 2002. "Gandhism: The Doom of the Untouchables." In *The Essential Writings of B. R. Ambedkar,* edited by Valerian Rodrigues, 149–172. New Delhi: Oxford University Press.

Anand, S. 2012. "Silence Eva Jayate." *Outlook,* July 23. Available at http://www.outlook india.com/article/silence-eva-jayate/281646.

Anarkali of Arrah. 2017. Directed by Avinash Das. Promodome Films. DVD.

Andaz Apna Apna. 1994. Directed by Rajkumar Santoshi. Digital Entertainment. DVD.

Angry Indian Goddesses. 2015. Directed by Pan Nalin. Jungle Book Media. DVD.

Anjaria, Jonathan Shapiro. 2016. *The Slow Boil: Street Food, Rights, and Public Space in Mumbai.* Stanford, CA: Stanford University Press.

Anjaria, Ulka. 2006. "Satire, Literary Realism, and the Indian State: *Six Acres and a Third* and *Raag Darbari.*" *Economic and Political Weekly* 41 (46): 4795–4800.

———. 2012. *Realism in the Twentieth-Century Indian Novel: Colonial Difference and Literary Form.* Cambridge: Cambridge University Press.

———. 2015. "Introduction: Literary Pasts, Presents, and Futures." In *A History of the Indian Novel in English,* edited by Ulka Anjaria, 1–30. Cambridge: Cambridge University Press.

———. 2016a. "*Lady Lolita's Lover* Shows Us There Can Be No Great Indian Novel Right Now." *Scroll,* January 30. Available at https://scroll.in/article/802712/how-lady -lolitas-lover-shows-us-there-can-be-no-great-indian-novel-right-now.

———. 2016b. "Pakistan's Place in World Literature." *Public Books,* March 15. Available at http://www.publicbooks.org/pakistans-place-in-world-literature.

———. 2016c. "The Realist Impulse and the Future of Postcoloniality." *Novel: A Forum on Fiction* 49 (2): 278–294.

———. 2017a. "Great Aspirations." *Public Books,* July 31. Available at http://www .publicbooks.org/great-aspirations.

———. 2017b. "Twenty-First-Century Realism." *Oxford Research Encyclopedia of Literature,* July. Available at http://literature.oxfordre.com/view/10.1093/acrefore/ 9780190201098.001.0001/acrefore-9780190201098-e-194.

Anjaria, Ulka, and Jonathan Shapiro Anjaria. 2008. "Text, Genre, Society: Hindi Youth Films and Postcolonial Desire." *South Asian Popular Culture* 6 (2): 125–140.

———. 2013a. "The Fractured Spaces of Entrepreneurialism in Post-liberalization India." In *Enterprise Culture in Neoliberal India: Studies in Youth, Class, Work and Media,* edited by Nandini Gooptu, 190–205. London: Routledge.

———. 2013b. "Slumdog Millionaire and Epistemologies of the City." In *The "Slumdog" Phenomenon: A Critical Anthology,* edited by Ajay Gehlawat, 53–68. London: Anthem.

Ansen, David. 2004. "Sundance 2004: The Buzz and the Bores." *Newsweek,* January 22. Available at http://www.newsweek.com/sundance-2004-buzz-and-bores-125761.

"Anuja Chauhan: I Never Took Criticism Seriously." 2015. *India Today*, June 4. Available at http://indiatoday.intoday.in/story/anuja-chauhan-book-interview-the-house-that-bj-built-those-pricey-thakur-girls/1/442106.html.

Ashar, Meera. 2017. "Public." *South Asia: Journal of South Asian Studies* 40 (2): 385–388.

Ashcroft, Bill. 1999. "The Rhizome of Post-colonial Discourse." In *Literature and the Contemporary: Fictions and Theories of the Present*, edited by Roger Luckhurst and Peter Marks, 111–125. Essex, UK: Pearson Education.

Asokan, Ratik. 2016. "Sarnath Banerjee: The Full Texture of a City." *Guernica*, April 1. Available at https://www.guernicamag.com/the-full-texture-of-a-city.

Aw, Tash. 2013. *Five Star Billionaire*. New York: Spiegel and Grau.

Awaara. 1951. Directed by Raj Kapoor. Shemaroo Video Pvt. DVD.

Baabul. 2006. Directed by Ravi Chopra. Adlabs Films. DVD.

Baghban. 2003. Directed by Ravi Chopra. InNetwork Entertainment. DVD.

Bakhtin, M. M. 1981. *The Dialogic Imagination: Four Essays*. Translated by Caryl Emerson and Michael Holquist. Austin: University of Texas Press, 1981.

Bal, Hartosh Singh. 2014. "City of New Arrivals." *Outlook*, March 17. Available at https://www.outlookindia.com/magazine/story/city-of-new-arrivals/289740.

Balakrishnan, Ajit. 2013. "Chetan Bhagat, India's Dickens." *Business Standard*, January 20. Available at http://www.business-standard.com/article/opinion/ajit-balakrishnan-chetan-bhagat-india-s-dickens-112122700104_1.html.

Bandi, Swati. 2016. "'Sober Encounters': The Neoliberal Logics of Human Rights Documentary and Indian Feminist Documentary Filmmakers." *Feminist Media Studies* 16 (2): 1–16.

Bandopadhyay, Bibhutibhushan. (1929) 1999. *Pather Panchali: Song of the Road*. Translated by T. W. Clark and Tarapada Mukherji. New Delhi: HarperCollins.

Banerjee, Sarnath. 2015. *All Quiet in Vikaspuri*. Noida: HarperCollins India.

Bardhan, Pranab K. 2013. *Awakening Giants, Feet of Clay: Assessing the Economic Rise of China and India*. Princeton, NJ: Princeton University Press.

Barrett, A. Igoni. 2015. *Blackass*. Minneapolis, MN: Graywolf Press.

Barris, Kenya, creator. 2014. *Black-ish*. Wilmore Films. Television series.

Barthes, Roland. 1967. *Writing Degree Zero*. Translated by Annette Lavers and Colin Smith. New York: Hill and Wang.

———. 2011. *The Pleasure of the Text*. Translated by Richard Miller. New York: Hill and Wang.

Basu, Kunal. 2015. *Kalkatta*. New Delhi: Pan Macmillan India.

Basu, Srimati. 2011. "Sexual Property: Staging Rape and Marriage in Indian Law and Feminist Theory." *Feminist Studies* 37 (1): 185–211.

Baviskar, Amita. 2011. "Spectacular Events, City Spaces and Citizenship: The Commonwealth Games in Delhi." In *Urban Navigations: Politics, Space and the City in South Asia*, edited by Jonathan Shapiro Anjaria and Colin McFarlane, 138–161. New Delhi: Routledge.

Baweja, Vandana. 2015. "Architecture and Urbanism in *Slumdog Millionaire*: From Bombay to Mumbai." *Traditional Dwellings and Settlements Review* 26 (2): 7–24.

Beer and Biryani. 2015. "ED Issues Notice to Aamir Khan for Disproportionate Shedding of Tears over the Last Few Months." *Faking News*, November 27. Available at http://www.fakingnews.com/entertainment/ed-issues-notice-to-aamir-khan-for-disproportionate-shedding-of-tears-over-the-last-few-months-8607.

Berlant, Lauren. 2008. *The Female Complaint: The Unfinished Business of Sentimentality in American Culture.* Durham, NC: Duke University Press.

Bewes, Timothy. 2012. "Introduction: Temporalizing the Present." *Novel: A Forum on Fiction* 45 (2): 159–164.

Bhabha, Homi K. 1996. "Unsatisfied: Notes on Vernacular Cosmopolitanism." In *Text and Nation: Cross-disciplinary Essays on Cultural and National Identities,* edited by Laura García-Moreno and Peter C. Pfeiffer, 191–207. Columbia, SC: Camden House.

Bhagat, Chetan. 2004. *Five Point Someone: What Not to Do at IIT.* New Delhi: Rupa.

———. 2005. *One Night @ the Call Center.* New Delhi: Rupa.

———. 2008. *The 3 Mistakes of My Life.* New Delhi: Rupa.

———. 2009. *2 States: The Story of My Marriage.* New Delhi: Rupa.

———. 2011. *Revolution 2020: Love, Corruption, Ambition.* New Delhi: Rupa.

———. 2012. *What Young India Wants: Selected Essays and Columns.* New Delhi: Rupa.

———. 2013. "Letter from an Indian Muslim Youth." *Times of India,* June 30. Available at http://blogs.timesofindia.indiatimes.com/The-underage-optimist/entry/letter-from-an-indian-muslim-youth.

———. 2014a. "Bestselling English Author: I Write about an India That the West Is Not Interested In." *Huffington Post,* July 17. Available at http://www.huffingtonpost.com/chetan-bhagat/bestselling-english-author_b_5575570.html.

———. 2014b. *Half Girlfriend.* New Delhi: Rupa.

———. 2015. *Making India Awesome.* New Delhi: Rupa.

Bhagwat, Vidyut. 1995. "Bombay in Dalit Literature." In *Bombay: Mosaic of Modern Culture,* edited by Sujata Patel, 113–125. Bombay: Oxford University Press.

Bhagwati, Jagdish, and Arvind Panagariya. 2014. *Why Growth Matters: How Economic Growth in India Reduced Poverty and the Lessons for Other Developing Countries.* New York: PublicAffairs.

Bhan, Gautam. 2005. "Challenging the Limits of Law: Queer Politics and Legal Reform in India." In *Because I Have a Voice: Queer Politics in India,* edited by Arvind Narrain and Gautam Bhan, 40–48. New Delhi: Yoda Press.

Bharucha, Rustom. 2006. *Another Asia: Rabindranath Tagore and Okakura Tenshin.* New Delhi: Oxford University Press.

Bhatt, Neha. 2017. "Why Crime Fiction Is Turning Out to Be the Best Way to Depict Indian Cities in Novels." *Scroll,* March 12. Available at https://scroll.in/article/831564/why-crime-fiction-is-turning-out-to-be-the-best-way-to-depict-indian-cities-in-novels.

Bhaumik, Kaushik. 2004. "A Brief History of Cinema from Bombay to 'Bollywood.'" *History Compass* 2:1–4.

"Big Fat Indian Wedding." 2012. *Satyamev Jayate,* season 1, episode 3. Aired May 20. Star Plus.

Bird, Emma. 2015. "*Beautiful Thing*: Literary Reportage and Bombay." *Journal of Postcolonial Writing* 51 (4): 380–394.

Birtchnell, Thomas. 2011. "*Jugaad* as Systemic Risk and Disruptive Innovation in India." *Contemporary South Asia* 19 (4): 357–372.

BOMgAY. 1996. Directed by Riyad Vinci Wadia and Jangu Sethna. Wadia Movietone. DVD.

Boo, Katherine. 2012. *Beyond the Beautiful Forevers: Life, Death and Hope in a Mumbai Undercity.* New York: Farrar, Straus and Giroux.

Bose, Derek. 2006. *Brand Bollywood: A New Global Entertainment Order.* New Delhi: Sage.

Braudy, Leo. 1999. "Genre: The Conventions of Connection." In *Film Theory and Criticism: Introductory Readings*, 5th ed., edited by Leo Braudy and Marshall Cohen, 613–629. New York: Oxford University Press.

Brooks, Peter. 1976. *The Melodramatic Imagination: Balzac, Henry James, Melodrama, and the Mode of Excess*. New Haven, CT: Yale University Press.

Brouillette, Sarah. 2014. "On the Entrepreneurial Ethos of Aravind Adiga's *The White Tiger*." In *Re-Orientalism and South Asian Identity Politics: The Oriental Other Within*, edited by Lisa Lau and Ana Cristina Mendes, 40–55. London: Routledge.

———. 2017. "Neoliberalism and the Demise of the Literary." In *Neoliberalism and Contemporary Literary Culture*, edited by Mitchum Huehls and Rachel Greenwald Smith, 277–290. Baltimore: Johns Hopkins University Press.

Brown, Nicholas. 2016. "The Plain Viewer Be Damned: Or, Modernism on TV." In *The Contemporaneity of Modernism: Literature, Media, Culture*, edited by Michael D'Arcy and Mathias Nilges, 178–189. New York: Routledge.

Brown, Wendy. 1999. "Resisting Left Melancholy." *boundary 2* 26 (3): 19–27.

Brueck, Laura R. 2017. "Bending Biography: The Creative Intrusions of 'Real Lives' in Dalit Fiction." *Biography* 40 (1): 77–92.

Buckley, Jerome Hamilton. 1974. *Season of Youth: The Bildungsroman from Dickens to Golding*. Cambridge, MA: Harvard University Press.

Buford, Bill. 1997. "Declarations of Independence: Why Are There Suddenly So Many Indian Novelists?" *New Yorker*, June 23, pp. 6–8.

Carroll, Rachel. 2015. "How Soon Is Now: Constructing the Contemporary/Gendering the Experimental." *Contemporary Women's Writing* 9 (1): 16–33.

Chakraborty, Madhurima. 2017. "Introduction: Whose City?" In *Postcolonial Urban Outcasts: City Margins in South Asian Literature*, edited by Madhurima Chakraborty and Umme Al-wazedi, 1–20. New York: Routledge.

Chakraborty, Samhita. 2012. "The Nine Pointer." *The Telegraph*, February 6. Available at https://www.telegraphindia.com/1120206/jsp/entertainment/story_15098363.jsp#.UTDJsRlPHYX.

———. 2015. "Author Ravinder Singh Is Busy with His 'Baby,' and Is Planning Reunion No. 3." *The Telegraph*, April 24. Available at https://www.telegraphindia.com/1150424/jsp/t2/story_16241.jsp#.WF1tTZJ-hFc.

Chakravartty, Paula, and Sreela Sarkar. 2013. "Entrepreneurial Justice: The New Spirit of Capitalism in Emergent India." *Popular Communication* 11 (1): 58–75.

Chakravarty, Sumita. 1993. *National Identity in Indian Popular Cinema: 1947-1987*. Austin: University of Texas Press.

Chakravarty, Suparna. 2013. "Globalization, Youngistan and Chetan Bhagat." In *The Indian English Novel of the New Millennium*, edited by Prabhat K. Singh, 97–104. Newcastle upon Tyne, UK: Cambridge Scholars.

Chakravorty, Mrinalini. 2014. *In Stereotype: South Asia in the Global Literary Imaginary*. New York: Columbia University Press.

Chandra, Nandini. 2010. "Young Protest: The Idea of Merit in Commercial Hindi Cinema." *Comparative Studies of South Asia, Africa and the Middle East* 30 (1): 119–132.

Chandra, Vikram. 2000. "The Cult of Authenticity." *Boston Review*, February 1. Available at http://bostonreview.net/vikram-chandra-the-cult-of-authenticity.

———. 2006. *Sacred Games*. London: Faber and Faber.

Chandrashekhar, Vaishnavi. 2013. "Could Gang-Rape Protests Mark Beginning of an Age of Activism for India?" *Christian Science Monitor*, January 3. Available at

https://www.csmonitor.com/World/Asia-South-Central/2013/0103/Could-gang
-rape-protests-mark-beginning-of-an-age-of-activism-for-India.

Chatterjee, Partha. 2012. "The Movement against Politics." *Cultural Critique* 81:117–122.

Chaudhuri, Amit. 2006. "'I Wish Indian Writing in English Were Less Triumphant.'" *DW*, October 3. Available at http://www.dw.com/en/i-wish-indian-writing-in -english-were-less-triumphant/a-2186200-1.

———. 2014. *Odysseus Abroad*. New Delhi: Penguin.

———. 2016. "Consider the Writer." *Indian Express*, January 6. Available at http:// indianexpress.com/article/lifestyle/books/consider-the-writer.

Chaudhuri, Maitrayee. 2010. "Indian Media and Its Transformed Public." *Contributions to Indian Sociology* 44 (1–2): 57–78.

Chauhan, Anuja. 2008. *The Zoya Factor*. New Delhi: HarperCollins India.

———. 2010. *Battle for Bittora*. Noida: HarperCollins India.

———. 2013. *Those Pricey Thakur Girls*. Noida: HarperCollins India.

———. 2015. *The House That BJ Built*. Chennai: Westland.

———. 2017. *Baaz*. Noida: HarperCollins India.

"Check Out: Vidya Balan's Dirty Picture on Cover of Manohar Kahaniya." 2011. *Bollywood Hungama*, December 1. Available at http://www.bollywoodhungama.com/ news/features/check-out-vidya-balans-dirty-picture-on-cover-of-manohar -kahaniya/.

Chennai Express. 2013. Directed by Rohit Shetty. UTV Motion Pictures. DVD.

Chopra, Anupama. 1999. "Movie Review: Deepa Mehta's '1947—Earth,' Starring Nandita Das, Aamir Khan." *India Today*, September 27. Available at http://indiatoday .intoday.in/story/movie-review-deepa-mehtas-1947-earth-starring-nandita-das -aamir-khan/1/255282.html.

Chopra, Neeti. 2015. "15 Times Shah Rukh Khan Played 'Raj' or 'Rahul' Onscreen." *Huffington Post*, November 2. Available at http://www.huffingtonpost.in/2015/11/ 02/shah-rukh-khan-movies_n_8450182.html.

Choudhury, Kushanava. 2017. *The Epic City: The World on the Streets of Calcutta*. London: Bloomsbury.

Chua, Jocelyn. 2016. *In Pursuit of the Good Life: Aspiration and Suicide in Globalizing South India*. Berkeley: University of California Press.

Chutel, Lynsey. 2017. "Groundbreaking African Architecture Is Shedding a Colonial Past and Identifying Its Own Aesthetic." *Quartz Africa*, September 23. Available at https://qz.com/1084845/african-architecture-awards-recognizes-ghana-congo -senegal-designs.

Cilano, Cara. 2009. "'Writing from Extreme Edges': Pakistani English-Language Fiction." *ARIEL* 40 (2–3): 183–201.

Consolaro, Alessandra. 2011. "Resistance in the Postcolonial Hindi Literary Field: *Mohan Dās* by Uday Prakāś." *Orientalia Suecana* 60:9–19.

Coolie. 1983. Directed by Manmohan Desai. Time-N-Tune. DVD.

Cowie, Elizabeth. 1999. "The Spectacle of Actuality." In *Collecting Visible Evidence*, edited by Jane Gaines and Michael Renov, 19–45. Minneapolis: University of Minnesota Press.

"The Criminalization of Politics." 2014. *Satyamev Jayate*, season 2, episode 5. Aired March 30. Star Plus.

Dabangg. 2010. Directed by Abhinav Kashyap. Eros International. DVD.

Daiya, Kavita. 2011. "Visual Culture and Violence: Inventing Intimacy and Citizenship in Recent South Asian Cinema." *South Asian History and Culture* 2 (4): 589–604.

Dalvi, Mustansir. 2017. "Amitabh Bachchan Was a Part of My Growing Up Years, Which Is Why I Will Never Watch 'Sooryavansham.'" *Scroll*, October 11. Available at https://thereel.scroll.in/853677/amitabh-bachchan-was-a-part-of-my-growing-up-years-which-is-why-i-will-never-watch-sooryavansham.

Dangal. 2016. Directed by Nitesh Tiwari. UTV Motion Pictures. DVD.

Daniels, Christina. 2012. *I'll Do It My Way: The Incredible Journey of Aamir Khan*. Noida: Om Books.

D'Arcy, Michael, and Mathias Nilges. 2016. "Introduction: The Contemporaneity of Modernism." In *The Contemporaneity of Modernism: Literature, Media, Culture*, edited by Michael D'Arcy and Mathias Nilges, 1–14. New York: Routledge.

Dasgupta, Rana. 2014. *Capital: The Eruption of Delhi*. New York: Penguin.

Dasgupta, Shougat. 2013. "Leading the Idiocracy." *Tehelka*, April 5. Available at http://old.tehelka.com/leading-the-idiocracy.

Davis, Mike. 2006. *Planet of Slums*. London: Verso.

Dawson Varughese, Emma. 2013. *Reading New India: Post-millennial Indian Fiction in English*. London: Bloomsbury.

Deb, Siddharta. 2011. *The Beautiful and the Damned: A Portrait of the New India*. New York: Faber and Faber.

Deewaar. 1975. Directed by Yash Chopra. Trimurti Films. DVD.

Desai, Anita. 1980. *Clear Light of Day*. New York: Harper and Row.

Desai, Kiran. 2006. *The Inheritance of Loss*. New York: Atlantic Monthly Press.

Deshpande, Sudhavna. 2005. "The Consumable Hero of Globalised India." In *Bollyworld: Popular Indian Cinema through a Transnational Lens*, edited by Raminder Kaur and Ajay J. Sinha, 186–203. New Delhi: Sage.

de Souza, Eunice. 2015. "Book Review: The Adivasi Will Not Dance." *Times of India*, October 16. Available at http://timesofindia.indiatimes.com/life-style/books/features/Book-Review-The-Adivasi-Will-Not-Dance/articleshow/49374930.cms.

Dhaliwal, Nirpal. 2014. "Chetan Bhagat: Bollywood's Favourite Author." *The Guardian*, April 24. Available at https://www.theguardian.com/books/2014/apr/24/chetan-bhagat-interview-bollywood-favourite-author-india.

Dhar, Shobita. 2014. "Hindi Fiction Writes a New Story." *Times of India*, January 19. Available at http://timesofindia.indiatimes.com/home/sunday-times/deep-focus/Hindi-fiction-writes-a-new-story/articleshow/29033359.cms.

Dhar, Subir. 2013. "Inspiring India: The Fiction of Chetan Bhagat and the Discourse of Motivation." In *Writing India Anew: Indian English Fiction 2000–2010*, edited by Krishna Sen and Rituparna Roy, 161–169. Amsterdam: Amsterdam University Press.

Dhillon, Amrit. 2008. "Indians Fear Aravind Adiga's 'The White Tiger' Says Too Much about Them." *The Telegraph*, October 18. Available at http://www.telegraph.co.uk/news/worldnews/asia/india/3222136/Indians-fear-Aravind-Adigas-The-White-Tiger-says-too-much-about-them.html.

Dhobi Ghat. 2011. Directed by Kiran Rao. Reliance Entertainment. DVD.

Dhoom 3. 2013. Directed by Vijay Krishna Acharya. Yash Raj Films. DVD.

"Dhoom 3 Movie Review." 2016. *Times of India*, April 26. Available at https://timesofindia.indiatimes.com/entertainment/hindi/movie-reviews/dhoom-3/movie-review/27677238.cms.

Dickey, Sara. 2007. *Cinema and the Urban Poor in South India*. Cambridge: Cambridge University Press.

Dil. 1990. Directed by Indra Kumar. Maruti International. DVD.

Dil Chahta Hai. 2001. Directed by Farhan Akhtar. Excel Entertainment. DVD.

Dil Hai Ke Manta Nahin. 1991. Directed by Mahesh Bhatt. T-Series. DVD.

Divakaruni, Chitra Banerjee. 1997. *The Mistress of Spices.* New York: Doubleday.

"Domestic Violence." 2012. *Satyamev Jayate,* season 1, episode 7. Aired June 17. Star Plus.

Dore, Bhavya. 2018. "Reviving the Past: A Literary Collective Is Translating 100 Classic Novels across Indian Languages." *Scroll,* May 26. Available at https://scroll.in/article/879423/reviving-the-past-a-literary-collective-is-translating-100-classic-novels-across-indian-languages.

Dubey, Manish. 2016. *A Murder in Gurgaon.* New Delhi: Srishti.

Duggal, Ashima. 2013. "Conversations of the Everyday Political in Paromita Vohra's Documentary Films." *Chapati Mystery,* October 25. Available at http://www.chapatimystery.com/archives/potpurri/conversations_of_the_everyday_political_in_paromita_vohras_documentary_films.html.

Dum Laga Ke Haisha. 2015. Directed by Sharat Katariya. Yash Raj Films. DVD.

Dwivedi, Om Prakash, and Lisa Lau. 2014. "Introduction: The Reception of Indian Writing in English (IWE) in the Global Literary Market." In *Indian Writing in English and the Global Literary Market,* edited by Om Prakash Dwivedi and Lisa Lau, 1–9. Basingstoke, UK: Palgrave Macmillan.

Dwyer, Rachel. 2005. "The Saffron Screen? Hindu Nationalism and the Hindi Film." In *Religion, Media, and the Public Sphere,* edited by Birgit Meyer and Annelies Moors, 273–289. Bloomington: Indiana University Press.

———. 2011. "The Case of the Missing Mahatma: Gandhi and the Hindi Cinema." *Public Culture* 23 (2): 349–376.

———. 2012. "*Zara Hatke* ('Somewhat Different'): The New Middle Classes and the Changing Forms of Hindi Cinema." In *Being Middle-Class in India: A Way of Life,* edited by Henrike Donner, 184–208. London: Routledge.

———. 2016. "Mumbai Middlebrow: Ways of Thinking about the Middle Ground in Hindi Cinema." In *Middlebrow Cinema,* edited by Sally Faulkner, 51–68. London: Routledge.

Dyer, Richard. 2011. *Stars.* Basingstoke, UK: Palgrave Macmillan.

Earth. 1999. Directed by Deepa Mehta. Zeitgeist Films. DVD.

East, Ben. 2015. "Newsmaker: Aamir Khan, the Thinking Man's Hero." *The National,* November 26. Available at http://www.thenational.ae/arts-life/film/newsmaker-aamir-khan-the-thinking-mans-hero.

Echanove, Matias, and Rahul Srivastava. 2009. "Taking the Slum out of 'Slumdog.'" *New York Times,* February 21. Available at https://www.nytimes.com/2009/02/21/opinion/21srivastava.html.

Edelman, Lee. 2007. *No Future: Queer Theory and the Death Drive.* Durham, NC: Duke University Press.

Ek Haseena Thi. 2004. Directed by Sriram Raghavan. R. R. Venkat. DVD.

Ellis, John. 2015. *Visible Fictions: Cinema, Television, Video.* Abingdon, UK: Routledge.

English, James F. 2016. "Now, Not Now: Counting Time in Contemporary Fiction Studies." *Modern Language Quarterly* 77 (3): 395–418.

Erber, Pedro. 2013. "Contemporaneity and Its Discontents." *Diacritics* 41 (1): 28–49.

Eshel, Amir. 2013. *Futurity: Contemporary Literature and the Quest for the Past.* Chicago: University of Chicago Press.

Fabian, Johannes. 1983. *Time and the Other: How Anthropology Makes Its Object.* New York: Columbia University Press.

Fanaa. 2006. Directed by Kunal Kohli. Yash Raj Films. DVD.

"Fawad Khan's Statement on Pak Artistes Ban Garners Mixed Reactions." 2016. *Business Standard*, October 8. Available at https://www.business-standard.com/article/news -ani/fawad-khan-s-statement-on-pak-artistes-ban-garners-mixed-reactions -116100800099_1.html.

Felski, Rita. 2015. *The Limits of Critique.* Chicago: University of Chicago Press.

"Female Foeticide." 2012. *Satyamev Jayate*, season 1, episode 1. Aired May 6. Star Plus.

Ferguson, James. 2015. *Give a Man a Fish: Reflections on the New Politics of Distribution.* Durham, NC: Duke University Press.

Fernandes, Naresh. 2014. "Cities in Motion: Why Mumbai's New Air Terminal Has Gone off the Rails." *The Guardian*, February 20. Available at http://www.theguardian .com/cities/2014/feb/20/cities-in-motion-mumbai-air-terminal-rails.

"Fighting Rape." 2014. *Satyamev Jayate*, season 2, episode 1. Aired March 2. Star Plus.

"First World Problems." 2011. *Know Your Meme.* Available at http://knowyourmeme .com/memes/first-world-problems.

Foltz, Mary Catherine. 2008. "The Excremental Ethics of Samuel R. Delany." *SubStance* 37 (2): 41–55.

Friedman, Milton. 2012. *Capitalism and Freedom.* Chicago: University of Chicago Press.

Frota, Monica. 1996. "Taking Aim: The Video Technology of Cultural Resistance." In *Resolutions: Contemporary Video Practices*, edited by Michael Renov and Erika Suderburg, 258–282. Minneapolis: University of Minnesota Press.

Gabbar Is Back. 2015. Directed by Krish. Viacom 18 Motion Pictures. DVD.

Gadihoke, Sabeena. 2012. "Secrets and Inner Voices: The Self and Subjectivity in Contemporary Indian Documentary." In *The Cinema of Me: The Self and Subjectivity in First Person Documentary*, edited by Alisa Lebow, 144–157. New York: Wallflower Press.

Gaines, Jane M. 1999. "Political Mimesis." In *Collecting Visible Evidence*, edited by Jane Gaines and Michael Renov, 84–102. Minneapolis: University of Minnesota Press.

Gajarawala, Toral Jatin. 2009. "The Last and the First." *Economic and Political Weekly* 44 (50): 21–23.

———. 2012. "The Casteized Consciousness: Literary Realism and the Politics of Particularism." *Modern Language Quarterly* 73 (3): 329–349.

———. 2013. *Untouchable Fictions: Literary Realism and the Crisis of Caste.* New York: Fordham University Press.

———. 2015. "Caste, Complicity, and the Contemporary." In *A History of the Indian Novel in English*, edited by Ulka Anjaria, 373–387. Cambridge: Cambridge University Press.

Ganguly, Debjani. 2016. *This Thing Called the World: The Contemporary Novel as Global Form.* Durham, NC: Duke University Press.

Ghajini. 2008. Directed by A. R. Murugadoss. Reliance Entertainment. DVD.

Ghosh, Amitav. 1988. *The Shadow Lines.* London: Bloomsbury.

———. 1992. *In an Antique Land.* Harmondsworth, UK: Penguin.

———. 2000. *The Glass Palace.* New Delhi: Ravi Dayal.

———. 2015. *Flood of Fire.* New Delhi: Penguin.

Ghosh, Paramita. 2013. "The Revolutionary Ideal Persists in India: Sanjay Kak." *Hindustan Times*, May 11. Available at http://www.hindustantimes.com/movie-reviews/ the-revolutionary-ideal-persists-in-india-sanjay-kak/story-UdlD1D8xihFBr MSTKEdeNJ.html.

Ghulam. 1998. Directed by Vikram Bhatt. Vishesh Films. DVD.

Gilroy, Paul. 2013. "'. . . We Got to Get Over before We Go Under . . .': Fragments for a History of Black Vernacular Neoliberalism." *New Formations* 80–81 (Winter): 23–38.

Gledhill, Christine. 1991. "Signs of Melodrama." In *Stardom: Industry of Desire*, edited by Christine Gledhill, 207–229. London: Routledge.

Goodlad, Lauren M. E. 2004. *Victorian Literature and the Victorian State: Character and Governance in a Liberal Society.* Baltimore: Johns Hopkins University Press.

Gooptu, Nandini. 2013. "Introduction." In *Enterprise Culture in Neoliberal India: Studies in Youth, Class, Work and Media*, edited by Nandini Gooptu, 1–24. London: Routledge.

Gooptu, Nandini, and Rangan Chakravarty. 2013. "Reality TV in India and the Making of an Enterprising Housewife." In *Enterprise Culture in Neoliberal India: Studies in Youth, Class, Work and Media*, edited by Nandini Gooptu, 140–236. London: Routledge.

Gopal, Sangita. 2012. *Conjugations: Marriage and Film Form in New Bollywood Cinema.* Chicago: University of Chicago Press.

———. 2015. "'Coming to a Multiplex near You': Indian Fiction in English and New Bollywood Cinema." In *A History of the Indian Novel in English*, edited by Ulka Anjaria, 359–372. Cambridge: Cambridge University Press.

Gopalan, Lalitha. 2002. *Cinema of Interruptions: Action Genres in Contemporary Indian Cinema.* London: British Film Institute.

Goswami, Dev. 2017. "Chetan Bhagat Wants Diwali Celebrated with Firecrackers: Because, Tradition." *India Today*, October 9. Available at http://indiatoday.intoday.in/story/chetan-bhagat-diwali-firecrackers-supreme-court-twitter/1/1064571.html.

Goswami, Manu. 2012. "The American Dream Outsourced: India and the Genre of Growth." *Public Books*, December 12. Available at http://www.publicbooks.org/the-american-dream-outsourcedindia-and-the-genre-of-growth.

Goyal, Divya. 2016. "How Aamir Khan Followed the Calorie-Count Method to Lose around 25kg for Dangal." *Indian Express*, November 29. Available at http://indianexpress.com/article/lifestyle/fitness/aamir-khan-weight-loss-story-secret-for-dangal-2857618.

Goyal, Yogita. 2014. "Introduction: Africa and the Black Atlantic." *Research in African Literatures* 45 (3): v–xxv.

Greaney, Michael. 2006. *Contemporary Fiction and the Uses of Theory: The Novel from Structuralism to Postmodernism.* Basingstoke, UK: Palgrave Macmillan.

Griffin, Peter. 2009. "An Interview with Chetan Bhagat." *Forbes*, December 23. Available at http://www.forbesindia.com/interview/magazine-extra/an-interview-with-chetan-bhagat/8452/1.

"Guardian Books Podcast: Africa and Post-post-colonialism." 2011. *The Guardian*, November 18. Available at https://www.theguardian.com/books/audio/2011/nov/18/africa-books-post-colonialism-podcast.

Guerrero, Lisa A. 2006. "'Sistahs Are Doin' It for Themselves': Chick Lit in Black and White." In *Chick Lit: The New Woman's Fiction*, edited by Suzanne Ferriss and Mallory Young, 87–102. New York: Routledge.

Gulaab Gang. 2014. Directed by Soumik Sen. Benaras Mediaworks. DVD.

Gupta, Dipankar. 2013. *Revolution from Above: India's Future and the Citizen Elite.* New Delhi: Rainlight.

Gupta, Kanishka. 2017. "While You Weren't Looking (or Reading), Savi Sharma Sold 100,000 Copies of Her Romance." *Scroll*, January 15. Available at https://scroll.in/

article/826723/while-you-werent-looking-or-reading-savi-sharma-sold-100000 -copies-of-her-romance.

Gupta, Sukanya. 2015. "*Kahaani, Gulaab Gang* and *Queen*: Remaking the Queens of Bollywood." *South Asian Popular Culture* 13 (2): 107–123.

Gupta, Suman. 2012. "Indian 'Commercial Fiction' in English, the Publishing Industry and Youth Culture." *Economic and Political Weekly* 47 (5): 46–53.

Gupta, Trisha. 2016. "'People Not Going to Literature Is One of the Reasons We See This Intolerance Today.'" *Scroll*, March 5. Available at http://scroll.in/article/804589/ people-not-going-to-literature-is-one-of-the-reasons-we-see-this-intolerance -today.

Guttman, Anna. 2017. "New Capital? Representing Bangalore in Recent Crime Fiction." In *Postcolonial Urban Outcasts: City Margins in South Asian Literature*, edited by Madhurima Chakraborty and Umme Al-wazedi, 257–272. New York: Routledge.

Haag, Laurie L. 1993. "Oprah Winfrey: The Construction of Intimacy in the Talk Show Setting." *Journal of Popular Culture* 26 (4): 115–121.

Hamid, Mohsin. 2013. *How to Get Filthy Rich in Rising Asia*. New York: Riverhead Books.

Hansen, Kathryn. 1981. "Renu's Regionalism: Language and Form." *Journal of Asian Studies* 40 (2): 273–294.

Hansen, Thomas Blom. 2001. *Wages of Violence: Naming and Identity in Postcolonial Bombay*. Princeton, NJ: Princeton University Press.

Harindranath, R., and Sukhmani Khorana. 2014. "Civil Society Movements and the 'Twittering Classes' in the Postcolony: An Indian Case Study." *South Asia: Journal of South Asian Studies* 37 (1): 60–71.

Harzewski, Stephanie. 2006. "Tradition and Displacement in the New Novel of Manners." In *Chick Lit: The New Woman's Fiction*, edited by Suzanne Ferriss and Mallory Young, 29–46. New York: Routledge.

Hasan, Anjum. 2009. *Neti, Neti, Not This, Not This*. New Delhi: Roli Books.

———. 2014. "On Recovering the Literary through Literary Activism." *Caravan*, December 26. Available at http://www.caravanmagazine.in/vantage/recovering-literary -activism.

———. 2015a. *The Cosmopolitans*. Gurgaon, India: Penguin.

———. 2015b. "Provincial Self-Fashioning in Fiction—Then and Now." *American Book Review* 36 (6): 6–22.

———. 2016. "Building Up the Alphabet Again." *Public Books*, July 15. Available at http:// www.publicbooks.org/fiction/building-up-the-alphabet-again.

Herman, Jeanette. 2005. "Memory and Melodrama: The Transnational Politics of Deepa Mehta's *Earth*." *Camera Obscura 58* 20 (1): 107–147.

Hoad, Phil. 2015. "Aamir Khan's Religious Satire PK Becomes India's Most Successful Film." *The Guardian*, January 7. Available at https://www.theguardian.com/film/ 2015/jan/07/global-box-office-pk-the-hobbit-big-hero-6-unbroken.

Holmes, Christopher. 2013. "The Novel's Third Way: Zadie Smith's 'Hysterical Realism.'" In *Reading Zadie Smith: The First Decade and Beyond*, edited by Philip Tew, 141–153. London: Bloomsbury.

Holmes, Su. 2011. "'All You've Got to Worry About Is the Task, Having a Cup of Tea, and Doing a Bit of Sunbathing': Approaching Celebrity in *Big Brother*." In *Understanding Reality Television*, edited by Su Holmes and Deborah Jermyn, 111–135. London: Routledge.

Holmes, Su, and Deborah Jermyn. 2011. "Introduction: Understanding Reality TV." In *Understanding Reality Television*, edited by Su Holmes and Deborah Jermyn, 1–32. London: Routledge.

Hoskote, Ranjit. 2010. *Sudhir Patwardhan, the Complicit Observer*. Mumbai: Sakshi Gallery.

Huang, Yibing. 2007. *Contemporary Chinese Literature: From the Cultural Revolution to the Future*. New York: Palgrave Macmillan.

Huehls, Mitchum. 2016. *After Critique: Twenty-First-Century Fiction in a Neoliberal Age*. Oxford: Oxford University Press.

Huehls, Mitchum, and Rachel Greenwald Smith. 2017. "Four Phases of Neoliberalism and Literature: An Introduction." In *Neoliberalism and Contemporary Literary Culture*, edited by Mitchum Huehls and Rachel Greenwald Smith, 1–18. Baltimore: Johns Hopkins University Press.

"I Can Never Cry with the Help of Glycerine: Sonam Kapoor." 2013. *Hindustan Times*, June 14. Available at http://www.hindustantimes.com/bollywood/i-can-never-cry-with-the-help-of-glycerine-sonam-kapoor/story-sRRLHrT66mZ7wr3WswqcCJ.html.

"I'm Battling 'Elitist Bullying' in Literature: Chetan Bhagat." 2016. *Sakshi Post*, October 16. Available at http://english.sakshi.com/editors-picks/2016/10/16/im-battling-elitist-bullying-in-literature-chetan-bhagat.

"I'm Not the Best Writer, but the Bestselling Writer: Chetan Bhagat." 2014. *Indian Express*, October 19. Available at http://indianexpress.com/article/entertainment/bollywood/im-not-the-best-writer-but-the-bestselling-writer-chetan-bhagat.

Irr, Caren. 2014. *Toward the Geopolitical Novel: U.S. Fiction in the Twenty-First Century*. New York: Columbia University Press.

Ishq. 1997. Directed by Indra Kumar. Eros Multimedia Pvt. DVD.

Ivanova, Natalia. 2009. "That Elusive Contemporaneity: Russian Literature of the Twentieth and Twenty-First Centuries: From 'Outside the Mold' to Post-Soviet, Now Global." *Russian Studies in Literature* 45 (3): 30–52.

Jai Ho. 2014. Directed by Sohail Khan. Eros International. DVD.

Jain, Anuja. 2013. "The Curious Case of the Films Division: Some Annotations on the Beginnings of Indian Documentary Cinema in Postindependence India, 1940s–1960s." *Velvet Light Trap* 71:15–26.

Jain, Mayank. 2014. "'I Find Chetan Bhagat Honest and Raw.'" *Scroll*, November 8. Available at https://scroll.in/article/685859/i-find-chetan-bhagat-honest-and-raw.

Jameson, Fredric. 2008. "New Literary History after the End of the New." *New Literary History* 39 (3): 375–387.

———. 2010. "Realism and Utopia in *The Wire*." *Criticism* 52 (3–4): 359–372.

———. 2013. *The Antinomies of Realism*. London: Verso.

Jauregui, Beatrice. 2014. "Provisional Agency in India: *Jugaad* and Legitimation of Corruption." *American Ethnologist* 41 (1): 76–91.

Jayashankar, K. P., and Anjali Monteiro. 2016. *A Fly in the Curry: Independent Documentary Film in India*. New Delhi: Sage.

Jeffrey, Craig. 2013. "No Country for Young Men?" *Economic and Political Weekly* 48 (24): 33–35.

Jeffrey, Robin. 2008. "The Mahatma Didn't Like the Movies and Why It Matters: Indian Broadcasting Policy, 1920s–1990s." In *Television in India: Satellites, Politics, and Cultural Change*, edited by Nalin Mehta, 13–31. London: Routledge.

"JNU Prof Makarand Paranjape Asks Kanhaiya Kumar: Did You Check Facts before Making the Speech?" 2016. *India*, March 8. Available at http://www.india.com/news/india/jnu-prof-makarand-paranjape-asks-kanhaiya-kumar-did-you-check-facts-before-making-the-speech-1014519.

Jo Jeeta Wohi Sikandar. 1992. Directed by Mansoor Khan. Jorden Electronics. DVD.

Joseph, Manu. 2010. *Serious Men*. New Delhi: HarperCollins.

———. 2012. *The Illicit Happiness of Other People*. New Delhi: Fourth Estate.

———. 2016. "Depression or Oppression: What Led to Rohith Vemula's Suicide?" *Hindustan Times*, January 25. Available at http://www.hindustantimes.com/columns/depression-or-dalit-what-s-the-bigger-factor-behind-rohith-s-suicide/story-q2BuU7LZTxChdxhGLeOY8N.html.

———. 2017. "Activism as a 'Blue Whale Challenge.'" *Live Mint*, August 26. Available at http://www.livemint.com/Leisure/eH5UQ2kmjBJUskw4tXmGnN/Activism-as-a-Blue-Whale-Challenge.html.

Joseph, Tony. 2014. "The Real Reason Indian Intellectuals Are Backing Narendra Modi." *Quartz*, May 2. Available at http://qz.com/205367/the-real-reason-indian-intellectuals-are-flocking-to-modi.

Joshi, Namrata. 2012. "'I'm Not a 24×7 Social Activist.'" *Outlook*, May 21. Available at http://www.outlookindia.com/article/im-not-a-24x7-social-activist/280889.

Joshi, Priya. 2010. "Bollylite in America." *South Asian Popular Culture* 8 (3): 245–259.

———. 2015. "Chetan Bhagat: Remaking the Novel in India." In *A History of the Indian Novel in English*, edited by Ulka Anjaria, 310–323. Cambridge: Cambridge University Press.

Kaala Patthar. 1979. Directed by Yash Chopra. Yash Raj Films. DVD.

Kabhi Khushi Kabhie Gham. 2001. Directed by Karan Johar. Yash Raj Films. DVD.

Kabir, Ananya Jahanara. 2015. "'Handcuffed to History': Partition and the Indian Novel in English." In *A History of the Indian Novel in English*, edited by Ulka Anjaria, 119–132. Cambridge: Cambridge University Press.

Kahaani. 2012. Directed by Sujoy Ghosh. Viacom 18 Motion Pictures. DVD.

Kapoor, Mini. 2014a. "My Competition Is Apps like Candy Crush or WhatsApp, Says Chetan Bhagat." *India Today*, August 29. Available at http://indiatoday.intoday.in/story/chetan-bhagat-unplugged/1/379759.html.

———. 2014b. "What Makes Chetan Bhagat the One-Man Industry and Change Agent That He Is." *India Today*, August 28. Available at http://indiatoday.intoday.in/story/chetan-bhagat-novel-half-girlfriend-two-million-copies-set-to-roll-off-press/1/379631.html.

Kapur, Geeta. 2008. "A Cultural Conjuncture in India: Art into Documentary." In *Antinomies of Art and Culture: Modernity, Postmodernity, Contemporaneity*, edited by Terry Smith, Okwui Enwezor, and Nancy Condee, 30–59. Durham, NC: Duke University Press.

Kapur, Jyotsna. 2003. "Why the Personal Is Still Political—Some Lessons from Contemporary Indian Documentary." *Jump Cut: A Review of Contemporary Media* 46. Available at http://www.ejumpcut.org/archive/jc46.2003/indiandocs.kapur/index.html.

———. 2006. "Love in the Midst of Fascism: Gender and Sexuality in the Contemporary Indian Documentary." *Visual Anthropology* 19:335–346.

———. 2013. *The Politics of Time and Youth in Brand India: Bargaining with Capital*. London: Anthem Press.

Karimi, Faith. 2016. "'An African City' Web Series Generates Buzz, Dismantles Stereo-types." *CNN*, August 25. Available at http://edition.cnn.com/2014/04/18/world/africa/ghana-african-city.

Karnicky, Jeffrey. 2007. *Contemporary Fiction and the Ethics of Modern Culture.* New York: Palgrave Macmillan.

Kaur, Pawanpreet. 2012. "The Sad Demise of Hindi Pulp Fiction." *Sunday Guardian*, March 18. Available at http://www.sunday-guardian.com/artbeat/the-sad-demise-of-hindi-pulp-fiction.

Kaur, Ravinder, and Thomas Blom Hansen. 2016. "Aesthetics of Arrival: Spectacle, Capital, Novelty in Post-reform India." *Identities: Global Studies in Culture and Power* 23 (2): 265–275.

Kazan, Patricia. 1998. "Sexual Assault and the Problem of Consent." In *Violence against Women: Philosophical Perspectives*, edited by Stanley French, Wanda Teays, and Laura Purdy, 27–42. Ithaca, NY: Cornell University Press.

Kesavan, Mukul. 2016. "Before the Change: When Austerity, Simplicity Ruled Everyday Middle Class Life." *Hindustan Times*, July 24. Available at http://www.hindustantimes .com/india-news/before-the-change-when-austerity-and-simplicity-ruled-everyday -middle-class-life/story-PuanuEB9aMkrD4doqtzI4N.html.

Khair, Tabish. 2008. "Indian Pulp Fiction in English: A Preliminary Overview from Dutt to Dé." *Journal of Commonwealth Literature* 43 (3): 59–74.

———. 2015. "The Cosmopolitanism of Small Towns." *American Book Review* 36 (6): 4–5.

Khair, Tabish, and Sébastien Doubinsky. 2015. "The Politics and Art of Indian English Fantasy Fiction." In *A History of the Indian Novel in English*, edited by Ulka Anjaria, 337–347. Cambridge: Cambridge University Press.

Khan, Aamir, creator. 2012–2014. *Satyamev Jayate*. Aamir Khan Productions. Television series.

Khan, Naveeda. 2012. *Muslim Belonging: Aspiration and Skepticism in Pakistan*. Durham, NC: Duke University Press.

Khan, Shahnaz. 2009a. "Nationalism and Hindi Cinema: Narrative Strategies in *Fanaa*." *Studies in South Asian Film and Media* 1 (1): 85–99.

———. 2009b. "Reading *Fanaa*: Confrontational View, Comforting Identifications and Undeniable Pleasures." *South Asian Popular Culture* 7 (2): 127–139.

Khanduri, Ritu Gairola. 2012. "Picturing India: Nation, Development and the Common Man." *Visual Anthropology* 25:303–323.

Khatun, Nadira. 2016. "Imagining Muslims as the 'Other' in Muslim Political Films." *Journal of Arab and Muslim Media Research* 9 (1): 41–60.

King, Barry. 1991. "Articulating Stardom." In *Stardom: Industry of Desire*, edited by Christine Gledhill, 167–182. London: Routledge.

King, Frederick D. 2012. "Queer Spaces and Strategic Social Constructions in Rao's *The Boyfriend*." *Community and Dissent* 1 (1): 35–45.

"Kings Every Day." 2014. *Satyamev Jayate*, season 2, episode 4. Aired March 23. Star Plus.

Kishore, Shweta. 2013. "Beyond Cinephilia: Situating the Encounter between Documentary Film and Film Festival Audiences; The Case of the Ladakh International Film Festival, India." *Third Test* 27 (6): 735–747.

———. 2017. "Interview with Paromita Vohra: Remaking the 'Political' in Social Documentary." *Camera Obscura 94* 32 (1): 167–177.

Kraidy, Marwan M. 2009. *Reality Television and Arab Politics: Contention in Public Life*. Cambridge: Cambridge University Press.

Kulkarni, Damini. 2017. "Meet Bollywood's Avenging Angels, from Rekha to Vidya Balan." *Scroll*, April 23. Available at https://thereel.scroll.in/835383/meet-bollywoods-avenging-angels-from-rekha-to-vidya-balan.

Kumar, Akshaya. 2014. "*Satyamev Jayate*: Return of the Star as a Sacrificial Figure." *South Asia: Journal of South Asian Studies* 37 (2): 239–254.

Kumar, Amitava. 2012. *Bombay, London, New York*. New York: Routledge.

Kumar, Avinash. 2013. "*Kai Po Che*: Reigniting Memories." *Economic and Political Weekly* 48 (13): 38–40.

Kumar, Shailesh. n.d. "Aamir Khan Speaks on 'Mangal Pandey.'" *Planet Bollywood*. Available at http://www.planetbollywood.com/displayArticle.php?id=072705022256 (accessed June 9, 2017).

Lagaan. 2001. Directed by Ashutosh Gowariker. B4U Entertainment. DVD.

Lage Raho Munnabhai. 2006. Directed by Rajkumar Santoshi. Vidhu Vinod Chopra. DVD.

Lahiri, Jhumpa. 2003. *The Namesake*. New York: Houghton Mifflin.

———. 2013. *The Lowland*. New York: Knopf.

Larkin, Brian. 1997. "Indian Films and Nigerian Lovers: Media and the Creation of Parallel Modernities." *Africa* 67 (3): 1–20.

Lau, Lisa, and Om Prakash Dwivedi. 2014. *Re-Orientalism and Indian Writing in English*. Basingstoke, UK: Palgrave Macmillan.

Lee, Summer Kim. 2017. "Wrong Impressions." *ASAP/Journal* 2 (2): 261–264.

Lewis, Tania, Fran Martin, and Wanning Sun. 2016. *Telemodernities: Television and Transforming Lives in Asia*. Durham, NC: Duke University Press.

Liang, Lawrence. 2005. "Cinematic Citizenship and the Illegal City." *Inter-Asia Cultural Studies* 6 (3): 366–385.

London, Dianca. 2016. "Beyoncé's Capitalism, Masquerading as Radical Change." *Death and Taxes*, February 9. Available at https://archive.is/9yusZ.

Love Aaj Kal. 2009. Directed by Imtiaz Ali. Eros International. DVD.

Lowdon, Claire. 2013. "*Americanah* by Chimamanda Ngozi Adichie: An Issues Novel Unashamedly Open about Its Intentions." *New Statesman*, July 19. Available at http://www.newstatesman.com/culture/2013/07/americanah-chimamanda-ngozi-adichie-issues-novel-unashamedly-open-about-its-intentio.

Lu, Hsiao-peng. 1997. "Art, Culture, and Cultural Criticism in Post–New China." *New Literary History* 28 (1): 111–133.

Luckhurst, Roger, and Peter Marks. 1999. "Hurry Up Please It's Time: Introducing the Contemporary." In *Literature and the Contemporary: Fictions and Theories of the Present*, edited by Roger Luckhurst and Peter Marks, 1–11. Essex, UK: Pearson Education.

Luo, Shao-Pin. 2013. "The Way of Words: Vernacular Cosmopolitanism in Amitav Ghosh's *Sea of Poppies*." *Journal of Commonwealth Literature* 48 (3): 377–392.

Maatr. 2017. Directed by Ashtar Sayed. CDB Musical. DVD.

Madaari. 2016. Directed by Nishikant Kamat. Reliance Big Pictures. DVD.

Mahboob, Tahiat. 2013. "Interview: Novelist Manu Joseph Explores Family Happiness, 'Illicit' and Otherwise." *Asia Blog*, January 7. Available at http://asiasociety.org/blog/asia/interview-novelist-manu-joseph-explores-family-happiness-illicit-and-otherwise.

Main Azaad Hoon. 1981. Directed by Tinnu Anand. Nadiawala Sons. DVD.

Maity, Saheli. 2015. "List of Movies Where Amitabh Bachchan Played the Character Named 'Vijay.'" *Koimoi.com*, March 7. Available at http://www.koimoi.com/bollywood-popular/list-of-movies-where-amitabh-bachchan-played-the-character-named-vijay.

"Major Focus on Translations among Publishing Houses in India." 2018. *The Quint*, February 8. Available at https://www.thequint.com/news/hot-news/major-focus-on-translations-among-publishing-houses-in-india.

Majumdar, Neepa. 2010. *Wanted Cultured Ladies Only! Female Stardom and Cinema in India, 1930s–1950s*. New Delhi: Oxford University Press.

Majumdar, Saikat. 2015a. "Introduction to Focus: Little India—the Provincial Life of Cosmopolitanism." *American Book Review* 36 (6): 3–4.

——. 2015b. *Prose of the World: Modernism and the Banality of Empire*. New York: Columbia University Press.

——. 2016. "Indian Writers under Siege: A Roundtable." *Public Books*, March 1. Available at http://www.publicbooks.org/interviews/indian-writers-under-siege-a-roundtable.

Majumder, Sanjoy. 2015. "India Porn Ban: How the Government Was Forced to Reverse Course." *BBC News*, August 8. Available at http://www.bbc.com/news/world-asia-india-33810775.

"The Making of Satyamev Jayate." 2017. *Satyamev Jayate*. Available at http://www.satyamevjayate.in/fromteamsmj/season1-making.aspx.

Mallya, Vinutha. 2016. "Numbers and Letters: The Possibilities and Pitfalls before India's Publishing Industry." *The Caravan*, April 1. Available at http://www.caravanmagazine.in/reviews-essays/numbers-and-letters-india-publishing-industry.

Mangal Pandey: The Rising. 2005. Directed by Ketan Mehta. Yash Raj Films. DVD.

Mankekar, Purnima. 2000. *Screening Culture, Viewing Politics: Television, Womanhood and Nation in Modern India*. New Delhi: Oxford University Press.

——. 2013. "'We Are like This Only': Aspiration, *Jugaad*, and Love in Enterprise Culture." In *Enterprise Culture in Neoliberal India: Studies in Youth, Class, Work and Media*, edited by Nandini Gooptu, 27–40. London: Routledge.

Manto, Saadat Hasan. 2012. "Odor." In *Manto*, edited by Ayesha Jalal and Nusrat Jalal, 94–100. Lahore: Sang-e-Meel Publications.

Mantri, Geetika. 2016. "Superheroes with Scars: Priya's Mirror, a Comic Featuring Real-Life Acid Attack Survivors." *News Minute*, September 30. Available at http://www.thenewsminute.com/article/superheroes-scars-priyas-mirror-comic-featuring-real-life-acid-attack-survivors-50664.

"March on Women: In Conversation with Columnist Paromita Vohra, Activist Trupti Desai." 2016. *YouTube*, March 12. Available at https://www.youtube.com/watch?v=uECpTNimUz8.

Mardaani. 2014. Directed by Pradeep Sarkar. Yash Raj Films. DVD.

Maslin, Janet. 2013. "Braiding Hair and Issues about Race." *New York Times*, May 19. Available at http://www.nytimes.com/2013/05/20/books/americanha-by-chimamanda-ngozi-adichie.html.

Matzner, Deborah. 2014. "*Jai Bhim Comrade* and the Politics of Sound in Urban Indian Visual Culture." *Visual Anthropology Review* 30 (2): 127–138.

Mazumdar, Ranjani. 2007. *Bombay Cinema: An Archive of the City*. Minneapolis: University of Minnesota Press.

——. 2013. "Dream Merchants." *Frontline*, October 18. Available at http://www.frontline.in/arts-and-culture/cinema/dream-merchants/article5179476.ece.

Mazza, Cris. 2006. "Who's Laughing Now? A Short History of Chick Lit and the Perversion of a Genre." In *Chick Lit: The New Woman's Fiction*, edited by Suzanne Ferriss and Mallory Young, 17–28. New York: Routledge.

Mazzarella, William. 2009. "Making Sense of the Cinema in Late Colonial India." In *Censorship in South Asia: Cultural Regulation from Sedition to Seduction*, edited by

Raminder Kaur and William Mazzarella, 63–86. Bloomington: Indiana University Press.

———. 2013. *Censorium: Cinema and the Open Edge of Mass Publicity.* Durham, NC: Duke University Press.

McCarthy, Anna. 2007. "Reality Television: A Neoliberal Theater of Suffering." *Social Text* 25 (4): 17–42.

McGuire, Meredith Lindsay. 2013. "The Embodiment of Professionalism: Personality-Development Programmes in New Delhi." In *Enterprise Culture in Neoliberal India: Studies in Youth, Class, Work and Media,* edited by Nandini Gooptu, 109–123. London: Routledge.

McGurl, Mark. 2011. *The Program Era: Postwar Fiction and the Rise of Creative Writing.* Cambridge, MA: Harvard University Press.

———. 2016. "Everything and Less: Fiction in the Age of Amazon." *Modern Language Quarterly* 77 (3): 447–471.

Mehrotra, Palash Krishna. 2012. *The Butterfly Generation: A Personal Journey into the Passions and Follies of India's Technicolour Youth.* New Delhi: Rupa.

Mehta, Ritesh. 2012. "Flash Activism: How a Bollywood Film Catalyzed Civic Justice toward a Murder Trial." *Transformative Works and Cultures,* no. 10. Available at http://journal.transformativeworks.org/index.php/twc/article/view/345/271.

Mehta, Suketu. 2004. *Maximum City: Bombay Lost and Found.* New York: Vintage.

Mendes, Ana Cristina. 2010. "Exciting Tales of Exotic Dark India: Aravind Adiga's *The White Tiger.*" *Journal of Commonwealth Literature* 45 (2): 275–293.

Miller, Sam. 2009. *Delhi: Adventures in a Megacity.* London: Jonathan Cape.

Minerva, Kelly A. 2017. "The Fiction of Anosh Irani: The Magic of a Traumatized Community." In *Postcolonial Urban Outcasts: City Margins in South Asian Literature,* edited by Madhurima Chakraborty and Umme Al-wazedi, 239–256. New York: Routledge.

Mishra, Pankaj. 2014. "Narendra Modi and the New Face of India." *The Guardian,* May 16. Available at https://www.theguardian.com/books/2014/may/16/what-next-india-pankaj-mishra.

———. 2017a. *Age of Anger: A History of the Present.* London: Farrar, Straus and Giroux.

———. 2017b. "India at 70, and the Passing of Another Illusion." *New York Times,* August 11. Available at https://mobile.nytimes.com/2017/08/11/opinion/india-70-partition-pankaj-mishra.html.

Mishra, Pankaj, and Aman Sethi. 2015. "In Conversation: Pankaj Mishra and Aman Sethi." *Granta,* May 18. Available at https://granta.com/in-conversation-pankaj-mishra-aman-sethi.

Mistry, Rohinton. 1991. *Such a Long Journey.* London: Faber and Faber.

———. 1995. *A Fine Balance.* New York: Vintage.

Mitra, Sreya. 2013. "From Heroine to 'Brand Shilpa': Reality Television, Transnational Cultural Economics, and the Remaking of the Bollywood Star." In *Transnational Stardom: International Celebrity in Film and Popular Culture,* edited by Russell Meeuf and Raphael Raphael, 187–206. New York: Palgrave Macmillan.

Mohabbatein. 2000. Directed by Aditya Chopra. Yash Raj Films. DVD.

Mohra. 1994. Directed by Rajiv Rai. Bombino Video Pvt. DVD.

Mohutsiwa, Siyanda. 2016. "I'm Done with African Immigrant Literature." *Okay Africa,* February 8. Available at http://www.okayafrica.com/news/im-done-with-african-immigrant-literature.

Mom. 2017. Directed by Ravi Udyawar. Zee Studio. DVD.

Monbiot, George. 2016. "Celebrity Isn't Just Harmless Fun—It's the Smiling Face of the Corporate Machine." *The Guardian*, December 20. Available at https://www.the guardian.com/commentisfree/2016/dec/20/celebrity-corporate-machine-fame-big -business-donald-trump-kim-kardashian.

Mongia, Padmini. 2014. "Speaking American: Popular Indian Fiction in English." *Comparative American Studies* 12 (1–2): 140–146.

———. 2015. "What about Shobhaa Dé? Indian Pulp Fiction Meets Indian Writing in English." In *Vernacular Worlds, Cosmopolitan Imagination*, edited by Stephanos Stephanides and Stavros Karayanni, 103–120. Leiden, Netherlands: Brill Rodopi.

Moore, Terron. 2014. "What *Black-ish* Gets Right about Black Manhood in America." *Esquire*, October 30. Available at http://www.esquire.com/entertainment/tv/a30612/ black-ish-black-manhood.

Morality TV aur Loving Jehad: Ek Manohar Kahani. 2007. Directed by Paromita Vohra. Parodevi Pictures. DVD.

Moss, Stephen. 2017. "Aravind Adiga: 'I Was Afraid the White Tiger Would Eat Me Up Too.'" *The Guardian*, August 25. Available at https://www.theguardian.com/books/ 2017/aug/25/aravind-adiga-books-interview-selection-day-the-white-tiger.

Mother India. 1957. Directed by Mehboob Khan. British Film Institute. DVD.

Mr. India. 1987. Directed by Shekhar Kapur. Eros International. DVD.

Msiska, Mpalive. 1999. "The Dialectic of Myth and History in the Post-colonial Contemporary: Soyinka's *A Dance of the Forests*." In *Literature and the Contemporary: Fictions and Theories of the Present*, edited by Roger Luckhurst and Peter Marks, 126–138. Essex, UK: Pearson Education.

Mukherjee, Meenakshi. 1993. "The Anxiety of Indianness: Our Novels in English." *Economic and Political Weekly* 28 (48): 2607–2611.

Mukherjee, Rahul. 2010. "A Reply to Terrorism on a Wednesday: A Citizen Vigilante's Prescriptions for Governing Terrorism." In *Sarai Reader 08: Fear*, edited by Monica Narula, Shuddhabrata Sengupta, and Jeebesh Bagchi, 242–247. Delhi: Centre for the Study of Developing Societies.

Mukherjee, Sujit. 1981. *Translation as Discovery and Other Essays on Indian Literature in English Translation*. New Delhi: Allied.

Mulkerrins, Jane. 2017. "Issa Rae: 'So Much of the Media Presents Blackness as Fierce and Flawless. I'm Not.'" *The Guardian*, August 5. Available at https://www.the guardian.com/tv-and-radio/2017/aug/05/issa-rae-media-presents-blackness-fierce -flawless-insecure.

Munnabhai MBBS. 2003. Directed by Rajkumar Hirani. Vinod Chopra Productions. DVD.

Muqaddar ka Sikandar. 1978. Directed by Prakash Mehra. Eros International. DVD.

Nagaraj, D. R. 1993. *The Flaming Feet: A Study of the Dalit Movement in India*. Bangalore: South Forum Press.

Nandy, Ashis. 2002. "Introduction: Indian Popular Cinema as a Slum's Eye View of Politics." In *The Secret Politics of Our Desires: Innocence, Culpability and Indian Popular Cinema*, edited by Ashis Nandy, 1–18. New Delhi: Oxford University Press.

Nathan, Archana. 2015. "And I Make Documentaries." *The Hindu*, April 2. Available at http://www.thehindu.com/features/friday-review/and-i-make-documentaries -paromita-vohra/article7061461.ece.

Ndebele, Njabulo S. 1994. *South African Literature and Culture: Rediscovery of the Ordinary*. Manchester, UK: Manchester University Press.

Nerlekar, Anjali. 2016. *Bombay Modern: Arun Kolatkar and Bilingual Literary Culture.* Evanston, IL: Northwestern University Press.

Neutill, Rani. 2010. "Bending Bodies, Borders and Desires in Bapsi Sidhwa's *Cracking India* and Deepa Mehta's *Earth.*" *South Asian Popular Culture* 8 (1): 73–87.

Nichols, Bill. 1991. *Representing Reality: Issues and Concepts in Documentary.* Bloomington: Indiana University Press.

No One Killed Jessica. 2011. Directed by Raj Kumar Gupta. UTV Motion Pictures. DVD.

Nowak, Mark. 2016. "The Essentials of Socialist Writing: An Interview with Vijay Prashad." *Jacobin*, December 20. Available at https://www.jacobinmag.com/2016/12/socialist-writing-publishing-books-reading.

Orsini, Francesca. 2015. "*Dil Maange More*: Cultural Contexts of Hinglish in Contemporary India." *African Studies* 74 (2): 199–220.

Osborne, Peter. 2013. *Anywhere or Not at All: Philosophy of Contemporary Art.* London: Verso.

Pal, Deepanjana. 2012. "The Hunt for the Next Chetan Bhagat." *DNA*, July 15. Available at http://www.dnaindia.com/mumbai/report-the-hunt-for-the-next-chetan-bhagat-1715210.

Pandian, Anand. 2015. *Reel World: An Anthropology of Creation.* Durham, NC: Duke University Press.

Patel, Sujata. 2003. "Bombay and Mumbai: Identities, Politics, and Populism." In *Bombay and Mumbai: The City in Transition*, edited by Sujata Patel and Jim Masselos, 3–30. New Delhi: Oxford University Press.

Patke, Rajeev. 2016. "Arun Kolatkar: A Singular Poetry in Two Languages." In *A History of Indian Poetry in English*, edited by Rosinka Chaudhuri, 284–298. New York: Cambridge University Press.

Paul, Arunima. 2013. "'They Point Guns for Money, We Run the Country!': Provincial Modernities in *Hatke* Cinema." *Studies in South Asian Film and Media* 5 (2): 113–130.

Peepli Live. 2010. Directed by Anusha Rizvi. UTV Motion Pictures. DVD.

Perera, Sonali. 2015. *No Country: Working-Class Writing in the Age of Globalization.* New York: Columbia University Press.

Perry, Alex. 2013. "The Young Turk." *Time*, October 27. Available at http://content.time.com/time/world/article/0,8599,2053802,00.html.

"Persons with Disabilities." 2012. *Satyamev Jayate*, season 1, episode 6. Aired June 10. Star Plus.

Phadke, Shilpa. 2017. "Women, Too, Have the Right to Fun." *Live Mint*, January 19. Available at http://www.livemint.com/Opinion/8bZu3L4PiQKNFfonpxKEfN/Women-too-have-the-right-to-fun.html.

Phadke, Shilpa, Sameera Khan, and Shilpa Ranade. 2011. *Why Loiter? Women and Risk on Mumbai Streets.* New Delhi: Penguin.

Philips, Deborah. 2015. "The New Miss India: Popular Fiction in Contemporary India." *Women: A Cultural Review* 26 (1–2): 96–111.

Pink. 2016. Directed by Aniruddha Roy Chowdhury. NH Studioz. DVD.

Pinto, Jerry. 2017. *A Murder in Mahim.* New Delhi: Speaking Tree.

Pinto, Jerry, and Naresh Fernandes, eds. 2003. *Bombay, Meri Jaan: Writings on Mumbai.* New Delhi: Penguin.

PK. 2014. Directed by Rajkumar Hirani. UTV Motion Pictures. DVD.

Poduval, Satish. 2012. "The Affable Young Man: Civility, Desire and the Making of a Middle-Class Cinema in the 1970s." *South Asian Popular Culture* 10 (1): 37–50.

"Police." 2014. *Satyamev Jayate*, season 2, episode 2. Aired March 9. Star Plus.

Poon, Angelia. 2017. "Helping the Novel: Neoliberalism, Self-Help, and the Narrating of the Self in Mohsin Hamid's *How to Get Filthy Rich in Rising Asia.*" *Journal of Commonwealth Literature* 52 (1): 139–150.

Prakash, Gyan. 2010a. "Imaging the Modern City, Darkly." In *Noir Urbanisms: Dystopic Images of the Modern City*, edited by Gyan Prakash, 1–14. Princeton, NJ: Princeton University Press.

———. 2010b. *Mumbai Fables.* Princeton, NJ: Princeton University Press.

Prakash, Shiv. 2012. "It Was a Great Show, but Missed Dr. Ambedkar: Dr. Kaushal Panwar." *Merinews*, July 13. Available at http://www.merinews.com/article/it-was-a -great-show-but-missed-dr-ambedkar-dr-kaushal-panwar/15872223.shtml.

Prakash, Uday. 2001. *Peeli chhatri wali ladki.* New Delhi: Vani Prakashan.

———. (2005) 2006. *Mohan Das.* New Delhi: Vani Prakashan.

———. 2008. *The Girl with the Golden Parasol.* Translated by Jason Grunebaum. New Delhi: Penguin.

———. 2012. "Mohandas." In *The Walls of Delhi: Three Stories*, translated by Jason Grunebaum, 43–129. Gurgaon, India: Hachette.

Prashad, Vijay. 2014. "India's Left Will Be Back." *The Guardian,* May 23. Available at http://www.theguardian.com/commentisfree/2014/may/23/india-communists-bjp -neoliberalism-left.

Pullen, Christopher. 2011. "The Household, the Basement and *The Real World*: Gay Identity in the Constructed Reality Environment." In *Understanding Reality Television*, edited by Su Holmes and Deborah Jermyn, 211–232. London: Routledge.

Punathambekar, Aswin. 2010. "Reality TV and Participatory Culture in India." *Popular Communication* 8:241–255.

Qadri, Monisa, and Sabeha Mufti. 2015. "Films and Religion: An Analysis of Aamir Khan's *PK.*" *Journal of Religion and Film* 20 (1): 1–29.

Qayamat Se Qayamat Tak. 1988. Directed by Mansoor Khan. B4U Entertainment. DVD.

Queen. 2013. Directed by Vikas Bahl. Viacom 18 Motion Pictures. DVD.

Raakh. 1989. Directed by Aditya Bhattacharya. T-Series. DVD.

Radjou, Navi, Jaideep Prabhu, and Simone Ahuja. 2012. *Jugaad Innovation: A Frugal and Flexible Approach to Innovation for the 21st Century.* Noida: Random House India.

Rae, Issa, creator. 2016. *Insecure.* HBO Entertainment. Television series.

Rai, Amit. 2009. *Untimely Bollywood: India's New Media Assemblage.* Durham, NC: Duke University Press.

Raj, Ashok. 2010. *Hero.* Vol. 2, *Amitabh Bachchan to the Khans and Beyond.* London: Hay House.

Rajagopal, Arvind. 2009a. "Afterword: Fast-Forward into the Future, Haunted by the Past: Bollywood Today." In *Global Bollywood*, edited by Anandam P. Kavoori and Aswin Punathambekar, 300–306. New Delhi: Oxford University Press.

———. 2009b. *Politics after Television: Hindu Nationalism and the Reshaping of the Public in India.* Cambridge: Cambridge University Press.

Rajagopal, Arvind, and Paromita Vohra. 2012. "On the Aesthetics and Ideology of the Indian Documentary Film: A Conversation." *BioScope: South Asian Screen Studies* 3 (7): 7–20.

Raja Hindustani. 1996. Directed by Dharmesh Darshan. Tips Industries. DVD.

Ramberg, Lucinda. 2016. "Backward Futures and Pasts Forward: Queer Time, Sexual Politics, and Dalit Religiosity in South India." *GLQ: Journal of Lesbian and Gay Studies* 22 (2): 223–248.

Ramnath, Nandini. 2013. "*Connected Hum Tum*: Preeti Kochar's Brave New World." *Live Mint*, July 4. Available at http://www.livemint.com/Leisure/X4lJ22G0qwZt HoR5iyQmNN/Preeti-Kochars-brave-new-world.html.

Rang De Basanti. 2006. Directed by Rakeysh Omprakash Mehra. UTV Motion Pictures. DVD.

Rangeela. 1995. Directed by Ram Gopal Varma. Shemaroo Video. DVD.

Rann. 2010. Directed by Ram Gopal Varma. PVR Pictures. DVD.

Rao, R. Raj. 1999. "Underground." In *Yaraana: Gay Writing from India*, edited by Hoshang Merchant, 97–98. New Delhi: Penguin.

———. 2003. *The Boyfriend*. New Delhi: Penguin.

Rao, Sandhya. 2005. "India." In *Global Entertainment Media: Content, Audiences, Issues*, edited by Anne Cooper-Chen, 131–144. Mahwah, NJ: Lawrence Erlbaum Associates.

Rege, Sharmila. 2002. "Conceptualising Popular Culture: 'Lavani' and 'Powada' in Maharashtra." *Economic and Political Weekly* 37 (11): 1038–1047.

Ricoeur, Paul. 1980. "Narrative Time." *Critical Inquiry* 7 (1): 169–190.

Roberts, Gregory David. 2003. *Shantaram*. New York: St. Martin's Griffin.

Ross, Oliver. 2014. "Communal Tensions: Homosexuality in Raj Rao's *The Boyfriend*." *Rupkatha* 6 (1): 108–119.

Roy, Anjali. 2000. "*Microstoria*: Indian Nationalism's 'Little Stories' in Amitav Ghosh's *The Shadow Lines*." *Journal of Commonwealth Literature* 35 (2): 35–49.

Roy, Arundhati. 1997. *The God of Small Things*. New York: Random House.

Roy, Devapriya. 2016. "Ravinder Singh Has Written This Novel That Feels Right (and That's a Huge Surprise)." *Scroll*, August 23. Available at https://scroll.in/article/ 814634/ravinder-singh-has-written-this-novel-that-feels-right-and-thats-a-huge -surprise.

Roy, Nilanjana S. 2013. "Bhagat Brandwagon." *Business Standard*, January 25. Available at http://www.business-standard.com/article/opinion/nilanjana-s-roy-the-bhagat -brandwagon-112082100003_1.html.

Roy, Sandip. 2016. "The City." *Kindle*, May 2. Available at http://kindlemag.in/city-india -forgot.

Roy, Sumana. 2012. "Jaya Hey to Jai Ho to Jayate: Sumana Roy." *Kafila*, May 27. Available at https://kafila.online/2012/05/27/jaya-hey-to-jai-ho-to-jayate-sumana-roy.

Rushdie, Salman. 1981. *Midnight's Children*. New York: Avon Books.

———. 1983. *Shame*. London: Picador.

———. 1988. *The Satanic Verses*. New York: Henry Holt.

Sadana, Rashmi. 2012. *English Heart, Hindi Heartland: The Political Life of Literature in India*. Berkeley: University of California Press.

Said, Edward. 1993. *Culture and Imperialism*. New York: Knopf.

Saldanha, Alison. 2016. "Disaster Risks Grow as India's Cities Flounder." *Scroll*, January 16. Available at https://scroll.in/article/801920/disaster-risks-grow-as-indias-cities -flounder.

Saldívar, Ramón. 2011. "Historical Fantasy, Speculative Realism, and Postrace Aesthetics in Contemporary American Fiction." *American Literary History* 23 (3): 574–599.

Salgaocar, Isheta. 2012. "The Problem with Aamir Khan's 'Satyamev Jayate.'" *Wall Street Journal*, July 4. Available at https://blogs.wsj.com/indiarealtime/2012/07/04/the -problem-with-aamir-khans-satyamev-jayate.

Sandhu, Sukhdev. 2013. "On the Itinerant as Philosopher: An Interview with Aman Sethi." *Public Books*, June 20. Available at http://www.publicbooks.org/on-the -itinerant-as-philosopher-an-interview-with-aman-sethi.

Sanga, Jaina C. 2001. *Salman Rushdie's Postcolonial Metaphors: Migration, Translation, Hybridity, Blasphemy and Globalization.* Westport, CT: Greenwood Press.

Sankaran, Lavanya. 2013a. "A Conversation with Lavanya Sankaran." In *The Hope Factory,* 353–355. London: Tinder Press.

———. 2013b. *The Hope Factory.* London: Tinder Press.

Santhya, K. G., Nicole Haberland, F. Ram, R. K. Sinha, and S. K. Mohanty. 2007. "Consent and Coercion: Examining Unwanted Sex among Married Young Women in India." *International Family Planning Perspectives* 33 (3): 124–132.

Sarda, Shveta, trans. 2010. *Trickster City: Writings from the Belly of the Metropolis.* New Delhi: Penguin.

Sarfarosh. 1999. Directed by John Mathew Matthan. Eros International. DVD.

Sarin, Jeetendra. 2016. "Dadri Lynching: Allahabad HC Stays Arrest of Ikhlaq's Family, except Brother." *Hindustan Times,* August 26. Available at http://www.hindustantimes.com/india-news/dadri-lynching-case-hc-stays-arrest-of-ikhlaq-s-family-members/story-GvPUN2tKsC49PRoCnhdF5K.html.

Sarkar. 2005. Directed by Ram Gopal Varma. Sahara One. DVD.

Satya. 1998. Directed by Ram Gopal Varma. Digital Entertainment. DVD.

Sawhney, Hirsh, ed. 2009. *Delhi Noir.* Noida: HarperCollins.

Secret Superstar. 2017. Directed by Advait Chandan. Essel Vision Productions. DVD.

Sen, Atreyee, and Neha Raheja Thakker. 2011. "Prostitution, Pee-ing, Percussion, and Possibilities: Contemporary Women Documentary Film-makers and the City in South Asia." *South Asian Popular Culture* 9 (1): 29–42.

Sen, Pat, and Paromita Vohra. 2017. "What Indian Men Feel about Their Penis." Agents of Ishq, April 26. Available at http://agentsofishq.com/indian-men-feel-penis.

Sen, Rajyasree. 2014. "Forget Satyamev Jayate: Why Mission Sapne Is the Must-See Sunday Show." *Firstpost,* April 28. Available at http://www.firstpost.com/bollywood/forget-satyamev-jayate-why-mission-sapne-is-the-must-see-sunday-show-1499703.html.

Senapati, Fakir Mohan. (1899) 2006. *Six Acres and a Third (Chha Mana Atha Guntha).* Translated by Rabi Shankar Mishra, Satya P. Mohanty, Jatindra K. Nayak, and Paul St-Pierre. New Delhi: Penguin.

Seth, Vikram. 1993. *A Suitable Boy.* New York: HarperCollins.

Sethi, Aman. 2011. *A Free Man.* Noida: Random House.

"A Seven Course Feast for the Eyes: Sudhir Patwardhan's Bombay Ballad." 2015. *Junoon,* September 29. Available at https://junoontheatre.wordpress.com/2015/09/29/a-seven-course-feast-for-the-eyes-sudhir-patwardhans-bombay-ballad.

Shah, Anushka. 2017. "Vigilantism and Mob Justice Are Glorified by Bollywood and That Is a Big Problem." *The Wire,* July 18. Available at https://thewire.in/158716/vigilantism-mob-justice-bollywood-movies.

Shahani, Parmesh. 2008a. *Gay Bombay: Globalization, Love and (Be)Longing in Contemporary India.* New Delhi: Sage.

———. 2008b. "The Mirror Has Many Faces: The Politics of Male Same-Sex Desire in *BOMgAY* and *Gulabi Aaina.*" In *Global Bollywood,* edited by Anandam P. Kavoori and Aswin Punathambekar, 146–163. New York: NYU Press.

———. 2015. "Mumbai, the Ultimate Jugaad City." *The Hindu,* December 2. Available at http://www.thehindu.com/opinion/op-ed/mumbai-the-ultimate-jugaad-city/article7937636.ece.

Shankar, Karthik. 2017. "These Are the Calcutta Stories That Stare Everyone in the Face but Most Don't Write About." *Scroll,* September 14. Available at https://scroll.in/

article/850487/these-are-the-calcutta-stories-that-stare-everyone-in-the-face-but -most-dont-write-about.

Sharma, Aparna. 2016. "From Angry Young Man to Icon of Neo-liberal India: Extra-cinematic Strategies That Make Amitabh Bachchan India's Lasting Super-star." In *Lasting Screen Stars: Images That Fade and Personas That Endure*, edited by Lucy Bolton and Julie Lobalzo Wright, 11–25. New York: Palgrave Macmillan.

Sharma, Swati. 2018. "Ta-Nehisi Coates on Cornel West's One-Sided War." *The Atlantic*, January 17. Available at https://www.theatlantic.com/entertainment/archive/2018/ 01/ta-nehisi-coates-cornel-west/550727.

Shekhar, Hansda Sowvendra. 2015. *The Adivasi Will Not Dance*. New Delhi: Speaking Tiger.

Shingavi, Snehal. 2013. *The Mahatma Misunderstood: The Politics and Forms of Literary Nationalism in India*. London: Anthem.

———. 2014. "Capitalism, Caste, and Con-Games in Aravind Adiga's *The White Tiger*." *Postcolonial Text* 9 (3): 1–16.

Sholay. 1975. Directed by Ramesh Sippy. Eros Entertainment. DVD.

Shri 420. 1955. Directed by Raj Kapoor. R. K. Films. DVD.

Shukla, Shrilal. 1968. *Raag Darbari*. New Delhi: Rajkamal Prakashan.

Shukla, Vandana. 2016. "Nothing Literary about English Books Bazaar." *The Tribune*, March 5. Available at http://www.tribuneindia.com/news/comment/nothing -literary-about-english-books-bazaar/204648.html.

Sidhwa, Bapsi. 1988. *Ice-Candy-Man*. London: Heinemann.

Simonds, Wendy. 1996. "All Consuming Selves: Self-Help Literature and Women's Iden-tities." In *Constructing the Self in a Mediated World*, edited by Debra Grodin and Thomas R. Lindlof, 15–29. Thousand Oaks, CA: Sage.

Singh, Jai Arjun. 2009. "The End of Pretension." *Biblio: A Review of Books*, March–April, pp. 27–28.

———. 2012. "'I'm a Cartoonist Who Can't Draw.'" *The Hindu*, September 15. Available at www.thehindu.com/books/"I'm-a-cartoonist-who-can't-draw"/article12633755 .ece.

Sitapati, Vinay. 2011. "What Anna Hazare's Movement and India's New Middle Classes Say about Each Other." *Economic and Political Weekly* 46 (30): 39–44.

Slumdog Millionaire. 2008. Directed by Danny Boyle. Warner Bros. DVD.

Smith, Faith. 2015. "Strolling in the Ruins." Talk given at Brandeis University, Waltham, MA, February 4.

Smith, Terry. 2006. "Contemporary Art and Contemporaneity." *Critical Inquiry* 32 (4): 681–707.

———. 2008. "Introduction: The Contemporaneity Question." In *Antinomies of Art and Culture: Modernity, Postmodernity, Contemporaneity*, edited by Terry Smith, Okwui Enwezor, and Nancy Condee, 1–19. Durham, NC: Duke University Press.

Sontag, Susan. 1996. "The Decay of Cinema." *New York Times*, February 25. Available at http://www.nytimes.com/books/00/03/12/specials/sontag-cinema.html.

Spivak, Gayatri Chakravorty. 1985. "Three Women's Texts and a Critique of Imperial-ism." *Critical Inquiry* 12 (1): 243–261.

———. 1988. "Can the Subaltern Speak?" In *Marxism and the Interpretation of Culture*, edited by Cary Nelson and Lawrence Grossberg, 271–315. Urbana: University of Illinois Press.

———. 1999. *A Critique of Postcolonial Reason: Toward a History of the Vanishing Pres-ent*. Cambridge, MA: Harvard University Press.

———. 2012. "Why Study the Past?" *Modern Language Quarterly* 73 (1): 1–12.

Srinivas, Lakshmi. 2002. "The Active Audience: Spectatorship, Social Relations and the Experience of Cinema in India." *Media, Culture and Society* 24 (2): 155–173.

Srinivasan, Ragini Tharoor. 2014. "Complicity and Critique." *Public Books*, October 15. Available at http://www.publicbooks.org/complicity-and-critique.

———. 2017. "Unmoored: Passing, Slumming, and Return-Writing in New India." In *Postcolonial Urban Outcasts: City Margins in South Asian Literature*, edited by Madhurima Chakraborty and Umme Al-wazedi, 95–112. New York: Routledge.

Srivastava, Sanjay. 2015. *Entangled Urbanism: Slum, Gated Community and Shopping Mall in Delhi and Gurgaon*. New Delhi: Oxford University Press.

———. 2016. "The Unsmart City: Gurgaon Remains a Tragic Case Study in How Not to Urbanise." *Scroll*, July 31. Available at https://scroll.in/article/812853/the-unsmart-city-why-gurgaon-remains-a-tragic-case-study-in-how-not-to-urbanise.

Stacey, Jackie. 2003. "Feminine Fascinations: Forms of Identification in Star-Audience Relations." In *Stardom: Industry of Desire*, edited by Christine Gledhill, 141–163. London: Routledge.

Stadtler, Florian. 2005. "Cultural Connections: *Lagaan* and Its Audience Responses." *Third World Quarterly* 26 (3): 517–524.

Staiger, Jeffrey. 2008. "James Wood's Case against 'Hysterical Realism' and Thomas Pynchon." *Antioch Review* 66 (4): 634–654.

Strubbe, Bill. 2003. "Getting Serious about Laughter." *World and I* 18 (3): 132–139.

Suggu, Kanchana. 1999. "'I Just Like to Do Films.'" *Rediff*, December 24. Available at http://m.rediff.com/movies/1999/dec/24aamir.htm.

Sundaram, Ravi. 2010. "Imaging Urban Breakdown: Delhi in the 1990s." In *Noir Urbanisms: Dystopic Images of the Modern City*, edited by Gyan Prakash, 241–260. Princeton, NJ: Princeton University Press.

Sunder Rajan, Rajeswari. 2011. "After *Midnight's Children*: Some Notes on the New Indian Novel in English." *Social Research* 78 (1): 203–230.

Suneetha, P. 2012. "Double Vision in Aravind Adiga's *The White Tiger*." *ARIEL* 42 (2): 163–175.

Taare Zameen Par. 2007. Directed by Aamir Khan. UTV Motion Pictures. DVD.

Talaash. 2012. Directed by Reema Kagti. Reliance Entertainment. DVD.

Tejpal, Tarun J. 2010. *The Story of My Assassins*. Brooklyn, NY: Melville House.

Thomas, Robin. 2010. "Mid-Day Ups Focus on Circulation, Readership; Hikes Ad Rates by 15 Pc." *Exchange4media*, April 1. Available at https://www.exchange4media.com/media-print-news/mid-day-ups-focus-on-circulationreadershiphikes-ad-rates-by-15-pc-37677.html.

Thomas, Rosie. 1998. "Melodrama and the Negotiation of Morality in Mainstream Hindi Film." In *Consuming Modernity: Public Culture in a South Asian World*, edited by Carol Appadurai Breckenridge, 157–182. Minneapolis: University of Minnesota Press.

3 Idiots. 2009. Directed by Rajkumar Hirani. Reliance Entertainment. DVD.

Tickell, Alex. 2015. "Some Uses of History: Historiography, Politics, and the Indian Novel." In *A History of the Indian Novel in English*, edited by Ulka Anjaria, 237–250. Cambridge: Cambridge University Press.

———. 2016. "'An Idea Whose Time Has Come': Indian Fiction in English after 1991." In *South-Asian Fiction in English: Contemporary Transformations*, edited by Alex Tickell, 37–58. London: Palgrave Macmillan.

Tiwari, Nishi. 2015. "'India Is a Semi-literate Country and Chetan Bhagat Is the Best It Can Do.'" *Rediff*, February 5. Available at http://uswww.rediff.com/news/interview/

aatish-taseer-india-is-semi-literate-and-chetan-bhagat-is-the-best-it-can-do/
20150205.htm.

"Top 20 Highest Grossing Bollywood Movies of Alltime Worldwide by Gross Box Office Collection." 2018. *Bollymoviereviewz.com*, September 18. Available at http://www .bollymoviereviewz.com/2013/05/top-10-bollywood-movies-of-alltime-by.html.

"Toxic Food." 2012. *Satyamev Jayate*, season 1, episode 8. Aired June 24. Star Plus.

Turner, Elen. 2012. "Gender Anxiety and Contemporary Indian Popular Fiction." In "New Work in Comparative Indian Literatures and Cultures," edited by Mohan G. Ramanan and Tutun Mukherjee. Special issue, *CLCWeb: Comparative Literature and Culture* 14 (2). Available at http://docs.lib.purdue.edu/clcweb/vol14/iss2.

Tyrewala, Abbas. 2012. "Chachu at Dusk." In *Mumbai Noir*, edited by Altaf Tyrewala, 75–85. Noida: HarperCollins.

Tyrewala, Altaf, ed. 2012. *Mumbai Noir.* Noida: HarperCollins.

Ungli. 2014. Directed by Rensil D'Silva. Dharma Productions. DVD.

Unlimited Girls. 2002. Directed by Paromita Vohra. Parodevi Pictures. DVD.

"Untouchability." 2012. *Satyamev Jayate*, season 1, episode 10. Aired July 8. Star Plus.

Varma, Pavan K. 1998. *The Great Indian Middle Class.* New Delhi: Viking.

Varma, Rashmi. 2004. "Provincializing the Global City: From Bombay to Mumbai." *Social Text* 22 (4): 65–89.

Vasudevan, Ravi S. 1995. "Addressing the Spectator of a 'Third World' National Cinema: The Bombay 'Social' Film of the 1940s and 1950s." *Screen* 36 (4): 305–324.

———. 1996. "Shifting Codes, Dissolving Identities: The Hindi Social Film of the 1950s as Popular Culture." *Third Text* 102 (34): 59–77.

———. 2001. "An Imperfect Public: Cinema and Citizenship in the 'Third World.'" In *Sarai Reader 01: The Public Domain*, edited by Raqs Media Collective, 57–67. Delhi: Centre for the Study of Developing Societies.

———. 2011. *The Melodramatic Public: Film Form and Spectatorship in Indian Cinema.* New York: Palgrave Macmillan.

Vermeulen, Pieter. 2015. *Contemporary Literature and the End of the Novel: Creature, Affect, Form.* New York: Palgrave Macmillan.

Virdi, Jyotika. 2004. *The Cinematic ImagiNation: Indian Popular Films as Social History.* Delhi: Permanent Black.

Viruddh. 2005. Directed by Mahesh Manjrekar. Amitabh Bachchan Corporation. DVD.

Viswamohan, Aysha Iqbal. 2013. "Marketing Lad Lit, Creating Bestsellers: The Importance of Being Chetan Bhagat." In *Postliberalization Indian Novels in English: Politics of Global Reception and Awards*, edited by Aysha Iqbal Viswamohan, 19–29. London: Anthem Press.

Viswanath, Gita. 2007. "The Multiplex: Crowd, Audience and the Genre Film." *Economic and Political Weekly* 42 (32): 3289–3291, 3293–3294.

Viswanathan, Shiv. 2012. "Anna Hazare and the Battle against Corruption." *Cultural Critique* 8:103–111.

———. 2017. "The Lure of the Dera." *The Hindu*, August 28. Available at http://www .thehindu.com/opinion/op-ed/the-lure-of-the-dera/article19571254.ece?utm _source=RSS_Feed&utm_medium=RSS&utm_campaign=RSS_Syndication.

Vohra, Paromita. n.d. "What You Find Is, Your Real Battle Is Not in Other People Finding You Attractive but in You Believing That They Can Find You Attractive." *Spool.* Available at http://thespool.in/paromita-vohra (accessed May 9, 2017).

———. 2008. "Separation Anxiety: The Schisms and Schemas of Media Advocacy; An Indian Filmmaker Working in the World." *Signs: Journal of Women in Culture and Society* 33 (2): 418–423.

——. 2010. "Time for a Lesson." *Mid-Day*, May 2. Available at http://www.mid-day.com/articles/time-for-a-lesson/80263.

——. 2011. "Dotting the I: The Politics of Self-Less-Ness in Indian Documentary Practice." *South Asian Popular Culture* 9 (1): 43–53.

——, creator. 2013a. *Connected Hum Tum*. Zee TV. Television series.

——. 2013b. "No Sex Please, We're Indian." *Mid-Day*, March 17. Available at http://www.mid-day.com/articles/no-sex-please-were-indian/204501.

——. 2013c. "Pushpa, I Hate Jokes." *Mid-Day*, December 22. Available at http://www.mid-day.com/articles/pushpa-i-hate-jokes/245584.

——. 2014a. "Dostana, Karela and Social Change." *Mid-Day*, September 28. Available at https://www.mid-day.com/articles/dostana-karela-and-social-change/15640155.

——. 2014b. "The Family Favourite." *Mid-Day*, January 6. Available at http://www.mid-day.com/articles/the-family-favourite/15015004.

——. 2014c. "Foreigners in Their Own Land." *Mid-Day*, August 10. Available at http://www.mid-day.com/articles/foreigners-in-their-own-land/15520154.

——. 2014d. "Irony-Clad Claws." *Mid-Day*, July 13. Available at http://www.mid-day.com/articles/irony-clad-claws/15444157.

——. 2014e. "King of Queen." *Mid-Day*, March 16. Available at http://www.mid-day.com/articles/king-of-queen/15162051.

——. 2014f. "Two States of T2." *Mid-Day*, May 11. http://www.mid-day.com/articles/two-states-of-t2/15287179.

——. 2014g. "With Respect to Fandry." *Mid-Day*, March 2. Available at http://www.mid-day.com/articles/with-respect-to-fandry/15133059.

——. 2015a. "Anarkali Apne Disco Chali." *Mid-Day*, June 28. Available at http://www.mid-day.com/articles/anarkali-apne-disco-chali/16325169.

——. 2015b. "Finding Indian Love: Dum Lagake Pyar Kar." *Bangalore Mirror*, March 5. Available at http://bangaloremirror.indiatimes.com/columns/others/dum-lagake-haisha-love-stories/articleshow/46469836.cms?.

——. 2015c. "Kadva Sach." *Mid-Day*, November 8. Available at http://www.mid-day.com/articles/kadva-sach/16664177.

——. 2015d. "Let's (Not) Talk about Sex, Maybe." *Mid-Day*, August 9. Available at http://www.mid-day.com/articles/lets-not-talk-about-sex-maybe/16438187.

——. 2015e. "Paanch Saal Paro-Normal." *Mid-Day*, April 19. Available at http://www.mid-day.com/articles/paanch-saal-paro-normal/16148193.

——. 2015f. "Remake in India." *Mid-Day*, October 4. Available at http://www.mid-day.com/articles/remake-in-india/16582198.

——. 2015g. "See See TV." *Mid-Day*, March 15. Available at http://www.mid-day.com/articles/see-see-tv/16062192.

——. 2016a. "Art as Ishq: Internet as Art." Presentation for "Mumbai Local" series, Mumbai, May 7.

——. 2016b. "The Final Word on Why Women Love Fawad Khan." *Scroll*, March 16. Available at https://scroll.in/reel/805186/the-final-word-on-why-women-love-fawad-khan.

——. 2016c. "Paromita Vohra: Dial N for Neyappam." *Mid-Day*, June 12. Available at http://www.mid-day.com/articles/paromita-vohra-dial-n-for-neyappam/17326187.

——. 2016d. "Paromita Vohra: In Whose Shoes?" *Mid-Day*, July 31. Available at http://www.mid-day.com/articles/paromita-vohra-in-whose-shoes/17483163.

——. 2016e. "Paromita Vohra: Rakhi Bandhan." *Mid-Day*, August 14. Available at http://www.mid-day.com/articles/paromita-vohra-rakhi-bandhan/17525169.

———. 2016f. "Paromita Vohra: The Rules." *Mid-Day*, May 1. Available at http://www
.mid-day.com/articles/paromita-vohra-the-rules/17185197.

———. 2016g. "Paromita Vohra: So What?" *Mid-Day*, May 8. Available at http://www
.mid-day.com/articles/paromita-vohra-so-what/17209182.

———. 2016h. "Paromita Vohra: Son Preference." *Mid-Day*, March 27. Available at http://
www.mid-day.com/articles/paromita-vohra-son-preference/17076156.

———. 2016i. "Paromita Vohra: Truth Out." *Mid-Day*, July 3. Available at http://www
.mid-day.com/articles/paromita-vohra-truth-out/17395180.

———. 2016j. "'A Prayer Thali of Cultural Aphrodisiacs': Writer/Filmmaker Paromita
Vohra's Sensory Storm." *Junoon*, April 25. Available at https://junoontheatre
.wordpress.com/2016/04/25/a-prayer-thali-of-cultural-aphrodisiacs-writerfilmmaker
-paromita-vohras-sensory-storm.

———. 2016k. "Tracking SRK's Film Journey Is to Map the Growth of the Indian Middle
Class." *Indian Express*, July 24. Available at http://indianexpress.com/article/
entertainment/bollywood/shah-rukh-khan-on-svreen-journey-2932000.

———. 2017a. "The Mystery of the Half-Girlfriend and the Double Chetan." *Ladies
Finger*, April 12. Available at http://theladiesfinger.com/half-girlfriend-double
-chetan.

———. 2017b. "Our Playlist Morphs into Khajuraho It's Sanskari." *Outlook*, January 2.
Available at http://www.outlookindia.com/magazine/story/our-playlist-morphs
-into-khajuraho-its-sanskari/298293.

———. 2017c. "Paromita Vohra: More Books in That (C)Bag." *Mid-Day*, April 30. Available at https://www.mid-day.com/articles/paromita-vohra-more-books-in-that
-cbag/18209172.

———. 2017d. "Paromita Vohra: The Sense of a (Financial Year) Ending." *Mid-Day*, April
9. Available at http://www.mid-day.com/articles/paromita-vohra-the-sense-of-a
-financial-year-ending/18148176.

———. 2017e. "Paromita Vohra: Yes Means Yes." *Mid-Day*, April 2. Available at http://
www.mid-day.com/articles/paromita-vohra-yes-means-yes/18129185.

Waheed, Mirza. 2014. *The Book of Gold Leaves*. New Delhi: Penguin.

Wainaina, Binyavanga. 2011. *One Day I Will Write about This Place*. Minneapolis:
Graywolf Press.

Wanzo, Rebecca. 2016. "Precarious-Girl Comedy: Issa Rae, Lena Dunham, and Abjection Aesthetics." *Camera Obscura 92* 31 (2): 27–59.

"Water." 2012. *Satyamev Jayate*, season 1, episode 12. Aired July 22. Star Plus.

Waters, Frances Cudjoe. 2014. "'Black-ish': Horrible Parody of Black Family Life." *Huffington Post*, September 25. Available at http://www.huffingtonpost.com/frances
-cudjoe-waters/blackish-horrible-parody-_b_5882622.html.

Waugh, Thomas. 2002. "'I Sleep behind You': Male Homosociality and Homoeroticism
in Indian Parallel Cinema." In *Queering India: Same-Sex Love and Eroticism in
Indian Culture and Society*, edited by Ruth Vanita, 193–206. New York: Routledge.

A Wednesday. 2008. Directed by Neeraj Pandey. UTV Motion Pictures. DVD.

Werbner, Pnina. 2016. "Paradoxes of Postcolonial Vernacular Cosmopolitanism in
South Asia and the Diaspora." In *The Ashgate Research Companion to Cosmopolitanism*, edited by Maria Rovisco and Magdalena Nowicka, 107–123. London: Routledge.

"When Masculinity Harms Men." 2014. *Satyamev Jayate*, season 3, episode 6. Aired
November 9. Star Plus.

Where's Sandra? 2006. Directed by Paromita Vohra. Parodevi Pictures. DVD.

"Why Is Aamir Shedding Tears without Glycerin in His Eyes?" 2015. *News Minute*, August 24. Available at http://www.thenewsminute.com/article/why-aamir-khan-shedding-tears-without-glycerin-his-eyes-33637.

Williams, Linda. 1991. "Film Bodies: Gender, Genre, and Excess." *Film Quarterly* 44 (4): 2–13.

Williams, Raymond. 2009. *Marxism and Literature*. Oxford: Oxford University Press.

Wolf, Nicole. 2013. "Foundations, Movements and Dissonant Images: Documentary Film and Its Ambivalent Relations to the Nation State." In *Routledge Handbook of Indian Cinemas*, edited by K. Noti Gokulsing, Wimal Dissanayake, and Rohit K. Dasgupta, 360–374. London: Routledge.

Woloch, Alex. 2003. *The One vs. the Many: Minor Characters and the Space of the Protagonist in the Novel*. Princeton, NJ: Princeton University Press.

———. 2016. *Or Orwell: Writing and Democratic Socialism*. Cambridge, MA: Harvard University Press.

Yousufi, Mushtaq Ahmed. (1990) 2015. *Mirages of the Mind*. Translated by Matt Reeck and Aftab Ahmad. New York: New Directions.

Zamindar, Vazira Fazila-Yacoobali. 2017. "Why the Partition Is Not an Event of the Past." *The Wire*, September 10. Available at https://thewire.in/175868/partition-not-thing-past.

Zanjeer. 1973. Directed by Prakash Mehra. Eros Entertainment. DVD.

Zelliot, Eleanor. 1978. "*Dalit*—New Cultural Context for an Old Marathi Word." In *Language and Civilization Change in South Asia*, edited by Clarence Maloney, 77–97. Leiden, Netherlands: E. J. Brill.

Index

Ulka Anjaria is Professor of English at Brandeis University. She is the author of *Realism in the Twentieth-Century Indian Novel: Colonial Difference and Literary Form* and *Understanding Bollywood: The Grammar of Hindi Cinema,* and editor of *A History of the Indian Novel in English* and, with Anjali Nerlekar, of *The Oxford Handbook of Modern Indian Literatures.*

www.ingramcontent.com/pod-product-compliance
Lightning Source LLC
Chambersburg PA
CBHW021354090426
42742CB00009B/847